Great October
and
Today's World

Great October
and
Today's World

by

N. I. LEBEDEV

Rector of the Institute for
International Relations, Moscow

Translated by

Y. S. Shirokov and Y. S. Sviridov

PERGAMON PRESS

OXFORD · NEW YORK · TORONTO · SYDNEY · PARIS · FRANKFURT

U.K.	Pergamon Press Ltd., Headington Hill Hall, Oxford OX3 0BW, England
U.S.A.	Pergamon Press Inc., Maxwell House, Fairview Park, Elmsford, New York 10523, U.S.A.
CANADA	Pergamon Press Canada Ltd., Suite 104, 150 Consumers Rd., Willowdale, Ontario M2J 1P9, Canada
AUSTRALIA	Pergamon Press (Aust.) Pty. Ltd., P.O. Box 544, Potts Point, N.S.W. 2011, Australia
FRANCE	Pergamon Press SARL, 24 rue des Ecoles, 75240 Paris, Cedex 05, France
FEDERAL REPUBLIC OF GERMANY	Pergamon Press GmbH, 6242 Kronberg-Taunus, Hammerweg 6, Federal Republic of Germany

First edition 1981

British Library Cataloguing in Publication Data

Lebedev, N.I.
Great October and today's world.
1. Russia — Foreign relations — 1917-
I. Title   II.   Velikii oktīabr' i perestroika mezhdunarodnykh otnosnenii. *English*
327.47   DK266
ISBN 0-08-023607-3

Library of Congress Catalog Card No.: 81-82519

Printed in Great Britain by A. Wheaton & Co. Ltd., Exeter

Preface to the English Edition

THE Russian edition of this book was published in 1978. Preparing its English edition for publication by Pergamon Press, the author has naturally made certain amendments suggested by the rapid course of political developments in the modern world. As for the main principles related to the interpretation of peaceful co-existence, *détente*, and the objective necessity of restructuring international relations, they have remained unchanged.

The last two chapters and Conclusion are intended specially for the English edition. They contain an assessment of the present phase of international relations, the problems and prospects of *détente*. A few abridgements were made, and new facts and figures added to bring the book as far as possible up to date.

Moscow
N. I. LEBEDEV
September 1980

Contents

Contents

Introduction

THE third Russian Revolution of October 1917, which has come to be known as the Great October Socialist Revolution, was a turning-point in mankind's development. It opened a new chapter in world history — one of transition from capitalism to socialism. By blazing the trail to a new civilization it has influenced radically all historical progress. The fresh winds of that revolution are sweeping every field of social life and their force is growing day by day. The field of international relations and diplomacy is no exception.

The birth of the world's first socialist state put an end to the unchallenged rule of imperialism in world politics. In Lenin's phrase, the development of "the world system of states" was now determined by a contest between socialism and capitalism. "Unless we bear that in mind, we shall not be able to pose a single. . . problem correctly, even if it concerns a most outlying part of the world."[1]*

This contest between the two socio-economic systems has a profound and steadily growing impact on the development of world revolution and on international relations. With the growth of the influence of socialism, the revolutionary and democratic forces, the forces committed to peace and progress, democratic and humane norms and customs are being increasingly adopted in the international community, while the methods of imperialist diplomacy are being discredited and falling out of use. "The radical changes in the balance of world forces are responsible for a profound restructuring of the entire system of international relations"[2] said the Central Committee of the Soviet Communist Party in the resolution on the occasion of the 60th anniversary of the October Revolution of 1917. A new system of

---

*Superscript figures indicate references at end of book.

1

international relations should be founded "on an honest and consistent adherence — free of all foul play and ambiguities — to the principles of sovereignty, noninterference in the internal affairs of foreign nations, and faithful compliance with the treaties and agreements in force", Leonid Brezhnev said in this context.[3]

The three main streams of modern revolution — world socialism, the working-class and Communist movement in the advanced capitalist countries, and the national-liberation movement — are steadily undermining the foundations of imperialism and setting the stage for a continuous restructuring of international relations on democratic principles — a major objective of the efforts to establish an international community free from imperialism and neo-colonialism.

Soviet foreign policy over the last 60 years has been marked by an indefatigable and purposeful struggle for peace, and for a renovation of international relations on the basis of Lenin's conception of a just and democratic peace. The effort to reshape international relations pursues the dual objective of securing peace and social progress. Referring to the link of Soviet foreign policy with revolutionary theory and practice, Leonid Brezhnev said that Lenin, the founder of the Soviet State and the architect of its foreign policy, "was the first in history to unite the theory of scientific communism with the conduct of state foreign policy. This union of Leninist theories and Leninist practice gave rise to the principles and methods underlying the socialist policy in the international arena by which we, his pupils and followers, are and shall always be guided."[4]

Soviet foreign policy, initiated by the October Revolution, has accumulated all the earlier experience gained by the proletariat in the struggle against bourgeois foreign policy and diplomacy, against the system of international relations established by capitalism and called upon to perpetuate the exploitation of man by man and suppress the liberation movement of the peoples.

Lenin gave a new dimension to Communist theory and the revolutionary struggle of the proletariat in the stage of monopoly capitalism. He attached first priority to foreign policy planning by the working class which had come to power in Russia, a lone island in a sea of capitalist states. As he emphasized, "...from the very beginning of the October Revolution, foreign policy and international relations have been the main questions facing us".[5] In the transition period, when moribund capitalism and burgeoning socialism exist side by side, this is a life-and-death question, involving the need to establish inter-state relations between the two opposite socio-economic systems to preserve peace among nations and provide a favourable climate for the continuous development of the world revolutionary process.

Lenin's conception of international relations in the transition period envisaged all-round co-operation between all states on a basis of equality. Its next premise was the need to involve in broad international intercourse all peoples and countries liberating themselves from colonial bondage to make international relations truly worldwide and free from colonial fetters. Ever since it was founded, the world's first socialist state has consistently and unswervingly abided by the Leninist foreign policy principles of proletarian internationalism and peaceful co-existence. A tireless and dedicated champion of peace and friendship among nations, it struggles against aggression, for respect for the sovereignty of each and every nation, for recognition of the right of any people to shape its own destiny, to choose the social and political system under which it will live. The beneficial influence of these new principles of international relations has been felt in world politics since the early days of socialist Russia.

As socialism grew into a world system and the alignment of world forces changed in favour of socialism, its revolutionizing influence on international relations tended to increase. Lenin's prevision that in the future socialism would be "...capable of exercising a decisive influence upon world politics as a whole" has come true.[6] Today the socialist community of nations is a crucial factor in world politics, the main motive force in the process of reshaping international relations on democratic principles dictated by the realities of life in the period of transition from capitalism to socialism.

The evolution of new, socialist international relations has produced a profound impact on the entire system of relations among nations. Not only has socialism opposed a new foreign policy of peace to capitalism but it has evolved its own model of truly democratic international relations alien to a policy of war and coercion. The relations between the socialist sister nations are based on socialist internationalism, comradely mutual assistance, respect for the equality and sovereignty of each nation, non-interference in its internal affairs.

In the 60 years since the October Revolution the relations between countries having different social systems have changed considerably. They have run a meandering course: the débâcle suffered by the imperialist military intervention in Soviet Russia led to a period of her diplomatic recognition by the major capitalist powers; in the pre-war period, attempts were made to organize co-operation between the USSR and the Western Powers to repulse Nazi aggression; although the USSR, the USA and Great Britain formed the anti-Hitler coalition which stood the test of the war against the Axis Powers, the post-war period was keynoted by the Cold War of imperialism against the socialist community of nations, with the menace of world thermonuclear war constantly threatening mankind.

The cardinal changes in the balance and alignment of forces on the world scene admittedly made the seventies a turning-point in the development of international relations. There is ample reason to speak of the advent of a new stage in the relations between the capitalist and the socialist countries — a stage dictated by the need to prevent nuclear missile war and to promote peace, security and international co-operation, which brings about political co-operation between states having opposite social systems. This is exemplified by the agreement on regular bilateral political consultations at various levels between the USSR and Western states. The trend towards wider multilateral co-operation is increasingly gaining ground, expressing the global character of vital international problems, including among others the ecological, economic, scientific and technological.

Today's international relations are distinctive in that the West has recognized the need for action jointly with the socialist countries to forestall military conflicts and safeguard peace, to check the arms race and reduce the menace of nuclear war. It is now clearer than ever before that national security can be safeguarded only by peaceful co-operation instead of by a contest in building up military might and stockpiling ever more sophisticated tools of warfare.

The growing power of the socialist community of nations makes it increasingly difficult for the imperialists to resort to military force to achieve their foreign-policy objectives. This lends crucial importance to diplomacy, a negotiated political settlement of international conflicts. Western foreign-policy theoreticians tend to agree that the time of settlement of international disputes by force of arms has passed never to return. In the nineteenth century military victories were a means of gaining diplomatic superiority and recognition, as is stated in a book published in the United States. In our day the situation has changed. The leaders of states, its author says, are coming to realize "...the increasing obsolescence of military solutions to international problems.... It follows that the next decade will be, *par excellence*, an era emphasizing and depending upon diplomacy and diplomatic skills."[7] Such admissions are highly significant. Indeed, it was but recently that Western strategists proclaimed force, especially military force, to be the decisive factor in world politics. Today they are talking of the "paradox of power" which it is impossible to use to achieve the intended result on the international scene.

A truly lasting peace is based not on force but on respect for the sovereignty, lawful rights and interests of all countries, large and small, without exception. It is thus a question of banishing the use of force from world politics. This is one of the central tasks in reshaping international relations initiated by the October Revolution.

In our day the principles of peaceful co-existence have taken good hold in international affairs as the only realistic and sensible ones. Factors making for this are the change in the alignment of forces in the world, primarily the increase in power and international prestige of the Soviet Union and the entire socialist community of nations; the successes achieved by the international working-class and national-liberation movements; and, finally, the understanding of the new realities by a definite part of the ruling quarters of the capitalist world.

At the same time, it is the sum total of the enormous work carried out during the last few years by the Soviet Union and other member states of the socialist community with a view to reshaping international relations and making the principles of peaceful co-existence an inviolable norm in relations between the capitalist and the socialist countries.

In his report on the occasion of the 60th anniversary of the October Revolution, President Brezhnev said:

> The changes for the better in the world, which have become especially appreciable in the 1970s, we refer to as international *détente*. These changes are tangible and specific. They come in the recognition and enactment in international documents of a form of code of rules for honest and fair relations between countries, which erects a legal and moral-political barrier against those given to military gambles. They come in the achievement of the first agreements — modest though they may be for the moment — for blocking some of the channels of the arms race. They come in a whole system of agreements covering many areas of peaceful co-operation between states with different social systems.[8]

The widening recognition of the new principles and standards of international relations is also noted in the activities of international organizations, primarily the United Nations, in the negotiated settlement of a number of extremely complicated problems and acute international crises, in the growing awareness of the need to limit the arms race and solve the disarmament problem, in the realistic approach to many other vital international issues.

In the field of foreign policy the Soviet Union throughout its history has accumulated diversified experience of enormous value and unique historical novelty, which vividly reflects the epoch-making innovative role of socialism in world politics. The mission of renovating international relations on democratic principles devolves precisely on the socialist countries. This is expressed above all in the proclamation of the maintenance of peace as the principal aim of Soviet foreign policy. Banishing war and preserving lasting peace among nations is an ideal of socialism.

The Soviet Union's peace policy is intended to safeguard the fundamental right of man — the right to life. This is an expression of the great humanitarian and democratic principles of socialist foreign policy, its historical contribution to the development of international relations. "Democracy is most clearly manifested in the fundamental question of war and peace", Lenin said.[9] The Soviet Union's efforts to make international relations more humane, to implant such standards of international law that would provide the most favourable conditions for protecting not only the political but also the vital social rights of the individual — the right to work, education, health care, etc., demonstrate the truly democratic essence of Soviet foreign policy, in which the struggle for peace is organically linked with the struggle for socialism.

The successes in the democratic renovation of the system of international relations, its restructuring on the Leninist principles of peaceful co-existence should be considered in the context of revolutionary changes in the world. The groundwork for them was laid by the October Revolution and the growth of socialism into a global system. Lenin pointed out that bourgeois governments can agree to peace "...in any way satisfactory to democracy and the working class" only after "...being 'taught' a lesson... by a series of revolutions".[10] Imperialism today has been taught a good enough lesson. This is precisely what made it possible to normalize relations between the socialist and the capitalist states and what constitutes the historical root-causes of *détente*.[11] Thus, the very process of historical development laid the objective foundation for the radical changes in international relations since October 1917.

It is necessary to emphasize the importance of the activities of the CPSU and the fraternal Communist parties, which are guided by Marxist– Leninist theory in analysing the laws governing the development of international relations and in applying these laws to promote the cause of peace and social progress. This stamps the foreign-policy programmes of the 24th and 25th Congresses of the CPSU — programmes which have given a strong impetus to reshaping international relations on democratic lines.

The new Constitution of the USSR has ratified the fundamental principles of Soviet foreign policy, its class-oriented, revolutionary character determined by the nature of the socialist state. This policy pursues the following objectives: to secure a favourable international situation for building a communist society in the USSR, to protect the national interests of the USSR, to consolidate the positions of world socialism, to support the struggle of the peoples for national liberation and social progress, to prevent wars of aggression, to achieve general and complete disarmament and to implement consistently the principle of peaceful co-existence of states having different social systems. Andrei Gromyko, Politburo member and Foreign Minister of the USSR, said in this context: "It should be emphasized that the peaceful essence of our foreign policy is a corollary of its class-oriented character. Peace is the wish of all peoples, of humanity as a whole, and has always been a common human ideal. It is this that determines the true humanism of Soviet foreign policy.[12]

The new Constitution contains a chapter on foreign policy. This is motivated by the cardinal changes in the position of the USSR on the international scene and its immensely increased influence on world development. By formulating the democratic principles of international law on which the USSR develops its relations with other states, the Constitution gives the force of law to all the ten principles of international relations laid down in the Final Act of the European Conference at Helsinki.

The affirmation in international law of the principles of peaceful co-existence of states having different social systems, for instance, in the UN Charter, the Final Act of the Helsinki Conference and other international documents, is vivid evidence of success in the struggle for democratic international relations initiated by the October Revolution and of progress in the relaxation of world tensions.

The 60-year history of the theory and practice of Soviet foreign policy based on an analysis of the objective deep-seated processes of world development, the dynamic change in the alignment of forces of the two opposite socio-economic systems on the international scene testifies to the growing democratic influence of socialism on international relations.

The march of time tends to bring into focus the system of international relations taking shape in the period of transition from capitalism to socialism under the influence of the three revolutionary mainstreams of today, lends clarity to the meaning and scale of changes in progress, and sheds light on the root causes of the landslides in world politics over the 60 years since the Great October Socialist Revolution.

The present work is an attempt to analyse from Marxist–Leninist positions the changes in international relations in the modern period under the impact of the dynamic and purposeful foreign policy of the world's first socialist state, to show the stages of the struggle waged by the international working class against the foreign policy of the bourgeoisie, to bring to light the main factors in reshaping the global system of international relations on the universal democratic principles of peaceful co-existence of states having different socio-economic systems, and to reveal the link between the struggle for *détente* and the prospects for social progress.

Under present conditions foreign policy and international relations have assumed crucial importance in the process of revolutionary remaking of the world, since the main contradiction of the current epoch — the antagonism between socialism and capitalism — is manifest primarily on the international scene. The contest between the two systems, which has become pivotal in international affairs, conditions not only the foreign policy of states having different social systems but also the development of the entire system of international relations. As is pointed out in a study published by the Institute of World Economics and International Relations under the USSR Academy of Sciences, "the character of the epoch, the deep-going changes affecting all aspects of social life, the spectacular progress of productive forces stimulated by the current revolution in science and technology tend to intensify and widen the interrelationship and interaction of foreign policy and international relations with the world revolutionary process".[13]

In this present work the author continues his research into the history and theory of international relations. Some of its results have been published earlier in his book *A New Stage in International Relations** and in a series of articles in Soviet and foreign journals and newspapers.

The author's specific purpose is to trace the history of the struggle for reshaping international relations on democratic principles, as well as to show the essence of the processes taking place in world politics, to reveal new trends in international relations and their development prospects. He had not confined himself to a concrete historical analysis of the major phenomena of international life but has pursued the wider objective of summing them up theoretically on the basis of Marxist-Leninist methodology.

Scientific analysis, theoretical comprehension of the principal trends in world politics assumes added urgency in view of the intense

---

*Pergamon Press, 1978

ideological struggle over the issues of *détente,* the various aspects of this process, in particular its causes, content and prospects. Ideologists of capitalism, for example, seek to misrepresent the part played by the socialist world in the advent of a new stage of world relations. The most "objective" bourgeois authors do not go further than the following interpretation: *détente* has been made possible by the retreat of the USA and the USSR from their former positions, since each of them has stockpiled enough overkill weapons to wipe out one another many times over. According to this conception *détente* is governed by the "technological factor", the "nuclear stalemate", etc., which have induced the antagonists to back down from military confrontation.[14]

This conception, like many other bourgeois conceptions and theories, attempts to attribute the causes of *détente* to many factors, which often look plausible but ignore the main factor — the change in the alignment of forces in favour of socialism that has compelled imperialism to accept the principles of peaceful co-existence promulgated by the Soviet State in its early days — in Lenin's Decree on Peace. Capitalism is unwilling to admit that it does not steer the course of social progress today; hence, its ideologists make every effort to cast aspersions on *détente* and distort its meaning. In this light the ideological struggle over *détente* has assumed the global character of a class confrontation of the two systems in the international arena.

The author criticizes the views of bourgeois foreign-policy theoreticians concerning the character of the processes now in evidence in world politics. He makes a point of exploding the works of Western anti-Communist authors who misinterpret the development of Soviet foreign policy and go out of their way to play down its beneficial influence on the international situation, its decisive contribution to reshaping the system of international relations on democratic lines. In the West the number of publications on the history of world politics since the October Revolution is growing year after year. Various theories are invented to present the changes in the world in a light favourable to capitalism. As justly noted by a British bourgeois analyst, the abundance of such works is evidence not so much of fruitful theoretical research as of fruitless attempts to evolve a truly scientific theory of international relations.[15] Bourgeois theories of international relations cannot stand the test of time, a confrontation with history, so to say. Divorced from reality, at odds with the historical processes, they are incapable of objectively analysing and forecasting the development of world politics. Bourgeois science cannot measure up to this task.

Marxism–Leninism alone holds the key to an understanding of the processes occurring in all fields of social life, international relations included. In his research on this subject the author was guided by Lenin's interpretation of the active role of socialist foreign policy in reshaping the entire system of international relations which had existed before October 1917. Documents of the CPSU, particularly those of the 24th and 25th Party Congresses, speeches of Leonid Brezhnev, General Secretary of the CPSU Central Committee and President of the Presidium of the USSR Supreme Soviet, are an enormous creative contribution to the Marxist–Leninist theory of international relations. They afford an in-depth analysis of the changes in the world economy and politics, the main trends in evidence within the present world order.

1

The Proletariat and the Foreign Policy of the Bourgeoisie in the Pre-October Period

Marx's and Engels' Ideas of International Proletarian Policy

AS far back as the period before the October Revolution the proletariat had waged a struggle against bourgeois foreign policy, against the system of international relations which had taken shape under the unchallenged rule of capitalism and had served the objective of perpetuating capitalist exploitation and suppressing the national liberation movement. Formulated by Marx and Engels, the international policy of the working class was dictated by its national and international interests as a class. It pursued the objective of creating the most favourable conditions for victory of a worldwide proletarian revolution, for international unity of the working class in the interest of overthrowing the rule of international capital. The essence of this policy was expressed in their slogan: "Workers of the world, unite!", in the principle of proletarian internationalism.

Marx pointed out that the working class alone could solve the problem of reshaping international relations on democratic lines and "...vindicate the simple laws of morals and justice, which ought to govern the relations of private individuals, as the rules paramount to the intercourse of nations".[1]

Marx and Engels believed that to bring about a radical change in the character of a nation's foreign policy the social system based on the exploitation of man by man must be abolished and replaced with a socialist system. "In proportion as the exploitation of one individual by another is put an end to, the exploitation of one nation by another will also be put an end to"[2] they said in the Communist Manifesto. On this path it will be possible to banish war from the life of society: "...in contrast to old society, with its economic miseries and its political delirium, a new society is springing up, whose International rule will be *Peace,* because its national ruler will be everywhere the same — *Labour!*"[3] They had in mind the establishment of a worldwide socialist system of international relations free from exploitation and oppression of nations; at the same time, they regarded proletarian internationalism as the sole principle of the foreign policy of socialist states.

Marx and Engels saw the objective foundation of a common policy of the working class on the international scene in that the class interests of the proletariat in world politics are united and inseparable regardless of the affiliation of a given contingent of the working class to its nationality or state. Engels wrote in this connection: "Since the basic relations between labour and capital are the same everywhere, and the political domination of the propertied classes over the exploited classes is omnipresent, the principles and aim of proletarian policy will be the same everywhere... ."[4] This applies to both the home and foreign policy of the proletariat.

International relations are a key sphere of the proletariat's struggle to achieve its revolutionary objectives. Marx and Engels analysed the class struggle in this sphere with a view to its specifics: the laws of this struggle take a form somewhat different from what is in evidence on the national scene, because they are modified by a great many international, inter-state and other factors. In contrast to the system of the social links within every nation, international relations are "secondary and tertiary phenomena, in general derived, and transmitted, i.e. non-primary" social relations.[5] "To put it differently, recognition of the primacy of domestic relations and of their organic link with international relations does not rule out essential distinctions between them and gives no reason to deny the relative autonomy of international relations as social relations of the secondary and tertiary order."[6]

The classics of scientific communism considered home and foreign policies organically interlinked as an expression — differing in form but identical in content — of the interests of the class in power. If the situation permits, the exploiter class extends the social relations of domination and subordination existing on the home scene to the sphere of international intercourse, so much so that a foreign nation is assimilated to the exploited class of its own nation.

Marx and Engels proved that the foreign policy of a bourgeois state is largely shaped by factors generated by the class struggle between the proletariat and the bourgeoisie. The latter regards foreign policy as a tool by which to preserve and consolidate its gains and positions abroad as well as to achieve its selfish class objectives at home. The class function performed by bourgeois foreign policy on the domestic scene is "...to paralyse democratic energies, to deflect attention from itself, to dig conduits for the fiery lava of the revolution and forge the weapon of suppression within the country."[7]

The discovery by Marx and Engels of the class character of international relations entailed the vital task of working out on scientific principles a consistent foreign-policy programme of the working class, which was coming on the historical scene "...no longer as servile retainers, but as independent actors, conscious of their own responsibility, and able to command peace where their would-be masters shout war".[8]

The close link between the task for the proletariat to pursue its own independent international policy and the Marxian theory of socialist revolution was pointed out in many works, in particular, in the Inaugural Address of the Working Men's International Association, which said that it was the duty of the world proletariat

> ...to master themselves the mysteries of international politics; watch the diplomatic acts of their respective Governments; to counteract them, if necessary by all means in their power...
>
> The fight for such a foreign policy forms part of the general struggle for the emancipation of the working classes.[9]

The foreign policy of the national contingents of the proletariat, internationalist in essence, was not limited to its class objectives but expressed the national interests in general, since it was determined by the requirements of society's most progressive class.

The struggle of the world proletariat for "the simple laws of morals and justice" to be affirmed in international relations meant in effect a struggle to establish the general democratic principles in world politics — the right of nations to self-determination, respect for their sovereignty, non-interference in the internal affairs of other states and peoples, renunciation of wars of conquest, etc. This task was put forward because once it had come to power the bourgeoisie discarded in its home and foreign policies the slogans of liberty, equality, and fraternity it had proclaimed when leading the people's assault on the feudal bastilles. In its foreign policy the bourgeoisie exhibited the wide gulf between word and deed characteristic of this class. Posing as guardians of national interests and peacemakers, the bourgeois leaders contributed to the establishment on earth of an unprecedented universal system of oppression of nations, lawlessness, and coercion. The bourgeoisie widely used its ostensible commitment to democratic slogans to mislead the masses and conceal its selfish ends.

No sooner had the bourgeois governments consolidated their power than they embarked on a policy of wars of conquest, violence and coercion in international politics. The government of the Directoire which came to power in France after the fall of the revolutionary dictatorship of the Jacobins converted the revolutionary wars of the French Republic into predatory raids in the interest of the French bourgeoisie. In Great Britain the names of Prime Minister Palmerston and Gladstone have long come to stand for the cynical lie, for insidiousness and sanctimonious hypocrisy. In Germany Chancellor Bismarck invariably camouflaged his wars of conquest against neighbouring states, which followed one another in rapid succession, with appeals for defence of German national interests. This ideological brainwashing of the masses had reached its climax on the eve of the First World War, when the bourgeoisie, using patriotic slogans, hoodwinked millions of workers in all countries and turned them into cannon fodder.

Guided by the principles of proletarian internationalism, the world working class from its early days opposed this corrupt antipopular system of international relations where war was a "lawful" means of attaining the predatory goals of the bourgeoisie. The national contingents of the proletariat took a determined stand against the foreign policy and diplomacy of the exploiter classes. But with the bourgeoisie holding unchallenged sway over the world, the working class had a limited possibility to influence international relations and foreign policy. What was most important, the world proletariat had no power to force the capitalists to abandon their policy of wars of conquest and enslavement of other countries and peoples. In our day, this power is wielded by real socialism, which has come on the historical scene as a world system co-existing with capitalism. Even in the period before the October Revolution, however, the proletariat had at times vigorously interfered in the foreign policy of bourgeois states.

The imperative need for the proletariat to oppose the foreign policy of the bourgeoisie was emphasized in the Inaugural Address of the International Working Men's Association, which read in part: "If the emancipation of the working classes requires their fraternal concurrence, how are they to fulfil that great mission with a foreign policy in pursuit of criminal designs, playing upon national prejudices, and squandering in piratical wars the people's blood and treasure?"[10] In a letter to Engels of 25 February 1865, Marx wrote that the proletariat must pursue its own foreign policy, in which it should "by no means be guided by what the bourgeoisie considers appropriate".[11]

The leaders of the international proletariat, Marx and Engels set up a model for exposing the true essence of the foreign policy of exploiter states. Engels wrote in 1848 that the skill and activities of all earlier governments and their diplomacy had boiled down to fomenting strife between nations, using one nation to oppress another so as to prolong the existence of absolute rule. In a series of pamphlets Marx levied scathing criticism on Britain's foreign policy and with annihilating sarcasm laid bare Lord Palmerston's diplomatic ploys.

The involvement of the working class in international politics became more active after the foundation of the First International. The workers of Europe took a determined stand against the European bourgeoisie intervening in the American Civil War on the side of the slave-owners of the South. As it was stated in a message to President Lincoln from the International Working Men's Association, written by Marx, the European proletariat had taken that action, fully aware that the struggle against slave-ownership in the USA was a cause for the international working class.[12]

The First International took a principled stand on the Franco–Prussian War of 1870-71 as well. The class-conscious workers of the European countries angrily protested against the annexation of Alsace-Lorraine. One of the appeals issued by the First International in connection with the Franco–Prussian war read in particular: "If they forsake their duty, if they remain passive, the present tremendous war will be but the harbinger of still deadlier international feuds, and lead in every nation to a renewed triumph over the workman by the lords of the sword, of the soil, and of capital."[13]

Marx and Engels paid keen attention to the struggle against the foreign policy of Russian tsarism, which had long been the bulwark of international reaction. In an article "The Foreign Policy of Russian Tsarism" published in 1890, Engels pointed out that by her constant interference in the affairs of the West Russia delayed the development of European revolution and made victory of the European proletariat largely impossible.[14] Hence the deep-rooted interest of the West European proletariat in overthrowing Russian absolutism.[15]

It should be noted that this assessment, which the Second International applied by rote to Russia of the late nineteenth and early twentieth century, was not true to fact: the decay of tsarism, its defeat in the Crimean War of 1853-56 and the rise of the revolutionary movement no longer allowed Russia to play that role. The main force in world politics now was the most advanced imperialist powers — Britain, France, Germany, the United States, Italy, and Japan — which pursued a predatory colonial policy and initiated a redivision of the world through war.

It would also be wrong to assess all foreign-policy moves of tsarist Russia as reactionary. In a few cases they contributed objectively to the liberation of some oppressed nations from the yoke of foreign exploiters. This is not at all surprising. As far back as 1860, Engels wrote of the possibility of circumstances where the subjectively reactionary becomes in foreign policy the objectively revolutionary.[16] That was precisely the case in the Balkans by reason of Russia's involvement. For all the subjectively reactionary plans of tsarism, Russia performed the objectively progressive mission of liberating the peoples of the Balkan Peninsula from the yoke of Ottoman Turkey.

Lenin later referred to Russia's drastically lessened influence on world and European affairs. In an article of 1909 commenting on Tsar Nicholas II's visit to Europe, he pointed out that half a century ago Russia had become widely notorious as an "international policeman", and that the leaders of the international proletariat, Marx and Engels, since the 1840s had repeatedly described tsarism as the main bulwark of reaction in the whole civilized world.

> Beginning with the last three decades or so of the nineteenth century, the revolutionary movement in Russia gradually altered this state of affairs. The more tsarism was shaken by the blows of the growing revolutionary movement at home, the weaker it became as the enemy of freedom in Europe. But in the meantime another international reactionary force had taken definite shape in Europe — the bourgeois governments, which had witnessed insurrections by the proletariat, had realized that a life-and-death struggle between labour and capital was inevitable and would welcome any adventurer or brigand on the throne for the sake of joining forces against the proletariat."[17]

The situation had changed: formerly the Tsar had helped Europe's counter-revolutionary bourgeois governments to suppress democracy, now Europe's bourgeois reaction was helping the Tsar to suppress revolution. This was strikingly exemplified in the help afforded the tsarist government by the "democratic" bourgeois states in defeating the first Russian Revolution of 1905-07.

The new era, one of transition from capitalism to imperialism, which followed defeat of the Paris Commune required Marxists and labour organizations further to develop the strategy and tactics of foreign policy.

In the last third of the nineteenth century the aggressive ambitions of the capitalist states tended to grow and the redivision of the world among the great powers was completed. The main imperialist blocs which later plunged the world into the First World War had also began to take shape at that time. Hence the steadily growing interest in international affairs on the part of the working class, its national and international organizations. The socialist movement focused its attention on the attitude of the working class to war and militarism, invasion, armies, and colonial conquest.

The arms race begun in the late nineteenth century in preparation for a world war faced the proletariat with the urgent need to campaign for disarmament. In the article "Can Europe Disarm?" published in March 1893 Engels warned the working class of the danger of a general war of annihiliation which would inevitably follow the arms race and the growth of the standing armies in the capitalist countries of Europe.[18] To the question posed in the title, he answered: "I believe that disarmament and thus a guarantee of peace are possible."[19] Thus, as far back as the late nineteenth century he formulated one of the main foreign-policy tasks still facing the international working-class movement, the entire peace-loving humanity — the struggle for disarmament, without which peace cannot be assured.

The Bolshevik Party Line on Foreign Policy before October 1917

In the new historical situation where capitalism developed into imperialism the foreign policy of the imperialist powers assumed a more clear-cut anti-popular and anti-national character, and the entire system of international relations became an instrument of domination by a handful of colonial powers. Wars followed one another in rapid succession from the late nineteenth to the early twentieth century: the Franco–Prussian War of 1870-71, the Serbo–Turkish War of 1877-78, the Russo–Turkish War of 1877-78, the Sino–Japanese War of 1894-98, the Spanish–American War of 1898, the Anglo–Boer War of 1899-1902, the Russo–Japanese War of 1904-05, the Italo–Turkish War of 1911-12, the Balkan Wars of 1912-13, and finally the imperialist First World War.

On the eve of the First World War imperialism had reached the zenith of its power. Almost 1000 million people of the world's population of 1600 million lived in colonies and semi-colonies.[20] London, Paris, Washington and Berlin were the main centres of world politics. Rape of small countries and peoples became "legitimized" in world politics.

Used for the method of handling international affairs employed by US imperialism "gunboat diplomacy" became a common term in the history of diplomacy. The methods of imperialist diplomacy changed, but their essence — coercion and dictatorialness — remained the same. The right way in international affairs, said President Theodore Roosevelt, is to speak kindly but have a big stick at the ready. His successor, Willie Taft, supplemented the big-stick policy with the so-called "dollar diplomacy".

Suppression of the revolutionary struggle of the proletariat and the national liberation movement in the colonial and dependent countries became a major foreign policy objective of imperialism. This is admitted by many bourgeois authors today. For instance, in the book *A Hundred Years of International Relations* published in the USA in 1971 it is stated that the system of international relations before the First World War had been predominantly European and based on the premise of the racial superiority of the peoples in the old continent, the use of coercion in relations with the countries of Asia, Africa, and Latin America. Its purpose was to safeguard the "security" of Europe against danger from abroad and revolutionary explosions at home.[21]

In developing the theory of Marx and Engels to bring it up to date in the imperialist era, Lenin planned the foreign policy of the proletariat in general and the working class of Russia and the Bolshevik Party in particular. Lenin's approach to the proletariat's foreign policy was characterized by, first, its all-round analysis of the current historical situation, the international situation, the balance of power between states or groups of states, and the contradictions between them; and secondly, by its awareness of the struggle between classes on the national and international scale and their movement, awareness, in the first place, of the position of the proletariat as today's most progressive and revolutionary class holding the key to the future. Lenin's conception of the international policy of the proletariat in the period before the October Revolution was essentially that it should promote international solidarity, should struggle for peace and against imperialist wars, and should take advantage of political crises caused by war to facilitate the victory of revolution.

The Bolshevik party-line on foreign policy before the October Revolution was one of a class opposition party coming out against the tsarist policy of conquest and was directed to securing the triumph of socialism in Russia and on the international scene.

Guided by an analysis of the revolutionary forces, Lenin widened the concept of proletarian internationalism. He pointed out that in the imperialist era the national liberation movement in the colonial and semi-colonial countries merged with the struggle of the international proletariat in a common revolutionary mainstream. "The foreign policy of the proletariat is alliance with the revolutionaries of the advanced countries and with all the oppressed nations against all and any imperialists."[22]

The objectives and methods of the Bolshevik Party's international policy were profoundly democratic. The reasons are obvious. The revolutionary movement of the proletariat meets the interests of the mass of the people; therefore, the Communist Party's activities in general and its foreign policy programme in particular are in complete accord with these interests. The Communists have no need to conceal their foreign policy from the people. They can implement it only with their massive support and direct involvement.

In accordance with Lenin's instructions, the Communist Party has invariably planned its foreign policy with the interests of the masses in the foreground, involving them in the work to set its guidelines and resolutely opposing the methods of bourgeois secret diplomacy. Lenin pointed out the need "...to denounce this diplomatic farce, bring the truth to the people, expose international anti-proletarian reaction!"[23]

The Bolshevik Party's foreign policy based on the principles of proletarian internationalism was expressed in its attitude to international events in the late nineteenth and early twentieth century. A typical example was the Party's stand in relation to the imperialist intervention of Britain, Germany, Austria-Hungary, Japan, the United States, France, Russia, and Italy in China, where an uprising flared up in 1899. In the article "The War in China" published in the first issue of the newspaper *Iskra* (Spark), Lenin stigmatized the interventionists' atrocities against Chinese civilians. He exposed the falsity of the bourgeois propaganda campaign which justified the imperialist intervention in China by a hue and cry about the "yellow peril", and said that it was the duty of the class-conscious workers "...to rise with all their might against those who are stirring up national hatred and diverting the attention of the working people from their real enemies".[24] Lenin expressed the full solidarity of the working people of Russia with the Chinese people's liberation struggle.

Coming out in support of the national liberation movement, the Leninist Party had to fight on two fronts — against the undisguised imperialists, and against the opportunists who opposed the principle of the right of nations to self-determination in favour of a "socialist colonial policy". Lenin described this stand of the right-wing Social-Democrats as a direct defection to the bourgeois point of view, which meant "...subordinating the proletariat to bourgeois ideology, to bourgeois imperialism."[25]

When after the defeat of the First Russian Revolution tsarism unleashed a new reign of terror against the oppressed national minorities, the Bolsheviks led by Lenin took a determined stand in defence of their rights. Russia's Social-Democrats angrily denounced the attempts of tsarism to deprive Finland of her autonomy.[26] The Prague Conference of the RSDLP in 1912 passed a special resolution "On the Policy of Tsarism Towards Finland". The resolution denounced the adoption by the Tsar and the State Duma of laws ignoring the rights of the Finnish people. It emphasized the common interests of the workers of Finland and Russia, and expressed strong confidence that it was only through their joint efforts that tsarism could be overthrown and the Russian and Finnish peoples could achieve their freedom.[27] This resolution reinforced what Lenin had formulated in his articles "The Tsar Against the Finnish People" (1909) and "The Campaign Against Finland" (1910) as the position of Russia's working class, which had a vital interest in supporting Finland's freedom and reasonably believed that the problem of her independence was closely bound up with its own revolutionary struggle.[28]

One of the resolutions of the Prague Conference emphasized the worldwide significance of the Chinese people's revolutionary struggle and denounced the stance of the Russian liberals in support of the tsarist policy of conquest. Russia's proletariat, the resolution said, followed the successes of the revolutionary people in China with profound inspiration and complete sympathy.[29]

The policy of the Russian Tsar *vis-à-vis* Iran was also angrily denounced.

> The Russian Social-Democratic Party protests against the predatory policy of
> the tsarist gang, who have determined to stifle the Persian people's freedom and

have not stopped at the most barbarian and heinous acts to achieve their ends. The Conference declares that an alliance of Russia's proletariat with the British Government so loudly advertised and supported by the Russian liberals is aimed primarily against the revolutionary movement of Asian democracy and that this alliance makes the British Liberal government an accomplice in the bloody atrocities committed by tsarism.[30]

Lenin's assessment of the aggressive, imperialist essence of the Anglo–Russian alliance of 1907 was along the same lines as his assessment of the Entente as a whole. When the French socialist Jaurès declared that he regarded the Entente as a guarantee of peace, Lenin expressed his solidarity with Rosa Luxemburg[31] who had strongly opposed the attempts to whitewash the alliance of the imperialist predators preparing for a redivision of the world.

The Prague Conference of the Bolsheviks demonstrated the truly internationalist approach of Russia's proletariat to the problem of international politics, its opposition to the existing system of international relations, its determination to struggle against imperialism, for the right of the peoples to be masters of their own destinies, and to live in conditions of peace and security. The Prague Conference unambiguously went on record in favour of strengthening fraternal solidarity with the proletarians in all countries. The Conference decisions were based on the principles of proletarian internationalism.

In his works on international politics before the First World War Lenin paid keen attention to the problems of Europe's "powder keg", the Balkan Peninsula. In essence, the Balkan problem was linked to the efforts of a counter-revolutionary coalition of European powers to check the national democratic movement of the Balkan peoples. Hence, it was a task for the class-conscious proletariat of Russia to explain to the masses the reactionary essence of the Balkans policy of the European powers and to oppose any interference by the imperialists in the affairs of the Balkan states. "The Balkans for the Balkan Peoples!" was the slogan formulated by the leader of the Russian and international proletariat.[32]

Lenin stressed that it was not the bourgeois diplomats but the progressive workers, the democratic forces in the Balkans, the mass of the people, who were to have their say concerning freedom for the

Balkan states.[33] He welcomed the victory of Serbia, Bulgaria, Montenegro, and Greece over Turkey, which was backed by Europe's imperialist powers. Lenin called this victory a new chapter in world history, a step towards the freedom of the Balkan peoples.

Support for the national liberation movement is the main line of the proletariat's foreign policy. Lenin and the Bolshevik Party viewed this question as follows:

> Socialists must not only demand the unconditional and immediate liberation of the colonies without compensation — and this demand in its political expression signifies nothing else than recognition of the right to self-determination. They must also render determined support to the more revolutionary elements in the bourgeois democratic movements for national liberation in these countries and assist their uprising — or revolutionary war, in the event of one — *against* the imperialist powers that oppress them.[34]

According to Lenin, the national liberation movement will be successful if it is firmly allied with the international working-class movement. He said that after its coming to power the proletariat should not only grant the rights of all colonial and dependent peoples to self-determination but also help them overcome their economic backwardness. The working class should make common cause with under-developed nations of Asia and Africa setting out on the road to independent development and give them disinterested assistance. It should help them come over to the application of machinery, the lightening of work, to democracy and socialism.[35]

These ideas of Lenin's laid the basis for the Bolshevik Party's policy towards the national liberation movement. They have fully kept their meaning for today.

The high-principled stand on the disarmament problem taken by the Bolsheviks on the eve of the First World War, at the congresses of the Second International in particular, was of crucial importance for the struggle against the aggressive policy of imperialism. Lenin declared that "Disarmament is the ideal of socialism".[36] At the same time, he appealed for disarmament as a democratic measure to lessen the risk of war between states. The slogan of and the movement for disarmament undermined the positions of militarism and imperialism, and their possibilities for making war.

In the years before the First World War, when the arms race had intensified, the Bolsheviks exposed those who lined their pockets by it.

GOTW - C

Lenin pointed out that the arms race benefited only the arms manufacturers who extracted fabulous super-profits from military contracts.

> Armstrong in Britain, Krupp in Germany, Creusot in France, Cockerill in Belgium — how many of them are there in all the 'civilized' countries?...
>
> These are the ones *who stand to gain* from the whipping up of chauvinism, from the chatter about 'patriotism' (cannon patriotism), about the defence of culture (with weapons destructive of culture) and so forth![37]

The Bolshevik representative in the State Duma, A.E. Badayev, declared at a meeting of its Budget Committee on 12 June 1913 that the Social-Democratic deputies would vote against the war budgets. He declared that socialism alone would uproot the causes of the arms race and war and went on to say that within the framework of the existing society "we are determined to do our utmost to lighten the burden of militarism and ease the struggle waged by the working class for its complete emancipation.[38]

Lenin regarded the problem of war and peace as central to the theory and practice of foreign policy. To banish war from the life of society was a historic task of the Communist movement outlined by Marx and Engels. Lenin considered the struggle for peace not only in conjunction with the struggle for socialism but also as an independent task in the international policy of the working class. It was precisely this class that was destined to perform the mission of waging this struggle in the interest of all mankind. Lenin repeatedly emphasized the immense contribution of the working class to the peace movement. He wrote that "The one guarantee of peace is the organised, conscious movement of the working class... there is no other champion of peace and liberty in the world than the international revolutionary proletariat".[39]

The International Socialist Congress at Basel in November 1912 discussed the problem of the war menace and called on all workers to oppose the efforts of the imperialists to unleash war, to use both the parliamentary and non-parliamentary means of struggle to demonstrate the proletariat's commitment to peace.

The Bolshevik Party consistently abided by this decision in its activities. It launched a wide-scale anti-war propaganda campaign. Lenin came forward with exposures of the war preparations which were in progress in the capitalist countries on the plea of defence of the national interests. "Russian chauvinists are being used to scare the Germans, and German chauvinists, the Russians!"[40] Speaking in the State Duma on behalf of the Bolsheviks in July 1914, Badayev declared that the working class would do everything in its power to avert war, which was against the interest of the workers and aimed at the heart of the world's working class. "The International Socialist Congress at Basel", he said, "resolved on behalf of the proletariat to wage a determined struggle against war should it break out. 'A war on war' is our slogan. We genuine representatives of the working class will fight under this slogan."[41]

Lenin emphasized that the Socialists had invariably condemned war as a barbarous and atrocious business. While opposing with strong determination wars of conquest for a redivision of the world, and the suppression of the national liberation movement by the colonial powers, the Bolsheviks at the same time openly declared their solidarity with those waging a just war for their liberation.

During the First World War the opportunistic leaders of the Second International defected from internationalist positions to the camp of the imperialist bourgeoisie. The Social-Democrats of Germany, Britain, France, and other countries came out in support of their bourgeois governments, proclaiming "a civil peace" within their nations. The Bolsheviks alone remained loyal to the sacred banner of proletarian internationalism. They held up to shame social-chauvinism and those who, like G.V. Plekhanov, called on Russia's proletariat to defend the bourgeois-monarchist fatherland.[42]

The Bolshevik Party was guided by Lenin's high-principled assessment of the First World War. "A struggle for markets and for freedom to loot foreign countries, a striving to suppress the revolutionary movement of the proletariat and democracy in the individual countries, a desire to deceive, disunite, and slaughter the proletarians of all countries by setting the wage slaves of one nation against those of another so as to benefit the bourgeoisie — those are the only real content and significance of the war," Lenin wrote in September 1914.[43]

Showing the link between the imperialist First World War and the preceding home and foreign policies of the bourgeois states and governments, Lenin quoted Clausewitz's dictum that war is the continuation of politics by other means. In the decades before the war, the imperialist states had been pursuing a policy of plundering the colonies, oppressing foreign nations, putting down the labour movement. As Lenin emphasized it was this very policy that was continuing in the present war.[44]

Proceeding from the definition of the character of the war as imperialist and anti-popular, Lenin worked out a tactic of the party, of the working class, which was in effect its policy in relation to that war. "A revolutionary class cannot but wish for the defeat of its government in a reactionary war, and cannot fail to see that the latter's military reverses must facilitate its overthrow," he wrote.[45] The slogan advanced in this connection called for the defeat of one's own government and for the imperialist war to be turned into a civil war. That truly internationalist, revolutionary policy of the working class towards the First World War was in full harmony with the tactics of opposition to an eventual imperialist war worked out at the congresses of the Second International.

Foreign social-chauvinists, not to speak of representatives of the Russian bourgeoisie, accused the Bolsheviks of lacking patriotism and love of the homeland. Lenin gave them a fitting rebuff in the article "On the National Pride of the Great Russians", in which he showed how patriotism should be interpreted and combined with a class-oriented, internationalist approach to the events of world politics. "We love our language and our country, and we are doing our very utmost to raise *her* toiling masses (i.e. nine-tenths of *her* population) to the level of a democratic and socialist consciousness."[46] He wrote that ". . . full of a sense of national pride, we Great-Russian workers want, come what may, a free and independent, a democratic, republican and proud Great Russia, one that will base its relations with its neighbours on the human principle of equality, and not on the feudalist principle of privilege, which is so degrading to a great nation."[47] These words express the essence of the international policy of the proletariat opposing dictatorship and coercion, inequality and subordination of one country to another.

Committed to peace in principle, the Bolsheviks at the same time patiently explained the inconsistency and even harmfulness of a pacifist approach to the slogan of peace with the First World War in progress. "At the present time," Lenin warned, "The propaganda of peace unaccompanied by a call for revolutionary mass action can only sow illusions and demoralize the proletariat, for it makes the proletariat believe that the bourgeoisie is humane, and turns it into a plaything in the hands of the secret diplomacy of the belligerent countries."[48]

At the end of 1916 there was a turn in world politics from the imperialist war to an imperialist peace settlement. The working class and the labouring masses of the whole world desired withdrawal from the war through a democratic process, a democratic and just peace settlement. The only way to achieve such settlement was for the proletariat to convert the imperialist into a civil war. Even before that, Lenin had pointed out that "...the idea of a so-called democratic peace being possible without a series of revolutions is profoundly erroneous".[49]

This remark of Lenin's helps one realize that it is impossible to reshape the traditional pattern of international relations without a socialist revolution winning in several countries. This idea of the great theoretician of scientific communism has been borne out by history: it was not until the triumph of the October Revolution and the formation of the world's first workers' and peasants' state — the Soviet Republic — that it became possible to begin reshaping international relations on the Leninist principles of a just and democratic peace.

The Bolshevik Party staunchly upheld Lenin's programme of withdrawal from the imperialist war through a revolution. In his "Letters from Afar" Lenin urged a struggle for denunciation of the Tsar's treaties, their publication, an immediate armistice, a peace settlement on condition that the colonies, dependent, oppressed and under-privileged peoples be granted freedom, and called on the workers of all countries to overthrow their governments and take over power, to refuse to repay the loans received by the bourgeois governments for the conduct of the war.[50] In his "April Theses" Lenin also discussed the ways of withdrawing from the war and called for explaining to the masses that unless the rule of capital was abolished it was impossible to end the war by a democratic peace settlement.[51]

After the victory of the bourgeois-democratic revolution of February 1917 in Russia Lenin suggested a concrete plan for the withdrawal of Russia and other belligerent powers from the world war. He expounded it in detail in "The Mandate to Deputies of the Soviet of Workers' and Soldiers' Deputies Elected at Factories and in Army Regiments". It demanded that the government should immediately and unconditionally, without any evasions or delay, openly propose a peace settlement to all belligerent powers on condition that all oppressed national minorities be granted freedom. Lenin explained this as meaning that Russia would not hold any people through coercion, direct or indirect. At the same time, the Bolsheviks were in favour of a fraternal union of all nations, their integration in a common state by mutual consent.

Lenin believed that the workers of other countries should take up the same internationalist attitude to the problem of ending the imperialist war. For instance, the German workers ought to fight for Germany's withdrawal from all conquered lands. Simultaneously with Russia she should pull out her forces from foreign territory and allow every people to decide freely in what state, a separate or a federated one, they would prefer to live. Germany, of course, should give up her colonies.

The "Mandate" also contained proposals to be implemented by the British workers. Under the terms of a peace settlement Britain should also give up immediately and unconditionally all occupied foreign lands, in particular the German colonies in Africa, as well as the Turkish lands and Mesopotamia, and all her colonies. Britain, just as Russia and Germany, should pull out her forces from the conquered lands, from her colonies (among them Ireland), and allow every people to decide in what kind of state, separate or federated, they would prefer to live.

Lenin deemed it necessary for every state involved in the war, all the belligerents, to make peace immediately on the same terms in principle. "This criminal war must be brought to a speedy end, *not* by a separate peace with Germany, *but by a universal peace,* not by a capitalist peace, but by a peace of the working masses *against* the capitalists. There is only one way to do this, and that is by transferring all state power to the Soviets of Workers', Soldiers', and Peasants'

Deputies both in Russia and in other countries."[52] Such were the foreign policy guidelines for the Russian and international working class set by Lenin after the February Revolution in Russia.

Lenin's plan of struggle against the imperialist war, for withdrawal from it through revolution, vividly revealed the fundamental principles of the foreign policy of a working-class party: its commitment to revolution, internationalism, democracy, humanism, and peace.

Leninism implies organic harmony between socialist and democratic ideas in the fields of home and foreign policy. Just as the general revolutionary programme of the Marxist–Leninist party combined the socialist aims as such with the general democratic tasks, its foreign-policy programme also included along with the socialist idea of proletarian internationalism the general democratic idea of a just peace.

Lenin's idea of a democratic peace, which was totally remote from abstract pacifism, was embodied in the programme of the revolutionary party of the proletariat not only as the corollary of the specific conditions of the First World War. The struggle for peace had always been a principle of the proletariat's international policy, an inalienable part of the common struggle for labour emancipation. What is more, both before and after the October Revolution Lenin definitely considered the idea of a democratic peace as an aim which had independent significance. "An end to wars, peace among the nations, the cessation of pillaging and violence — such is our ideal", he said when Russia was still on her way to a socialist revolution.[53] In combination with other democratic principles (the right of nations to self-determination, equality, sovereignty, non-interference in the internal affairs of other nations, renunciation of annexation, and of all violence and coercion in relations between nations, etc.), in the post-October period Lenin's idea of a just and democratic peace became the keynote of a consistent programme of reshaping international relations on democratic principles.

2

The October Revolution —
Towards a New Global System of
International Relations

The Soviet Foreign Policy Principles as Laid Down and Developed by Lenin

MARX and Engels took it as axiomatic "The communist revolution will . . . be no merely national one; it will be a revolution taking place simultaneously in all civilized countries, that is, at least in England, America, France and Germany".[1] With this concept of the world revolutionary process a simultaneous abolition of capitalism implied the overthrowing of the bourgeois system and the establishment of a socialist global system of international relations. In this new system of international relations free from the exploitation and oppression of nations, proletarian internationalism alone could be the sole principle of foreign policy.

As capitalism developed into imperialism, however, the conditions and the very course of the world revolutionary process changed. Lenin proved that in the monopoly stage of capitalism the objective and subjective prerequisites for a world socialist revolution could not mature in all countries simultaneously. In his articles "On the Slogan of a United States of Europe" (1915) and "The Military Programme of the Proletarian Revolution" (1916) he set forth the conclusion to the effect that uneven economic and political development, which is an absolute law under capitalism, makes victory of socialism impossible in all capitalist countries simultaneously. A socialist revolution will win initially in one or several countries, while the others will remain capitalist or pre-capitalist for a certain period of time.

Lenin's theory of socialist revolution suggests conclusions of enormous importance for the proletariat's strategy in the foreign policy field. First, the very character of the world revolutionary process makes a historical period of co-existence of the two opposite socio-economic systems inevitable; it is in the interest of socialism for this co-existence to be peaceful, because it is precisely in peacetime that the advantages of the socialist system can be brought into full play. Second, the system of international relations taking shape under these conditions and comprising both socialist and non-socialist states will have the character of transition from the bourgeois to a socialist system. Third, in the period of transition from capitalism to socialism the socialist states must work for reshaping the global system of international relations on democratic lines to secure peace and social progress.

The triumph of the socialist revolution in Russia confirmed the correctness of Lenin's revolutionary theory, which incorporates as its organic component his conception of peaceful co-existence of states having different social systems in the period of transition from capitalism to socialism. The October Revolution initiated the struggle of socialism against the bourgeois system of world relations, which no longer corresponded to the realities of the socially heterogeneous world that faced mankind after the establishment of the world's first workers' and peasants' state.

The historic significance of the October Revolution stems from the fact that its victory brought about a qualitative change in mankind's eternal problem of war and peace. The 60-year history of the Soviet State from the first fundamental act of Soviet government — Lenin's Decree on Peace — to the new Constitution of the USSR proves conclusively that the first state of triumphant socialism has forever inscribed on its banner the word 'peace' as the supreme principle of its foreign policy meeting the interests of its own people and all the other peoples on earth.

In the Decree on Peace the Soviet Government denounced the

imperialist war as the most heinous crime against humanity and solemnly declared "its determination immediately to sign the terms of a peace settlement ending this war on the aforesaid terms equally fair to all peoples without exception". It contained a clear-cut definition of a just and democratic peace — a peace without annexations and indemnities. The document explained that "the government interprets annexation or conquest of foreign lands as any annexation to a large and strong state of a large or small people without its precisely and clearly-worded voluntary consent regardless of when this forcible annexation took place, and irrespective of how developed or underdeveloped is the nation forcibly annexed or forcibly held within the borders of a given state. Regardless, finally, of whether this nation lives in Europe or in a faraway overseas land."[2]

Thus, the very definition of annexation formulated the general democratic principles followed by a socialist state in international affairs. These are as follows: complete renunciation of aggression in whatever form, recognition of the right of nations to self-determination, denunciation of colonialism, respect for the principle of equality of all states and peoples, both large and small.

"We will, of course, insist upon the whole of our programme for a peace without annexations and indemnities. We shall not retreat from it; but we must not give our enemies an opportunity to say that their conditions are different from ours and that therefore it is useless to start negotiations with us. No, we must deprive them of that advantageous position and not present our terms in the form of an ultimatum", Lenin declared in his report on peace on 26 October 1917.[3]

This statement forcefully demonstrated the willingness of the Soviet State to settle international problems through negotiation, so as to ensure the peaceful co-existence of the socialist state with the capitalist countries.

The Declaration of Rights of the Working and Exploited People drafted by Lenin and approved by the Third All-Russia Congress of Soviets in January 1918 reaffirmed an inflexible determination to deliver mankind from "the most criminal of all wars", to achieve at all costs a democratic peace among nations, without annexations or indemnities, on the principle of self-determination of nations. The

Soviet Government declared its "...complete break with the barbarous policy of bourgeois civilization, which has built the prosperity of the exploiters belonging to a few chosen nations on the enslavement of hundreds of millions of working people in Asia, in the colonies in general, and in the small countries".[4] Another important document was the appeal "To All Muslim Working People of Russia and the East", which proclaimed their right to organize their national life freely and without obstruction. "You must know", the Soviet Government solemnly assured them, "that your rights and the rights of all peoples of Russia are protected by the full power of the revolution and its organs — the Soviets of Workers', Soldiers' and Peasants' Deputies."[5]

Just as the Decree on Peace, so the other first foreign-policy acts of Soviet Russia, which laid the foundation of socialist foreign policy, organically combined the principles of peaceful co-existence and proletarian internationalism. The Decree on Peace emphasized the class character of Soviet foreign policy by declaring that the proletarian state would conduct it "in accordance with the law consciousness of democracy in general and the labouring classes in particular".[6] The fact, which was without precedent in history, that the Decree on Peace was addressed not only to the governments but also to the peoples of the belligerent powers, particularly to the progressive class-conscious workers of Britain, France, and Germany strikingly demonstrated the proletarian internationalism of Soviet foreign policy. That was an appeal to the masses to take a direct part in the struggle for peace, to interfere actively in world politics.

Lenin's conception of peaceful co-existence, substantiated theoretically before October 1917 and formulated in the Decree on Peace as the foundation of Soviet foreign policy towards the capitalist countries, was designed to protect the national and international interests of the world's first socialist state. This policy was based on general democratic principles and recognition of equality between the two systems of ownership. The policy of peaceful co-existence expressed essentially the dedication of the Bolshevik Party and the Soviet Government to their internationalist duty: the peaceful co-existence of states having different social systems ensures favourable conditions for the struggle of all revolutionary forces against imperialism, for peace and social progress.

In Lenin's interpretation, peaceful co-existence is a form of the class struggle between socialism and capitalism on the international scene. However, it is radically different from the forms in which the states of the exploiter classes struggled in the sphere of international relations. In contrast to these forms — military intervention, economic blockade, etc. — socialism calls into being qualitatively new forms of this struggle, abiding by the general democratic principles of relations between states having different social systems.

Needless to say, their application necessarily implies a constant struggle against imperialism. First, because imperialism seeks to undermine and suppress democracy wherever possible it follows that the struggle for democracy invariably offers a rebuff to the aggressive designs and ambitions of imperialism. Second, the struggle against imperialism, for the ideals of democracy in world politics is inevitable, because the very notion of democracy is differently interpreted by different classes; consequently, even the recognition by capitalist states of certain democratic norms does not yet settle the question of how consistent this recognition is and what meaning is actually attached to these norms. This question can also be settled only through the clash and struggle between different class-motivated points of view.

Peaceful co-existence implies that the superiority of a social system must be determined not through war or preparation for war but through competition in the economic, political, social and spiritual fields, mutually beneficial co-operation in definite fields between states having different social systems. Peaceful co-existence is not a mechanical combination of "struggle and cooperation", where these two components are on an equal footing, so to say. The contest between states with opposite social systems which Lenin had in mind has always been and remains in essence a question of relations in the class war regardless of the fact that within the framework of such a specific form of this war as peaceful co-existence this essence is expressed in co-operation between states on a wide range of problems.

The term "peaceful co-existence" was first used in official documents of the Soviet Government in 1920. Speaking at a meeting of the All-Russia Central Executive Committee in June 1920, the People's Commissar for Foreign Affairs, G.V. Chicherin, declared: "Our slogan has always been 'peaceful co-existence with other governments whatever they may be'. The realities of life have led us and other states to the necessity of setting up long-term relations between the workers' and peasants' government and the capitalist governments."[7]

At the climax of the Civil War and foreign military intervention the question of peaceful co-existence of socialism and capitalism could not be in the foreground, the Soviet political scientist G.A. Arbatov points out.[8] Whereas from the time of her birth Soviet Russia sought, in Lenin's phrase, "to live together", "to co-exist" with the surrounding capitalist world, the international bourgeoisie went to war against her in an effort to restore the socio-economic order which had existed in the world prior to October 1917.

It was not enough just to proclaim a policy of peaceful co-existence for it to become the basis for relations between Soviet Russia and the capitalist countries encircling her. It was necessary to "win", as Lenin repeatedly emphasized, the right to exist side by side with the capitalist world. In the "Military Programme of the Proletarian Revolution" (September 1917), he warned that the victory of a socialist revolution initially in one or several countries, with the exploitative system surviving in the rest of the world was bound "to create not only friction, but a direct attempt on the part of the bourgeoisie of other countries to crush the socialist state's victorious proletariat".[9] The record of foreign military intervention against Soviet Russia confirmed his prediction.

Even after the interventionists had been defeated, the Soviet Government had to wage a long struggle to affirm the principles of peaceful co-existence in the practice of international relations. Lenin had foreseen this difficulty: "We never imagined that with the fighting over and the advent of peace, the capitalist wolf would lie down with the socialist lamb. No, we did not".[10] The final acceptance of the principles of peaceful co-existence — the independence, sovereignty and equality of all peoples and states, non-interference in their internal affairs — could be achieved only through a change in the alignment of forces on the international scene, which has made it impossible for imperialism to go to war against socialism.

Not only did Lenin discover and substantiate the principle of peaceful co-existence as the foundation of interstate relations between socialist and capitalist countries. In a new historical situation he developed and deepened the principle of proletarian internationalism, which became a principle of national policy as soon as the Soviet government came to power. The victory of the October Revolution meant that proletarian internationalism had been put on a material foundation in the form of a state of proletarian dictatorship. This elevated it to a new and higher stage and added to it a qualitatively new dimension, which the "left" and right-wing opportunists failed to comprehend. Clinging to the outdated concepts of the past historical epoch, they sought to prove that proletarian internationalism required either a world revolutionary war through the "export of revolution" (the concept of the "left") or the abandonment of socialist revolution in Russia should it fail to be reinforced simultaneously by victorious socialist revolutions in the majority of capitalist countries (the concept of the right-wing Social-Democrats).

Lenin laid bare the theoretical untenability of these concepts and pointed out the need for a radical re-evaluation of the concept of internationalism in the new conditions of the revolutionary struggle of the working class created by the victory of the October Revolution.

Lenin gave an exhaustive definition of the essence of proletarian internationalism and strongly emphasized that it "...demands, first, that the interests of the proletarian struggle in any one country should be subordinated to the interests of that struggle on a world-wide scale, and, second, that a nation which is achieving victory over the bourgeois should be able and willing to make the greatest national sacrifices for the overthrow of international capital".[11] "There is one, and only one, kind of real internationalism, and that is — working whole-heartedly for the development of the revolutionary movement and the revolutionary struggle in *one's own* country, and supporting (by propaganda, sympathy and material aid) *this struggle*, this, *and only this*, line, in *every* country without exception."[12]

Lenin proved theoretically, and history confirmed, that in the new conditions proletarian internationalism outstepped the bounds of the working-class movement in the industrialized countries, gradually extending, in addition to the working-class struggle, to the national liberation movement of the peoples oppressed by imperialism. Reflecting the link between these movements, the international communist movement and the Third International advanced the slogan: "Workers of all countries and all oppressed peoples, unite!" "We now stand," Lenin said, "not only as representatives of the proletarians of all countries but as representatives of the oppressed peoples as well. A journal of the Communist International recently appeared under the title of *Narody Vostoka*. It carries the following slogan issued by the Communist International for the peoples of the East: 'Workers of all countries and all oppressed peoples, unite.'"[13]

The basic principles of Soviet foreign policy laid down by Lenin logically follow from Lenin's conception of international relations in the epoch of transition from capitalism to socialism. They have now had 60 years of fierce attack from the "right" and from the "left".

Critics of the principle of peaceful co-existence, both bourgeois and those acting under the guise of leftist phraseology, accuse Lenin of distorting Marxism on the ground that to the sole international principle of the proletariat — that of proletarian internationalism — established by Marx and Engels he "added arbitrarily" the principle of peaceful co-existence, which is allegedly incompatible with it. Herbert Marcuse, for instance, bluntly declares that Lenin's conception of peaceful co-existence represents an "anomalous situation" in Marxism, and that it is a revision of the Marxist doctrine.[14]

There is not, nor can there be, a contradiction between the principles of peaceful co-existence and proletarian internationalism. The consistent efforts to translate the ideas of peaceful co-existence into reality are an expression of the democratic and internationalist spirit of Soviet foreign policy. The Decree on Peace which called on the progressive workers "to ensure success for the cause of peace as well as the cause of liberation of the labouring and exploited masses from all slavery and exploitation"[15] demonstrated that the fundamental principles of peaceful co-existence and proletarian internationalism form an organic unity in Soviet foreign policy.

The American Sovietologist Frederick C. Barghoorn interprets the policy of peaceful co-existence as the product of a temporary weakness of the Soviet State. He writes that Soviet Russia's desire of peace was merely "anxiety reflecting the harsh struggle of the Soviet regime to survive against both domestic and foreign enemies".[16] The falsity of this allegation is especially clear today when the Soviet Union, which has grown into a mighty power and in alliance with the fraternal socialist nations is exerting a decisive influence on world politics, is pursuing as before its policy of peaceful co-existence.

J.M. Mackintosh, the author of *Strategy and Tactics of Soviet Foreign Policy*, alleges the absence of a relationship between Lenin's theory of the world revolutionary process in the era of imperialism and the conception of peaceful co-existence. He attributes the latter's appearance to the abandonment of the idea of world revolution after the "collapse of the German and Hungarian revolutions".[17] These allegations are meant to disprove the objective need for peaceful co-existence as a stage in the development of international relations in the transition period and to prove that the Soviet State was forced by circumstances to pursue a policy of peaceful co-existence with the capitalist countries.

The efforts of our ideological adversaries to denigrate the Soviet policy of peaceful co-existence and depict it as a "treacherous" tactical ruse of the Bolsheviks seeking to "lull" the vigilance of the West are to no avail. It is for over 60 years that the Soviet Union in its relations with the capitalist countries has been unswervingly following the line of peaceful co-existence. In his report on the sixtieth anniversary of the October Revolution, Leonid Brezhnev said in particular: "...Soviet power was established under the sign of Lenin's Decree on Peace, and ever since then our country's entire foreign policy has been one of peace. Objective historical conditions have dictated its concrete expression as the peaceful co-existence of states with different social systems".[18]

The principle of proletarian internationalism — another corner-stone of Soviet foreign policy — is subject to no less vicious attacks and distortions. A number of Western experts on Soviet foreign policy have called in question the objective character of the theory of proletarian internationalism in general. According to the American authors F. Jan Triska and David D. Finley, "proletarian internationalism may be... a slogan or a motto...; it may be a reliable tool, . . . a set of principles, an outlook and even a policy, but it is not a theory". They allege that no Marxist–Leninist doctrine of internationalism does or can exist.[19]

It is a long-standing tradition in Sovietology to interpret the principle of proletarian internationalism in Soviet foreign policy as a "theoretical substantiation" or "camouflage" of the "export of revolution" imputed to the Communists. This tradition arose immediately after the victory of the October Revolution as the myth of the "Bolshevik menace", "perfidious schemes of Red diplomacy" and other fabrications of this kind. Carried at times to absurdity by the bourgeois press, this myth long influenced the mind of the Western man in the street. The primitive concoctions of newsmen preying on sensations of the day, however, could not satisfy the ruling quarters in the capitalist countries. And then the potential of bourgeois science was brought into play.

Many books in which the principle of proletarian internationalism is deliberately distorted and presented as an analogue of the "export of revolution" are available on the market in growing numbers. In one of them even the Decree on Peace is described as a thinly veiled call for a worldwide revolution,[20] that is, as an instrument for the "export of revolution".

Some Sovietologists maintain that the international Communist movement and the principle of proletarian internationalism were employed by the Bolsheviks to achieve the traditional foreign policy objectives of tsarist Russia, which were allegedly preserved in Soviet foreign policy and constituted its "national-state" aspect. This idea is peddled in a book by H.J. Morgenthau.[21] The principle of proletarian internationalism is described as masking and legitimizing Soviet foreign policy in all periods of its history — from the October Revolution to date. In a work published in France, it is alleged, for instance, that under cover of Communist internationalism Soviet foreign policy seeks to secure for Russia strong positions which were the coveted goal of the monarchy for five centuries.[22]

Equating proletarian internationalism, which implies consistent defence of the right of a nation to shape its own destiny, with the "export of revolution", bourgeois students of Soviet foreign policy accuse Lenin of adherence to the "export of revolution". To lend credibility to their allegations they quote some of his statements concerning the need for armed assistance to the workers' struggle in other countries in certain situations. However, these statements made in the period of the imperialist military intervention against Russia and other countries where the working people had taken over power (Finland, Hungary, etc.) were to the effect that the revolution developing in several countries "had already assumed (on the initiative of world imperialism) the character of armed resistance of the working people in several countries to the actions of the allied bourgeoisie... In such a situation armed assistance has nothing in common with the 'export of revolution'."[23] Dedication to proletarian internationalism implies not the "export of revolution" but determined opposition to attempts of the counter-revolutionary bourgeoisie to "export counter-revolution".

At one time Lenin and the party under his leadership rejected the demands of the "left-wing" Communists and the Trotskyites to the effect that a "revolutionary war" levied by the working class which has assumed power in a given country (or countries) upon the bourgeoisie of other nations should be made the main instrument of assistance to a revolution. Arguing against the "left-wing" Communists in 1918, Lenin inquired rhetorically if they believed that the interests of world revolution demanded it to be pushed, and that the push could be nothing but war and by no means peace, which could only impress the masses as something like legalizing imperialism, and answered: "Such a 'theory' would be completely at variance with Marxism, for Marxism has always been opposed to 'pushing' revolutions, which develop with the growing acuteness of the class antagonisms that engender revolutions."[24] In one of its official statements in June 1920 the People's Commissariat for Foreign Affairs re-emphasized: "We do not spread our system or our power by the bayonet, and this is known to all...."[25]

Having taken a principled stand against the "export of revolution", the world's first socialist state nevertheless did all in its power to assist the revolutionary and national-liberation struggle waged by the people in other countries. Elevated to the status of national policy, proletarian internationalism marked Soviet Russia's relations with Mongolia from the time of the democratic revolution there in 1921. It was also put at the basis of Soviet Russia's policy in relation to the short-lived Bavarian, Hungarian and Slovak Soviet Republics.

The Resolution of the All-Russia Central Executive Committee of 11 November 1918, which instructed the "local institutions to begin immediately raising a special fund for assistance to our comrades-in-arms — the workers and soldiers of Germany" is a stirring document pervaded with the spirit of proletarian internationalism.[26] To prevent the "export of counter-revolution" to Germany, the Soviet Government was preparing to resist it by every means at its disposal, including armed force. "We are all ready to die to help the German workers advance the revolution which has begun in Germany...", Lenin wrote. The Party set the task of raising the strength of the Red Army to 3 million men towards the spring of 1919 to suppress the internal counter-revolution and "help the international workers' revolution".[27] In a message of greetings to the 4th Congress of the Comintern, Lenin wrote: "Soviet Russia considers it a matter of the greatest pride to help the workers of the whole world in their difficult struggle to overthrow capitalism."[28] For its part, the world proletariat deemed it its internationalist duty to give every assistance and support to the young Soviet Republic in its struggle against the internal and external counter-revolution. Karl Liebknecht in a leaflet published in Germany in the period of foreign intervention against Soviet Russia wrote that the world proletariat cannot allow the home of revolution to be destroyed unless it wants to see its own hopes and strength exhausted. The fall of Soviet Russia would mean a defeat for the world proletariat.

In response to the Soviet Government's appeals to the working people of all countries not to relax their pressure on the bourgeois government "so as to prevent them from strangling the people's revolution in Russia", a movement under the slogan "Hands off Soviet Russia!" was mounting in the capitalist countries, and giant demonstrations and strikes were held in defence of the world's first socialist state.

Many prisoners of war held in Russia went over to the side of the Soviet Government after the October Revolution and fought in the ranks of the Red Army. Between 1917 and 1920 Red Army units enlisted about 80,000 Hungarians, up to 40,000 Chinese, roughly

30,000 Yugoslavs, thousands of Czechs, Poles, Germans, Koreans, Romanians, Bulgarians, and Finns. Units of the Red Guard were formed of prisoners of war in 400 towns of Soviet Russia.

Having denounced the bourgeois foreign policy of conquest, Soviet Russia advanced and started to carry into effect the new principles of peaceful co-existence and proletarian internationalism, which were organically interlinked in the international policy of the working class which had seized power in one country. This link has been maintained in Soviet foreign policy to this day. In his speech at the World Congress of Peace Forces in 1973, Leonid Brezhnev stated in particular: "By promoting the principles of peaceful co-existence we are working for something which billions of people all over the world cherish most of all: the right to life itself, and deliverance from the danger of its destruction in the flames of war. At the same time, we are thereby also working to ensure favourable international conditions for the social progress of all countries and peoples."[29]

Guided by these principles, Lenin and the Party immediately after the overthrow of the exploitative system in Russia began to campaign for a new system of international relations conforming to the realities of the period of transition from capitalism to socialism.

Lenin's Conception of a New System of International Relations

The October Revolution made a breach in the chains of imperialist domination and triggered off the collapse of the global system of capitalist international relations. The laws and standards of international relations which had taken shape in conditions of the unchallenged supremacy of imperialism, the so-called "rules of the game" in world politics, could no longer apply to Soviet Russia. After October 1917 their sphere of operation narrowed considerably.

Before October 1917 the imperialist system of international relations had been based on a definite balance of forces of similar class origin. The emergence of the world's first socialist state upset this balance beyond repair and led to a realignment of socio-political, economic and military forces on the international scene. In a situation where the dividing line between the capitalist and socialist systems became the main watershed in international relations the structure of these relations changed. With the new alignment of forces in the world, not only the balance between the state forces existing within national boundaries but also the balance between the antagonistic class forces on the national and international scale assumed importance in world politics. Lenin pointed out this circumstance in these words: "We have an international alliance, an alliance which has nowhere been registered, which has never been given formal embodiment, which from the point of view of 'constitutional law' means nothing, but which, in the disintegrating capitalist world, actually means everything."[30]

The concurrent existence of two socio-political systems in the world meant in itself the emergence of a new system of international relations. Needless to say, this new system of world relations could not rest on the traditional principles of imperialist politics. However, socialism, which had been established in only one-sixth of the world's habitable area could not impose its foreign-policy principles on the capitalist countries either. Therefore, the new system of international relations which had begun to take shape after October 1917 was of necessity a transitional system expressing, so to say, the historical compromise between socialism and capitalism in the sphere of world politics — the peaceful co-existence of states having opposite socio-economic systems. This transitional system of world relations is characterized by a process of democratization and by the gradual elimination from international affairs of imperialist methods of dictation and aggression which is directly dependent on the growing power and influence of socialism in the world.

As soon as it came into being, Soviet Russia took a determined stand against the imperialist system of international relations in which war, plunder, and rape of nations were all organic components. The Soviet Government's programme of action in the sphere of international relations was formulated in general outline in its first foreign-policy statement — the Decree on Peace, which upheld the idea of a just and democratic peace. Lenin urged a struggle for a "democratic organization of international relations". Although in the early years following the October Revolution the possibilities for solving this problem were quite limited, its urgency was perfectly obvious. It was important that after proclaiming this goal the Soviet Government immediately started a campaign for practical steps to be taken in this direction.

Lenin's idea of a just and democratic peace, the idea of setting up a system of international relations based on general democratic principles met the vital interests of the working class and the working people of the whole world. Lenin was confident that the working class was the most dependable guarantor of peace and democratic principles in world politics; on the other hand, he believed that a just and democratic peace in the system of inter-state relations would provide the most favourable conditions for successful development of the world revolutionary process.

These conclusions, which are with full reason accepted today as axioms of Marxist–Leninist policy, are among the greatest discoveries of Lenin, who converted a general theoretical concept of the international policy of the revolutionary proletariat into a politically concrete expression of the theory of socialist revolution applied to international relations.

The renunciation of secret diplomacy was a *sine qua non* of the new system of international relations advocated by Soviet Russia. The Decree on Peace proclaimed its abolition and the Soviet Government's strong determination to conduct negotiations quite openly, before the whole people. Accordingly, the newly established People's Commissariat for Foreign Affairs published tsarist Russia's secret treaties, including the Anglo–Russian secret treaty and convention of 1907 on "demarcation" of the spheres of interest of Russian tsarism and British imperialism in the Middle East, the agreements to carve up Turkey between Britain, France, and tsarist Russia concluded in the spring of 1916, etc. The publication of these treaties caused a political shock in the capitals of the Western powers. Lenin commented on the significance and meaning of the publication of the secret treaties as follows: "The bourgeois gentlemen are beside themselves because the people see why they have been driven to the slaughter . . . we can and have to work hand in hand with the revolutionary class of working people in all countries. That is the path the Soviet Government has taken by making public the secret treaties and showing that the rulers of all countries are brigands."[31]

The renunciation of secret diplomacy meant that from now on for the first time in history a government's words would not show a discrepancy from its deeds, that the Soviet Government was truly pursuing the objectives it had proclaimed for all to hear.

It would be wrong to conclude, however, that the Soviet Government refused to hold confidential discussions and keep secret information whose publication might interfere with the implementation of its foreign policy of peace.

Laying the foundations for a new system of world relations, Lenin's Decree on Peace aimed to convert relations between governments, which the relations between states had actually amounted to before October 1917, into truly international relations. This followed from the very fact of the Soviet Government's peace proposals to the governments and peoples of the belligerent states. In the capitalist countries, Lenin said, "Everywhere there are differences between the governments and the peoples, and we must therefore help the peoples to intervene in questions of war and peace."[32] Such an appeal had no precedent in the international diplomatic practices of imperialism. On the part of the workers' and peasants' state it was a perfectly logical step, reflecting its determination to involve the masses in the struggle for the triumph of the equitable, democratic principles of international relations.

The Decree on Peace fully deserves to be described as the first foreign-policy programme of the Soviet State. The aims of securing a just and democratic peace formulated in it were tantamount to a revolution in the system of international relations and outlined the way of reshaping them.

The fundamentally new socialist foreign policy required the selection of new diplomatic personnel and the institution of a new diplomatic service capable of translating into reality Lenin's ideas of a just and democratic peace and waging a successful struggle for a new system of international relations. Lenin personally handled matters involved in selecting Soviet diplomatic cadres. His article "How We Should Reorganize the Workers' and Peasants' Inspection" pointed out that "...the Foreign Commissariat is working under the direct guidance of our Central Committee. This, as a matter of fact, is the only one of our commissariats that has been fully renovated and that is really working for the workers' and peasants' government and in the spirit of that government.''[33]

Lenin's instructions concerning the need for an absolute and consistent break with the capitalists in home and foreign policies were of great importance for the struggle to be launched by the Soviet State for a new system of international relations.[34] This did not rule out, however, a definite continuity in the sphere of international relations. Lenin referred to it in his speech at the Second Congress of Soviets: ''...We reject all clauses on plunder and violence, but we shall welcome all clauses containing provisions for good-neighbourly relations and all economic agreements; we cannot reject these.''[35] The border issues were resolved on this basis already in the early years of Soviet government. Lenin, who was personally involved in settling them, staunchly upheld the territorial integrity of the world's first socialist state. "Under all possible *changes* of state frontiers we put in the forefront the interests of the workers' class struggle.''[36]

The first foreign-policy acts of the October Revolution which proposed in fact a programme of reshaping the system of international relations on general democratic principles evoked a worldwide response and had a tremendous influence on the peoples in various countries. They gave the peoples of Central and South-east Europe a powerful stimulus to begin a struggle for self-determination and the formation of independent national states.*

---

*Bourgeois historiographers, in the United States in particular, are completely silent on this fact. They give full credit for the emergence of Yugoslavia, Austria, and Hungary from the ruins of the Austro-Hungarian monarchy, for the constitution of Poland and other small European nations as independent states to the United States and President Woodrow Wilson. They stubbornly adhered to this view at the conference of the American Historical Association held in New York in 1957 on the subject "Wilson, Lenin and the Formation of States in Central and South Europe". Ignoring the facts of history, American bourgeois scholars alleged that it was not the October Revolution, nor Lenin's Decree on Peace, nor other historic acts of Soviet Russia implementing in her foreign policy the principle of the right of nations to self-determination that changed the political map of Europe and the world after the First World War, but the "fourteen points" of President Wilson's declaration. (see: *Problems of History of International Relations and the Ideological Struggle*, Ed. A.O. Chubaryan, Moscow, 1976, p.1). The efforts of our ideological opponents to belittle the impact of the October Revolution on the development of international relations in general and on the solution of post-war problems in Europe and other parts of the world are to be seen in a series of works by American authors. (For instance, N. Levin, *Woodrow Wilson and World Politics. America's Response to War and Revolution*, New York, 1968.)

The US Secretary of State Robert Lansing wrote President Woodrow Wilson at the time that the presentation of peace terms by the Bolsheviks "may well appeal to the average man".[37] To offset the influence of Soviet Russia's foreign policy the capitalist world was compelled to put forward its own programme of a post-war settlement. President Wilson submitted his Fourteen Points in a message to Congress in January 1918. In the pictorial phrase of the American historian William A. Williams, commenting on the reaction of American ruling quarters to the October Revolution, Wilson's Fourteen Points were "written on a table shaken by that revolution".[38]

Wilson's declaration, intended as the "ideological counterweight" to Lenin's Decree on peace, demagogically proclaimed "peace without annexations", the right of small nations to self-determination and the formation of their national states, "equality of trade", and "freedom of navigation". Its watchword was disarmament and it proposed an association of "free nations" to be established with the object of granting "mutual guarantees of political independence and territorial integrity to great and small states alike". It was declared that Russia should be allowed to determine without any obstruction whatsoever her political development and national policy, and that she would be assured of a sincere welcome if she joined the association of "free nations". The point relating to the freedom of the colonies read that a free, open-hearted and absolutely impartial adjustment of all colonial claims, based upon a strict observance of the principle that in determining all such questions of sovereignty the interests of the populations concerned must have equal weight with the equitable claim of the government whose title is to be determined.[39]

It was significant that Wilson came forward with his peace programme precisely at a time when the publication of secret treaties began in Soviet Russia. The bourgeois press went out of its way to extoll the allegedly democratic character of Wilson's "fourteen points". The President himself, however, made no bones about the true objective of his diplomatic initiative called upon to counteract the impression created by the revolutionary diplomacy of the Soviet government. The venom of Bolshevism, he said in a discussion with Secretary of State Lansing, has become so widespread only because it was a protest against the system governing the world. Now it is our turn, and we must defend the new order at the peace conference by good, if possible, by evil, if necessary.[40]

America's "peace programme" was intended as a cover-up for the hegemonistic ambitions of American imperialism on the international scene. The anti-Soviet orientation of the "fourteen points" was frankly admitted in the secret commentaries compiled in the same year 1918 by Colonel House, one of Wilson's closest aides, and approved by the President himself. It followed from them that the United States and other imperialist powers of the First World War were making plans for military intervention in Soviet Russia's affairs with the object of destroying the Soviet Government and dismembering and enslaving her.

The imperialists had no intention of establishing a just peace and remaking on democratic lines the system of international relations which had taken shape before the First World War. They viewed the Soviet socialist state as an "unnatural phenomenon" doomed to destruction and were doing whatever they could to this end. "No real harmony between Bolshevism and the present civilization is possible. The baby must be strangled in its cradle", Winston Churchill wrote in a letter to Lloyd George. (Translated from the Russian).[41]

Lenin had foreseen that the Soviet Government's policy of peaceful co-existence of states having opposite social systems would be bitterly resisted by the imperialists. Indeed, this policy has stood severe, even cruel tests of history. Imperialism has employed every means at its disposal to fight socialism and democracy. Lenin never doubted, however, that the idea of peaceful co-existence would eventually get the upper hand. His confidence was based on a profound analysis of the laws governing world social development in the epoch of transition from capitalism to socialism. He said that as long as two systems of ownership remained, in particular, such an outdated one as capitalism with the economic chaos and war that it generated, peaceful co-existence would be the only right way out of difficulties, chaos and the danger of war.

The Peace Treaty of Brest-Litovsk was a milestone event in the Soviet Republic's foreign ,policy. Opening the peace talks with imperial Germany, the Soviet Government declared from the outset that its objective was the conclusion of a general rather than a separate peace. In its "Appeal to the Labouring Masses in All Countries", the All-Russia Central Executive Committee stated that Soviet Russia would not agree to a peace settlement that would sanctify the old injustices and that she desired "a democratic and just peace".[42] Such a peace, however, could be achieved only through a revolutionary struggle waged by the people in all countries. Thus, the struggle of the masses was regarded as the decisive factor in securing a just and democratic peace.

Faced by the refusal of the Entente powers to negotiate a general peace settlement, Soviet Russia alone entered into peace talks with Germany, Austria-Hungary, Bulgaria and Turkey. At the very first plenary meeting the Soviet delegation proposed that the ideas formulated in the Decree on Peace be made the basis of the agenda. The six points of the Soviet declaration at the Brest–Litovsk peace talks were as follows:

1. No forcible annexation of territories invaded during the war shall be allowed.
2. The political independence of the nations deprived of their independence during the current war shall be completely restored.
3. The national minorities denied political independence before the war shall be guaranteed freedom of choice of affiliation with a given state or national independence through a referendum.
4. In territories inhabited by more than one nationality, the rights of the minority shall be protected by special legislation to safeguard its national culture and, wherever possible, administrative autonomy.
5. None of the belligerent powers shall pay war indemnities to other countries.
6. The colonial problems shall be settled in compliance with the principles proclaimed in points 1, 2, 3 and 4.[43]

The German imperialists declined these proposals and imposed humiliating peace terms on Soviet Russia. The Soviet Government agreed to sign the peace treaty of Brest–Litovsk to protect the vital interests of the working people of Russia and the rest of the world.

Lenin frankly stated that "...we were making and were obliged to make great national sacrifices for the sake of the supreme interests of the world proletarian revolution".[44] Russia's working class and its revolutionary party proved in practice their dedication to proletarian internationalism.

Lenin's efforts to achieve a peace settlement at Brest–Litovsk were a striking testimony to his understanding of the dialectical unity of the national and the international in the world revolutionary process, the worldwide historic implications of the first socialist revolution. To save the revolution and the Soviet Republic, Lenin insisted on the acceptance of the extortionist terms of the Brest–Litovsk peace treaty as unavoidable.

In those years the whole notion of the socialist state's commitment to peace repeatedly came under bitter attack from the Trotskyites, the "left-wing" Communists and other exponents of petty bourgeois revolutionism. Theoreticians of "leftism" saw only one thing: that war could stimulate revolution, and turned a blind eye to the fact that wars had often delayed the onset of revolutions. Moreover, they completely ignored another fact: that socialism creates a fundamentally new system of values, chief among which is the working people's life and well-being. The Party resolutely rejected the proposals of the "leftists" that peace and millions of lives should be sacrificed to the adventuristic idea of spurring world revolution. "The price of the blood of our workers and soldiers is too high for us; we shall pay... a heavy tribute as the price of peace; we consent to a heavy tribute to preserve the lives of our workers and peasants", Lenin said in this connection.[45]

This is an expression of the profound humaneness of Soviet foreign policy stemming from its class character and the very essence of the socialist system.

Soviet foreign policy at the time of the Brest–Litovsk peace talks showed the wisdom of the Leninist line of peaceful co-existence, to which there is no reasonable alternative in the period of transition from capitalism to socialism. In Lenin's view, the conclusion of the Brest–Litovsk peace treaty and the establishment of business relations with the capitalist world was motivated by the historical inevitability and objective necessity for socialism and capitalism to co-exist peacefully for a more or less prolonged period of time. He said that if it refused to accept this reality "a socialist republic surrounded by imperialist powers... could not exist at all, without flying to the moon".[46]

The vast experience of Soviet foreign policy and diplomacy gained in negotiating the Brest–Litovsk peace treaty showed that the question of political compromises between Soviet Russia and the capitalist powers was of crucial importance for success in the struggle for a new system of international relations. Compromises are necessary, Lenin said, but it is important "through all compromises, when they are unavoidable, to remain true to one's principles, to one's class, to one's revolutionary purpose".[47]

Reviewing the activities of the Party and the Soviet Government in the foreign-policy field in that period, Soviet historians point out that Lenin's arsenal of foreign-policy methods was created and enriched by the solution of the following problems: the permissibility of a compromise between the socialist state and its capitalist counterparts, the necessity of setting up and developing political relations between states having different social systems; the establishment of trade and economic relations on a basis of equality; the possibility to take advantage of contradictions between capitalist powers to consolidate peace; to work out forms of association and methods of diplomacy on democratic foreign-policy principles.[48] This was of paramount importance for planning Soviet foreign policy and diplomacy, and for socialism to produce a revolutionizing impact on the entire pattern of world relations.

Lenin's conception incorporated broad and all-round co-operation on a basis of equality between all nations of the world as a major component of a new system of international relations. In his view, the policy of the socialist state should help eradicate mistrust between nations and states implanted through the centuries of oppression of nations, colonial domination, and imperialist plunder. "...Only exclusive attention to the interests of various nations can remove grounds for conflicts, can remove mutual mistrust, can remove the fear of any intrigues and create that confidence, especially on the part of workers and peasants speaking different languages, without which there absolutely cannot be peaceful relations between peoples or anything like a successful development of everything that is of value in present-day civilization."[49] The idea of national sovereignty and equality runs through the theory and practice of Soviet foreign policy with its aim of reshaping international relations on democratic lines. Lenin wrote about the aspirations of the nations and countries oppressed by imperialism towards "a system of equal nations".[50] By virtue of its ideology, the proletariat which has come to power cannot but make a stand against unequal relations, against the oppression of one state by another. "The unity and fraternal alliance of the workers of all countries are incompatible with the use of force, direct or indirect, against other nationalities."[51] It is respect for the sovereignty and equality of states and nations that should make the basis for a new system of international relations aimed at organizing their co-operation with a view to preserving peace. The new system of international relations advocated by Soviet Russia ruled out as a matter of principle the use of force in settlement of international conflicts.

The emergence of the Soviet Republic enabled formally independent small states, colonial and semi-colonial countries to struggle for and uphold successfully their sovereign rights against oppression and encroachments by imperialist powers. Lenin pointed out that the existence and policy of the Soviet State "groups around the Soviet Republic capitalist states being suffocated by imperialism",[52] affords them possibilities of gaining an equal status within the system of bourgeois inter-state relations. That had an immediate effect on the position, for instance, of Finland, Poland, the Baltic Republics, in part of Germany, which had been forced to sign the Treaty of Versailles, and especially of Iran, Afghanistan, and Turkey.

In his efforts towards a new system of international relations Lenin attached special significance to developing relations between the Soviet State and the colonial countries. Describing socialist international policy, Lenin wrote in the early days of Soviet government that "...the Bolsheviks are establishing completely different international relations which make it possible for all oppressed peoples to rid themselves of the imperialist yoke".[53] The Soviet Government repeatedly declared its intention to develop relations with the Eastern nations on the principles of equality, mutual respect and friendship, and expressed its willingness to give them friendly assistance in their struggle against imperialism.

Soviet Russia regarded the oppressed nations as allies of the working class in the anti-imperialist struggle, in her efforts towards a new system of international relations based on a just and democratic peace. Even before the October Revolution, Lenin had predicted that a political alliance between the proletariat of the West and the working people of the East would become an important factor in the anti-imperialist struggle. Explaining the programme of Russian Social-Democracy, Lenin said in particular: "We shall exert every effort to foster association and merger with the Mongolians, Persians, Indians, Egyptians. We believe it is our duty and in our interest to do this."[54]

The world's first workers' and peasants' state gave close attention to the question of rendering all-round assistance to the nations oppressed by imperialism. Addressing the Second Congress of the Comintern, Lenin declared "It is unquestionable that the proletariat of the advanced countries can and should give help to the working masses of the backward countries, and that the backward countries can emerge from their present stage of development when the victorious proletariat of the Soviet Republics extends a helping hand to these masses and is in a position to give them support."[55] Loyal to its internationalist duty, the Soviet State, despite its severe economic plight and the ravages of the Civil War and foreign military intervention, rendered not only political and moral but also great material support to Turkey, Afghanistan, Iran, and other countries in their struggle for liberation from the imperialist yoke.

Leonid Brezhnev has pointed out: "Throughout its history the Soviet Union has resolutely supported the struggle of the Asian peoples against imperialism and colonialism, for freedom and independence."[56] This assistance grew along with the consolidation of the socialist state, and stimulated the national-liberation movement.

The stand taken by the socialist state in support of the national-liberation struggle is not a tactical manoeuvre or a cunning diplomatic ploy in pursuit of some ulterior objectives. In this, just as throughout its foreign policy, the Soviet State is guided primarily by considerations of principle, by Communist ideology which is irreconcilably hostile to all kinds of oppression of classes or nations. The peoples of the East could see for themselves that Soviet foreign policy was not motivated by any considerations of the moment or propaganda purposes, but followed from the very nature of Soviet power.

The opposition of the young socialist state to the imperialist policy of oppression and coercion of nations was part and parcel of its struggle for a new system of international relations ruling out subjugation of one nation by another. This struggle, which won the Soviet Republic immense prestige, was a key factor in strengthening its ties of brotherhood and alliance with the national liberation movement. Lenin pointed out that the Soviet Republic enjoyed tremendous prestige among all peoples of the East precisely because they regarded it as a staunch fighter against imperialism.[57] Lenin deemed it necessary to change radically the position of these countries within the system of international relations and involve them in active efforts to solve world political problems.

The October Revolution produced a tremendous impact on the peoples of Asia, Africa and Latin America. The victories of the Soviet people, of the Red Army over the interventionists dispelled the myth of the invincibility of imperialism. "Up to now, the Eastern peoples may have been like sheep before the imperialist wolf, but Soviet Russia was the first to show that, despite her unparalleled military weakness, it is not so easy for the wolf to get his claws and teeth into her. This example has proved to be catching for many nations. . . ",[58] Lenin wrote. The labouring masses of the colonial countries, which constitute the vast majority of the world's population, were awakened to political life after 17 October. Lenin's policy of assistance to the Eastern nations in their struggle for political and economic independence was strikingly exemplified by the abrogation of all unequal treaties and agreements between the Russian Empire and these countries. In a note of 4 (17) January 1918 to the Government of Iran it was pointed out that Soviet Russia's policy was "diametrically opposite to the East policy of the imperialist powers and motivated by a desire for independent economic and political development of the Eastern nations to which it gives every support. . . . The Soviet Government of Russia regards it as its mission and its calling to be a natural and selfless friend of the nations struggling for their complete independence, economic and political freedom."[59]

Fully opposed to the policy of imperialism and colonialism, the Soviet Government on 26 June 1919 abolished all privileges for Russian nationals in Iran, renounced all concessions and control over Iran's state revenue, and handed over to the Iranian people, without compensation, the banks, railways and highways, port facilities on Iran's Caspian coast and other property which had belonged to Russia.* The first equal treaty with a European power in the history of Iran — the treaty of friendship between Soviet Russia and Iran — was signed on 29 February 1921. It contained articles which guaranteed the independence of Iran and the security of the Soviet border. The significance of the Soviet–Iranian Treaty of 1921 extended far beyond the framework of their bilateral relations: it demonstrated the new element introduced by Soviet Russia into the practice of world politics.

Soviet Russia developed her relations on the principles of internationalism and national self-determination also with Turkey where an anti-imperialist movement and struggle against international reaction had started under the leadership of Kemal Atatürk. Under the Soviet-Turkish Treaty of Friendship and Alliance signed on 16 March 1921, the contracting parties undertook "not to recognize any peace treaties or other international acts that the other High Contracting Party would be under pressure to accept through coercion".[60] Kemalist Turkey received from the Soviet Republic generous economic, financial, and military aid which enabled her to bring her national liberation struggle to successful completion.[61] In a message to Lenin, Kemal Atatürk expressed his profound gratitude to the Soviet Republic for this aid: "As long as I live Turkey will not forget what Lenin has done and continues to do for her. I consider Turkey's friendship with Soviet Russia the corner-stone of our independence."[62]

---

*These measures not only alleviated Iran's economic situation but also gave an impulse to her people's struggle against British imperialism. The treaty of 19 August 1919 imposed upon Iran by Great Britain, which gave London powers to appoint British advisers to the Iranian Government and Army and in fact reduced Iran to the status of a British protectorate, was thwarted.

The Soviet-Afghan Treaty based on the common goals of the two countries in their struggle against imperialism and colonialism was concluded in the spring of 1921. Soviet Russia began helping Afghanistan to develop its economy by extending to it interest-free loans and assigning specialists to work there. It should be emphasized that Soviet Russia developed her friendly ties with Afghanistan and other countries of the East on the principle of equality without any interference in their internal affairs whatsoever. That was reaffirmed in categorical terms in a letter of 3 June 1921 from the Soviet Foreign Minister Chicherin to the Soviet Ambassador in Kabul, who was instructed to make the following statement to the Afghan Government: "We do not interfere in the internal affairs of other nations, nor do we encroach on the independence of your people.... We have no intention whatsoever of imposing on your people a programme that is alien to them...."[63]

The ideas of a new system of international relations, the new principles proclaimed and applied by Lenin and the Party in world politics also highlighted Soviet Russia's attitude to China, the biggest country in Asia, which had languished under the yoke of imperialist powers for long decades. The "Message of the Soviet Government to the Chinese people and the Governments of South and North China" of 25 July 1919 read in part: "We bring nations liberation from the yoke of the foreign bayonet, from the yoke of foreign gold, which are strangling the enslaved nations of the East, the Chinese people first and foremost. If the Chinese people wants to be free like the Russian people and avoid the lot prepared for it by the Allies at Versailles with the object of converting China into a second Korea or a second India, it will understand that the Russian workers and peasants and their Red Army are its only friend and ally in the struggle for freedom."[64] The Soviet Republic was willing to establish friendly relations with China, but the Chinese Government, then under the influence of foreign capitalists, was indifferent to the interests of the Chinese people and took no steps to meet Soviet Russia half-way.

*   *   *

When the political realities after October 1917 corroborated Lenin's theoretical conclusion, made even before the October Revolution, concerning the inevitability of a certain historical period of co-existence of states belonging to different social systems, the Soviet Government came forward with proposals for establishing relations with the capitalist countries on the basis of Lenin's idea of "equality between the two systems of property". The very possibility of peaceful co-existence was the result of the struggle waged by the revolutionary forces headed by the first socialist country. "Without having gained an international victory, which we consider the only sure victory, we are in a position of having won conditions enabling us to exist side by side with capitalist powers.... In the course of this struggle we have won the right to an independent existence," Lenin wrote.[65] Guided by the principle of peaceful co-existence, Soviet Russia from the early days of her history sought to develop trade and economic co-operation with the capitalist countries.

Such co-operation was an objective necessity dictated by the process of international division of labour. In the Central Committee's report to the 11th Party Congress, Lenin said that "...the most urgent, pressing and practical interests that have been sharply revealed in all the capitalist countries during the past few years call for the development, regulation and expansion of trade with Russia. Since such interests exist, this fundamental economic necessity will... make a way for itself."[66] Some time earlier he had declared: "...we know that the economic position of those who blockaded us has proved to be vulnerable. There is a force more powerful than the wishes, the will and the decisions of any of the governments or classes that are hostile to us. That force is world general economic relations, which compel them to make contact with us."[67]

Lenin emphasized that the development of Soviet Russia's economic relations with the capitalist states helped consolidate her position on the international scene. He pointed out that "The entry of the socialist country into trade relations with capitalist countries is a most important factor ensuring our existence in such a complex and absolutely exceptional situation."[68]

The conclusion in March 1921 of a treaty of commerce with Britain, which was tantamount to *de facto* recognition of the Soviet Republic, was an important success in the efforts to affirm the principle of peaceful co-existence of the socialist and the capitalist states. The two contracting parties undertook to refrain from hostile actions and propaganda against one another "outside their national frontiers".

That meant the failure of the imperialists' attempts to restore the global supremacy of imperialism and the former world order. The accession of the socialist state to the "world community" could not but have changed "the rules of the game" within it, although initially the imperialists, aware of their military and economic superiority over the world's first socialist state, had tried to dictate their terms to it. The Soviet Republic resolutely opposed such attempts. Addressing himself to those who sought to take advantage of developing economic ties with the Soviet Republic to undermine her foundations and those who were unwilling to establish economic relations with her because of their hostility to the socialist system, Lenin said: "Whether they like it or not, Soviet Russia is a great power.... America will gain nothing from the Wilsonian policy of a pious refusal to do business with us on the ground that our government is unpalatable to them."[69] His words are as true today as they were in his time.

Lenin advanced the idea of remaking the world on "a rational economic foundation".[70] Already in that period the Soviet Republic was campaigning for a new form of international economic relations on the principle of mutually beneficial co-operation of nations based on equality, was opposing autarchy and advocating participation in the international division of labour within the framework of an integrated world system of economy. In an interview with an American correspondent on 21 February 1920, Lenin said: "I know of no reason why a socialist commonwealth like ours cannot do business indefinitely with capitalistic countries. We don't mind taking their capitalistic locomotives and farming machinery, so why should they mind taking our socialistic wheat, flax and platinum."[71]

A factor of crucial importance for organizing international economic co-operation was the recognition by the capitalist world of the equality of the two systems of ownership, which was obtained by persistent Soviet diplomatic efforts ruling out any compromise on this question. The Cannes Conference of the Entente powers in January 1922 declared its resolution that no state may usurp the right to dictate to others the principles on which they must organize their system of ownership, internal economic life and mode of government. It was on this condition of principle, which laid the groundwork for normalizing relations between states belonging to opposite socio-economic systems, that Soviet Russia agreed to take part in the international economic conference at Genoa in 1922.

At that Conference the Soviet delegation put forward a comprehensive programme of consolidating peace and developing international co-operation, which had been drawn up with Lenin's personal participation and epitomized his ideas of peaceful co-existence and a new system of international relations. Referring to the historic significance of the Soviet proposals at the Genoa Conference in his report on the 50th anniversary of the October Revolution, Leonid Brezhnev said: "In 1922, in Genoa at the first international conference to which Soviet Russia received access, our country tabled a comprehensive programme of peaceful co-operation and disarmament."[72]

The Soviet programme provided for settlement of international disputes through negotiation, granting independence to the colonies and dependent countries, a revision of the Versailles system of peace settlement, a solution to the disarmament problems, etc. Much space was devoted to economic problems: relinquishment of all foreign debts, extension of loans on favourable terms to war-ravaged countries, co-ordination of measures to control inflation, organizing international co-operation to solve economic problems. Lenin proposed as a separate item a discussion ... on measures for coping with the fuel crisis and on measures for the most rational and economical use of power resources on the basis of unified planned electrification.[73]

At the Conference Chicherin read out a policy statement which said in part:

> Remaining loyal to the principles of Communism, the Russian delegation believes that in the present historical epoch, making possible the co-existence of the old and the emerging new socialist system of economic co-operation between states representing these two systems of ownership, is imperative for general economic recovery. Therefore, the Russian Government attaches supreme importance to the first point of the Cannes resolution concerning reciprocal recognition of the different systems of ownership and the different political and

economic structures existing in different countries today. The Russian delegation has arrived here not for propaganda of its own theoretical views but for entering into business relations with the governments and commercial and industrial circles of all countries on the basis of reciprocity, equality and complete and unconditional recognition.[74]

Soviet Russia called for democratization of world politics, for incorporation of all countries and peoples in a new system of international relations. Preparing on Lenin's instructions his statement at Genoa, Chicherin wrote:

Our international programme must involve all oppressed and colonial peoples in an international system. The right of secession should be granted to all peoples.... The novelty of the international system we propose is that the African and other colonial peoples should be allowed to take part in conferences and committees on an equal footing with European nations and have the right to oppose interference in their home affairs. Another novelty is participation of labour organisations.

Lenin underlined these phrases in Chicherin's letter and wrote in the margin "True!" He also agreed with Chicherin that "These two novelties, however, are not sufficient to protect the oppressed peoples and downtrodden countries from the domination of the imperialists....

"...another thing to be established is *the principle of non-intervention on the part of international conferences or congresses in the internal affairs of various peoples. Voluntary co-operation and aid for the weak on the part of the strong* must be applied without subordinating the former to the latter."[75]

At the Genoa Conference the Soviet delegation supported the British Prime Minister Lloyd George's idea concerning international conferences to be called periodically, and emphasized the need to widen the range of their participants by including representatives of all nations. Chicherin said in his statement that general peace could be established by a world congress convened on the principle of complete equality of all nations and recognition of their right to shape their own destinies and attended by representatives of labour organizations.[76]

The Soviet delegation at Genoa called for a revision of the Covenant of the League of Nations with a view to converting it into an international organization without domination of one country by another or division into victors and vanquished.*

At the Genoa Conference the Soviet delegation also tabled proposals for a general reduction in armaments and armies, for a total ban on the most barbarous means of warfare, the use of war gases, aerial warfare, and other means of destruction directed against the civilian population. Thus, Soviet Russia came forward with the first practical initiative on the disarmament problem. The Soviet Government called for implementing any measures that could serve as preliminary steps towards general and complete disarmament. The Soviet delegation at Genoa declared that revolutionary Russia was determined to support any proposal for lightening the burden of militarism.

Lenin pointed out that only the growth and development of the political class forces would make it possible to reach agreement on effective disarmament measures. He viewed the practical tasks of the Soviet Republic's struggle for disarmament in that situation primarily as isolation of the aggressive militaristic wing of the bourgeoisie, as demonstration of the essence of the socialist policy of peace and enlistment of an ever-greater number of supporters of this policy. He called for steps to be taken ". . .in order to split the pacifist camp of

---

*The League of Nations set up in 1919 as a component part of the Versailles peace settlement was very far, even in form, from the ideal of an international organization within the framework of which all states and peoples could co-operate on an equal footing to promote peace. First of all, it was not of a universal character: a number of states were not admitted to the League of Nations. Soviet Russia's absence from it emphasized the anti-Soviet orientation of that body, in which the victorious powers of the First World War called the tune. Secondly, the thesis on racial equality was expunged from the Covenant of the League of Nations. Thirdly, the Covenant articles which introduced the mandate system in Germany's and Turkey's colonial possessions and placed them under the administration of the imperialist victor powers were intended to perpetuate the disgraceful colonial system. Fourthly, disarmament, without which "international peace" proclaimed by the founders of the League of Nations was inconceivable, was defined in very nebulous terms. The Covenant of the League of Nations graphically demonstrated the demagogic character of Wilson's promise to give mankind "an instrument of peace". The tasks of the League of Nations, Academician Minz points out, were "reduced to protection of the new system of international relations against revolution" (*History of Diplomacy*, vol. 3, Moscow, 1945, p. 32). As regards its "rules of the game", that new system differed but little from the pre-war one. The main changes in the pattern of international relations at the time of the Treaty of Versailles were, in addition to the emergence of the socialist state, a realignment of forces in the imperialist camp, where the contradictions between the victors and the vanquished had intensified.

the international bourgeoisie away from the gross-bourgeois, aggressive-bourgeois, reactionary-bourgeois camp".[77]

The existence of the socialist state created the material prerequisites for transferring disarmament problems to the realm of practical solution. However, the Soviet Government was under no delusion that a policy of disarmament would be immediately and unconditionally adopted by the capitalist countries. It was guided by Lenin's instructions concerning the need to achieve specific, however limited, measures to facilitate progress towards the ideal of socialism — general and complete disarmament. There is much talk and many declarations and sometimes even solemn oaths against war throughout the world, Lenin noted. "On this, and on similar questions, we should like to see a minimum of general assurances, solemn promises and grandiloquent formulas, and the greatest possible number of the simplest and most obvious decisions and measures that would certainly lead to peace, if not to the complete elimination of the war danger."[78]

These ideas of Lenin's illustrate the parameters and essence of the new system of international relations advocated by Soviet Russia opposing imperialist aggression, dictatorialness and coercion. They are fully valid today when a fundamental reshaping of international relations is in progress due to a change in the alignment of forces in favour of socialism, the collapse of the disgraceful colonial system, the enhancement of the role played by the masses in history in general and in international politics in particular.

Soviet Russia's willingness to co-operate with the capitalist world in the interests of all nations was expressed in Chicherin's statement on the principled approach of the Soviet Communists to the problems on the agenda of the Genoa Conference:

> Naturally, we have no illusions concerning the possibility to eliminate effectively the causes of war and economic crises given the present general state of things; for all that, however, we are prepared to contribute to a common effort in the interests of Russia and all Europe and scores of millions of people exposed to unbearable privations and suffering caused by economic disorder, as well as to support any attempt to bring about at least a palliative improvement in the world economy and put an end to the menace of new wars.[79]

Through the efforts of the French and American imperialists, their accomplices and minions the Genoa Conference in fact came to naught. The capitalist world, torn by antagonisms, was still seeking to dictate to the young Soviet Republic. However, it suffered a major setback. Taking advantage of the contradictions between the imperialist powers, Soviet Russia concluded a bilateral treaty with Germany. Lenin described it as follows: "True equality of the two property systems — *if only as a temporary state, until such time as the entire world abandons* private property and the *economic chaos* and wars engendered by it for the higher property system — is found only in the Treaty of Rapallo."[80] In the efforts to consolidate the Soviet Republic's position on the international scene Lenin attached great importance to exploiting the contradictions between imperialist powers. He described the role played by Soviet diplomacy in the period of the Civil War and foreign intervention in these words: "We have made use of this divergence of imperialist interests all the time. We defeated the interventionists only because their interests divided them, thereby enhancing our strength and unity."[81]

This refers to deep-seated contradictions rooted in fundamental economic causes. "If we try to exploit minor and fortuitous differences, we shall be behaving like petty politicians and cheap diplomats. There is nothing of value to be gained by that",[82] Lenin warned. Soviet diplomacy takes advantage of those contradictions in relations between capitalist countries that affect the essence of these relations and are central at a given time. As an objective factor these contradictions are exploited by Soviet diplomacy to promote peace among nations, not to instigate war as is the case with bourgeois diplomacy.

Although in the period 1917-24 no radical change was achieved in international political and diplomatic practices, and no progress in the efforts to reshape the traditional system of international relations on the principles of a just and democratic peace, Lenin's ideas left a deep imprint on the minds of people and gave momentum to the process of democratization of international life which has been continually developing since the October Revolution and has been boosted tremendously in our day by the radical change in the alignment of forces on the world scene in favour of socialism.

It would be wrong, however, to ignore the gigantic changes in the sphere of world politics. As far back as the years immediately following the October Revolution, the foreign policy principles and diplomatic activity of the Soviet Republic had an impact not only on the character of relations taking shape between socialism and capitalism but also on relations within the capitalist world. These latter relations became more democratic, outwardly at any rate. As the international positions of socialism were consolidated, its revolutionizing influence on international relations steadily increased.

3

The Struggle of the USSR for Peace and Social Progress in the Inter-war Period

Lenin's Foreign Policy Continued

DURING the temporary stabilization of capitalism, Soviet foreign policy continued to follow the line based on the principles of peaceful co-existence and proletarian internationalism just as it had done in the period of the revolutionary storms of 1917-23. From the formation of the Union of Soviet Socialist Republics in December 1922 onward, this Leninist policy began to exert a steadily growing influence on the entire pattern of international relations.

The message of the Presidium of the USSR Central Executive Committee of 13 July 1923 "To All Nations and Governments of the World" set out the aims and tasks of Soviet foreign policy:

> ... The Union State created thereby on the principle of fraternal co-operation between the peoples of the Soviet Republics aims to preserve peace with all nations.... . As a natural ally of the oppressed nations, the Union of Soviet Socialist Republics seek peaceful and friendly relations and economic co-operation with all nations. The Union of Soviet Socialist Republics aims to promote the interests of the working people of the whole world. In a vast area extending from the Baltic, from the Black and White Seas to the Pacific Ocean it has established a brotherhood of nations and a reign of labour, seeking at the same time to contribute to friendly co-operation between all nations of the world.[1]

The foreign policy of peace pursued by the Party and the Soviet Government was resisted not only by the imperialists opposed to the

Soviet Union's equality in the sphere of world politics. It was continuously attacked by the Trotskyites and other opportunists, who denied the possibility of peaceful co-existence of states with different socio-economic systems.

In opposition to the Party line of building socialism in the Soviet Union in the conditions of capitalist encirclement, a line of peaceful co-existence of the socialist and the capitalist states, the Trotskyites advocated a line of instigating world revolution. They alleged that orientation on the triumph of socialism in one country was tantamount to a betrayal of proletarian internationalism and to "national narrow-mindedness". The Party demolished the ostensibly ultra-revolutionary but in effect capitulationist position of Trotsky and his followers, who did not believe in the ability of the working class to build socialism in the Soviet Union. The defeat of Trotskyism meant that the Leninist line of peaceful co-existence was preserved as one of the fundamental principles of Soviet foreign policy.

Although over half a century has passed, the present-day "leftists" and ideologists of imperialism continue their attacks against the Soviet policy of that period, drawing on the arguments of Trotskyism. Distorting historical facts, they allege that the defeat of Trotskyism meant a "renunciation" of the principle of proletarian internationalism and the triumph of "nationalism" in Soviet foreign policy.[2]

The American Sovietologist R. Braham writes that the Bolsheviks reoriented themselves when their hopes for victorious revolutions in the Western countries had been dashed. He says that the ideological demands for world revolution were gradually replaced by an empirical policy designed to achieve the national objectives of the USSR struggling for existence in a world based on the national state system.[3]

Other Western critics of Soviet foreign policy are seeking to prove the "incompatibility" of the principles of peaceful co-existence and proletarian internationalism, which are allegedly in constant conflict.[4] Adam B. Ulam maintains that "the policy of Soviet Russia in the 1920s contained a very basic paradox that has continued down to our own day. On the one hand, the Soviet Union more than any large state required peace and international stability, both political and economic.... . On the other hand.... stability diminished the prospects of Communism. Lack of international tension would mean the isolation of the Soviet Union, its inability to play off one capitalist country against another."[5]

Such interpretations of Soviet foreign policy are motivated by a desire to represent the principle of proletarian internationalism as identical to the concept of "export of revolution", with which it has nothing in common. Nor, in its turn, can loyalty to the principle of peaceful co-existence be taken as evidence of the "priority" of national before international interests in the foreign policy of the socialist state.

In a situation where the Soviet Union was the only state of proletarian dictatorship in the world, the struggle to build socialism in one country, to strengthen the bulwark of world revolution, was a truly internationalist policy, for which peaceful co-existence provided the most favourable conditions.

The multifarious activities of the Bolshevik Party in the period between the two world wars were marked by concern for the development of the world Communist movement, for promoting international solidarity among the working people of all countries. This was exemplified by its participation in the work of the Communist International. The character of the relations between the Comintern and the Soviet Union was clearly defined in a document of the Comintern Executive Committee: "It is not the International that is a tool of the Soviet Republic but Soviet Russia that is the strongest bulwark of the Communist International. This cannot be otherwise, since the destinies of the Soviet Republic and the Communist International are governed by responsible political leaders."[6] The Communist International invariably emphasized in its documents the duty of every proletarian revolutionary to defend the Soviet Union against attacks from international reaction. The definition of the internationalist as a staunch defender of the Soviet State has retained its significance to date.

All Soviet foreign policy was pervaded with proletarian internationalism. The Soviet Union's struggle for peace was an expression of the internationalism of Soviet foreign policy aimed at safeguarding peace — the main condition for social progress. The Party and the Soviet Government were guided by the principle of proletarian internationalism in assisting their class comrades abroad.

The Soviet State used all its power and influence to protect the victims of the bourgeois reign of terror in Germany, Italy, Japan, Poland, Romania, Hungary, Bulgaria, and Yugoslavia. The activities of such organizations as MOPR (International Organization for Aid to Workers) and MEZHRABKOM (International Workers' Committee) were a striking demonstration of international proletarian solidarity; Soviet people raised funds for assistance to working people in other countries. Such was the case during the British workers' general strike in 1926, the Japanese earthquake, etc. And this was done at a time when the Soviet people themselves had not yet sufficient means to meet their daily needs.

Adhering to the principle of peaceful co-existence of the two opposite socio-economic systems, the Soviet Union in the inter-war period set an example of implementing the ideas of proletarian internationalism in practice. This was expressed above all in the Soviet people's selfless work to build socialism in the country, as well as in the many-sided assistance and support given by the Soviet State to the struggle of the proletariat in the capitalist states and the national liberation movement in the colonial and dependent countries. In Lenin's view, the internationalist duty of the Soviet working class, its contribution to the cause of world revolution consists not only in building a new society successfully. The Soviet State is the bedrock and bulwark of all international revolutionary, democratic and progressive movements. It is the internationalist duty of the working class in power to render constant moral, political and material support to various contingents of the international working-class and national liberation movements, to develop and strengthen its fraternal ties with the working people of all countries.

In planning its foreign-policy strategy the Party combined consistency and revolutionary dedication with keen political realism. It never forgot that the existence of the two opposite social systems caused the constant menace of a capitalist blockade, other forms of economic coercion, armed intervention, and restoration of the old order. Lenin warned that although ". . . we are in a position of having won conditions enabling us to exist side by side with capitalist powers",[7] "we are always a hair's breadth away from invasion".[8] It was necessary to take full advantage of the respite and to gain time to strengthen the new socialist system.

The only guarantee of final victory of socialism, i.e. a guarantee against restoration of the old order, is victory of a socialist revolution in several countries. "We are living not merely in a state, but *in a system of states,* and it is inconceivable for the Soviet Republic to exist alongside the imperialist states for any length of time. One or the other must triumph in the end."[9]

Guided by these instructions of Lenin's, the Party and the Soviet Government pursued a foreign policy based on the struggle for peace. In an interview with a correspondent of the French newspaper *Temps* on 26 January 1924, Chicherin said:

> Lenin charted the path we are following and will continue to follow. The main idea of our policy we invariably reaffirm is the idea of peace. We desire peace ourselves and we want to contribute to universal peace. . . . Our peace policy is a constructive policy. We are telling our people that the Soviet Republic means peace. Peace required for developing not only our own productive capacity but also world production, of which our production is an inalienable part. These ideas which we uphold at Genoa are a creation of the genius of Lenin. It was precisely to speed up the growth of our productive capacity that he introduced the New Economic Policy inside the country and — on the external plane — economic co-operation with foreign capital. To attract the latter through an agreement satisfactory to both sides, to share in its profits without falling into its clutches — such is one of Lenin's main ideas. And it remains our programme for the future.[10]

At the 1922 Genoa Conference the imperialists failed in their efforts to enmesh Soviet Russia in financial obligations and loans on fettering terms so as to weaken her economically and prepare the ground for the restoration of capitalism. Unable to strangle Soviet Russia, imperialism "has been compelled to recognize her officially or semi-officially", ". . . has been obliged. . . to conclude trade agreements with her".[11] The task of Soviet foreign policy was to exploit its success at Genoa and achieve *de jure* recognition of the Soviet Republic. Without that, it was unthinkable to set up a new system of international relations within the framework of which the Soviet Republic would enjoy complete equality with the capitalist states.

The Versailles–Washington system established by the victorious powers after the First World War was of a frankly anti-Soviet character, its purpose being to perpetuate the unequal and isolated position of the Soviet Republic on the international scene. One of the central tasks of that system, which ran counter to the objective tendencies of world development, was to check the further spread of socialist ideas. It could not be a durable system, because it was torn apart by irreconcilable imperialist contradictions and pregnant with another world war. The perennial source of conflict were the different interests of its members: the bitter resentment of vanquished Germany, the disgruntlement of Italy and Japan, which considered themselves robbed of their fair share of the German and Turkish colonial inheritance, the indignation of the small countries against their high-handed treatment by the imperialist powers, the contradictions between Great Britain and France, and so on. Lenin's phrase to the effect that the Treaty of Versailles was ''. . .the heaviest blow the capitalists and imperialists. . . could possibly have struck at themselves''[12] proved truly prophetic.

A new system of world relations was thus to be created only on the principles of peaceful co-existence of states having different social systems. Hence the special importance attached to the question of diplomatic recognition of the USSR and of establishing normal relations with it on an accepted footing in international law — respect for sovereignty, non-interference in internal affairs, mutually beneficial co-operation, etc. It was necessary to secure diplomatic recognition of the world's only socialist state as a means of affirming the principle of peaceful co-existence in international affairs.

Chicherin said in this context: "Many mistakenly believe that we are soliciting a high international rank. We don't need it. We don't think of prestige symbols. We are interested in *de jure* recognition only as a technical and practical step that will facilitate our economic relations. This, however, is necessary not only to us but to our partners as well."[13] The establishment of normal diplomatic relations was a *sine qua non* for developing broad and comprehensive co-operation between the USSR and the capitalist countries.

On 2 February 1924 the British Government declared its recognition of the Soviet Government. Recognition in itself, however, did not mean an automatic improvement in Anglo–Soviet political and economic relations. It was necessary to settle a number of complicated outstanding problems and place the development of commercial relations on a solid legal basis. That was the purpose of the Anglo–Soviet conference held in London between April and August

1924. The Soviet delegate declared at the conference: "We believe that the difference between the social structures of the two countries will not be an obstacle to their political and economic co-operation."[14]

At the London Conference the Soviet Government expressed its desire to table for discussion, in addition to questions concerning relations between the two countries, important international political problems, such as a general arms reduction, an expansion of international co-operation, a revision of the Treaty of Versailles and related treaties. For instance, the "Bessarabian Protocol" had sealed the annexation of part of Soviet territory by bourgeois-feudal Romania and was therefore not recognized by the Soviet Union.

The Italian Premier Mussolini tried to sell *"de Jure* recognition of the Russian Republic" at a high price. He said that for this "Russia must give me something. I demand a good trade treaty. I demand a concession in raw materials Italy needs."[15] The Soviet stand on this issue was quite definite: "We will not embark on buying *de jure* recognition.... . In our negotiations with Italy we will not agree to more than mutual concessions for mutual benefits."[16] On 7 February 1924 the Italian Government declared a resumption of political relations with the USSR.

During 1924 diplomatic relations with the USSR were established by Norway, Austria, Sweden, Greece, and Denmark. On 28 October 1924 France expressed her willingness to establish immediately normal diplomatic relations with the USSR at ambassadorial level. The USSR Central Executive Committee replied on the same day that it attached prime importance to concluding between the USSR and France "a general agreement that could provide a solid basis for friendly relations in accordance with the constant desire of the USSR for effective guarantees of universal peace in the interest of the labouring masses in all countries and for friendship with all nations".[17]

The USSR was the one major power to insist that a China liberated from imperialist domination should take her lawful place as a sovereign state within the system of international relations. The Sino–Soviet talks to normalize relations greatly discomfited the governments of France, the United States and Japan, apprehensive lest a Sino–Soviet agreement concluded on a basis of equality undermine the inequitable treaties according imperialist powers a privileged status in Chinese territory. In the "Agreement on the General Principles of Settlement of Disputes Between the Union of Soviet Socialist Republics and the Republic of China" signed on 31 May 1924 the USSR reaffirmed its renunciation of consular jurisdiction, extraterritoriality and other imperialist privileges of the tsarist government. The East China Railway built by the tsarist government at the expense of the Russian people was proclaimed a purely commercial enterprise and placed under joint Sino–Soviet management on a parity basis. The Soviet Government declared null and void all treaties, agreements and other acts concluded by the tsarist government with a third party to the prejudice of the sovereign rights or interests of China. The Sino–Soviet agreement, which was a striking expression of the principles of Soviet foreign policy, contributed to the Chinese people's struggle against imperialism.

In January 1925 the USSR and Japan concluded a convention on the basic principles of their bilateral relations whereby the two contracting parties proclaimed their desire of peace and friendship, undertook to abide by the principle of non-interference in internal affairs, and to abstain from any hostile activity against each other. Japan was to withdraw her troops from Northern Sakhalin.

> Unable at the time to remedy the consequences of Russia's defeat in the Russo-Japanese War, the Soviet Government was compelled to concede the validity of the Portsmouth Treaty of 5 September 1905, in particular its territorial clauses on the surrender to Japan of Southern Sakhalin, historically Russian territory. At the time of signing the convention, the Soviet Government published a special declaration to the effect that "its recognition... of the Portsmouth Treaty as valid... by no means implies that the Soviet Government shares political responsibility with the former tsarist government for the conclusion of the above treaty".

This reservation evidenced that the recognition of the Portsmouth Treaty was of a temporary character.

The imperialists took a hostile stance towards the Soviet–Japanese Convention. The American *Evening Post* wrote editorially in a tone of anger and animosity that the USSR had forged an effective weapon to break the iron ring in the Pacific established by the Washington Conference.[18]

The Soviet Union also did much to establish diplomatic, economic and cultural relations with the Latin American countries. Mexico was the first of them to normalize relations with the USSR in August 1924. "The Mexican people and government completely agree with the Soviet-policy principles of respect for the sovereignty of small nations and renunciation of imperialist policy", declared Badilla, the first Mexican envoy to the Soviet Union.[19] Presenting his credentials to the Mexican President, the Soviet Ambassador said that the people of the USSR felt solidarity with the Mexican people in their struggle for independence against imperialist powers. Diplomatic relations between the Soviet Union and Uruguay were also set up at that time. The attempt to resume relations with Argentina, however, failed. As the Argentine Chargé d'Affaires in Berlin said to a Soviet representative, "on this issue Argentina will not take an independent stand and will follow in the footsteps of the United States".[20]

As far back as the twenties, the peoples of Latin America could see for themselves that the Soviet Union was their loyal friend and defender of their national independence, an ally in their anti-imperialist struggle. Convincing proof of this was the resolute denunciation of the US intervention early in 1927 against the small Central American republic of Nicaragua.[21]

In 1924/5 the USSR established diplomatic relations with thirteen states in Europe, Asia and Latin America, and concluded a number of new trade treaties. That was a serious setback for the policy of boycott and isolation of the USSR from world affairs. The normalization of relations between the Soviet Union and a number of capitalist countries resulted in a further growth of Soviet influence on international relations.

The period of diplomatic recognition of the Soviet Union ushered in a new stage in the relations between the countries of the two opposite systems. Evaluating the significance of the agreement signed by the British and Soviet Governments in his statement at a plenary meeting of the Moscow Soviet on 20 August 1924, Chicherin described it as the first step on the new path of our relations and hence the first step on the path of new world relations. These new world relations were being built on the solid foundation of the principle of peaceful co-existence, the universally accepted standards and principles of international law.

Seeking diplomatic recognition by the leading Western powers, which gave tone to the attitude of the capitalist world towards the

USSR, the Soviet Government invariably adhered to the fundamental principles of Soviet foreign policy. It never tried to ingratiate itself with them or attempted to buy their favour by abandoning its Communist ideals. That position ensured support for the Soviet Republic by the world revolutionary and national liberation movements, and, despite her relative weakness in those years, enabled her to take her rightful place within the global system of international relations.

The Comintern Executive Committee in a letter to members of the Communist Workers' Party of Germany duly rebuffed the malicious insinuations against the Russian Communist Party (Bolsheviks), which had allegedly turned the Communist International into a tool of Soviet Russia's foreign policy and was attempting to

> "pursue within the International a watery policy of compromise so as to curry favour with the Western capitalists. Such ideas can enter only politically naïve heads. The Russian comrades have enough experience in politics to realise that no decorous conduct or readiness for repentance can win the sympathy of capitalists for the Soviet Republic. They realize that any concession can be wrested from the capitalist states by force alone, and this force lies in the strength of Soviet Government, the Red Army and largely in the revolutionary energy and revolutionary successes of the proletariat in all capitalist states."[22]

The Soviet Union, faithful as it was to its internationalist duty, continued to render assistance to the peoples fighting against imperialist domination, for their national and social liberation. In the period when an anti-imperialist and anti-feudal revolution began in China, the Soviet Union, at the request of the Chinese revolutionary government of Sun Yat-sen in Canton, immediately sent it arms and ammunition by sea and commissioned a group of military and political advisers (V.K. Blyukher, M.M. Borodin, and others) to help it. In many Soviet cities, factory and office workers contributed a day's pay to the assistance fund for the Chinese people. The Central Committee of the Soviet Communist Party in a resolution of April 1926 emphasized that the Soviet state must do its utmost to hinder the formation of a common imperialist front against China. The Central Committee pointed out the need to pursue a line motivated by great attention to the rights of China and respect for her sovereignty.[23] The Soviet Union's assistance to the Chinese revolutionaries enraged the imperialist powers seeking to perpetuate their sway over China.

M.M. Litvinov, Commissar for Foreign Affairs, in a statement at the session of the USSR Central Executive Committee on 21 February 1927, declared: "We did not conceal in the past, nor do we conceal now our sincere sympathy for the Chinese people's liberation movement, their struggle for independence.... . We would only welcome the establishment of relations between China and other countries on new principles of equality."

The Soviet Union's position helped China, Turkey and other countries to do away with the regime of capitulations and other forms of semi-colonial enslavement — clear evidence of success in the struggle to reshape international relations on democratic principles.

The contours and parameters of a new system of international relations based on strict adherence to the principle of self-determination of nations and international co-operation on a basis of equality were outlined in the Soviet proposals at the Lausanne Conference in September 1923, which boiled down to the following three points:

1. Satisfaction of Turkey's national aspirations.
2. Closure of the Black Sea straits to all warships in peacetime and wartime.
3. Full freedom of commercial navigation.[24]

Loyal to Leninist foreign-policy principles, the Soviet Union also came out in support of the Republic of the Riffs (Northern Morocco) against the Spanish and French colonialists, and expressed its solidarity with the Syrian people's heroic struggle during the national uprising of 1925-27. The Soviet Union called for abolishing the colonial system in whatever form, including the so-called protectorates and mandates, and for granting to all nations freedom of political and economic self-determination.

The Soviet Union's relations with the Middle East countries developed on the principles of equality, which created an atmosphere of mutual trust and respect. In 1925-27 the Soviet Union signed treaties of neutrality and non-aggression with Turkey, Afghanistan and Iran, which were another step in developing these relations. On 1 November 1928 the Soviet Union concluded a treaty of friendship and commerce with Yemen.

*   *   *

The Versailles–Washington system of post-war peace settlement became increasingly unstable year after year. Peace and co-operation among nations were constantly threatened by the foreign policy of the imperialist powers. The 15th Congress of the Soviet Communist Party held between 2 and 19 December 1927, in its resolution on the Central Committee Report, declared:

> The last two years of world development have shown again that the efforts of bourgeois and pacifist politicians to "unite" and "reconcile" powers on a capitalist basis have proved futile. The endless conciliatory conferences and commissions of the League of Nations, the so-called "Manifesto of Bankers" (a declaration against the Versailles postwar customs barriers), the international economic conference, the pacifist project of "pan-Europe", the tripartite Geneva disarmament conference, all have exposed themselves as just another deception of the working class. The conciliatory attempts only covered up the imperialists' frantic rivalry behind the scenes, their infighting over the colonial loot, the incessant arms race, the knocking together of secret and open military blocs in direct preparation·for new imperialist wars.[25]

There was also an exacerbation of contradictions between the capitalist countries and the Soviet Union, which by its triumphant development was undermining the mainstays of world imperialist domination. The growth of socialism in the Soviet Union, the frustrated hopes of the bourgeoisie for a degeneration of the proletarian dictatorship, along with an increase in the revolutionary influence of the Soviet Union on the international scene were the main factors in that exacerbation. Thus, the development of capitalism as a whole tended to shorten the historical time of the peaceful "respite" and to speed up the advent of a new period of great imperialist wars.

In view of the trends prevailing in the international situation, the 15th Congress of the Soviet Communist Party formulated the foreign-policy guidelines for the Party and the Soviet Government. These were as follows:

1. Continued implementation of a steadfast peace policy as a policy of fighting the menace of imperialist war and as the main condition for further growth of socialism in the USSR.

2. All-round extension of the friendly ties of the workers of the USSR with the workers of the West European states and the labouring masses in the oppressed countries.

3. Further systematic development of economic links with the

capitalist states while securing the Soviet Union's growing economic independence.

The foreign policy guidelines set by the 15th Congress of the Soviet Communist Party evidenced that in world politics the Soviet Union continued to abide by the Leninist principles of peaceful co-existence and proletarian internationalism, on the basis of which it sought to restructure international relations in the period of transition from capitalism to socialism.

The struggle for peace and for preventing war is inconceivable without a struggle for disarmament. The Genoa Conference, at which the world's first socialist state came forward with a comprehensive programme on this problem, was followed by the Moscow Disarmament Conference in December 1922 convened on a Soviet initiative. It was attended by Soviet Russia, Poland, Finland, Estonia, Latvia, and Lithuania. At the Conference, the Soviet delegation proposed a 75 per cent reduction in the armed forces of the states represented at the Conference to be effected within 18 months to 2 years, and agreed to cut the strength of the Red Army from 800,000 to 200,000 men and to disband irregular troops. It also proposed a ceiling on average military spending per serviceman and neutral zones to be established along the borders, where no troops were to be stationed. Significantly, the bourgeois partners at the Conference declined the Soviet proposals on the plea of the need for preliminary "moral disarmament", anticipating thereby the present-day hypocritical appeals of bourgeois ideologists and politicians for "ideological reconciliation" as a precondition for *détente* and restructuring international relations today.

At the Anglo-Soviet conference of 1924 the Soviet Union raised disarmament problems. The Soviet delegation stated with profound regret that the hopes for the abolition of militarism after the war had proved unfounded. Military budgets continued to consume the greater part of the national income, and the governments' attention was focused on war preparations.

> Never before has the human mind achieved such sophistication in search of new weapons of destruction as today. All competent people agree that should it break out, a new war, thanks to the progress of war chemistry, aviation, ship-building and artillery, will be the most destructive of all wars in history. We believe,

therefore, that the disarmament problem should be raised before all governments in a completely clear and categorical form. Disarmament should be implemented to the greatest possible extent.[26]

As far as the USSR was concerned, between 1921 and 1924 it reduced the strength of its army from 6 million to 500,000 men, and was prepared to take further resolute steps towards disarmament along with other states and to contribute in every way to a general reduction of naval armaments.

From 1927 the Soviet Union was actively involved in the work of the Preparatory Committee for an international disarmament conference set up at a session of the League of Nations Council, although the USSR was not yet a member of the League of Nations. At the very first meeting the Soviet delegation made public a declaration on general and complete disarmament to be implemented under a convention to be concluded immediately. The Soviet delegation proposed disbandment of all land, naval and air forces, destruction of all armaments, ammunition, chemicals and other lethal weapons, closing down of munition factories, a ban on military appropriations, abolition of War Ministries and General Staffs, etc.

The Soviet proposal for general and complete disarmament helped effectively to lay bare the hypocrisy of the imperialist powers. The 6th Congress of the Communist International in its thesis "On Measures to End the Menace of Imperialist War" declared in this context: "The Soviet Government has proposed that the imperialists engaged in cynical talk of disarmament should in actual fact disarm, and has torn the mask of pacifism off their face. It goes without saying that no Communist expected the imperialists to accept the Soviet disarmament plan. Nevertheless, the Soviet Government's proposal was not hypocritical, but was made in a spirit of complete sincerity, since it is not at variance with the home and foreign policies of the workers' state, whereas the imperialists' phraseology about 'disarmament' is inconsistent with the policy of the bourgeois states — a policy of oppression and plunder."[27] The Soviet proposal, the thesis read, "expresses one of the goals of socialism, which the revolutionary proletariat will accomplish after its victory on a world-wide scale."[28]

The Soviet proposal for general and complete disarmament was turned down through the efforts of the delegations of Great Britain, France, Japan, and the United States which described the Soviet approach to disarmament as "oversimplified" and intended for "the man in the street". Indeed, as the American newspaper *Baltimore Sun* said, the Soviet proposals were welcomed by ordinary people everywhere.[29] The British Labour Party leader George Lansbury expressed his assurance that if the Russian proposals were presented to a meeting of ordinary men and women, they would unanimously vote for them. He described the Soviet declaration as the most momentous event on record in the struggle for peace.[30] After its plan of general and complete disarmament had been rejected, the Soviet Union submitted to the 5th session of the preparatory committee for a disarmament conference in March 1928 a "Draft Convention on Arms Reduction". It provided for a progressive and proportional reduction in all kinds of armaments and for a permanent international control commission to implement such reduction to be made up of representatives of all states party to the convention. This Soviet plan, however, was also declined by the capitalist states, which were unwilling, as the 5th Congress of Soviets pointed out, to make "even a small step in the direction of arms reduction".

In its campaign for a lasting peace and prevention of another war, the Soviet Union supported the idea of renunciation of war as an instrument of national policy, which was the basis for the so-called Kellogg–Briand Pact. Initially, the imperialist powers had excluded the USSR from the range of member states of the Pact. This created the impression that the principle of renunciation of war, i.e. the principle of peaceful co-existence, could not be made the basis for relations between the capitalist countries and the Soviet Union, while the Pact itself was to be used as an instrument for preparing war against the USSR. Apprehensive of exposure of their anti-Soviet designs, the Western powers were obliged to invite the USSR to join the Kellog–Briand Pact when it had been signed by fifteen states.

Not only did the Soviet Government accept this invitation but on its initiative a protocol on early ratification of the Pact was signed in Moscow on 9 February 1928 by the USSR, Estonia, Latvia, Poland, and Romania. After some time Turkey, Iran, and Lithuania followed suit. The conclusion of the protocol helped to a definite extent to strengthen peaceful relations between the USSR and neighbouring countries and was one of the measures required to set up a new system of international relations. It demonstrated again the Soviet Union's desire of lasting peace and peaceful co-existence, its willingness to have war banished for good as a method of settling disputes between nations.

In the years of the Great Depression of 1929-33 when the danger of another war had sharply increased, the Soviet Union persistently continued to campaign for disarmament, regarding it as the chief factor of peace among nations. The Soviet Government repeatedly stated that "under present conditions disarmament, or at least a maximum arms reduction, can be the only guarantee of peace".[31] At the World Disarmament Conference in 1932 the Soviet Union again tabled its proposals which had been earlier submitted to the Preparatory Committee.

Referring to the importance of an urgent solution of the disarmament problem, the chief Soviet delegate called attention to the fact that the disarmament conference had opened to the accompaniment of thundering guns: Japan was waging a war of aggression against China in Manchuria. "Two states which are party to the pact of the League of Nations and the Treaty of Paris of 1928", he said, "have been at war *de facto* if not *de jure* for five months now. The war has not yet been registered and certified by a lawyer, but a vast territory of one of the belligerent powers has been invaded by the armed forces of the other, and their regular troops are fighting battles involving all arms and services, with thousands of casualties in dead and wounded."[32]

The statement of the Soviet delegation was an appeal to all states attending the conference to renounce war as an instrument of national policy, to find means of "making war impossible in principle", to "put an end to war" because it causes suffering to the mass of the people throughout the world.[33] This appeal, however, was ignored by the delegates of the capitalist countries, whose governments sought to take advantage of the disarmament conference to consolidate their military–political positions, preserve their own armed forces and armaments and correspondingly to weaken their rivals and potential foes.

Aware of the fact that by giving lip service to disarmament the capitalist powers were seeking to cover up the arms race, the Soviet delegation insisted that practical solutions be found without further delay and procrastination to the disarmament problem, which should no longer be thrown like a tennis ball from one committee or sub-committee to another, from one session of the conference to another.

The significance of the disarmament campaign waged by the USSR can hardly be overestimated. The whole world for the first time, as a matter of first priority, was faced with the task of implementing genuine disarmament by a government which sought earnestly and not only in words to achieve this goal. A proposal for general and complete disarmament, that is, for making war impossible, was without precedent in history. The Soviet Union once again demonstrated its desire for peace, for peaceful co-existence with the capitalist states and its willingness to do away with war as an instrument for settling disputes between nations. The situation prevailing in that period, the alignment of forces on the world arena prevented this programme being translated into reality, but this does not detract from its historic significance.

Another important event in the history of the Soviet Union's struggle for a new system of international relations was its proposal for the conclusion of a protocol on economic non-aggression submitted at a meeting of the European Commission in May 1931. The protocol was to ban all forms of economic aggression by a country or a group of countries against any other country or group of countries as well as appeals for boycotting the foreign commerce of any country. This would contribute to the development of economic co-operation between states irrespective of their social systems and to acceptance of the principle of peaceful co-existence. The *ad hoc* committee of the European Commission on 5 November 1931 adopted a resolution saying that: first, the Committee approves of the general idea of the Soviet proposal for an economic non-aggression pact; second, the Committee acknowledges the possibility of peaceful co-existence of states having a different economic and social structure; third, the Committee underlines the necessity for states to be motivated in their economic relations solely by the requirements of economic life, ignoring considerations following exclusively from differences in their social and political systems.[34]

An economic non-aggression pact, along with the Kellogg–Briand Pact, could have served as a means of affirming the principles of peaceful co-existence, which were to make the basis for restructuring the post-war system of international relations. The imperialist circles still hoping to do away with the socialist state and restore the rule of capitalism throughout the world, refused to carry into effect the peace-asserting provisions of these pacts.

The Soviet Policy of Collective Resistance to Fascist Aggression

In the early thirties the international situation began to change essentially. In the Soviet Union the question "who will win?" was being decided in favour of socialism in the course of a bitter class struggle. During the early 5-year plans the Soviet Union consolidated its economic position and defence capability. At the same time, the Great Depression of 1929-33 put an end to the period of relative stabilization of capitalism. The class struggle intensified in the imperialist states. In certain of them, the ruling quarters began to search for a way out of their predicament via fascism and reckless expansion in wars of aggression. Fascism at home and a predatory policy abroad were generated by the same forces, namely, by the most reactionary circles of the financial oligarchy. In the van of imperialist reaction now stood the fascist and militaristic rulers of Germany, Italy, and Japan rather than the ruling circles of Britain and France. It was the emerging bloc of aggressive powers that became the main force hostile to the cause of peace and socialism, a force by which Soviet foreign policy was primarily confronted on the international scene in the pre-war period.

At the time of their coming to power the German Nazis already had a plan of establishing a system of international relations primarily by ending the division of the world — the conquest through war of the first socialist state. The ideologists of German nazism, who denied the Soviet Union even the right to statehood, went as far as to declare openly the complete legality of any war against the USSR. Hitler stated for instance:

> We National-Socialists deliberately reject the foreign policy line of the prewar period. We are resuming our advance in the direction where it was suspended six centuries ago. We are ending the Germans' traditional pressure on the south and west of Europe and turning our eyes to the lands in the East. Finally, we are completing the colonial and trade policies of the prewar years and coming over to the territorial policy of the future. But if we are speaking today of new lands in Europe, we imply in the first place only Russia and the neighbouring states under her control.

After the Nazi takeover of power in Germany Hitler reaffirmed in a series of statements and speeches his foreign policy programme set forth in *Mein Kampf*. For instance, at a secret conference with the commanders of all arms and services of Germany on 4 February 1933, he spoke of the need for "the conquest of *lebensraum* in the East and its ruthless colonization".[35]

Nazi Germany allied with fascist Italy and militarist Japan cherished the ambition of carving up the world by force of arms. Their programme, besides liquidating the USSR, provided for a revision of the results of the First World War in favour of the imperialist predators defeated or "unrewarded" in that war, for discarding in effect all standards of international law restraining imperialist expansion, for legitimizing the use of force in international intercourse and eventually the establishment of world supremacy by the three fascist predators — Germany, Italy, and Japan. Under the new world order which the fascist aggressors planned to establish in that way they were to be elevated to the status of rulers of whole continents, whose population was to be turned into slaves deprived of rights.

The formula for the world order put forward by the aggressive fascist states was intended in particular to destroy the Versailles-Washington system, to undermine the positions of dominance of American, British, and French imperialism. Hitler stated frankly: "We want it to be understood once and for all that our struggle against Versailles and our struggle for a new world order are one and the same thing and that we cannot halt at any point. We will enforce our system all over the world and impose it on all nations." (Translated from the Russian.)

In the struggle to establish his own system of international relations — "a new world order", which meant the world supremacy of fascism — Hitler assigned a conspicuous role to fascist foreign policy and diplomacy. "I am conducting a policy of coercion, employing any means without bothering about ethics or the 'code of honour'...," Hitler said. "In politics I recognize no laws. Politics is a game in which any trick is justifiable, and its rules vary with the skill of the players." Preparing to use fascist diplomacy on a wide scale, Hitler as far back as 1932 described the arsenal of its means as follows:

> I have already taken steps to organize my own diplomatic service. I have ordered a card index of all influential personalities in the world to be compiled and all relevant information to be gathered about them. Mr. So-and-so: does he take bribes? How can he be bribed? Is she ambitious? What are his erotic predilections? What kind of women does he prefer? Is he homosexual? This category deserves special attention; such people can be firmly kept on a leash. Has he anything in his past to conceal? Does he yield to blackmail?... In this way I am conducting a real policy, winning over people, forcing them to work for me, and secure for myself infiltration and influence in every country. The political successes I need are achieved by systematic corruption of the classes in power. (Translated from the Russian.)[36]

What was the attitude of the leaders of the United States, Britain, and France to the plans of the fascist aggressors? The only word for it is ambivalent. On the other hand, the anti-Soviet programme of Nazi Germany and her allies perfectly agreed with them. Turning a blind eye to the mortal danger posed to their nations by the expansion of fascist aggression, the ruling quarters of the bourgeois-democratic states cherished the hope that they would manage to provoke a conflict between Nazi Germany and Japan on the one hand and the Soviet Union on the other, thereby killing two birds with one stone: destruction of the Soviet state and a blow to formidable rival imperialists in the course of an anti-Soviet war. This line was supported and approved by the most influential circles in the United States, the "Cliveden set" in Britain (Chamberlain, Simon, Wood, Halifax, Hoare, and others), and by politicians like Daladier and Reynaud in France.

More far-sighted political leaders in these countries, however, realized that Hitler's policy threatened to undermine Britain's colonial monopoly and to wrest from France whatever she had obtained as a result of the First World War; that Mussolini's ambitions to turn the

Mediterranean into an "Italian lake" was prejudicial to the interests of Britain and France; that Japan's aggression in China jeopardized American and British interests in the Far East. Among such politicians were Churchill, Lloyd George, Eden, Duff-Cooper, Amery, and Beaverbrook in Great Britain; Louis Barthou, Jean-Paul Boncour, and Edouard Herriot in France. Politicians of this kind were prone to seek some form of agreement with the Soviet Union to hold back fascist aggression.

Although in the 'thirties Western foreign policy was shaped by advocates of the first trend, who came to be known as the "Munichites", important changes took place in the attitude of Britain, France, and the United States towards the USSR. Formerly, any reluctant recognition by the West of the functioning of the socialist state within the system of international relations amounted to admitting that it could not be crushed by force of arms. Now, however, the leaders of the bourgeois-democratic countries of the West adopted a view of the Soviet Union as a force that could be opposed to the "exorbitant claims" of Germany, Italy, and Japan, and their ambitions for world supremacy.

The year 1933 was a turning-point in the Soviet Union's relations with the capitalist states. This was primarily due to the consolidation of the power of the socialist state, its increased influence on world affairs, as well as to the emergence on the international scene of a group of states which had openly taken the path of preparing for war in order to carve up the world. Between 1933 and 1935 a number of capitalist countries established diplomatic relations with the USSR. Among them were the United States, Romania, Bulgaria, Belgium, Colombia and Albania.

On 16 November 1933 President Roosevelt and the Commissar for Foreign Affairs Litvinov (who had succeeded Chicherin in 1930) exchanged letters in which they expressed the hope that the relations now established between the two nations could forever remain normal and friendly and that the two nations could co-operate in the future for their mutual benefit and for safeguarding peace throughout the world.

The normalizing by the United States of its relations with the Soviet Union in the sixteenth year of the latter's existence was motivated by considerations of home and foreign policy. Referring to them in his memoirs, Secretary of State Cordell Hull said that the world was entering a dangerous period of its development both in Europe and Asia. Russia could in time greatly help to stabilize the situation, when the war menace grew more and more formidable.[37]

The normalization of Soviet–American relations extended far beyond the framework of bilateral relations. Pointing out their importance, the 17th Congress of the Soviet Communist Party declared: "This act is indisputably of crucial significance for the entire system of international relations."[38]

The Soviet Union, which from the outset had taken a determined stand against the fascist aggressors, on 6 February 1933 proposed at the Geneva Disarmament Conference that the latter adopt an international document defining aggression. The Soviet draft suggested the following definition: (1) Declaration of war against another state. (2) An invasion by armed forces of the territory of another state without a declaration of war. (3) An attack by land, naval or air forces, without a declaration of war, against the territory, ships or aircraft of another state. (4) A sea blockade of the coast or ports of another state. (5) Support for armed bands formed in the territory of one state and invading the territory of another state or a refusal to comply with a request of the invaded state to take whatever measures may be necessary to deny these bands any assistance or patronage in the territory of the former state. "No considerations of a political, strategic or economic nature, nor an interest in utilizing in the territory of the state under attack its natural resources or in obtaining other advantages or privileges of whatever kind, just as no reference to large investments of capital or to any other vested interests likely to exist in that territory, nor denying it the distinctive qualifications of a state shall be invoked to justify an attack...," said the Soviet draft. It listed sixteen of the most common grounds that were not to justify military attack.[39]

The adoption of the Soviet proposal could and surely would have been a new instrument in the struggle to deliver mankind from bloody wars and create a more secure system of international relations. The Soviet initiative, however, was cold-shouldered by the leading powers at the disarmament conference. As a result in July 1933 the Soviet

Union, jointly with its neighbour-countries (Estonia, Latvia, Turkey, Persia, Poland, Romania, Afghanistan, Czechoslovakia, and Lithuania), signed a convention on the definition of aggression. Later the convention was joined by Finland. It was not until many years later, in the new conditions of a normalized political climate in the world and intensified activity of the peace forces, that it became possible to implement this idea. The 29th UN General Assembly in December 1974 adopted a definition of aggression drafted on the initiative and with the active participation of the USSR.

The Soviet Union believed as before that general and complete disarmament would be the most effective guarantee of a lasting peace. However, the rejection of the Soviet proposals on this question at the Geneva Disarmament Conference and the increased war menace from the fascist states dictated a search for new ways of averting war and fascist aggression. In December 1933 the Central Committee of the Soviet Communist Party adopted the historic decision to launch a campaign for setting up a workable collective-security system in Europe with the object of preserving peace and preventing aggression. The idea of collective security was perfectly realistic and acceptable both to the Soviet Union and to the capitalist countries interested in peace being maintained. That is why the Soviet Government advanced then the formula "peace is indivisible", which won international recognition.

The thesis on the indivisibility of peace was based on the Leninist principle of peaceful co-existence of states belonging to different socio-economic systems. The establishment of a collective security system in Europe and on other continents would deal a blow to the designs of the fascist aggressors.

In compliance with this decision, the People's Commissariat of Foreign Affairs drew up a programme of setting up a collective security system in Europe, which was approved by the Politburo of the Central Committee of the Soviet Communist party on 19 December 1933. The programme was as follows:

> 1. The USSR is prepared on certain terms to join the League of Nations. 2. The USSR has no objections to a regional convention being concluded within the framework of the League of Nations for mutual defence against aggression from Germany. 3. The USSR consents to the participation in this convention of

Belgium, Czechoslovakia, Poland, Lithuania, Latvia, Estonia, and Finland but with indispensable participation of France and Poland. 4. Negotiations to specify the commitments under the future convention on mutual assistance may be started when a draft convention has been submitted by France which is the initiator of the whole venture.[40]

Clause 6 of the programme contained proposals for a revision of some articles of the Convenant of the League of Nations, in particular those which sanctioned war as a means of settling international disputes. The Soviet demand for recognition of the racial and national equality of all member states of the League of Nations merits special attention.

The Soviet plan of collective security in Europe together with the Soviet proposal for a regional Pacific Pact to be concluded between the USSR, the United States, Japan, China, and other states, which had been submitted to the US government in November 1933, embodied the conception of the indivisibility of peace, the principles of peaceful co-existence and co-operation between the USSR and the capitalist countries, and indicated the right way of safeguarding peace by the joint efforts of states belonging to different socio-economic systems.

In September 1934, on the initiative of France, the governments of thirty member states of the League of Nations in a telegram addressed to the Soviet Government declared that "the task of maintaining peace which is the main duty of the League of Nations requires co-operation of all states. In view of this, the undersigned invite the USSR to join the League of Nations and contribute its valuable co-operation". The Soviet Government accepted the proposal. Communicating its consent to the President of the 15th Assembly of the League of Nations, the People's Commissar for Foreign Affairs of the USSR stated that the Soviet Government, which had made the maintenance and consolidation of peace the main task of its foreign policy, had never turned a deaf ear to proposals for international co-operation and that it interpreted the invitation as an expression of the real desire of peace by the League of Nations and as a recognition of the necessity to co-operate with the Soviet Union.[41]

At the 7th Congress of Soviets in January 1935 it was pointed out that the Soviet Union had to admit the usefulness of co-operation with the League of Nations, although the role played by such organizations should not be overestimated. The Soviet Union's former negative attitude to the League of Nations had been explained in his time by Lenin who said in an interview with Michael Farbman, a correspondent of the *Observer* and the *Manchester Guardian,* that it is "...marked by the absence of anything resembling the establishment of the real equality of rights between nations, anything resembling a real chance of their peaceful coexistence".[42] However, after Nazi Germany and militarist Japan had left the League of Nations and taken the path of war, there arose an opportunity for that international body to be converted into an effective obstacle to the warmongers. As a resolution of the Communist International stressed, the Soviet Union's accession to the League of Nations showed the masses that Soviet leaders were not dogmatists but dedicated Marxists who correctly assessed the balance of power in the capitalist world and were capable of taking advantage of even the slightest opportunity to widen their activities in defence of peace and in the interests of revolution.[43]

The Soviet Union's entry into the League of Nations was a milestone in Soviet foreign policy. It marked the changeover to political co-operation with the capitalist countries with the object of struggling against fascist aggression and concluding mutual assistance treaties with them. The efforts to organize such co-operation came up against formidable difficulties, bringing into sharp relief as they did the antagonism between the class interests of the bourgeoisie and the proletariat. It was not until the Soviet Union had grown much stronger in the course of socialist construction and the European countries had found themselves faced by the menace of fascist aggression that it became possible to implement the idea of political co-operation.

Already in the early days of its membership of the League the Soviet Union took vigorous steps to rally forces to a struggle against the menace of another war, for peace and security, for co-operation of states having different social systems on the Leninist principle of peaceful co-existence.

In November 1934 a war provoked by the imperialist forces was being fought between Paraguay and Bolivia, and the Soviet Union came forward in the League of Nations with a proposal for effective measures to be taken to settle the conflict.[44]

The Soviet Union urged the League to use economic sanctions against Italy which had attacked Ethiopia on 2 October 1935. The Soviet Union denounced all attempts to justify the Italian aggression. In a note to the Italian Government of 22 November, it condemned in strong terms the aggression against Ethiopia, which was a sovereign state like any other. A different view on this question, the note said, would mean "a rejection of the foundations of the League of Nations, a rejection of collective organization of security, encouragement of aggression in the future and denial of the possibility to display international solidarity in the cause of maintaining and strengthening universal peace, which is the basis for the policy of the Soviet Government and the purpose of its entry into the League of Nations".[45]

Within the framework of the League of Nations the Soviet Government applied strenuous efforts to set up a regional system of collective security in Europe — the so-called Eastern Pact, as well as to conclude a Pacific Pact. The opposition of the reactionary circles of the imperialist powers thwarted these projects. In 1935, however, the Soviet Union concluded mutual assistance treaties with France and Czechoslovakia, which laid a solid foundation for a collective rebuff to the aggressors.

The questions of organizing a struggle against fascism and the menace of another imperialist war were in the focus of attention of the international Communist movement. In the summer of 1935 these questions were discussed in comprehensive detail at the 7th Congress of the Communist International. The reports and resolutions of the 7th Congress became a militant programme for all Communist parties in their struggle against fascism and the menace of war. They emphasized the leading role played in this struggle by the Soviet Communist Party and the Soviet State. The resolution on "The Tasks of the Communist International in View of the Imperialist Preparations for Another World War" read in part:

> The main contradiction between the socialist and the capitalist worlds has intensified to a still greater degree. However, thanks to its growing power the Soviet Union averted an attack of the imperialist powers and their satellites and embarked on a consistent peace policy directed against all warmongers. This has made the Soviet Union the focus of attraction not only for the class-conscious

workers but also for all labouring people committed to peace in the capitalist and colonial countries. At the same time, the Soviet peace policy has not only frustrated the plans of the imperialists seeking to isolate the Soviet Union but also has laid the groundwork for its co-operation in the cause of safeguarding peace with small states, for which war, threatening their independence, poses an especially great danger, as well as with those countries which are interested in preserving peace at the present time.

The Soviet peace policy opposing proletarian internationalism to nationalist and racial strife is directed not only to defence of the Soviet Union, to safeguarding the security of socialist construction; it protects the lives of the workers in all countries, the lives of all oppressed and exploited people; it means defence of the national independence of small nations; it meets the vital interests of mankind; it protects culture against the barbarity of war.[46]

This resolution proves conclusively the organic interrelationship between the basic principles of Soviet foreign policy held to in the thirties — the principle of peaceful co-existence and that of proletarian internationalism. It exposed those who sought, by emasculating the class essence of Soviet foreign policy, to depict it as an unprincipled compromise between the USSR and the "Western democracies".

Palmiro Togliatti declared at the 7th Congress:

I believe that no working man, that no one at all, doubts that the Soviet Union's policy is a policy of peace. The fact that the Soviet Union pursues a peace policy is not accidental, nor is it motivated by transitory considerations of expediency. This policy is an organic phenomenon stemming from the very nature of Soviet government, from the entire history of its development, from everything that it represents and everything that it is doing. (Translated from the Russian).[47]

In the struggle against fascism and war, international proletarian solidarity assumed a new dimension. This was strikingly illustrated by the support of the international proletariat for the heroic struggle of the Spanish Republicans against fascism. Nationals of fifty-four countries fought in the international brigades on the side of the Spanish Republic.[48] Among them were Soviet citizens from various national republics, Germans and Austrians, Italians, Poles, Bulgarians, Frenchmen, Belgians, etc. The international brigades gave considerable moral, political and military aid to the Spanish Republicans in the struggle against the mutineers and the German–Italian fascist interventionists.

Performing its internationalist duty and acting in full compliance with the standards of international law, the Soviet Union rendered every assistance and support to the republican government of Spain right to the end.

The defeat of Republican Spain was the result of her forces being heavily outnumbered, as well as the notorious Anglo-French policy of "non-intervention" and "appeasement" of the aggressive fascist powers. In keeping with that policy the Chamberlain government of Britain sought to reach agreement with the fascist powers so as to canalize their aggression against the USSR. For that purpose, according to Lloyd George, it was prepared to sacrifice not only Spain but other countries as well.

The Soviet Union campaigned persistently to preserve and secure a lasting peace by joint efforts of states within and without the framework of the League of Nations. A hotbed of war existed not only in Europe but also in Asia, where Japan, which had conquered Manchuria in the early 'thirties, was preparing to invade the Mongolian People's Republic. To oppose these plans the Governments of the USSR and the MPR on 27 November 1934 reached an understanding on mutual assistance and support. On 12 March 1936 the Soviet Union and the Mongolian People's Republic formalized their relations of alliance in an official protocol published on the same day. This compelled the Japanese militarists to suspend for a time their attack on the MPR.

The next victim of Japanese aggression in July 1937 was China, where Japan in a series of lightning strikes captured important centres of commerce and industry — Shanghai, Peking, Tientsin, and elsewhere. Speaking at the League of Nations, the Soviet delegate urged its members to organize a rebuff to aggression against China. At an emergency international conference called at Brussels on 3 November 1937, the USSR proposed collective sanctions, not excluding military force, against Japan in conformity with Article 16 of the Covenant of the League of Nations. These proposals were rejected, however, the delegates of the United States and Britain preferring to provoke a war between the USSR and Japan than to take collective measures to repel the aggressor.

Commenting on the failure of the Brussels conference, the *New York Times* pointed to the responsibility of the American administration, saying that the world was allowed to know that the

United States was standing aloof, saving its own skin from the dangers directly threatening it; the dictators were allowed to feel that the group of American policy-makers were prepared to look on at the remaking of the world after the fascist pattern without interfering and without understanding that such remaking posed an eventual danger to the United States.[49]

The Soviet Union alone gave China diplomatic and other assistance at that time. On 27 August 1937 it signed a non-aggression pact with China, emphasizing its friendly feelings and preparedness to ease the burden of China's war against the Japanese invaders. In 1938-39 the USSR extended to China a total of 250 million dollars' worth of credits to supply her with 600 aircraft, 100 howitzers and other pieces of ordnance, more than 8000 machine-guns, etc. A total of 3665 Soviet military advisers took part in the just war waged by the Chinese people, and more than 200 Soviet volunteers were killed in action.[50] Even Chiang Kai-shek in a letter to Kliment Voroshilov in 1939 admitted that "Thanks to the sympathies and solidarity of the peoples of the Soviet Union, China has been given material aid, which is enabling her to fight a long war of liberation".[51]

The Soviet Union's attempts to convert the League of Nations into an effective international instrument for the struggle against aggression, for safeguarding peace and security by joint efforts, were undermined by circles in Britain and France pursuing the disastrous policy of "appeasement" of the fascist aggressors with the objective of securing their narrow class interests. Just this policy enabled Hitler to annex Austria to the Nazi Reich. The USSR denounced the Anschluss and declared its willingness to contribute to a collective effort to check the further expansion of aggression and eliminate the increased danger of another world war, to start immediate discussions with other powers at the League or elsewhere of practical steps dictated by the emergency circumstances. "It may be too late tomorrow", the Soviet statement said, "but today there is still time for action if all states, particularly the Great Powers, take a firm and unambiguous stand on the problem of collective preservation of peace."[52] Britain and France declined this proposal, while the United States simply ignored it.

A similar situation developed regarding the Nazi aggression against

Czechoslovakia. Neither the League of Nations, nor France as an ally of Czechoslovakia, moved a finger to prevent the implementation of the Nazi plans against her.

The Soviet Union alone, loyal to the obligations of alliance, offered to defend Czechoslovakia. The USSR officially informed the Czechoslovak government of its willingness to give her military aid in the event of German invasion if Czechoslovakia offered resistance and requested such help. Moreover, the Soviet Union moved up to its western border thirty infantry divisions and concentrated about 550 bombers and fighters within the Kiev and Byelorussian military districts alone.

The governments of Britain and France, however, resolved to sacrifice Czechoslovakia, using her as a pawn in the great imperialist game of making a deal with Hitler. That was the motive for calling the Munich Conference where Nazi Germany was offered a part of Czechoslovak territory as a price for her obligation to attack the USSR. In the opinion of the eminent British bourgeois historian J.W. Wheeler-Bennett, "the object of the Munich Agreement had been to eliminate Czechoslovakia as an independent military, political and economic factor and to prepare for further German expansion toward Poland and Russia".[53] The Munich agreement was supplemented with an Anglo-German and a Franco-German declaration, which were, in effect, non-aggression pacts. The Anglo-German declaration, for example, stated the desire of the two nations never again to go to war with each other. The Franco-German declaration contained an obligation of the governments to keep in touch and consult with one another in the event of a threat of complications in international relations.

The Munich policy of the Western powers pursued under the smokescreen of "non-intervention" was laid bare in the Political Report of the Central Committee to the 18th Congress of the Soviet Communist Party, in which it was described as connivance at aggression and at unleashing of war. "The policy of non-intervention reveals a desire not to hinder the aggressors from perpetrating their evil deeds, not to hinder, say, Japan from making war on China, or even better on the Soviet Union, to allow all belligerents... to drain and exhaust one another and then, when they are sufficiently weakened, to come on the scene with fresh forces, 'in the interests of peace', of course, and to dictate their own terms to the war-weary belligerents.''[54]

The USSR warned that this hazardous political gamble might end in disaster for the gamblers themselves.

On 15 March 1939 German forces conquered the whole of Czechoslovakia. The Czech lands were incorporated in the Nazi Reich under the name of "Protectorate of Bohemia and Moravia". Slovakia was separated from the Czech lands and made a puppet republic. And again the USSR alone angrily protested against this new act of fascist violence on the international scene. In a note of 18 March 1938, the Soviet Union declared that it "could not recognize the incorporation in the German Empire of the Czech lands in whatever form, as well as of Slovakia, as legitimate and consistent with the universally accepted standards of international law and justice or the principles of self-determination of nations."[55]

The Soviet Union's last attempt in the pre-war period to organize political co-operation with the Western bourgeois democracies with the object of preventing a war from being unleashed by the fascist powers was the Anglo–French–Soviet talks in Moscow in the spring and summer of 1939. There existed an objective reason for the conclusion of a military–political alliance between the USSR, Britain, and France: the common menace to these states from Nazi Germany. The stand taken by the Western powers, however, did not allow the objective necessity of such a common front to materialize in a military convention. A wide difference emerged in their approach to these talks: while the USSR sincerely wished a mutual assistance agreement, Britain and France were conducting negotiations just for show to bring pressure to bear upon Germany and force her into an agreement on an anti-Soviet basis. British documents of that period made public today evidence that during the Moscow talks the British Government was negotiating with Hitler through official and unofficial channels a broad Anglo–German agreement. That was what predetermined the disruption of the Anglo–French–Soviet talks in 1939.

As evidenced by the above-mentioned British documents, the Soviet Government emphasized that its interest in an alliance with Britain and France was not greater than the interest of these powers in an alliance with the USSR. It is stated there that though Russia "could in the long run win any war of defence single-handed, she could not prevent war in general. She was therefore ready to collaborate with other powers for this purpose".[56]

The Moscow talks with Britain and France revealed the complete unwillingness of the Western powers to co-operate with the USSR in organising resistance to the fascist aggressors.

In the Far East these powers were encouraging Japan to make war on the Soviet Union. In 1938 and 1939 Japanese forces battled against Soviet troops at Lake Khassan and at the river Khalkhin-Gol. Faced with the prospect of a war on two fronts — in the West against Nazi Germany and in the East against samurai Japan — the Soviet Government took the only correct decision under the circumstances. It accepted the German proposal for a non-aggression pact, and signed it on 23 August 1939.

The Soviet Union, however, was willing, as before, to continue negotiations for a mutual assistance pact with Britain and France. The USSR believed, an American document says, that a non-aggression pact with Germany was not inconsistent with a mutual defensive alliance between Great Britain, France, and the Soviet Union.[57] Indeed, the Anglo-German and the Franco-German declarations, equivalent to non-aggression pacts, were not an obstacle to the Moscow talks of 1939.

The eminent British bourgeois historian A.J.P. Taylor admits that the USSR sought to have guaranteed security in Europe. He writes that Soviet leaders did not trust Hitler and considered an alliance with the Western powers a safer arrangement. The Soviet Government, he says, turned towards Germany only when it had become convinced that it was impossible to conclude that alliance.[58]

The conclusion of the Nazi-Soviet pact in the extremely complicated situation prevailing in the summer of 1939 was an example of skilful exploitation of capitalist contradictions. It demonstrated the Soviet Union's flexibility in pursuing its high-principled foreign-policy line in an effort to prevent or at least delay the outbreak of war. The Party and the Soviet Government followed Lenin's instructions to the effect that the foreign policy of a socialist state· should be as flexible as

possible. Lenin wrote in this context: "...we have also learned
...flexibility, the ability to effect swift and sudden changes in tactics
if changes in objective conditions demand them, and to choose
another path for the achievement of our goal if the former path proves
to be inexpedient or impossible at the given moment."[59]

Though the pact did not free the USSR from the menace of fascist
aggression, it afforded the country time to strengthen national defence
and prevent the formation of a common anti-Soviet front.

By avoiding a war on two fronts simultaneously — against
Germany and Japan — the Central Committee of the Soviet
Communist Party and the Soviet Government fulfilled their duty not
only to the Soviet people, they also acted as internationalists to the
world proletariat, strengthening the security of the main bastion of
world socialism — the Soviet Union. The wisdom of that foreign-
policy act has been borne out by history.

Although the Western powers succeeded in thwarting the plans to
set up a collective security system involving the USSR, developments
in 1939 by no means followed the course charted by the Munichites.
The Second World War broke out within the capitalist world. The
fascist aggressors had come to the conclusion that it would be easier to
win a war against the Western powers than a war against the Soviet
Union.

*   *   *

Summing up the results of the Soviet Union's struggle in the inter-
war period for peace and the security of nations, for a system of
international relations based on the principles of peaceful co-existence
of states having different social systems, it should be emphasized that
it was closely bound up with the struggle for social progress. The
Soviet Union supported everywhere the revolutionary and democratic
forces, which were its natural allies in the struggle for peace and
international co-operation on a basis of equality.

For all its modest achievements in the efforts to set up a new system
of world relations, the Soviet State succeeded in the 'twenties in
securing its diplomatic recognition by the main countries of the
capitalist world except the United States. In the 'thirties the USSR
attempted to organize political co-operation with the Western powers,

dictated by its common interest with them in stemming the aggression of the fascist states. The formula of such international political co-operation was collective security, which the Soviet Union persistently advocated in the pre-war years. The Munichites opposed the Soviet strategy of "collective preservation of peace" with their disgraceful policy of "appeasement" of the aggressor, which essentially consisted in efforts to resolve, at the expense of the USSR, the imperialist contradictions exacerbated by the Great Depression of 1929-33.

The periods of political co-operation between the USSR and the Western bourgeois democracies with the object of safeguarding peace (the treaties with France and Czechoslovakia, the Soviet Union's contribution to the activities of the League of Nations, the Anglo– French– Soviet talks of 1939, etc.) indicated that the principles of peaceful co-existence provided the basis required for such co-operation. By their double-faced policy, however, the Western powers reduced this co-operation to naught. The whole point is that in the inter-war period the policy of the Western powers was aimed, as before, at liquidating the Soviet State.

With the alignment of world forces unfavourable to socialism at that time, the capitalist countries proved unreceptive to the idea of democratization of international relations, relying, as before, on the supremacy of military force, the main instrument of imperialist policy. Nevertheless, the Soviet Union's indefatigable efforts to affirm the principles of peaceful co-existence contributed to definite progress made towards democratization in the sphere of world politics.

4

Working Out a Democratic Peace Programme During the Great Patriotic War

The Prerequisites for Setting up the Anti-Hitler Coalition

DURING the Second World War, the Soviet Union continued consistently to abide by the Leninist principles of Soviet foreign policy. Wartime conditions naturally left their impress on the ways and means of implementing that policy, but its essence never changed: it was a struggle for peace, security, and social progress.

The specific character of Soviet foreign policy in the years of the Great Patriotic War was as follows: the Soviet State, while waging a bitter armed struggle against the fascist states which had attacked it, went on developing relations on the principles of peaceful co-existence with most of the capitalist states. Moreover, within the framework of the anti-Hitler coalition relations between countries of opposite social systems developed much more successfully than in the pre-war period. The USSR, the USA, and Britain were engaged in broad military, political, economic and other co-operation, which as regards its scope and content surpassed whatever positive results had been achieved earlier in the field of relations between the countries of the capitalist and socialist systems. Quantitatively and qualitatively, that was a new stage in the development of international relations, in the practice of peaceful co-existence.

That new stage — one of anti-fascist co-operation between states with different social systems — was dictated by their common vital interests. It became possible because the governments of Britain and the United States, aware of the formidable menace threatening them, had been obliged to agree to co-operation with the USSR in the war against Germany and Japan. As for the Soviet Union, it was proposing to the Western powers even before the war that they join it in action against the aggressors and now was persistently urging all anti-fascist forces to unite.

For the Soviet Communist Party and the Soviet State military and political co-operation with one group of capitalist states for the purpose of defence against another was a problem to which Lenin had given a clear answer in his time. He believed that a socialist state should not . . . reject military agreements with one lot of imperialists against the other in cases where such an agreement, without undermining the basis of Soviet power, could paralyse the attacks of any imperialist state.[1] That was the instruction of Lenin's which the Soviet Union was observing when it entered into coalition with the United States and Britain.

The predatory, inhuman policy of the German Nazis and their allies, who had frankly declared their intention to establish the world supremacy of the German "master race", was a factor which helped bind together the states and peoples whom Hitler's aggression was directed against. The conception of the Nazi "New Order" in its international aspect, i.e. a world order ensuring the complete and unchallenged domination of the world by German imperialism, envisaged the destruction of the very national existence of a number of countries, including those whose leaders had hoped to come to terms with Hitler. The enslaved peoples were to be deprived of elementary democratic rights and the occupied states, of their independence and sovereignty.

Thus, Hitler's plan of forcibly restructuring the world order rejected out of hand, without concern for formality, the bourgeois-democratic principles of international relations to which the United States, Britain, France, and other powers professed, ostensibly at any rate, their allegiance. As is justly pointed out by the West German historian Jakobsen, "the National–Socialist foreign policy, in which ideology and violence were inseparably interconnected", was aimed not only at territorial conquest, which had been the objective of other imperialist powers in earlier centuries, but at the eventual complete annihilation of their opponents, at the total spiritual enslavement of the peoples and at the creation of a new European continent "organized" on racist principles with qualitatively new ideals.[2]

The Nazi leaders considered the Soviet Union the chief obstacle in the way of establishing the "New Order". As far back as 1932 Hitler said: "It would be naïve to presume that we shall rise to supremacy in a direct way. We will change fronts and not only at war. Above everything else, however, we must hold to the notion that Bolshevism is our mortal enemy" (Translated from the Russian). "In the eyes of Hitler and many veteran National-Socialists", writes Hitler's General Butlar, "Soviet Russia remained as before the ideological enemy No. 1. The 'Russian sphinx', with its forces so hard to size up and with its ideology so dangerous, had an oppressive effect on Hitler and stood in his way." (Translated from the Russian.)[3]

Thus, the Soviet Union was the enemy No. 1 of Nazi Germany. However, Hitler's "indirect" way towards world supremacy lay, in his view, primarily through destruction of his opponents and rivals in the West. Hitler declared on 23 May 1939: "England is ...our enemy and the conflict with England will be a life and death struggle." The Munich policy of the British and French Governments had finally fortified his determination to start the war by attacking the Western powers and their allies. On 1 September 1939 Nazi Germany invaded Poland, which was followed by the entry into the war of the latter's "guarantors" — Britain and France. The Second World War had begun.

Their early successes in the war convinced the Nazis of their ability to redraw the map of the world and radically remodel international relations by establishing a New Order in the world. Another reason for the Nazis' grandiose ambitions was the attitude of the ruling circles of the Western powers, which after declaring war on Germany in practical terms did nothing to rescue their Polish ally. On the Western Front no effective hostilities were opened against Germany. The British and French Governments were conducting what came to be known as the "phoney war", hoping that they would somehow make it up with Hitler and encourage him to strike eastward, at the Soviet Union.

After conquering Poland, Nazi Germany in the spring of 1940 invaded Denmark and Norway. On 10 May 1940 Hitler put an end to the "phoney war" by launching a large-scale offensive against France, striking across the Low Countries and circumventing the heavily fortified French "Maginot Line". On 22 June 1940 the French Government headed by Marshal Pétain disgracefully capitulated to the advancing Nazi forces. Shortly before that, fascist Italy had joined in the war against France.

The débâcle suffered by the Anglo-French forces led not only to the establishment of Nazi supremacy over Western Europe but also changed the entire strategic situation in the world in favour of the Axis powers. To consolidate their victory and to formalize, as it were, the new system of international relations of the fascist type, Germany, Italy, and Japan concluded the Tripartite Pact on 27 September 1940. In it they declared a redivision of the world among themselves into their respective spheres of influence and undertook to "mutually assist and co-operate in their actions in Greater East Asia and in regions of Europe". Among its terms, Japan recognized the leadership of Germany and Italy in the establishment of a New Order in Europe, and Germany and Italy reciprocated with respect to Japan in "Greater East Asia". The Pact was soon joined by Hungary and Romania.

The Tripartite Pact was directed against all nations committed to peace, primarily against the USSR, although its anti-Soviet orientation was camouflaged with a special clause. Ribbentrop described the Pact as a double-edged weapon — "against Russia and against America".

*   *   *

While the "phoney war" was going on in the West and the Nazi Reich was seizing one country after another, gearing their economic and manpower resources to the service of its military machine, the Soviet Union was taking urgent steps to strengthen the security of its borders and to check the aggression of Nazi Germany wherever possible.

When the Polish Army had disintegrated under the blows of Nazi forces, the Red Army on 17 September 1939 entered Western

Byelorussia and the Western Ukraine, which became reunited with the Byelorussian and Ukrainian Soviet Socialist Republics.

The conquest of Poland by German troops, which had shown that the small countries neighbouring on the USSR were not in a position to check the spread of Nazi aggression on their own, led the Soviet Government to consider offering Estonia, Latvia, and Lithuania mutual assistance treaties. These were signed in the autumn of 1939 in complete accord with the vital interests of the Baltic nations, guarding them against the danger of Nazi aggression. The Soviet–Lithuanian treaty provided for joint defence of the Lithuanian frontier. In August 1940, at the request of their democratically elected parliaments Estonia, Latvia and Lithuania rejoined the USSR as equal Soviet Republics, as they had been in 1918-19 before Soviet government there was liquidated by the combined forces of the Entente powers, German troops and the Russian White Guards.

As far back as the spring of 1938 the Soviet Government acting through unofficial channels had offered the Government of Finland to conclude a mutual assistance pact. In March 1939 the Soviet Government made an attempt to guarantee the security of Leningrad by requesting Finland to lease certain islands in the Gulf of Finland to the Soviet Union. After the fall of Poland to the Nazis, the Soviet Government at negotiations in Moscow reiterated its proposal to Finland for a mutual assistance treaty. When the latter had declined this proposal the USSR requested a lease for 30 years of the port of Hango, a few islands in the Gulf of Finland and a part of the Karelian Isthmus with a total area of 2761 km^2 to guarantee a minimum of security for Leningrad in exchange for twice as large an area of Soviet territory. Having declined these, as U.K. Paasikivi said, "restrained and moderate" proposals, which "should have been accepted", the Finnish Government broke off the negotiations and provoked a series of border incidents which led to the outbreak of a war between Finland and the USSR on 30 November 1939.

The ruling circles of the Western powers, A.J.P. Taylor writes, took advantage of that "so that the war against Germany could be forgotten or even ended.[4] For this purpose a 150,000-strong Anglo–French expeditionary force was formed to be sent to Finland, and the "Southern Plan" was drawn up to bomb the Baku oil fields.

The signing on 12 March 1940 of a peace treaty between Finland and the USSR following the defeat of the main forces of the Finnish Army on the Karelian Isthmus frustrated the plans of an anti-Soviet crusade.

Although it was in a position to occupy the whole of Finland, the Soviet Union in negotiating the peace treaty confined itself to minimum demands required to guarantee the security of its borders in this area.

On 26 June 1940 the Soviet Government made a representation to 'the Romanian Government concerning the immediate return to the Soviet Union of Bessarabia which had been forcibly annexed in 1918 by the Romanian bourgeois-feudal government with the support of the Entente. Now that the rulers of Romania had decided to cast their country's lot with the fascist aggressors' bloc, a settlement of the long-drawn-out conflict could no longer be postponed.[5] "The Soviet Union", the Soviet note said,

> has never reconciled itself to the fact of the forcible annexation of Bessarabia, as the Soviet Government has repeatedly and openly declared to the whole world. Now that the military weakness of the USSR has become a thing of the past, and the prevailing international situation requires a speedy resolution of the outstanding problems inherited, the Soviet Union, animated by the wish to found at last a durable peace between the two nations, deems it necessary and timely in the interest of justice to take immediate steps jointly with Romania to settle the problem of restoring Bessarabia to the Soviet Union.
>
> The Soviet Government believes that the question of returning Bessarabia is organically linked with that of ceding to the Soviet Union that part of Bucovina whose population, in its vast majority, is connected with the Soviet Ukraine by a common language and ethnic composition

(the valid reasons for this request were also emphasized by the fact that as far back as November 1918 the People's Assembly of Bucovina in conformity with the clearly-expressed will of its population had voted for a reunion with the Soviet Ukraine. — N.L.)[6]

The Romanian Government was obliged to comply with the legitimate request of the USSR. The peaceful settlement of the Bessarabian dispute resulted in Bessarabia's reunification with Soviet Moldavia, which was proclaimed a Union Republic on 2 August 1940.

All these steps helped strengthen the military-strategic position of the USSR, having pushed its boundaries fairly far westward, which later played a helpful role in the early period of the Great Patriotic War.

Opposing the spread of Nazi aggression, the Soviet Government in the latter half of 1940 and early in 1941 repeatedly stated to the German Government that its expansion towards Romania, Bulgaria, and other countries threatened the security of the USSR. At the Soviet-German talks held in Berlin on 12-13 November 1940, it demanded the withdrawal of German forces from Finland and the cessation of German expansion in the Balkans and in the Middle East. The West German historian Holdak writes in connection with the Berlin talks that "Moscow had no intention to commit itself against the Western powers or connive at Germany's claims in Eastern Europe".[7]

The Soviet Government rejected Hitler's proposal for joining in recarving the world planned in the Tripartite Pact, for a "territorial expansion. . . south of the national territory of the Soviet Union in the direction of the Indian Ocean". In a message to the Soviet Ambassador in London about the results of the Berlin talks, the USSR Commissar for Foreign Affairs wrote:

> As became clear from the discussions, the Germans intend to lay their hands on Turkey on the pretext of guaranteeing her security Romanian style and to grease our palm with the promise of a Montreux Convention revised in our favour, offering their aid in this matter. We did not consent to this because we believe, first, that Turkey should remain independent and, secondly, that the regime in the Straits can be improved through our negotiations with Turkey rather than behind her back. The Germans and the Japanese would evidently much like to push us in the direction of the Persian Gulf and India. We declined a discussion of this question because we consider such counsel on the part of Germany inappropriate.[8]

To bar the way to Nazi aggression in the Balkans the Soviet Union offered some countries mutual assistance treaties, but this initiative was opposed by their ruling circles. In January 1941 the Soviet Union again declared to Germany that it considered the territory of Bulgaria and the Straits as a zone vital to Soviet security and could not look indifferently on developments in this area. On 5 April 1941 the Soviet Government concluded a treaty of friendship and neutrality with Yugoslavia, which was rightly interpreted as support for the Yugoslav people who fell victim to Nazi aggression on the next day.

The Soviet Union also continued to assist the Chinese people in their war against the Japanese invaders. In 1940 it extended two loans amounting to a total of 200 million dollars and in 1941 supplied 200 bombers and fighter planes to China. Soviet volunteer pilots were fighting on the Chinese side against Japan.

The Western powers took a different stance on Japan's aggression against China, still hoping to provoke Japan to go to war against the USSR. While the Japanese war machine was continually supplied with oil, iron, non-ferrous metals, machinery, etc., the journal *Amerasia* wrote in 1941, China's defenders were denied truly effective aid from the United States and Britain. The journal said that 10 years of American and British tolerance allowed Japan to pursue her openly declared campaign for subordination of Greater East Asia.[9]

The Soviet Union's consistent implementation in that difficult period of a policy of opposition to fascist aggression, of support for the peoples fighting for their freedom and independence, won it the respect of all peace-loving nations, who saw in it the main obstacle in the way of fascist aggression. When Nazi Germany treacherously attacked the USSR, the nations of the world took sides with the Soviet people.

The Programme of a Post-war Democratic Peace

In the early days of the Great Patriotic War the Soviet Union put forward a programme of mobilizing and uniting all anti-fascist forces to a struggle against the aggressors. In his message to the Soviet people of 3 July 1941, Joseph Stalin declared:

> This war with Fascist Germany cannot be considered an ordinary war. It is not only a war between two armies, it is also a great war of the entire Soviet people against the German Fascist forces. The aim of this national war in defence of our country against the Fascist oppressors is not only elimination of the danger hanging over our country but also aid to all peoples groaning under the yoke of German Fascism. In this great war we shall have loyal allies in the peoples of Europe and America, including the German people who are enslaved by Hitlerite despots. Our war for the freedom of our country will merge with the struggle of the peoples of Europe and America for their independence, for democratic liberties. It will be a united front of peoples standing for freedom and against enslavement and threats of enslavement by Hitler's Fascist armies.[10]

The stage for the formation of the anti-Hitler coalition was set by the conclusion in Moscow on 12 July 1941 of the agreement between the governments of the USSR and Great Britain on joint actions in the war against Germany, whereby the parties undertook to render mutual assistance in war as well as to renounce a separate peace with the enemy. Before the end of the month agreements were signed with the Czechoslovak and Polish governments-in-exile in London. In addition to the obligations in the Soviet– British Agreement, they contained articles whereby the Soviet Union allowed the formation in its territory of Czechoslovak and Polish national military units to fight against Germany.

The Soviet Union's agreements with Czechoslovakia and Poland gave legal form to the military alliance of their peoples and demonstrated their determination to bring the war against the fascist invaders to final victory, to restore the independence, sovereignty, and territorial integrity of states. The Soviet policy towards the small states conquered by the Nazi aggressors had been set out in a message to the Soviet Ambassador in London in the early days of the war. It said in particular:

> On the question of restoring the national states of Poland, Czechoslovakia, and Yugoslavia, you are instructed to adhere to the following position:
> A. We stand for the restoration of an independent Polish state within the national boundaries of Poland;
> B. We stand also for the restoration of the Czechoslovak and Yugoslav states on the principle that their systems of government are their internal affair.[11]

On 2 August 1941 the US government informed the Soviet Ambassador in Washington of its determination to render the Soviet Union every possible economic assistance in the struggle against armed aggression, being convinced that the stiffening of the armed resistance of the Soviet Union to the predatory attack of an aggressor threatening the security and independence not only of the Soviet Union but also of all other nations was consistent with the national security interests of the United States.[12]

The Soviet Union's entry into the Second World War and the objectives formulated by it required that the War Cabinet of Great Britain as well as the government of the United States, which, in the phrase of the American historians W.L. Langer and S.E. Gleason, was fighting "an undeclared war", come forward with their own declaration of principles.[13] This declaration of 14 August 1941, came to be known as the Atlantic Charter. It declared that the United States and Great Britain seek no aggrandizement, territorial or other; they desire to see no territorial changes that do not accord with the freely expressed wishes of the peoples concerned; they respect the right of all peoples to choose the form of government under which they will live; and they wish to see sovereign rights and self-government restored to those who have been forcibly deprived of them. After the final destruction of the Nazi tyranny, they hope to see established a peace which will afford to all nations the means of dwelling in safety within their own boundaries. All the nations of the world must come to the abandonment of the use of force. "Since no future peace can be maintained if land, sea, or air armaments continue to be employed by nations which threaten, or may threaten, aggression outside their frontiers, they believe, pending the establishment of a wider and permanent system of general security, that the disarmament of such nations is essential."

On the one hand, the Atlantic Charter showed the influence of the Soviet declaration on the war aims and the post-war settlement. From this angle the Atlantic Charter may be considered a positive factor in the history of international relations during the Second World War. Moreover, it expressed the determination of the United States and Britain to achieve the "final destruction of the Nazi tyranny".

On the other hand, the Atlantic Charter reflected the Anglo–American claim to world supremacy. The American historian Williams writes that the Atlantic Charter had been drawn up by Churchill and Roosevelt before the United States entered the war, but after the Nazi attack on Russia it was presumed that Britain and the United States would be responsible for the post-war settlement in all corners of the world.[14]

The Soviet Union determined its attitude to the Atlantic Charter at the Allied Conference in London on 24 September 1941 attended by representatives of the USSR, Czechoslovakia, Poland, Yugoslavia, Greece, Norway, the Netherlands, Belgium, Luxembourg, and "Free France".The Soviet declaration expressed agreement with the basic principles of the Atlantic Charter. However, it contained reservations to prevent that document being interpreted to the prejudice of the freedom and independence, sovereignty and territorial integrity of any state or people.

The central task was, the declaration emphasized, to achieve the speediest and most decisive defeat of the aggressors. Nothing short of complete and final victory over nazism could lay the groundwork for international co-operation and friendship in accordance with the aspirations and ideals of the freedom-loving nations.

Referring to the post-war peace settlement, the Soviet Government declared that it was "guided by the principle of self-determination of nations, upheld the right of every people to national independence and the territorial integrity of its country, the right to establish the social system and choose the form of government it considers rational and necessary for securing the economic and cultural prosperity of its country". The Soviet position was based on Lenin's well-known definition of the terms of a just and democratic peace, chief among which is a renunciation of conquest ". . . in the only correct sense that *every* nationality without any exception, both in Europe and in the colonies, shall obtain its freedom".[15]

In its declaration the Soviet Union again expressed itself in favour of collective actions against the aggressors, for disarmament, for peaceful and good-neighbourly relations with all countries, for assistance to the victims of aggression. In putting forward this programme for organizing post-war international relations, the Soviet Union placed emphasis on the principal task facing the anti-fascist coalition — "to concentrate all economic and military resources of the freedom-loving nations for the complete and earliest liberation of the peoples languishing under the yoke of the Nazi hordes".[16]

Loyal to its policy of all-out assistance to the peoples fighting against the fascist aggressors, the Soviet Union on 26 September 1941 recognized the "Free France" movement led by De Gaulle and stated its willingness to give it comprehensive assistance and support in the common war effort against Nazi Germany and her satellites. The Soviet Government expressed its strong determination to "see the independence and greatness of France completely restored" after winning common victory.[17]

The signing in Washington on 1 January 1942 of the Joint Declaration of the United Nations by representatives of the four great powers (the USSR, the USA, Britain, and China) and twenty-two other states was a milestone on the path of consolidating the alliance of nations in the war against the fascist aggressors.

They proclaimed the imperative need for complete victory over the fascist aggressors and pledged themselves to employ their full resources, military or economic, against those members of the Tripartite Pact and its adherents with which they were at war. The signatories undertook to co-operate with one another and not to make a separate armistice or peace with the enemies.

The Anglo–Soviet treaty of alliance in the war against Nazi Germany and her satellites in Europe and on post-war co-operation of 26 May 1942, as well as the Soviet–American agreement on the principles applicable to mutual assistance in the conduct of war against aggression of 11 June 1942 was of key importance in the series of agreements fortifying the anti-Hitler coalition.

In the second part of the Anglo–Soviet treaty which contained obligations concerning post-war co-operation in order to maintain peace and resist aggression, the parties undertook to take whatever measures might be necessary to prevent a recurrence of German aggression, and should it come about then to render military and other aid to each other. The treaty imposed on each party an obligation not to enter into alliances or coalitions directed against the other.

The association of the USSR and the Western powers in the anti-Hitler coalition did not and could not resolve the contradictions between them generated by the difference between their social systems. These contradictions, however, did not prevent the Soviet Union from abiding by its commitments as an ally, as was repeatedly admitted by the Western leaders, Roosevelt and Churchill in particular. The Allied military leader, Admiral William D. Leahy, said in his memoirs that "Russia had kept every military agreement made before...".[18] As the US ex-Secretary of War, Henry L. Stimson, testified, "the Russians were magnificent allies. They fought as they promised...".[19]

As for the Western powers, their policy clearly showed a different approach to their allied commitments. This was glaringly evident in their timing of the Second Front. As is known, motivated by their imperialist interests, the governments of Britain and the United States delayed the opening of a second front in Euope, relying on weakening of the USSR.

Although the governments of Britain and the United States were quite inconsistent in meeting their allied obligations, the very fact of forming the anti-Hitler coalition uniting nations of the two opposite systems was an event of crucial historic importance. The formation of this coalition helped strengthen and enlarge co-operation among the peoples of USSR, the USA, Britain, France, and China, the biggest powers fighting against the Axis. It contributed to the consolidation of all anti-fascist forces and broadened greatly the front of worldwide struggle against fascism.

The spectacular victories of the Soviet Army in the summer–autumn campaign of 1943, which turned the tide of hostilities not only for the Great Patriotic War but also for the Second World War as a whole, confronted Germany and her satellites with imminent catastrophe. The outline of a long-awaited peace began to loom more and more clearly on the political horizon. The problem of a post-war peace settlement was given increasing attention at international conferences and in the talks between the USSR, the United States, and Britain. Therefore, while going ahead with its consistent efforts to strengthen the anti-Hitler coalition, the alliance of all nations in the anti-fascist war, the Soviet Union came forward with a programme setting forth the principles of a just and democratic peace. It encompassed the following

1. the liberation of the peoples of Europe from the fascist invaders and assistance to them in the restoration of their national states;

2. granting the liberated peoples the right and freedom to choose their form of government by themselves;

3. severe punishment of the war criminals;

4. provision of the requisite conditions to prevent further aggression from Germany;

5. securing long-term economic, political and cultural co-operation between the peoples of Europe.[20]

The Soviet Union consistently upheld these democratic principles throughout the war and the post-war peace settlement, imbued as they were with concern for lasting peace and co-operation among nations, for social progress.

In the years of the Second World War the Soviet Union was confronted by the crucial task of doing away with the aftermath of fascist aggression, in particular, the carving-up of Europe's territory performed by the Axis powers on the eve of and during the war. That carving-up flagrantly violated the right of nations to self-determination, the sovereignty of national states, the basic democratic rights of European peoples.

In settling territorial questions the Soviet Union sought such borders to be established as would secure the most favourable conditions for friendly relations between neighbour states. The approach of the American and British circles was different: they tried to impose on nations such boundaries as would serve the objectives of consolidating world imperialist domination. At the end of 1941, during the visit to Moscow by the British Foreign Secretary Anthony Eden, the Western powers, under the pretext of compliance with the principles of the Atlantic Charter, indicated that they would not recognize the reunion with the USSR of Western Byelorussia, the Western Ukraine, the Baltic Republics, and certain other territories. The Soviet Government firmly opposed that move of the imperialists.

Problems of post-war frontiers loomed large on the agenda of all conferences held by the countries of the anti-Hitler coalition. The Moscow Conference of Foreign Ministers in October 1943 discussed some questions pertaining to the post-war settlement in Europe. The United States and Britain intended to establish federated associations of small and medium-sized states in Central and South-east Europe. These plans were designed to reshape the map of Europe in the interests of British and American imperialism contrary to the wish of the peoples concerned.

The Soviet Government could not consent to such projects. Soviet representatives at the Conference pointed out that liberation of the small countries and restoration of their independence and sovereignty were one of the major tasks of the post-war settlement in Europe and of establishing a lasting peace. The Soviet delegation declared that no foreign interference or external pressure could be tolerated in the process of shaping by the peoples of Europe of their post-war destinies. The Soviet delegation also stated that attempts to federate small countries on instructions from governments-in-exile failing to express the true wish of their peoples would be tantamount to imposing on them decisions running counter to their desires. Finally, the Soviet Government resolutely opposed all attempts to resurrect the anti-Soviet policy of *córdon sanitaire* which loomed behind the Western projects of federations. The Soviet viewpoint on the inadmissibility of dictation from the outside of the forms of association of small and medium-sized states in Europe completely accorded with the interests of guaranteed post-war security of the USSR and other states and with the right of the peoples of Eastern and Central Europe to shape their own destinies.

The Moscow Conference adopted the Declaration on Austria, which guaranteed the restoration of a sovereign Austrian state. The Declaration on Italy proclaimed a joint policy to be pursued by the Allies — the USSR, the USA, and Britain — with the object of complete destruction of fascism and the establishment of a democratic regime.

The Moscow Conference showed that the Soviet Union would have to fight a stiff diplomatic battle for a democratic peace settlement in Europe based on a just demarcation of frontiers between states.

The problem of post-war frontiers as a major component of a post-war settlement was also discussed at the Teheran Conference (28 November to 1 December 1943) attended by Stalin, Roosevelt and Churchill. At the Conference the Anglo-American side again raised the question of forming a federation of small states. The Soviet Union categorically opposed this plan as prejudicial to the interests of the peoples of Europe.

The question of Poland's borders was an important item on the agenda. The Soviet Government had come out for creating after the war an independent, democratic and strong Polish state. That was precisely why, as well as for the purpose of safeguarding a lasting peace in Europe, it was necessary to secure fair and historically justified borders of Poland, that would become a factor of security and durable peace in Europe. The Soviet Government proposed that Poland's eastern border be drawn along the "Curzon line", which coincided with the Polish people's ethnic boundaries, and her western border, along the "Oder line". At Teheran, the Soviet delegation, upholding the interests of the Polish people, insisted on the restoration to Poland of her historical western lands. As a result, the Teheran Conference adopted a decision to the effect that the "hearth of the Polish state and people must be situated between the so-called Curżon Line and the line of the Oder river''.[21]

The Soviet Union's consistent policy to help create favourable conditions for the resurrection of a strong and democratic Polish state was not limited to efforts to guarantee just borders for Poland. On 21 April 1945 the Soviet Government concluded a treaty of friendship, mutual assistance, and post-war co-operation with Poland. That was an event of historic significance. The treaty laid the groundwork for developing relations of a new type between the Soviet and Polish peoples and helped consolidate the positions of the Provisional Government of democratic Poland at home and abroad.

The principles of Soviet policy towards Poland applied also to other countries enslaved by fascism and liberated by the Soviet Army. As far back as 12 December 1943 the USSR signed a treaty of friendship, mutual assistance, and post-war co-operation with Czechoslovakia. The parties agreed on close co-operation after the war on the principles of mutual respect for their sovereignty and non-interference in each other's internal affairs.

Under the Soviet–Czechoslovak agreement of 8 May 1944 the territory of Czechoslovakia, as soon as it ceased to be an area of hostilities, was to come immediately under the sovereign administration of the Czechoslovak government and public agencies. The constitution, composition, and character of these agencies were under the exclusive jurisdiction of the Government of the Czechoslovak Republic.

The joint struggle against Nazi Germany was the strong basis for the development of fraternal friendship between the peoples of the USSR and Yugoslavia. On 11 April 1945 a Soviet–Yugoslav treaty of friendship, mutual assistance, and post-war co-operation was signed in Moscow. The treaty created the prerequisites for the further development of fraternal co-operation between the peoples of the USSR and Yugoslavia.

During General de Gaulle's visit to Moscow in December 1944 the Soviet Government concluded with France a treaty of alliance and mutual assistance, which fortified the military and political co-operation between the USSR and France and contributed to the consolidation of the sovereignty of the French Republic.

Soviet policy directed to restoring the sovereignty and territorial integrity of the countries invaded by the fascist aggressors combined organically with its policy of consolidating peace and security in post-war Europe and throughout the world, of setting up an international organization to maintain peace and security. As far back as 8 November 1941 the Soviet Government had suggested that the Allies reach an understanding "on the war aims and plans of a post-war peace settlement".[22] The Soviet Union was actively involved in drawing up the joint four-power declaration (by the USSR, the USA, Britain, and China) adopted at the Moscow Conference of 1943. The Declaration set the guidelines for a post-war peace settlement. The governments of the four powers declared the necessity of setting up as early as possible a universal international organization called upon to maintain peace and security and based on the principle of sovereign equality of all peace-loving states. The Declaration proclaimed that after the war the USSR, the USA, Britain, and China would not employ military force to settle disputes without mutual consultation. The governments of the four powers also declared their intention to co-operate with each other and with other member states of the United Nations to achieve a general agreement on post-war arms control.

The problems of post-war co-operation and ensuring a lasting peace was also discussed at the Teheran Conference. In their joint declaration the three powers expressed their determination to develop international relations on the principles of democracy and justice. The Declaration said in particular:

> And as to peace — we are sure that our concord will win an enduring peace. We recognize fully the supreme responsibility resting upon us and all the United Nations to make a peace which will command the good will of the overwhelming mass of the peoples of the world and banish the scourge and terror of war for many generations.... . We shall seek co-operation and active participation of all nations, large and small, whose peoples in heart and mind are dedicated, as our own peoples, to the elimination of tyranny and slavery, oppression and intolerance. (Translated from the Russian.)[23]

The programme of a just and democratic post-war peace settlement was expressed in concrete terms in the decisions of the Yalta Conference held in an atmosphere dominated by the immensely enhanced international prestige of the Soviet Union and its peace policy. The Soviet Union secured the adoption by the United States and Britain of a series of joint decisions aimed at a democratic organization of the post-war world order. The most important programme document of the conference was the Declaration on Liberated Europe. It proclaimed that the USSR, the USA, and Britain had agreed among themselves to co-ordinate their policies in the cause of aiding the peoples liberated from the rule of fascism in a democratic solution by them of the vital political and economic problems of their countries. "The establishment of order in Europe and the rebuilding of national economic life must be achieved by processes which will enable the liberated peoples to destroy the last vestiges of Nazism and fascism to create democratic institutions of their own choice." (Translated from the Russian.)[24] It was also a matter of rendering assistance in setting up provisional bodies of government widely representing the democratic sections of the people and called upon to establish as soon as possible freely elected governments in accordance with the will of the people.

Paradoxically, it was precisely these provisions of the Declaration on Liberated Europe that British and American representatives attempted to rely upon, seeking to reinstate in the East European countries their pre-war reactionary regimes which had discredited themselves by their hostility towards the USSR. Naturally, the Soviet Union resolutely opposed the imperialist attempts to export counter-revolution into the countries which had chosen the democratic path of development. In so doing the Soviet Union protected not only its own interests but also those of the countries concerned; restoration of the "cordon sanitaire" would have again jeopardized the security of the Soviet Union.

The Soviet victory in the Great Patriotic War against Nazi Germany was won at a price of 20 million lives. Three million Soviet officers and men laid down their lives for the liberation of the peoples of Europe and Asia. The Soviet casualties in fighting the Nazis neared 600,000 in Poland alone. Having played the decisive role in liberating the peoples of Europe and Asia, the Soviet Union could not allow the victory over fascism which had cost it so dearly to be usurped by its enemies.

Of crucial importance for the post-war peace settlement in the Far East was the document of the Yalta Conference containing the Soviet commitment to enter the war against Japan. Its three main clauses were as follows:

1. The *status quo* in Outer Mongolia (the Mongolian People's Republic) shall be preserved.
2. The former rights of Russia violated by the treacherous attack of Japan in 1904 shall be restored, which entails returning to the Soviet Union the southern part of Sakhalin as well as all islands adjacent to it.
3. The Kurile Islands shall be handed over to the Soviet Union.

The final declaration of the Yalta Conference reaffirmed the common determination of the Soviet Union, the United States, and Britain to maintain and strengthen in the peace to come that unity of purpose and of action that had made victory possible. The declaration stressed that "only with the continuing and growing co-operation and understanding among our three countries and among all the peace-loving nations can the highest aspiration of humanity be realized — a secure and lasting peace..."[25] For this purpose a permanent mechanism was to be set up for consultations between the three governments on vital world problems: the Conference of Soviet, American, and British Foreign Ministers to be convened periodically (once every 3 to 4 months).

By a decision of the Yalta Conference the San Francisco Conference was convened on 25 April 1945 for the establishment of the United Nations Organization. All states which had originally signed the Joint Declaration of the United Nations, as well as all countries which had acceded to it later and declared war on the Axis powers, were represented.

The deliberations of the Conference ran their course in a fairly complicated situation. Opponents of international co-operation, advocates of a "hard line" towards the USSR who were increasingly influencing US government policy, strewed obstacles in the path of successful resolution of the problems facing the Conference. Despite their obstructionist tactics, however, the Conference adopted the Charter of the United Nations serving the interests of peace and the security of all nations. The Charter emphasized the determination of the peoples of the United Nations "to save succeeding generations from the scourge of war, which twice in our lifetime has brought untold sorrow to mankind''.

The first conference of the United Nations proclaimed as the basic principles of its organization the equality and self-determination of nations, international co-operation and non-interference in the internal affairs of foreign states, settlement of international disputes by refraining from threatened or actual use of force in international affairs. The UN Charter ratified the principle of peaceful co-existence of states having different socio-economic systems.

As is admitted even by bourgeois historiographers of international relations, at the San Francisco Conference the Soviet Union made a stand against colonialism, for the rights of colonial and oppressed peoples. It was precisely on the initiative of the Soviet delegation that the clause on respect for the principle of equal rights and self-determination of peoples, human rights and fundamental freedoms for all without distinction as to race, sex, language, or religion was incorporated in Chapter 1 — "Purposes and Principles" — of the UN Charter. The Soviet Union was committed to secure such a procedure of activities for the Organization as would in truth make it serve the cause of peace and would preclude its use by any power or group of powers to their selfish ends as a tool against other states. Therefore, the Soviet Union applied every effort to have the Security Council decisions on measures to safeguard peace adopted by a unanimous vote of its five permanent members — the USSR, the USA, Britain, France, and China. This voting procedure in the Security Council ruled out dictatorialness and obliged the great powers to take agreed decisions through negotiation. This also expressed the recognition of the principle of peaceful co-existence of states having different social systems.

The San Francisco Conference laid the foundation of an international body which became a crucial element in the post-war world order. Referring to the role played by the United Nations in the modern world, Leonid Brezhnev has said: "The United Nations Organization has made a useful contribution to the implementation of the aims and principles proclaimed in its Charter. It has facilitated the resolution of a number of acute international crises."[26] The Soviet Union, which contributed decisively to the victory over the forces of fascism and reaction in the war, also made an outstanding contribution to the establishment of the United Nations Organization created as an instrument for the maintenance of peace, the security and co-operation of nations.

Another Milestone on the Path Towards a Democratic World Order

The Potsdam Conference

The selfless struggle of the peoples of the USSR and the Allied powers and of the peoples of Europe resulted in the total defeat of Nazi Germany. The problem of organizing the post-war world order assumed first priority. The Soviet Union's position at the Potsdam Conference of the heads of state and government of the USSR, the USA, and Britain held in July–August 1945 was motivated by concern for establishing a lasting and inviolable peace. In the face of opposition from Britain and the United States, the Soviet Union saw to it that the resolutions of the Potsdam Conference clearly formulate the principles of maintaining peace and security in Europe and the rest of the world. The Conference forcefully declared that the main prerequisite for European security was to prevent a revival of German militarism and nazism and that relations between states should be based on the principles of sovereignty and national independence, equality and non-interference in each other's internal affairs.

The Potsdam Conference was the final stage in the numerous and difficult negotiations between the governments of the USA, the USSR, and Britain on a wide range of problems concerning Germany's future. The decisions taken at the Potsdam Conference were of fundamental importance for the development of the entire system of international relations in the post-war period.

The course and outcome of the Potsdam Conference reaffirmed the Soviet Union's consistent stand in favour of complete eradication of the aftermath of the Nazi "New Order" and for a just and democratic peace. The Soviet Union's central aim at the Conference was also to secure favourable conditions for consolidating the sovereignty and independence of every European country, including Germany's former allies, and to make international relations in Europe truly universal and equal.

How did the ideas of a just and democratic peace, proclaimed in the Potsdam Conference decisions thanks to the strenuous diplomatic efforts of the USSR, take actual shape?

As is known, the problem of Germany's future had been discussed at all wartime Allied conferences. The Anglo–American side had repeatedly advocated a plan of partitioning Germany. The Western imperialist powers sought to weaken Germany, their economic and political rival, as much as possible. As far back as October 1944 Churchill had frankly told Stalin that Britain was determined to fill Germany's place in Europe after the war as a manufacturer of commodities for the smaller European countries.[27] Admiral Leahy, one of Truman's closest advisers, writes in his memoirs of the latter's intention to propose at Potsdam a plan of partitioning Germany into several states and of making the Rhineland, in particular, an independent state.[28]

It was precisely due to the Soviet Union's principled stand that the decisions of the Potsdam Conference clearly formulated the chief aim of the victorious powers in relation to Germany — her preservation and development as a united and democratic state committed to peace. It was stated in the communiqué of the Potsdam Conference that "German militarism and Nazism will be extirpated, and the Allies will take, in agreement together now and in the future, the other measures necessary to assure that Germany never again will threaten her neighbours or the peace of the world. It is not the intention of the Allies to destroy or enslave the German people. It is the intention of the Allies that the German people be given the opportunity to prepare for the eventual reconstruction of their life on a democratic and peaceful basis."[29]

The conference reached agreement on the political and economic principles of a co-ordinated Allied policy towards vanquished Germany. It envisaged in particular:

the complete disarmament and demilitarization of Germany, and the elimination or control of all Germany industry that could be used for military production;

the destruction of the National-Socialist Party and its affiliated and supervised organizations, dissolution of all Nazi institutions, ensuring that they are not revived in any way, and prevention of all Nazi and militarist activity or propaganda;

the abolition of Nazi laws, prohibition of discrimination on grounds of race, creed or political opinion;

the punishment of war criminals and those who have participated in planning or carrying out Nazi enterprises involving or resulting in atrocities or crimes;

the encouragement of all democratic political parties;

the decentralization of the German economy for the purpose of eliminating the present excessive concentration of economic power as exemplified in particular by cartels, syndicates, trusts, and other monopolistic arrangements.[30]

The Potsdam Conference decisions on Germany created favourable conditions for complete eradication of nazism and for her democratic development. Although at a later time the Western powers, once they had set a course for a division of Germany, reneged in fact on many of the earlier agreed positions, the Potsdam decisions retained their enormous historic significance. They expressed the determination of the peoples to prevent a revival of fascism on German soil, not to allow Germany again to become a hotbed of aggression.

The Potsdam decisions concerning Germany's eastern borders were of crucial importance for Europe's future. At Teheran agreement had been reached in principle on the question of determining historical precedent. The Potsdam Conference in a special resolution finally laid down these new frontiers. Thereby favourable conditions were created for a durable peace on the continent.

Another question of fundamental importance for developing international relations in the post-war period was a policy towards the European countries which had fought the war on the side of Germany but then had broken with her and contributed to the defeat of fascism. The Soviet policy in the countries which had formerly been Germany's satellites was based on a recognition of the sovereign rights of their peoples. At the Potsdam Conference the Soviet Union vigorously opposed the attempts of Britain and the United States to secure a "reshuffle" of the governments of the countries of Central and

Eastern Europe, where coalitions of the largest democratic parties had come to power with support from the vast majority of the population. The firm stand taken by the Soviet delegation on this issue protected these countries against imperialist intervention and safeguarded their national interests. The delegations of the United States and Britain had to withdraw their motion for a reshuffle as a preliminary condition for their diplomatic recognition of a number of East and Central European countries.

Soon after the Potsdam Conference the Soviet Government announced its decision to resume diplomatic relations with Romania, Bulgaria, and Hungary. This decision was of enormous significance for the democratic development of these countries freed from the fascist yoke. Having liberated the countries of Central and South-east Europe, the Soviet Union now gave their peoples a helping hand, assisting them to end their isolation on the international scene.

In keeping with its steadfast policy of strengthening the sovereignty of all countries in post-war Europe the Soviet Union gave a determined rebuff to the Western powers' efforts to bring up the question of "internationalization" of the Danube at the Potsdam Conference. The Soviet Union upheld the right of the Danubian states to have the river under their exclusive jurisdiction.

At Potsdam the Soviet Government demonstrated again its loyalty to its duty as an ally by reaffirming its pledge made at the Yalta Conference to enter the war against Japan. In accordance with this commitment the Soviet armed forces routed Japan's Kwantung Army. On 2 September 1945 the Japanese Government signed an unconditional surrender. The defeat of Japan delivered the peoples of Asia from Japanese oppression and put an end to the Second World War.

The Potsdam decisions were conclusive proof of the possibility of co-operation between countries with opposite social systems — both in war and peace. Their wartime alliance had helped to achieve victory in the mortal combat with fascism and was to become a guarantee of peace, security and co-operation of nations everywhere after the guns fell silent. "The Potsdam decisions embodied the will of the peace-loving nations of Europe, America, and other continents, their determination to prevent a recurrence of new war cataclysms. They were crucial political acts called upon to rally the efforts of states to winning peace after winning the war. . . . The basic principles of Potsdam are to this day the foundation of the post-war peace settlement in Europe", the Soviet Premier Alexei Kosygin said in marking the 25th anniversary of the Conference.[31]

The Potsdam Conference reflected a new alignment of forces in Europe and the world and demonstrated the steadily growing role of socialism and the Soviet Union in solving international problems in the interest of mankind.

At the same time, discussion of the problems on the Conference agenda indicated that the ruling circles of the Western powers had no intention of co-operating with the USSR in building a democratic world order. Their policy increasingly manifested anti-Soviet tendencies. That was connected with the elimination of the war menace from the now vanquished fascist powers and to the testing of the atom bomb in the United States. Referring to its significance for American foreign policy, Secretary of War Stimson discussed with President Truman "the revolutionay changes in warfare that might result from the atomic bomb and the possible effects of such a weapon on our civilization".[32] Relying on their "atomic diplomacy", the Western powers sought to infringe the Soviet interests as much as possible, to strengthen the positions of imperialism on the world arena. The deep-going social transformations which were in progress in the East European countries, the consolidation of the positions of the democratic forces in a number of West European countries, the mounting tide of the national liberation movement greatly alarmed imperialist circles, so much so that they started a "cold war", hoping to check the inexorable march of history.

The Soviet Union persistently struggled for a democratic post-war settlement. After the Potsdam Conference the central task of Soviet foreign policy was to secure the conclusion of equitable peace treaties with Germany's former wartime allies. Along with the decisions of the Yalta and Potsdam Conferences, these treaties helped to create a democratic post-war system of international relations in Europe.

The peace treaties with Italy, Romania, Bulgaria, Hungary, and Finland were drafted at three international meetings: the London session of the Council of Foreign Ministers in September-October 1945, the Moscow Conference of Soviet, American and British Ministers in December 1945, and the Paris session of the Council of Foreign Ministers in April-June 1946. At all of these and later sessions of the Council of Foreign Ministers the Soviet Union consistently advocated the implementation of the decisions made at Yalta and Potsdam. The Soviet Union took every step necessary to rule out the possibility of imperialist aggression and violence against peoples. It took a consistent and firm stand on the question of making truly democratic and equitable peace treaties with the vanquished countries to safeguard their political, economic, and national independence, their democratic development.

At the sessions of the Council of Foreign Ministers, the American and British delegations attempted to pursue the opposite line. They sought such peace treaties with Nazi Germany's former allies as would enable the United States and Britain to establish their political and economic control over these countries. As J.F. Dulles, a member of the American delegation, admitted later, the position of the United States and Britain on this issue meant the end of an epoch, the epoch of Teheran, Yalta, and Potsdam.[33]

After a hard-fought diplomatic struggle, the Soviet Union got the draft treaties with Germany's former allies worded in general consistently with the interests of their peoples.

These drafts were discussed at the Paris Peace Conference held between 29 July and 15 October 1946 in heightened international tension caused by the withdrawal of American and British ruling circles from co-operation with the USSR and their attempts to dictate to it from positions of strength. Speaking at the Conference, the chief Soviet delegate said: "This Conference is the scene of a struggle for a democratic peace settlement, which must be the goal of all democratic countries, but is not yet interpreted identically by the countries represented here. The Soviet delegation calls on the delegations of other countries to co-operate in the cause of establishing a democratic peace."[34]

The Conference concentrated on the problems of a political settlement in the defeated countries. By its persistent efforts the Soviet delegation ensured that the political provisions of the peace treaties with Nazi Germany's former allies were worded in a democratic spirit, did not infringe their sovereignty and independence, and created favourable conditions for their democratic development. The peace treaties with Italy, Romania, Bulgaria, Hungary, and Finland contained an obligation to guarantee human rights and fundamental freedoms to all citizens without discrimination on grounds of race, sex, language, or religion.

There were heated debates on territorial issues at the Paris Conference. The Greek ruling circles supported by the British and American delegations laid claim to a part of Bulgarian territory. The USSR came out in support of the territorial integrity of Bulgaria, which had broken off relations with Nazi Germany and taken a path of radical democratic reforms. "Bulgarians, don't worry. Your frontiers shall not be violated!" the Soviet delegation declared.[35] The Greek claims on Bulgaria were rejected by an overwhelming majority of votes in the Conference Political and Territorial Committee for Bulgaria. Britain's attempts at the New York session of the Council of Foreign Ministers between 4 November and 11 December 1946, where the draft peace treaties were to be finalised, to have Bulgaria's frontiers revised in favour of Greece were also effectively resisted.

At the Paris Peace Conference the US delegation also demanded a revision of the Finnish–Soviet and Bulgarian–Romanian frontiers. That calculated attempt to sow discord in Soviet–Finnish and Romanian–Bulgarian relations was duly rejected.

One of the most complicated problems of peace settlement was the issue of reparations. At the Conference the Soviet Union firmly insisted on terms of payment of reparations that would not inevitably enslave the defeated countries economically or undermine the development of their peacetime economies. The American and British governments took a different approach to the issue of reparations, seeing in them a tool for implementing their plan of economic control over Germany's former allies.

The determined Soviet stand frustrated this plan. Decisions concerning reparations had in the main an equitable character. They were formulated on democratic principles and prevented economic enslavement of Germany's wartime allies by the monopolistic bourgeoisie of the United States and Britain.

At Paris the Western powers reiterated their demands for "internationalization" and "equal opportunities" for shipping on the Danube. The Anglo-American bloc sought to restore the pre-war situation where Britain, France, Italy, and Belgium had been virtually in control of the river in accordance with the Danube Convention of 1921, while the interests of the riparian countries had in fact been ignored. Internationalization of the Danube would also allow the United States to join the non-Danubian countries which had formerly held sway over the Danube basin.

The opposition of the USSR thwarted the plans of the Western powers to establish dominance over the Danube basin. The texts of the treaties incorporated just a few general provisions for freedom of navigation on the Danube, equal harbour and navigation dues and other terms of commercial shipping. The Danube Shipping Convention was worked out at a conference of the seven riparian states in Belgrade in the summer of 1948.

The policy of economic subjugation of the defeated countries pursued by the Anglo-American bloc was epitomized by what they upheld as the "principle of equal opportunities" to be afforded to the capitalist monopolies in the countries which were Germany's former allies. The Soviet Union took a determined stand in defence of the economic independence of all defeated countries — not only the People's Democracies but Italy and Finland as well. The Soviet delegation was instructed to object resolutely to such economic claims on Italy as were incompatible with her sovereignty.[36] The Soviet delegation managed to reduce the "equal opportunities" claims of the Anglo-American bloc to a provision obliging the defeated countries to grant each of the United Nations most-favoured-nation treatment and national treatment on a basis of reciprocity in the fields of commerce, industry and shipping for a period of 18 months from the date on which the relevant peace treaty came into force.

The peace treaties with Italy, Romania, Bulgaria, Hungary, and Finland were signed on 10 February 1947. It was thanks to the active involvement in the peace settlement of the great socialist power — the Soviet Union — that for the first time in history peace treaties with countries defeated in war were not based on dictation and subjugation. The peace treaties with Nazi Germany's wartime allies in

Europe embodied the principles of a truly democratic and equitable post-war settlement. This settlement ensured the consolidation of the national sovereignty of European states' with a view to preventing another war of aggression, guaranteed the national rights, including territorial rights, of the states concerned, and contained no clauses infringing the political and economic independence of the defeated countries or humiliating the national dignity of their peoples.

The Yalta and Potsdam agreements, as well as the peace treaties of 1947, laid the groundwork for establishing a democratic and just post-war world order, for securing a peaceful life for the nations of the world. They meant a triumph of the Leninist principles of peaceful co-existence of states with different social systems, and were a milestone in the Soviet Union's campaign for reshaping international relations begun by the October Revolution.

However, just as in the inter-war period, the imperialist powers had no intention of collaborating with the Soviet Union in building a just and democratic world order. They still hoped that they would be able to "roll back" the Soviet Union and regain their supremacy in the world. The progressive forces and their vanguard the Soviet Union had still to fight long and hard for the Yalta and Potsdam decisions, the peace treaties of 1947 and the principles of peaceful co-existence to be implemented in international affairs.

5

The Two Lines in World Politics After the Second World War

THE Soviet people's victory in the Great Patriotic War, the rout of the Nazi aggressors, radically changed the face of the world and brought about essential qualitative shifts in the developmental pattern of international relations. It was not only the collapse of the plans of German, Japanese, and Italian imperialism to remake the pre-war system of world relations by wiping out the Soviet Union and establishing an unchallenged world supremacy of the Axis powers. The war also put an end to the Versailles–Washington system designed to consolidate the positions of imperialism, to secure the international isolation and the weakening of a Soviet Union surrounded with the "cordon sanitaire" of states governed by reactionary regimes.

Notwithstanding the enormous devastation and loss of life in the Great Patriotic War, the Soviet Union had defended its freedom and independence and consolidated its economic, political, and military power. Soviet international prestige and influence on the course of world development had grown immeasurably. This influence was the prime factor responsible for the cardinal democratic changes in the development of world relations in the early post-war years, for the establishment on universal democratic principles of such a vital instrument for maintaining international peace and security as the United Nations Organization, and for a just and democratic peace settlement with Nazi Germany's wartime allies and satellites.

Naturally, the complicated and many-sided process of change in the alignment of forces in the world, having been refracted in such a specific sphere as international relations, did not lead automatically to progress in reshaping these relations' on democratic lines, to advancement of the cause of peace and socialism. Imperialism did its level best to resist that. After the Second World War, however, its possibilities steadily diminished.

The most important outcome of the year was the extension of socialism beyond the boundaries of one country. The formation of the world socialist system as a result of the victorious revolutions in European and Asian countries and later in Cuba radically changed the alignment of forces of the two social systems on the international scene. Socialism became a factor which increasingly determined the course of world development. The post-war period was characterized by an unusually rapid process of historical change and multiple revolutionary landslides and cataclysms.

Whereas in the early stage of the general crisis of capitalism the world arena was dominated by imperialism, which often had a decisive impact on the nature of world development, the emergence of the world socialist system triggered radical changes in the situation. The aggressive ambitions of imperialism were now opposed by the powerful defence potential of world socialism. The complete futility of the attempted economic blockade of the socialist states became increasingly obvious.

With progress in the socialist remaking of society in the People's Democracies, their all-round co-operation with the Soviet Union on the basis of equality steadily increased. A military and political alliance of countries where the proletariat was in power was taking shape. It was formalized in a series of treaties of friendship, co-operation and mutual assistance concluded by the Soviet Union with other socialist states in the 'forties and early 'fifties. From the very outset such co-operation extended beyond the framework of military–political alliance into other fields. This was graphically illustrated by the founding of the Council for Mutual Economic Assistance (COMECON) in 1949.

Another important factor in the continued process of reshaping the system of international relations on democratic principles in the post-war period was an upsurge of the national liberation movement.

Under its pressure imperialism was forced to grant political independence to Syria, the Lebanon, India, Burma, Ceylon, Jordan, and certain other countries. The peoples of Vietnam and Indonesia were waging an armed struggle for their national freedom. The crisis of the colonial empires went over into disintegration. The newly independent states became more and more actively involved in international affairs, which helped convert a traditionally Eurocentric system of international relations into a truly global system. The common interests of the socialist and the newly independent states made them natural allies in the cause of democratization of international political and economic relations.

These great changes within the capitalist camp undermined its power and influence on international affairs. Both imperialist blocs (German–Italian–Japanese and Anglo–French) which started the Second World War had sustained irreparable losses.

The fascist states — Germany, Italy, and Japan — were defeated and surrendered, losing all their conquests and colonial possessions. They ceased for a long time to be active participants in the struggle on the world arena and lost their status as great powers.

France, though she ended the war in the camp of the victorious powers, also lost her former influence in the world. Her economy was undermined. The French colonial empire was in the throes of a deep-going crisis and beginning to break up. The position of Great Britain was increasingly aggravated by the incipient disintegration of her colonial empire. She had to request assistance from the USA and to abandon more and more often her independent role in world politics, turning into a "junior partner" of the United States. The part played by Britain in international affairs markedly diminished as compared with that in the pre-war period. Belgium and the Netherlands found themselves in a similar situation after the war.

The West European countries were swept by a powerful tide of revolution. The prestige and influence of the international Communist movement had grown tremendously. In the 'forties Communists took up cabinet posts in a number of capitalist countries. The general democratic movement took on unprecedented scope in these countries. One of its major component parts was the peace movement, which kept in check the instigators of another war.

Only one imperialist power — the United States of America — far from being weakened by the war, had emerged from it with a still greater potential. The American war casualties were small. As for American business, it had mushroomed. American economic power reached an all-time high, far beyond that any other imperialist country was able to attain. Not only separately but even combined these others were now unable to oppose their omnipotent American "partner". Moreover, in the early post-war years the United States possessed atomic-bomb monopoly. This resulted in an unprecedented situation where one imperialist power had unchallenged supremacy over the whole capitalist world.

For all the intensity of contradictions among the imperialists, the West European countries yielded to American coercion. They were pushed in this direction by their fear of revolution, and of their own peoples — fears that led them to direct betrayal of national interests.

Having achieved hegemony in the capitalist world, the United States put forward a programme for reshaping the world order with a view to establishing its world supremacy — a Pax Americana. The chief obstacle in the way of American imperialism was the Soviet Union and the socialist camp as a whole. Hence the extremely acute confrontation between the socialist and capitalist worlds which, in the history of international relations, has come to be known as the Cold War. It was generated by the refusal of American imperialism to accept the political and social realities of the post-war world, by its underestimation of the power and potentialities of socialism, and by its irresistible ambitions for world supremacy.

Thus, the post-war period saw a collision between two lines in international politics, two programmes of reshaping the system of international relations: the Soviet programme of their democratization on the principle of peaceful co-existence and the imperialist programme of revising the results of the Second World War, destroying the socialist system, and establishing the world dominion of US imperialism. The contest between these two lines governed the development of the entire system of world relations in the post-war decades.

America's Post-war World and Foreign-policy Strategy

While the Soviet Union was seeking to implement in the new conditions Lenin's idea of a just and democratic peace on the basis of co-operation between states of the anti-Hitler alliance, the great powers first and foremost, the United States opposed this policy with its own conception of a post-war world order designed to consolidate the positions of capitalism on a world-wide scale, to destroy the socialist states and to suppress the struggle of the peoples for their national and social liberation.

This imperialist line in international politics was expressed in a series of foreign-policy doctrines evolved by ideologists and politicians of American imperialism.

In the post-war period American foreign-policy doctrines evolved under the direct impact of the alignment of forces on the international scene that was steadily changing in favour of socialism. These doctrines are thus milestones in the development of both the foreign-policy thinking of America's ruling circles and their practical policies in post-war international relations.

Intoxicated with the power of the United States, its leaders in the years of the Cold War were cynically outspoken in formulating the tasks of establishing the world supremacy of American imperialism. As far back as 19 December 1945, President Truman in a message to Congress set out attainment of world leadership as the key aim of American foreign policy. The victory we have won, he said, has imposed on the American people the burden of permanent responsibility for leadership of the whole world.[1] The temporary US monopoly of the atomic weapon had a specific role to play in shaping this policy. The terrifying destructive power of the atomic bomb, as General Maxwell D. Taylor, formerly chairman of the Joint Chiefs of Staff of the US armed forces, has admitted, generated the opinion that the United States was in a position to police the world and impose on it a kind of Pax Americana.[2] The adventuristic policy proclaimed by the United States logically required that all those opposed to "American world leadership" should be tamed by force. As a country with an opposite social system and as the only real "power centre" beyond the sphere of influence of the United States, the Soviet Union evoked bitter hatred from American imperialists.

The first move in implementing the American foreign-policy line of reshaping the world order after the American model was the notorious Truman doctrine, which in effect declared war on all "non-American" socio-economic and political systems. The US ruling circles openly declared their intention to interfere in the internal affairs of other countries and peoples everywhere in the world so as to impose on them social orders and regimes suited to the United States and threatened any means, even war, to achieve their ends. The Truman doctrine embodied the anti-Communist postulates of American foreign policy and its expansionist claims to world supremacy. The much-vaunted Marshall Plan was the economic extension of the doctrine, which detailed and developed it. The objective of the plan was to stabilize the capitalist economy, to subordinate Western Europe to American monopolies and to attempt to enslave the European People's Democracies economically.

The doctrine of "containment" expounded in the journal *Foreign Affairs* in July 1947 was an attempt to camouflage the annexationist objectives of American imperialism with ideological propaganda in support of the Cold War policy. Its author, who concealed himself under the pseudonym "X" was the leading American ideologist and diplomat George Kennan, chief of the policy-planning staff at the US State Department.

The doctrine of containment was based on the postulate of "aggressive" Soviet foreign policy allegedly inspiring and using world revolution for its ulterior motives. From that false premise the necessity was derived of firm and vigilant containment of the Russian expansionist tendencies by means of skilful and determined use of counter-force.[3] In this way all aggressive moves of American imperialism were depicted as defensive and alleged to have been dictated by Soviet aggression.

The doctrine of containment called for a "policy from positions of strength" to be pursued against the socialist countries and for preparing war against them as the main obstacle to American world supremacy. At the same time, the United States employed this doctrine to perpetuate its positions of dominance in the capitalist world.

Although the doctrine of containment was unrealistic and reflected an organic defect of the bourgeois conceptions of international relations in modern times — underestimation of the power and potentialities of the socialist system — it was made the basis of American foreign policy in the early post-war years.

Following this doctrine American imperialism provoked a series of acute international conflicts aimed directly against the USSR and other socialist countries, resorted to open aggression and created the threat of another world war. One of the first acts of this kind was the Berlin crisis of 1948 provoked by the Western powers. It was followed by the division of Germany and the formation of a separate West German state, and the setting up of the aggressive North Atlantic Pact (NATO). Another, even more dangerous crisis was caused by the war of aggression against the Korean Democratic People's Republic in 1950. It was used to heighten anti-Communist psychosis in the West, to intensify militarization of the capitalist countries, to re-arm the FRG, to conclude the US–Japanese "mutual security" treaty, to consolidate the sway of American imperialism over Taiwan and South Korea, to find a pretext for broad American intervention in the affairs of Indochina, etc.

By establishing NATO the US ruling circles assumed a mission of "defence of Western civilisation", of guidance of the world. The Chairman of the US Senate Foreign Relations Committee, A.H. Vandenberg, said in a speech in 1949: "Now we are unavoidably the leader and the reliance of freedom throughout this free world. We cannot escape from our prestige nor from its hazard."[4] America's General Gunther, NATO Commander-in-Chief, declared later that whether Americans liked it or not, the mantle of world leadership lay on their shoulders. The success of this alliance [NATO] would mainly depend on how far they would prove capable of this leadership.

Thus, after renouncing the wartime alliance with the USSR, American ruling circles went over to "stiff confrontation" with the Soviet Union, to "containment" of socialism, to encirclement of the socialist countries with a chain of imperialist military bases and blocs. They started the Cold War based on the ideology of frantic anti-communism, through which prism any changes in the world unwelcome to the United States were interpreted as "masterminded by Moscow" and requiring immediate "counteraction by force". In view of that, the doctrine of a policy "from positions of strength" was sanctioned as the basis for American official foreign policy and the most effective means of implementing it.

The prime prerequisite for pursuing a policy "from positions of strength" was American monopoly of the atomic weapon. In the opinion of Washington it conferred enormous political and military advantages, guaranteed success in foreign policy, ensured the might of America and afforded an opportunity to remake the world to suit American interests.

However, the balance of power in the world arena quickly underwent substantive changes after the war brought about by the end to American atomic monopoly, by the steady consolidation of the economic and defence potential of the socialist countries. The moral and political unity of their peoples grew stronger. The untenability and ineffectiveness of the doctrine of containment became obvious. It was subjected to severe criticism and discarded as a principle of American foreign policy.

In place of the bankrupt doctrine of containment, American foreign-policy strategists employed new aggressive notions of "liberation", "rolling back communism", "massive retaliation", which were characterized by the same old defect — unwillingness to reckon with the realities of the post-war world, where the positions of socialism were steadily growing stronger. The new foreign-policy doctrines differed from the doctrine of containment not in their objective, which remained unchanged, but in methods of its achievement.

"Liberation", and "rolling back communism", meant liquidation in the socialist countries of a social system freely chosen by the people and restoration of the rule of the exploiter classes. Guided by the utterly fallacious idea of the "internal weakness" of the USSR and other socialist countries, the imperialists attempted to step up interference in their internal affairs, to undertake "localized" military actions against individual socialist countries, to stiffen the struggle against Communist ideas and parties throughout the world.

The doctrine of "massive retaliation", as that of "liberation", was based on the assumption of overwhelming military superiority of the United States, which was allegedly capable of dealing an annihilatory nuclear strike while remaining invulnerable to a retaliatory blow. The authors of the doctrine ignored the fact that the situation in the nuclear field was rapidly changing and by no means in favour of the United States. For instance, in 1953 the Soviet Union, having outstripped the United States, tested the first thermonuclear device. In 1957 the Soviet Union launched an intercontinental ballistic missile, which put an end to the legend of "invulnerability" of the United States.

The new military-strategic situation in the world reflected changes in the alignment of forces on the international scene in favour of socialism. It compelled the American ruling quarters to revise their foreign policy doctrine again. A definite part of the American scientific and political community gradually developed an awareness of the unrealistic character and danger of the continued policy towards American world supremacy and destruction of socialism by military force. The need for an American foreign policy conforming to the changed international situation became perfectly obvious.

The process of adaptation of American ruling circles to the actual situation in the world proved to be fairly long and contradictory. Realistic trends in American foreign policy had begun to show as far back as the mid-fifties in the "Geneva spirit", in the participation of a US delegation in the conference of heads of government of the four great powers in 1955. Meanwhile the momentum of the Cold War continued, which resulted in the cobbling together of the aggressive military blocs SEATO and CENTO, in support for the counter-revolution in Hungary and in provoking the Suez crisis of 1956. The doctrine of "liberation" still decisively influenced American foreign policy-making.

By orbiting the world's first artificial earth satellite, the Soviet Union not only shattered the postulates of American foreign-policy doctrines — US military-strategic superiority and the invulnerability of the American continent to a retaliatory nuclear missile strike — but also challenged American military, economic, scientific and technological superiority over the rest of the world. All mankind witnessed the spectacular economic, scientific, and technological progress of the USSR. This gave an impetus to developing new foreign-policy doctrines taking account of the mortal danger to the

United States of a nuclear missile war against the USSR and therefore offering a more flexible approach to the problem of struggle against world socialism. This was indisputably the reason for the decision of the American administration to open summit talks with the USSR in 1959.

However, the advocates of a policy "from positions of strength" still wielded much influence in the United States. Therefore, soon after the Soviet-American talks in 1959 the American government concentrated on measures to ensure US military superiority rather than on implementing the agreements reached. The Administration decided to continue the dialogue with the Soviet Union "from positions of strength". This was illustrated by another outbreak of war psychosis in the United States, an expansion of the arms build-up, and the provocative flights of American aircraft over Soviet territory, which resulted in the summit conference planned for 1960 being called off.

All this showed the misinterpretation by American ruling circles of the situation which had taken shape in the world towards the early 'sixties in consequence of the increased influence of the Soviet Union and other socialist countries, of all anti-imperialist forces, on the course of world development. As the Declaration of the Meeting of Communist and Workers' Parties in Moscow pointed out, "The superiority of the forces of socialism over those of imperialism, of the forces of peace over those of war, is becoming ever more marked in the world arena."[5]

In the late 'fifties and early 'sixties a new stage began in the general crisis of capitalism. One of its major factors was the consolidation of the positions of world socialism. At that time the People's Democracies were completing the building of the foundations of socialism. Their unity with the Soviet Union was growing stronger. The political, economic, scientific, technological, ideological, and cultural co-operation between the socialist countries had advanced to a higher level, and the process of levelling up their development was under way. At the same time, the socialist community of nations — the crucial factor in peace and social progress — was gaining strength.

The collapse of the colonial empires and the emergence of a large number of newly independent states on the world arena in the 'sixties was another striking manifestation of the crisis of world capitalism. This qualitative change in the structure of world relations further narrowed the sphere of imperialist domination.

Having lost its historical initiative and military-political superiority, imperialism was obliged to search for new methods to counteract the steadily growing forces of social progress and peace. The need for the West to revise its approach to major international problems, to the global strategy of imperialism itself, became crystal clear. In this connection differences of views on foreign-policy problems widened within the ruling circles of the Western powers, the United States first and foremost. Outspoken apologists of militarism were clamouring for a continued "balancing on the brink of war", while more sober-minded politicians, aware of the suicidal consequences of a global conflict with socialism, saw exclusive reliance on military force as hopeless.

That was how the new notion of "flexible response" came into being and was adopted by President Kennedy. It was based on recognition of the fact that with the nuclear parity existing between the USA and the USSR, nuclear conflict between them was unacceptable and undesirable. From this, however, no conclusion was drawn as to the need to stabilize this parity and to rule out the risk of future direct military conflict between the USA and the Soviet Union. On the contrary, the American leadership decided as a matter of top priority to regain its miltary superiority over the USSR.

The notion of flexible response relied as before on military force as the means of securing American foreign-policy objectives. In contrast to the doctrine of "massive retaliation" leading to a global nuclear war, it implied a limited application of military force, particularly on the periphery of the socialist community of nations and against the newly independent states. This was tantamount to a continued threat of new military conflicts likely to grow into a world thermonuclear war.

The result of the application of the doctrine of flexible response was the outbreak in 1961 of another Berlin crisis provoked by the United States and its allies, as well as an escalation of American aggression in Indochina. The crisis in the Caribbean provoked by the aggressive actions of the United States against revolutionary Cuba in 1962 pushed the world to the brink of global thermonuclear war. By adroit Soviet diplomacy combining high-principled firmness with tactical flexibility the plans of imperialism were frustrated. The failure of American aggression against Cuba demonstrated again the futility and senselessness of continuing the "positions of strength" policy towards the socialist community of nations.

The Cuban crisis, which showed the full dimensions of the danger of nuclear war, entailed an "agonizing re-evaluation" within the American ruling quarters. President Kennedy made an interesting remark in this connection. "The family of man can survive differences of race and religion. . . it can accept differences of ideology, politics, economics. But it cannot survive, in the form in which we know it, a nuclear war."[6] The spectacular achievements of the USSR in strengthening its defence capability were assessed in the capitalist world realistically enough. Its more sober-minded politicians became increasingly aware of the formidable danger the capitalist world exposed itself to by the continued reckless arms build-up and military confrontation with the USSR and other socialist countries. This prompted a search for new foreign policy and military-strategic conceptions of imperialism in its struggle against socialism.

For all the variety and outward dissimilarity of American foreign-policy doctrines employed as far as they could be in the American government's actions on the international scene, they had one thing in common: an ambition to achieve the world supremacy of imperialism, to dictate its terms to the socialist countries and eventually to do away with world socialism.

The implementation of American foreign policy was accompanied by constant appeals from American ruling circles to their NATO allies to pursue an "integrated foreign policy". At the same time, ideologists of American imperialism could not but realize that the making and carrying out of such policy was complicated by the unchallenged American domination of the North Atlantic alliance. Therefore, appeals that the USA abandon its domineering role in favour of a more equal co-operation were often voiced in the capitalist press and in statements of government and political leaders. However, the policy of so-called "Atlantic solidarity" meant in effect adjustment of the foreign policies of other Western powers to that of the United States, and the serving and justification of American policy. True, America's partners switched their roles in this show. Initially, Great Britain played the leading part among them. However, as her position in the capitalist world grew weaker, the place of leading American partner was taken over by West Germany, which spearheaded the struggle against the socialist and peace forces in Europe in the Adenauer era.

It was not till the 'sixties that the American position of dominance in the capitalist world began to decline, and other capitalist countries became capable of pursuing a more independent policy. That was an important symptom of how the attempt to set up a system of world relations under undisputed American domination had failed and of how conditions were taking shape for further democratization of international life.

In the early 'sixties a further shift was noted in American foreign policy towards realism and a dialogue with the USSR. More and more appreciable were the efforts of the United States to find safe ground for a negotiated settlement of outstanding problems, a search for compromise and a way to maintain relatively amicable relations with the Soviet Union.

In view of the progressive change in the alignment of forces in favour of socialism, the United States in its foreign policy towards the USSR and other socialist countries began shifting emphasis from military-power aspects to methods of so-called "peaceful infiltration". A new foreign-policy doctrine of "building bridges" with the socialist countries came into being. It was designed to undermine the unity of the socialist community of nations, the foundations of socialism in individual countries. The essence of that policy came into the open during the events in Czechoslovakia in 1968. Employing the method of creeping counter-revolution, the imperialists attempted to topple the socialist system in Czechoslovakia, and thereby deal a blow at the socialist community in Europe.

At the same time, however, imperialism stubbornly clung to various "classic principles" of its foreign policy. The frantic arms race continued unabated, generating tensions in the world. Imperialism did not stop its aggressive acts. For instance, at the end of 1964 a tripartite American–British–Belgian aggression was organized against the

Congo. In 1965 American troops landed in the Dominican Republic. In the latter half of the 'sixties the United States drastically widened its intervention in Vietnam, extending it to Laos and Cambodia. This escalation of American aggression was supported with the appropriate military doctrine envisaging a gradual expansion of the use of military force up to nuclear missile war.

However, the possibilities for imperialism to achieve its foreign-policy objectives by using military force steadily diminished. The outstanding achievements of the Soviet people led by the CPSU, the cohesion of the socialist community of nations, the growth of its defence potential, the active and purposeful socialist foreign policy were an insurmountable obstacle to the imperialist policy of military adventurism. It is these factors that realigned the world forces in favour of socialism, making the 'seventies a turning-point in international relations.

The imperialist foreign policy of the United States was gripped by a deep-seated crisis. It revealed the full bankruptcy of the imperialist ideological conceptions, which were designed in the final analysis to undermine and destroy socialism and communism. The imperialist strategy of reliance on military power suffered a fiasco. The global ambitions of the American ruling circles for US world supremacy came to naught.

In view of the bankruptcy of the old doctrines caused by the general erosion of the positions of imperialism, the foreign policy of the United States and its allies was subjected to a radical revision. This gave rise to a new American foreign-policy theory which came to be known as the "Nixon doctrine", whose core was a thesis on transition from the "era of confrontation" to an "era of negotiations". While remaining essentially an imperialist doctrine, it did, however, contain a not inconsiderable measure of realism, of level-headed insight into the character of the current international scene, and of assessment of the alignment of forces in the world arena.

As a result of the long evolution of American foreign policy under the impact of the growth of the socialist forces, it became possible to reach a fundamental mutual understanding between the world's two most powerful nations — the USSR and the USA — which in its turn largely cleared the way for *détente. Détente* set the stage for a fundamental reshaping of international relations in our time.

Soviet Foreign-policy Strategy in the Cold War Period

To understand the specific features of the post-war period in the Soviet Union's struggle for peace and the security of nations, for affirmation of the principles of peaceful co-existence of states with different social systems, it is important not to overlook the fact that this struggle was waged in a situation where the imperialist camp headed by the United States had started a "cold war" against the USSR and the People's Democracies.

Of course, when the world socialist system came into being, the peace and socialist forces consolidated their positions. This made it easier to oppose the aggressive designs of imperialism, and to continue the democratization of world politics. It is not only a matter of socialism, once it had extended beyond the boundaries of one country, assuming ever-greater economic and military power for the imperialists to reckon with. The emergence of a new type of international relations between the socialist countries was also vitally important. Opposed in principle to capitalist international relations based on oppression and subjugation of the weaker by the stronger states, these were bound to exert a democratizing influence on the global system of international relations. The impact of socialist international relations on world politics tended to increase along with the consolidation of the positions of the socialist system in the world.

The new post-war situation in which the CPSU and the Soviet State continued to pursue their Leninist foreign policy of peace and national freedom was characterized by the following distinctive features. First, the USSR was no longer alone in its fight for peace but was waging it in close co-operation with the socialist sister nations. Second, the positions of imperialism in the world had been undermined, but that by no means made it peace-minded. Third, the progressive disintegration of colonialism led to the appearance on the international scene of new allies — the newly independent states — in the struggle for reshaping international relations. Fourth, the peace movement in the capitalist countries after the war attained an unprecedented scale, frustrating the designs of the instigators of war. Expressing the historical trend for growth in the role played by the masses in history in general and in world politics in particular, this

world public movement was an important factor in the democratization of international life.

With these favourable circumstances came unfavourable ones. It
should be specifically emphasized that the forces of peace, democracy,
and socialism with the Soviet Union in the van were now opposed not
by separate and conflicting blocs of imperialist states but by a
common front of world capitalism under the unchallenged
domination of the United States. This made it quite hard to profit
from inter-imperialist contradictions in the interest of safeguarding
peace, the freedom and security of nations.

The maintenance of peace was a permanent strategic objective of
Soviet foreign policy. Although after the war the alignment of forces
on the world arena tended steadily to change in favour of socialism, in
the early post-war years it would have been inopportune to set the task
of banishing war from the life of society. At that time world socialism
took it as its task to avert the war being prepared by the imperialists,
to secure for the Soviet Union and the People's Democracies the
longest possible period of peace. By 1956, however, the 20th Congress
of the CPSU, in the light of the new alignment of forces on the
international scene, could conclude that prevention of a world war
was a realistic task under present conditions. The Congress declared in
its resolution: "As long as capitalism exists on the globe the
reactionary forces representing the interests of the capitalist
monopolies. . . may try and unleash war. Today powerful public and
political forces exist in the world, which are in possession of effective
means of preventing war from being unleashed by the imperialists,
and — should they try to start it — of giving a devastating rebuff to
the aggressors to thwart their adventuristic plans."[7] The 21st
Congress of the CPSU in 1959 stressed that even the combined forces
of imperialism were now unable to restore capitalism in the countries
of the socialist community. Although a world war was not fatally
inevitable, the unity of all peace forces and a tireless struggle against
the imperialist instigators of war were indispensable for preserving
and strengthening peace.

As is known, at the height of the Cold War the world was repeatedly
on the threshold of thermonuclear catastrophe. However, the
development of world socialism and the emergence of powerful forces

opposed to aggression stopped imperialism from giving free rein to its predatory ambitions. By compelling the imperialist powers in times of international crisis to assume a realistic stance these forces succeeded in preventing a third world war.

A crucial role in averting another world war was played by the consistent and high-principled but flexible foreign policy of the USSR, which took advantage of every opportunity to lessen international tensions in a situation where the alignment of forces had not yet changed irrevocably in favour of socialism. It should be also emphasized that Soviet foreign policy appealed to the broader popular masses, seeking to involve them in an active struggle for peace, against the menace of another world war.

It was believed within the international Communist movement that the peace forces were enormous, that they were capable of averting war and preserving peace. "However, we Communists believe that it is our duty to warn all the peoples of the world that the danger of a monstrous and annihilating war has not passed."[8] This meant that another world war could be prevented only if all peace forces relying on the strength of the socialist community of nations widened the scope of the anti-war movement.

In view of the prevailing international situation, the Soviet Union as far back as 1946 had met the plans of war advanced by the aspirants to world supremacy with a concrete plan of strengthening peaceful relations between all states on the principles of equality and friendly co-operation, respect for the sovereignty of other nations and non-interference in their internal affairs.

The Soviet foreign-policy programme provided for continued co-operation between the members of the wartime alliance which had jointly routed the Axis powers, for peaceful co-existence between countries having different social systems, for consolidation of the United Nations, for the withdrawal of troops from foreign territories, for a general arms reduction and a ban on atomic weapons. That was to strengthen peace and the freedom of nations, their right to shape their own destinies. In the post-war period as before, Soviet foreign policy linked organically the struggle for peace with the struggle for social progress.

The conclusion of the treaty of friendship, co-operation and mutual assistance between the Soviet Union and Finland set an example of co-operation of states belonging to different social systems. It was a concrete embodiment of Lenin's ideas of peaceful co-existence of states having different social systems, a model of equal, mutually beneficial relations between a large and a small state. Against the general background of international developments in that period, however, this example appeared quite exceptional. For the aforesaid reasons, the Western world as a whole under the pressure of American imperialism rejected out of hand the very idea of peaceful co-existence and the Soviet plans of democratic restructuring of post-war international relations.

The Soviet Union never desisted, not even for a moment, from its struggle to end the Cold War, to see the principles of peaceful co-existence adopted as a matter of course in practical international affairs. While laying bare the imperialist plans and determinedly opposing them, the Soviet Union at the same time expressed its willingness to normalize relations with the United States and other capitalist powers.

The war preparations of the American imperialists, ringing the USSR and other socialist countries of Europe with a chain of military bases, together with the formation of the aggressive NATO, CENTO, and SEATO military blocs, called for counter-measures to strengthen the security of the socialist countries. While remaining loyal in principle to the idea of a collective security system, the Soviet Union was obliged, however, jointly with other socialist countries of Europe, to form the integrated defensive Warsaw Pact Organization. It was established in May 1955 in response to the admission of the FRG to the North Atlantic alliance, whose slant against the USSR and other socialist countries had never been concealed by its founders.

The formation of an integrated defensive organization of the socialist countries as a counter-measure dictated by the need to guarantee their security was by no means an obstacle to organizing collective security in Europe and the rest of the world. The text of the Warsaw Pact contains a provision expressing consent to dissolve it in the event of a collective security system being established in Europe.[9]

The strategic direction of Soviet foreign policy in the post-war period was the struggle for disarmament, and an arms and troop reduction as a *sine qua non* for the maintenance of peace and creating an atmosphere of trust in relations between states.

On the disarmament issues the Soviet side invariably showed its sincere desire to reach mutually acceptable compromise agreements. It agreed, in effect, to any procedure and sequence of measures to liquidate weapons of mass destruction and limit conventional armaments and armed forces provided these were to be realistic measures of balanced disarmament implemented on the principle of parity. Advancing a programme of general and complete disarmament under effective international control as its ultimate objective, the Soviet Union has never adhered to the extreme "all or nothing" principle. The Soviet Union has invariably supported all proposals for measures to effect partial disarmament and lessen the danger of war.

To demonstrate its good will and commitment to peace, the Soviet Union has more than once unilaterally reduced its armed forces and announced a moratorium on atomic and thermonuclear weapons tests.

Possessed by its delusions of military grandeur, however, the United States rejected the Soviet disarmament proposals. It was not until the Soviet Union had built up a powerful nuclear missile arsenal that the leaders of the Western powers found it necessary to ponder over the risks involved in unleashing another world war. Only then was it possible to put arms limitation and disarmament talks on a more realistic basis. One of the first signs of change in this field was the Moscow treaty of 1963 between the three great powers banning nuclear weapons tests in the three media. This treaty was of fundamental importance, because it showed the way to check the reckless arms race.

Another main line of post-war Soviet foreign policy was to stamp out the seeds of war springing up here and there, to oppose acts of imperialist aggression. The principle that peace is indivisible, which had been formulated as a vital element of Soviet foreign-policy doctrine as far back as the 'thirties, assumed added significance in the post-war period. The extreme instability of the international situation caused by the Cold War being waged by the United States against the socialist world generated one international conflict after another. With the increased post-war internationalization of world affairs, a crisis situation at any point on the globe affected the interests of many countries and threatened the peace of the entire world. Its firmness and patience combined with tireless searching for the way out of a crisis more than once helped Soviet diplomacy to eliminate hotbeds of war and force the imperialists in various parts of the world to desist from their acts of aggression.

Socialist foreign policy implied that an international machinery for settlement of disputes between states should be devised and used to the best advantage both in attempts to deal with crisis situations and to promote the cause of peace in general. This referred primarily to the activities of the socialist countries in the United Nations. They vigorously opposed attempts to convert the UN from an organ of co-operation between equal states on the principle of peaceful co-existence, as is laid down in its Charter, into a tool of American foreign policy. As is known, the United States sought to gear the UN voting machinery to its objectives and attempted to revise the UN Charter as a *fait accompli* or, failing that, to circumvent it. The principled and firm stand of the Soviet Union frustrated these plans. The UN Charter was preserved intact thanks primarily to the efforts of the socialist countries, and the world body itself assumed greater universality.

The success of these efforts was largely facilitated by the post-war struggle waged by the USSR and other socialist countries for the abolition of colonialism, which was yet another of the key trends in reshaping international relations along democratic lines. The disorganization of imperialism's bases in the colonies changed the face of the world. The entry of the newly-independent states to the UN put an end to American domination of that body, shattering its "voting machine".

The USSR and other socialist countries fought their battle for the abolition of the colonial system of imperialism along three main lines. First, the line of denouncing colonialism as incompatible with international law. The Declaration on Granting Independence to the Colonial Countries and Peoples adopted by the UN General Assembly on a Soviet initiative created an intolerable atmosphere for preserving the disgraceful colonial system. Second, the line of rendering all-out assistance to the national liberation movements in their fight to throw off the colonial yoke, of determined opposition to imperialist acts of aggression against newly independent states. Third, the line of organizing economic, scientific, and technological co-operation on a basis of equality between the socialist and the newly independent states so as to help the latter achieve complete independence from imperialism and pursue an independent policy.

Developing economic, scientific, and technological co-operation based on equality between countries with different social systems was another main line of the foreign policy pursued by the USSR and other socialist countries in the post-war period. The economic interests of the capitalist countries compelled them to defy American objections and carry on mutually beneficial trade with the socialist world. However, the turnover of Soviet trade with the capitalist countries in the post-war years was relatively small. Trade and economic ties of the USSR and other socialist countries with the leading capitalist power — the United States — amounted to almost nothing. The reason was the introduction by the West in the Cold War period of severe restrictions and discrimination against the socialist countries in the field of commerce.

The Cold War indisputably caused a good deal of harm to the socialist world, because the Soviet Union and the People's Democracies had to invest heavily in defence at a time when resources were badly needed for post-war recovery and economic and cultural development. In the final analysis, however, the Cold War boomeranged on the states whose governments began it and conducted it.

The Specifics of International Relations During the Cold War

The development of world relations in the post-war period was determined by a conflict between two opposite policies. One was the consistent Soviet policy, initiated as far back as the October Revolution, supported by other socialist states and pursued with the object of affirming the principle of peaceful co-existence in daily international life, restructuring the system of international relations on the basis of respect for the sovereignty of all countries and peoples and non-interference in their internal affairs. The other was the policy followed by the United States and other Western powers with the aim of heightening international tensions, committing acts of aggression, and suppressing the liberation struggle of the peoples. To implement this policy, the imperialist powers led by the United States triggered off a frantic arms race. This race was the key factor in the Cold War.

Eventually the imperialist policy of the Western powers on the post-war international scene proved a failure. The USSR and its allies had succeeded in saving the world from thermonuclear catastrophe. Although at that time international relations could not be restructured in the spirit of Lenin's ideas of a just and democratic peace, it is to the credit of world socialism that even in the years of the Cold War there came periods in international relations known as "the thaw", in its way a prototype of the latter-day *détente*. In the 'fifties and 'sixties the Soviet efforts were rewarded with an understanding reached on a number of issues, the conclusion of agreements which put an end to military conflicts in certain flashpoint areas of the world and were a step in the direction of preventing a world war, of strengthening peace and stability.

Examining the post-war situation from this aspect, one cannot ignore the clear successes in the settlement of conflicts achieved in spite of the imperialist policy of the Western powers.

The efforts of the socialist countries were decisive in preventing so-called local conflicts from growing into a world war. Coming out for a negotiated settlement of vital international problems, the Soviet Union and other socialist countries thwarted many aggressive designs of imperialism, and helped to preserve peace. They worked persistently for easing international tensions. The change in the alignment of forces in favour of socialism curbed imperialism, nipping in the bud its attempts to restore capitalism in individual socialist countries and to suppress the national liberation movement.

It was precisely the Soviet Union's foreign-policy initiatives that were the crucial factor in ending the Korean War unleashed by the American imperialists and their South Korean puppets in June 1950. The American government had to agree to the proposal for armistice talks made by the Soviet Government in June 1950. The determined stand taken by the Soviet Union and other socialist countries, their growing aid to the Korean people fighting American aggression, forced the United States to back down from its escalation of the war and to sign an armistice agreement in July 1953.

The armistice in Korea put an end to the bloodshed which had been going on for 3 years, removed the threat of a world conflagration and contributed to a lessening of world tension. The ending of the Korean War was a major success for the Soviet efforts to preserve peace. At the same time, it furnished visible proof that it was impossible for the United States to settle vital international problems from "positions of strength", to enforce its line in international affairs. The end of hostilities in Korea was a grave setback for the United States and for its imperialist plans in Asia connected with the Korean War.

Another example of the effectiveness of the foreign policy of the socialist countries was the halting of French aggression against the peoples of Indochina. The Conference of Foreign Ministers called at Geneva in 1954 on a Soviet initiative put an end to French military operations in Vietnam, Cambodia, and Laos and consolidated the international position of the young socialist Democratic Republic of Vietnam. It is significant that the Geneva agreements on Indochina were reached in the face of resistance from the United States. The American government was opposed to a cease-fire agreement on Indochina, because a peace settlement in that area would mean another setback for the policy of "containment" of communism. The Geneva agreements banned the supply of arms and ammunition, the entry of foreign troops and military personnel into the countries of Indochina. Although the American government had not participated in the Geneva Conference, it was compelled by the pressure of world opinion to declare in July 1954 that it would abide by its decisions. Just a year later, however, the United States flagrantly violated the Geneva agreements by sending its military advisers and specialists to South Vietnam.

The Soviet Union gave a determined rebuff to the imperialist aggression against Egypt. At a critical moment the Soviet Government demanded that Britain, France, and Israel immediately end their military intervention against Egypt and warned them of the risks involved should it continue. The Soviet Union's firm stand forced these countries to end the war against Egypt. This was admitted in the *New*

York Herald Tribune of 12 November 1956. The newspaper said that the true motive for the decision of Britain, France, and Israel to withdraw was the Soviet warning note. Twenty-two hours after the Soviet Government's messages were delivered in London and Paris, Britain and France terminated hostilities in Egypt. The British, French, and Israeli authorities were forced to withdraw their troops from the occupied territories. The Anglo–French–Israeli aggression against Egypt ended in ignominious defeat. One of the local wars unleashed by the imperialists and threatening to plunge mankind into a world catastrophe was terminated by the joint efforts of the Egyptian people, the Soviet Union, and other forces committed to peace. This was an expression of both the growing influence of socialism on world development and its strengthing alliance with the national liberation movement.

The counter-revolutionary rebellion in Hungary engineered by the imperialists in the days of the Anglo–French–Israeli aggression was intended not only to distract the Soviet Union's attention from the events in the Middle East. As conceived by its masterminds, it was to wrest Hungary from the socialist community of nations and turn her into an imperialist bridgehead. Therefore, when the revolutionary workers' and peasants' government of Hungary appealed to the Soviet Army Command in Hungary for aid to the Hungarian people in defeating the counter-revolutionary forces and restoring law and order in the country, the Soviet Government, motivated by its desire to maintain peace and security and abiding by the principles of socialist internationalism, satisfied that request. The power of socialism checked this further instance of imperialist intervention aimed at exporting counter-revolution.

The failure of the counter-revolutionary rebellion in Hungary and of the imperialist aggression against Egypt showed that imperialism was no longer in a position to decide at will for or against war, was unable to restore the capitalist system in countries building socialism or reinstate the colonial order in countries which had won political independence. The Soviet Union, whose power was steadily growing, proved itself once more the staunch defender of the freedom and independence of nations, the main obstacle to imperialist aggression.

The Cuban crisis was a particularly vivid demonstration of the change in the alignment of forces in favour of socialism. The victorious revolution in Cuba infuriated the American imperialists, so much so that they threw into action their whole arsenal of political blackmail, economic coercion, and counter-revolutionary conspiracies. When in April 1961 Cuba was attacked by bands of interventionists provided with cover by American warships and aircraft, the Soviet Union expressed its strong determination to help the Cuban people to defend their freedom and independence and demanded that America end the aggression. The United States was obliged to retreat.

Before long, however, the United States started preparations for another attack, this time an open intervention by American armed forces. American ruling circles could not reconcile themselves to the fact that a socialist state should exist as a neighbour to the United States. In view of the threat of American invasion of Cuba, the Soviet Government at the Cuban Government's request took steps to strengthen her defence capability.

In its statement of 23 October 1962, the Soviet Government declared that the unprecedented aggressive actions of the American imperialists were pushing the world towards the abyss of a catastrophic war and called on all governments and peoples "to denounce resolutely these actions and erect a barrier in the way of thermonuclear war planned by the US Government". The statement also contained a stern warning to the US Government to the effect that "if the aggressors unleash a war, the Soviet Union would deal a devastating retaliatory blow".[10]

This crisis, unprecedented in all the post-war years for its gravity, and which brought mankind face to face with the threat of a world thermonuclear conflagration, was resolved. American imperialism was forced to abandon its plan of war against socialist Cuba.

The Cuban crisis demonstrated that it was impossible for American imperialism to use force, to accept the risk of direct military conflict with the USSR, without exposing itself to prohibitive casualties in a nuclear missile war. It was also evidence that in its actions the United States had largely gone over to political blackmail. The reason was that the growth of the defence potential of the socialist countries, primarily of the Soviet Union, was limiting the possibility of using

brute military force in America's post-war strategy and tactics.
Developments in Indochina also testified to the increased possibilities for the USSR and other countries of the socialist community to give assistance to the peoples victimized by imperialist aggression. After the beginning of American aggression against North Vietnam, the Soviet Union gave it diverse military and economic aid enabling the Vietnamese people to hold their ground in a war where the United States unleashed its full firepower. Soviet diplomacy took effective steps to isolate the aggressor on the international scene, to mobilize world opinion and all peace forces in support of the just struggle of the Vietnamese people. In July 1966 the Political Consultative Committee of the Warsaw Pact member states warned the American government of "the responsibility it bears in the eyes of all mankind by continuing and escalating this war, responsibility for all the unpredictable consequences likely to follow from it and which may harm the United States itself.[11]

Despite the growth of the forces of world socialism, its enemies did not desist from their attempts to subvert it. In 1968 the imperialists undertook one of their largest acts of subversion in Czechoslovakia, hoping to make a breach in the socialist community of nations and change to their advantage, if only partly, the alignment of forces in Europe. This time again they suffered a total defeat. Under the slogan "Defence of socialism is the internationalist duty of Communists!", the countries of the socialist community joined hands to assist fraternal Czechoslovakia. Their cohesion and internationalist solidarity proved stronger than those who had expected to reverse the history of the Czechoslovak people, to wrest power from the hands of the working class, of all working people. The entry of Warsaw Pact forces into the territory of Czechoslovakia frustrated the plans of the internal and external counter-revolution. This action in defence of the socialist achievements of the Czechoslovak people demonstrated to the whole world the loyalty of the USSR and its allies to the Leninist principles of socialist internationalism.

In the 'fifties and 'sixties the imperialists also resorted to military provocation and intervention against the Arab countries (Syria, Egypt, Jordan, Iraq, the Lebanon) and other newly independent states (Indonesia, Cyprus, Congo) in an effort to enforce on the international scene their policy of suppression of national liberation movements and of securing the interests of the monopoly bourgeoisie. This policy gave rise to a series of conflicts which threatened the peace of the world.

In all critical international situations the Soviet Union unhesitatingly used its international prestige and influence to stop the aggressor, to put an end to lawlessness and coercion in international politics. It was the Soviet Union that defended the sovereignty and independence of the newly independent peoples by its resolute opposition to imperialist aggression. Its support and assistance to the developing countries became an insurmountable obstacle to colonialism and neo-colonialism, forcing the imperialists to make certain concessions to the newly independent states.

The tense struggle against imperialist aggression and war preparations waged by the Soviet Union during the Cold War blended with its unswerving and consistent policy of implementing long-term tasks in radically reshaping the system of international relations on the principles of peaceful co-existence of states with different social systems. Striving to normalize crisis situations in international affairs, Soviet foreign policy pursued a task without precedent in significance and scope: to preclude the very possibility of such situations arising in the future.

The growth of the military–political and economic potential of socialism in the 'fifties and 'sixties provided the material basis for setting the task of a general relaxation of international tension. Leonid Brezhnev declared on 7 June 1969:

> The 1960s will occupy a special place in the history of world socialism. It was in this decade that many fraternal countries completed the foundations of socialism and went over to the building of developed socialist society. As it matures, the socialist system more and more fully reveals the advantages of its economic, social and political organization and its inherent genuine democracy. All this is a tangible and weighty contribution to our common cause, the cause of consolidating the anti-imperialist front.[12]

The joint actions and mutual support of the socialist countries in foreign-policy matters not only frustrated many aggressive designs of imperialism in the 'fifties and 'sixties but also contributed to an easing of international tension and laid the groundwork for effecting cardinal changes in international life in the 'seventies.

Among the political means of strengthening peace and restructuring international relations the Soviet Union attached first priority to collective security. The Soviet Union has always implied by collective security a joint opposition of states to aggression, an organization of all-round mutually beneficial co-operation through the use of suitable political mechanisms whose fundamental principle of operation is the collective responsibility of all the security of each. Thus, collective security means the maintenance of peaceful co-existence by the joint efforts of states belonging to different social systems.

In the final phase of the Second World War, when the Soviet Union's prestige and influence had grown immeasurably, it proved possible to implement a series of measures to organize a collective security system. This was expressed, in particular, by the foundation of the United Nations, whose Charter provides for the institution of a universal system of collective security, as well as the conclusion of bilateral treaties between European states containing their obligations to prevent aggression. As is justly stated by the Soviet historian V.K. Sobakin, these treaties concluded between the main European countries — the USSR, France, Britain, Czechoslovakia, Poland — could form the backbone of an all-European collective security system.[13] As is known, however, efforts to set up a collective security system were soon frustrated by the Western powers, which had embarked on a policy of cobbling together military blocs after the war.

The formation of the imperialist blocs, and NATO in particular, undermined the United Nations as an instrument for maintaining peace and international security, torpedoed the collective security system which had begun even during the war to take shape in Europe, and led to a situation of growing war danger. Alarmed by this fact, informed public opinion demanded a search for methods to guarantee European security, ruling out a confrontation of military blocs and rivalry between states in building up their military might.

On the Soviet Union's initiative, the question of setting up a European Security system was discussed at the Berlin Conference of Foreign Ministers (January-February 1954), the Geneva Conference of the heads of government of the four great powers (July 1955), and the Geneva Conference of Foreign Ministers (October-November

1955). The draft of an all-European collective security treaty submitted by the Soviet Union to the Berlin Conference provided for the establishment of a collective security system in Europe involving all countries of the continent regardless of their social system (the GDR and the FRG included). Although the draft in no way infringed the interests of the non-European countries, to meet the desires of the Western powers the Soviet Government in a note of 31 March 1954 expressed its consent to direct American participation in an all-European security system.

The persistent efforts of the USSR and other socialist countries brought about in the mid-fifties a certain relaxation of international tension, which came to be known as the "Geneva spirit". At the two Geneva conferences of 1955, the Western powers had to express themselves in favour of normalizing relations with the Soviet Union and other socialist countries, for finding mutually acceptable solutions to major international problems, including European security, the German problem, disarmament, and East–West contacts.

The Geneva Conference neither set up a European security system, nor settled the German problem. Nevertheless, it was one of the breakthroughs towards *détente* which the Soviet Union managed to achieve even during the Cold War. The "Geneva spirit" was conclusive proof of the possibility of co-operation between states with different social systems. It showed that, for all its zigzags, the foreign policy of the Western powers could occasionally tend towards a sober and realistic assessment of the world situation. The very appearance of that tendency was caused by the process of constant change in the alignment of forces in favour of socialism.

The peace settlement with Austria was another important step of the Soviet Government in the direction of lessening international tensions. Faced with the unwillingness of the Western powers to settle the Austrian problem on a collective basis, the Soviet Union opened direct negotiatons with Austria, which were held in Moscow in April 1955. They laid the foundation for a settlement of the Austrian problem and resulted in the conclusion of the State Treaty with Austria which guaranteed her neutrality. The State Treaty for the restoration of an independent and democratic Austria was signed by representatives of the four powers in Vienna in May 1955. Austria committed herself to a permanent neutral status, including an obligation to abstain from membership in military blocs and to allow no foreign military bases in her territory. As a result, another non-aligned country appeared in Europe. Thus, an agreement consistent with the cause of European security was reached through the Soviet Union's efforts.

The development of the international situation and particularly the change in the alignment of forces on the international scene in favour of socialism compelled statesmen of the Western powers, including the United States, to give more careful consideration to their position on the problems of war and peace. In the chief capitalist country of America, awareness was growing that it was time to get out of the quagmire of the Cold War and make a realistic assessment of today's realities in all their diversity.

The Soviet–American summit talks at Camp David in the autumn of 1959, and the understandings reached there, went into the record of international relations as favourably influencing the world situation. The "Camp David spirit" showed that the Soviet line in international affairs was exerting a steadily growing influence on the course of world politics, *détente* and international life, and assuming an ever more profound and multilateral character. The agreements reached at Camp David were, however, not destined to materialize. American reactionary circles succeeded in holding back progress towards Soviet–American co-operation. They thwarted the summit meeting between the USSR, the USA, Great Britain, and France which was to be held in Paris on 16 May 1960, and would have become a milestone on the path towards a settlement of the German problem and normalizing East–West relations.

Seeking to bury the Camp David spirit, the reactionary circles underestimated the profound motives behind another "breakthrough towards *détente*" on the international scene. The relative improvement in Soviet–American relations in 1959 had been brought about not by the good intentions of American leaders but by a real and tangible factor — the tilt in the balance of power in favour of socialism, primarily by the development in the USSR of nuclear missiles which put an end to the legend of American invulnerability to a retaliatory strike. It was quite legitimate, therefore, that after the defeat of the Republican Party in the presidential elections of 1960 and the inauguration of J.F. Kennedy as President, the question of improving relations with the USSR and hence the international climate in general again assumed first priority.

The abandonment of the Cold War in American foreign policy proved a very difficult matter. And small wonder. It is known that foreign policy has a degree of independence from the objective factors generating it, that foreign-policy logic is not a mechanical replica of world socio-economic development. Between them extends a complete chain of indirect, intermediate links, owing to which objective changes are not immediately and directly transformed into foreign-policy decisions. In the period under review, the momentum of the Cold War was still very strong. Western policy-makers could not change their minds at once and take a realistic stand on world affairs. That is why in the 'sixties American foreign policy was still not able to get itself completely out of the rut of the Cold War.

The zigzags in the foreign policy of imperialism in the 'sixties, manifested by alternations of periods of relaxation and heightening of international tension, were due to the viability of Cold War dogmas, which had become a material force in their own right. In the United States and other Western powers the Cold War had called into being a group having a vested interest in its continuation. These were national and international monopolies combining in the arms manufacturing field the interests of industrial and military élites, the scientific community involved in military R & D programmes, and politicians raised to prominence by the Cold War.

The Cold War stereotypes fiercely resisted the tendency towards the dissolution of military blocs and alliances which had turned into a dangerous and often autonomous force in international relations. The bloc-oriented approach of the imperialists hindered progress in individual areas and settlement of vital problems of world politics. There was also a psychological factor: the ringleaders of NATO had for so long been intimidating their peoples with the "Soviet menace" that they had become indoctrinated with their own propaganda.

It could not have been otherwise. Accustomed to settling all international problems by might and resorting to force at will, they applied their own yardstick to Soviet policy and were apprehensive of growing Soviet power.

The "China factor", the divisive activities of the Maoists, which generated in the West the illusion of a possible acute weakening of the positions of world socialism, also stimulated the activity of the Cold War and prolonged its death-throes.

All these factors taken together explain why the roads to peace were so arduous and the development of international relations so spasmodic in the sixties.

The position of the Western powers continued to bar the way towards the solution of the problems inherited from the Second World War. At a summit meeting in Vienna on 3-4 June 1961, the Soviet side went on record for a speedy settlement of the German problem and tabled specific proposals to this end. The American side, which had recognized for the first time the parity of US and Soviet forces, nevertheless tried to compel the USSR to abandon its efforts to set a seal on the Second World War in Europe. The military–industrial complex came out against concluding a German peace treaty and normalizing the situation in West Berlin, and set the Administration on the dangerous path to military confrontation with the Soviet Union. At a meeting of the National Security Council, however, President Kennedy declared that the United States should not refuse negotiations as a means of handling international affairs.[14]

In the autumn of 1961 and during 1962 Soviet and American representatives had a series of meetings in New York, Washington, and Geneva to discuss the whole range of problems involved in a German peace settlement. As a result the rift between the Soviet and American positions narrowed on many current matters relevant to a final settlement of the problems left by the Second World War. Among them were the problems of finalizing and ratifying the existing German frontiers, recognition of the sovereignty of the GDR, and renunciation of nuclear armament of the GDR and the FRG. Although the final settlement was still a long way off, it was increasingly obvious that the reactionary forces were powerless to implement their plans in German affairs, to infringe the interests of the GDR and other socialist countries. The efforts of the socialist community of nations to strengthen European security and achieve a

German peace settlement largely contributed to the trend towards a relaxation of international tensions.

The Soviet Union's policy of extending bilateral ties with the capitalist countries was a highly important part of the drive towards *détente*. The development of Soviet–Finnish relations attested to the broad opportunities for co-existence of states with different social systems. In 1955 a protocol was signed to prolong by 20 years the term of the Treaty of Friendship, Co-operation, and Mutual Assistance concluded between the USSR and Finland in 1948. In view of its good-neighbourly relations with Finland, the Soviet Union elected to relinquish its rights to the Porkkala–Udd military base due to expire in 1997. Having dismantled earlier its naval base at Port Arthur, the Soviet Union now closed down its last military base outside its national territory. This was further convincing evidence of its commitment to peace.

The restoration in October 1956 in the face of US opposition of diplomatic relations with Japan was an important step towards improving the international climate. The joint Soviet–Japanese declaration signed in October 1956 provided the basis for setting up good-neighbourly relations and developing economic and political ties between the two countries.

The Soviet Union's bilateral relations with France, Britain, Italy, and other capitalist countries were further developed in the 'fifties and 'sixties. The development of relations between the USSR and France, which were the forerunner of *détente,* was of especially great significance. The Soviet–French declaration signed at the end of General de Gaulle's visit to Moscow acknowledged that relaxation of tension was the first and indispensable stage in the desirable development of relations between the European countries irrespective of their political systems. The sides agreed to work for a normalization followed by gradual development of relations between all European countries on the principle of respect for the independence of each of them and non-interference in their internal affairs. To strengthen mutual trust and widen the areas of accord and co-operation between the USSR and France, the two governments agreed to hold regular political consultations.

The development of the Soviet Union's bilateral ties with capitalist countries largely contributed to setting the stage for a transition from the Cold War to *détente*. At the same time, it testified to the steadily growing influence of Soviet foreign policy on international affairs.

The 23rd Congress of the CPSU held in March 1966 outlined a series of specific measures to promote the trend towards *détente*. The Congress emphasized in its decisions that the Soviet State would consistently uphold the principle of peaceful co-existence of states having different social systems, resist with determination the aggressive forces of capitalism, and do all in its power to deliver mankind from the menace of another world war.[15]

The alignment of forces which took shape on the world arena in the late 'sixties, the vigorous joint actions of the socialist states to consolidate the peace of the world, created the prerequisites for a relaxation of international tension, for accelerating a fundamental restructuring of the entire system of international relations on an equitable and democratic basis. This required that *détente* be made not a transitory but a permanent process governing international relations.

6

The Key Factor in the Fundamental Reshaping of International Relations

The Growing Role of the Socialist Community of Nations

ALL progressive forces today — the socialist countries, the international working class and the national liberation movement — are interested in a just and democratic peace being established in the world. The three mainstreams of the world revolutionary movement, interacting with one another, are waging a struggle against imperialism, for reshaping international relations on democratic principles. This was emphasized at the Berlin Conference of Communist and Workers' Parties of Europe in June 1976: "The socialist countries, the non-aligned movement, the revolutionary and progressive forces in the developing countries, and the working-class and democratic movements are fighting for the establishment of new international political and economic relations on the basis of justice and equality."[1]

The main force in the struggle for peace and the security of nations, for a relaxation of international tension is the socialist community of nations, whose role in international affairs is steadily growing. On the whole in 1979 the socialist world had a territory of 35.6 million km^2 with a population of 1462 million, and accounted for over 40 per cent of world industrial production. The industrial output of the socialist countries is equivalent to over three-quarters of that of the economically advanced capitalist countries.[1]

The Soviet Union, which is a great socialist power, holds a special place in this world. Whereas imperial Russia produced slightly over 4 per cent of the world's industrial output in 1913, the Soviet Union's share today is equal to one-fifth. In 1979 Soviet industry produced more than the whole world had produced in 1950. Over the last decade Soviet gross industrial output has doubled. The Soviet output of key industrial products as compared with that of the United States is as follows: oil, 139 per cent; steel, 117 per cent; mineral fertilizers, 111 per cent; mainline diesel locomotives and electric locomotives, 175 per cent; tractors, 277 per cent; grain-harvesting combines, 355 per cent; cement, 158 per cent; cotton fabrics, 179 per cent; woollen fabrics, 456 per cent.[2] For many indicators Soviet industrial production is larger than that of Great Britain, the FRG, and France combined.

Agricultural production (in comparable prices) in 1979 was more than three times that of 1913. At the same time, manpower employed in agriculture had diminished almost by half.[3]

Speaking before the electorate of Moscow's Bauman District on 22 February 1980, Leonid Brezhnev said:

> The whole of the past decade was one of the continuous steady growth of the economic, scientific and technical potential of our homeland, of the capacities of our industry and agriculture. This made it possible to bring about a substantial rise in the living standards of the people, which has been and remains the main aim of all our economic activities. During the 'seventies the real per capita income of the population rose by 50 per cent. More than 108 million people have improved their housing conditions. And that, comrades, is more than 40 per cent of the country's population.
>
> The Soviet Union's defence might is also being maintained at the due level. Today on the eve of Soviet Army and Navy Day the Central Committee can assure the Soviet people that we have everything necessary to repel any armed provocations. The peaceful future of the Soviet state is secured, and reliably secured.[4]

The rapid progress of science and technology is a guarantee of successful development in all sectors of the Soviet economy. There were 11,600 research workers in 1913, 98,300 in 1940, and in 1979 the number of Soviet research personnel was 1,340,000, or one-quarter of the world's total.[5] Research appropriations in 1979 amounted to 20,200 million roubles.[6]

The political system of Soviet society is being developed on the basis of the new Constitution of the USSR. The purpose of this development is to ensure a steady and ever broader involvement of the working people in the management of all the affairs of society, to widen further the democratic foundations of Soviet nationhood, and to provide the requisite conditions for all-round personality development.

The growth of the economic and defence potential of the USSR, the consolidation of the moral and political unity of the Soviet people have made the Soviet Union a dependable guarantor of peace and international security, the main countervailing power restraining the forces of war and reaction. It is primarily to the Soviet Union that mankind owes its advance along the path of social progress. In this connection, Gus Hall, General Secretary of the US Communist Party, has said: "Before the Soviet Union appeared and consolidated its positions, imperialism had been master of the situation. The sun had never set over the British Empire, and the boots of the US Marines had trampled foreign shores with impunity. The great imperialist powers had been engaged in carving up the world — the population, lands and natural wealth of this planet as if it were their own pie.... . The Soviet Union became a counter-weight to imperialism politically, ideologically, diplomatically, militarily, economically, and commercially." (Translated from the Russian.)[7]

This role of the USSR in international affairs is recognized today not only by its friends but also by its ill-wishers. As is admitted in the book *The Soviet Impact on World Politics* published in the USA in the 'seventies, Soviet influence in the world has been steadily growing ever since the October Revolution.[8]

The international ties of the Soviet State have assumed a global character and scope and extended to all continents. Today no world problem or international issue of importance can be settled without the Soviet Union or in contravention of its interests and the interests of world socialism. As a world power the Soviet Union cannot take up an indifferent or passive attitude to developments which, even if distant from its borders, affect one way or other its security and the security of its allies, the prospects of peace and progress on earth. As was stated in the report of the Central Committee to the 25th CPSU Congress, "In the present conditions our Party's activity on the international scene is exceptionally broad and varied. In shaping our foreign policy we now have to reckon, in one way or another, with the state of affairs in virtually every spot on the globe.'"[9]

The member countries of the socialist community affiliated with the Council for Mutual Economic Assistance (Comecon) constitute a powerful force. Although they contain a mere 9.3 per cent of the world population, they account for one-third of the world's industrial output. Between 1950 and 1978 the growth rates of industry in the Comecon countries were four times those in the industrialized capitalist countries.

The progress of the countries of the socialist community is primarily due to their close economic and political co-operation and the relations of fraternal friendship, mutual assistance and support established among them. These embody the principles of socialist internationalism by which the fraternal parties of the countries of the socialist community are guided in their mutual relations. It is precisely due to socialist internationalism that the alliance, friendship, and co-operation of sovereign and equal states united by their common aims and interests and held together by their bonds of comradely solidarity and mutual assistance have been established between the countries of the socialist community.

Economic co-operation within the Comecon framework was given a powerful impulse by the adoption in 1971 of the Comprehensive Programme of Socialist Economic Integration and the implementation of long-term target-oriented co-operation programmes. This programme of further extending and improving co-operation and developing the socialist economic integration of the Comecon member countries enables them to utilize more completely the advantages of the socialist economic system and the international socialist division of labour in the interest of consolidating their economic and defence potential and improving the well-being of their peoples. Its implementation strengthens the unity and cohesion of the socialist commonwealth of nations and enhances their role in the struggle for social progress, peace, and international co-operation.

The 30th session of the Council for Mutual Economic Assistance took a crucially important decision to place co-operation within the Comecon framework on the foundation of a long-term plan by drawing up joint long-term target-oriented programmes for 10 to 15 years. In taking this decision the Comecon member countries expressed their willingness to use jointly in their national and common interests their natural wealth, material and manpower resources in accordance with the principles of co-operation pervaded with the spirit of socialist internationalism.

The 32nd session of the Council for Mutual Economic Assistance in 1978 approved the first three long-term target-oriented co-operation programmes providing for the construction of about 250 large projects. For instance, by 1990 a number of atomic power plants with a total capacity of 37 million kWh will have been built with Soviet technical assistance in the European member countries of Comecon and Cuba.

Under such long-term target-oriented programmes large integration enterprises are being built by joint efforts in Soviet territory: the Ust-Ilim woodpulp plant, the Kiembayev asbestos mining and enrichment complex (its first section with an annual capacity of 250,000 tons was commissioned in 1979), iron works using ores of the Kursk magnetic anomaly area, the "Soyuz" gas pipeline from Orenburg to the Western border of the USSR, the Yermakov ferroalloy plant, the Dnieper ore-dressing complex, and other projects to be completed between 1976 and 1980. The products of these enterprises will be distributed between the Comecon countries in proportion to their shares in deliveries of various materials and equipment to the Soviet Union.

Between 1976 and 1980, just as in the preceding period, the Comecon countries imported the bulk of modern energy carriers from the USSR: roughly 368 million tons of crude oil, 100,000 million m³ of gas, 67,000 million kWh of electric power.[10] In 1978 a 750-kWh power transmission line from Vinnitsa to Albertirs in Hungary, a distance of 842 km, was completed ahead of schedule.

The USSR has helped to build coal mines in Mongolia which supply steam coals to the thermal power plants outside Ulan-Bator and Choibalsan. The first section of the joint Soviet–Mongolian ore-dressing complex "Erdenet" has gone into operation. In Cuba Soviet specialists are helping to enlarge the capacity of a copper and nickel complex outside Santiago de Cuba, whose products are needed by the Comecon countries.

Bourgeois ideologists are going out of their way to discredit and denigrate the mutually beneficial economic co-operation of the Comecon countries. However, the record of co-operation within the framework of Comecon, the principles of its activities give the lie to the calumnies of anti-Soviet propaganda. The international economic organization of the fraternal countries is based on the principles of complete equality, respect for their sovereignty and national interests, mutual benefit and comradely mutual assistance. For example, Article IV of the Comecon Charter reads: "All recommendations and decisions of the Council shall be adopted exclusively with the consent of the Council member countries concerned, each country being entitled to declare its interest in any question under review in the Council."[11] In contrast to the Common Market where the votes of the member countries are unequal and depend on the economic contribution of each of them, Comecon unswervingly observes the principle of complete equality of its member countries irrespective of the size of the territory and population, the military, political and economic potential of each. The Council recommendations and decisions are binding only on those countries which have voted in favour of them. Comecon does not stipulate any preliminary conditions for the admission of members, nor does it make any unusual claims on them. Any member of Comecon is free to withdraw from it any time.[12]

The activities of Comecon are based on democratic principles. Its member countries are equally represented on the Council bodies regardless of the size of their population, economic potential, contributions to the Comecon budget, and other factors. Each of them determines the extent of its interests in the Comecon activities at discretion. Comecon recommendations adopted by member countries are carried into effect by a decision of authorized national agencies in accordance with established procedure. Comecon is an inter-state rather than supranational organization. The steady enhancement of the international economic interaction of the fraternal countries goes hand in hand with the consolidation of their national sovereignty.

Party and government leaders of the Comecon countries have emphasized that their economic co-operation accelerates the economic progress of each of them. In his report to the 12th Congress of the

Hungarian Socialist Workers' Party in February 1980, First Secretary János Kadar declared that co-operation with the Comecon framework facilitated the economic advance of the Council member states and that the "Hungarian People's Republic will continue to take an active part in the work of Comecon".[13] The First Secretary of the Central Committee of the Polish United Workers' Party, Edward Gierek, in his report to the 8th Congress of the PUWP in February 1980 stressed that in view of the economic and political significance of continued co-operation with the Comecon member countries Poland would seek to develop productive specialization and co-operation, a joint solution to the fuel and raw materials problems, and further integration of the economic potentials of the fraternal countries. He said in particular: "We will actively contribute to implementing the Comprehensive Programme of Socialist Economic Integration."[14]

Economic co-operation between the countries of the socialist community helps advance the living standards of the working people, improve their working and living conditions, widen housing construction, meet the demand of the population for foodstuffs and consumer goods. In 1978 productive *per capita* national income was 450 per cent that of 1950 in the Comecon member countries as a whole. The Comecon countries have solved the key social problem of full employment of the entire able-bodied population.[15]

In addition to cash income an important part in improving the well-being of the people is played by what is known as the social consumption funds used to meet the costs of free education, medical service, holidays for working people, pensions, and other social benefits. Between 1960 and 1978 these funds increased as follows: in Bulgaria and Hungary, more than 400 per cent; in the GDR, 170 per cent; in Mongolia, 310 per cent; in the USSR, 290 per cent; in Czechoslovakia, 230 per cent.[16]

The progress in the development of the USSR and other countries of the socialist community adds to the force of attraction socialism has for other peoples. The fact that the socialist economy develops without economic depressions and unemployment and secures a steady advancement of the living standards of the people has a tremendous impact on the working people in the industrialized capitalist countries. The working people of the whole world are being revolutionized by their awareness of the fact that the world socialist community of nations has abolished the exploitation of man by man and ethnic oppression, guaranteed the advancement of all its nations, large and small, and brought education and culture within reach of all sections of the population.

Economic co-operation between the countries of the socialist community throws into salient relief the new type of international relations, which not only rest on the universal democratic principles of equality, mutual trust among nations, respect for sovereignty and national independence, and mutually advantageous co-operation of states but also imply fraternal proletarian mutual assistance and mutual support, a socialist division of labour contributing to the consolidation of their combined economic potential and joint defence of world socialism.

The 33rd anniversary session of Comecon held in June 1979 expressed its high assessment of the record of this organization — the first of its kind in history — in multilateral economic, scientific and technical co-operation, which had for 30 years served to develop close economic ties between the fraternal countries, to consolidate the power and unity of the socialist community of nations, to promote the cause of socialist and communist construction. As the Comecon session stated in its declaration, the strong alliance of the ruling Communist and Workers' parties is the dependable political foundation on which the socialist nations are advancing their co-operation and concerting their efforts more and more closely in all spheres of social life. Thanks to the tireless work of these parties, the prevision of the great Lenin about friendship and fraternal relations among nations based on mutual understanding and mutual trust, on harmony between their vital interests and voluntary accord has come true.

The new forms of human community created by socialism are a model to all peoples of the world, and their influence on the international situation is steadily growing.

Comecon is open to membership for both socialist and capitalist countries. The principles of its activities are gaining increasing recognition throughout the world. In addition to the Comecon member states, Yugoslavia, the Korean Democratic People's

Republic, the People's Republic of Angola, Socialist Ethiopia, the Democratic Republic of Afghanistan, the People's Democratic Republic of Yemen and the People's Repubic of Mozambique are more and more broadly involved in the work of its agencies. In the 'seventies co-operation agreements with Comecon were concluded by Finland, Mexico, and Iraq. This is evidence of the steadily growing gravitation of countries outside the socialist community towards co-operation with Comecon.

The economic co-operation of the countries of the socialist community with the young developing states is constantly widening and growing stronger. The diverse forms of trade and economic ties with the socialist countries based on the principles of equality, non-interference in each other's internal affairs, mutual interest and benefit help the peoples of the young states to build an independent modern economy, to organize the process of extended reproduction on a national basis, to restructure their foreign economic relations.

The development of close co-operation between the socialist and the developing countries makes for the consolidation of peace and international security, and accelerates social progress. It is creating a situation where the process of reshaping international political and economic relations on democratic principles ruling out imperialist dictation is increasingly gaining momentum.

*   *   *

The close political co-operation among the countries of the socialist community, by strengthening each of them and the community as a whole, has turned the socialist world into a powerful factor in international relations. It is making steady progress, providing favourable conditions for socialist and communist construction and contributing to the consolidation of the positions of world socialism. This co-operation is implemented on a multilateral and bilateral basis.

The Warsaw Pact, set up in 1955 in response to the formation of the imperialist military bloc NATO, has greatly contributed to preserving peace during its history of over 25 years. As is pointed out in the document "For Peace, Security, Co-operation and Rapprochement of the Peoples of Europe", adopted in 1975 by representatives of the parliaments of the Pact member states at a meeting in Warsaw to mark the twentieth anniversary of that organization, its members have fought and are fighting actively to achieve an historic objective — to establish a system of relations and obligations effectively safeguarding the peace and security of Europe, to end the cold war, to lessen international tension, to strengthen the political and territorial law and order, which has taken shape as a result of the Second World War and post-war development, to perpetuate the principles of peaceful co-existence in relations between states regardless of differences in their social systems.[17]

Bourgeois ideologists allege that the Warsaw Pact is stepping up tension in Europe and limits the national independence and sovereignty of the socialist countries affiliated with it. The facts, however, completely disprove these slanderous fabrications. For over two decades now the Warsaw Pact has mounted guard over the peace and security of nations throughout the world. As declared by D.F. Ustinov, Politburo member and Defence Minister of the USSR,

> The Warsaw Pact differs radically in its content, aims and tasks from any bourgeois coalitions past or current. As a truly defensive alliance it reliably protects its member states, the interests of peace and socialism. Its formation was a response of the socialist states to the threat from the NATO aggressive bloc founded six years earlier. Progressive mankind has more than once seen for itself how wise and timely it was to have concluded the Warsaw Treaty, what an important role it plays in the maintenance of peace and the security of nations.[18]

The Warsaw Pact takes credit for the failure of many military provocations and conflicts organized by imperialist states.

Backed up by bilateral treaties of friendship, co-operation and mutual assistance between the socialist countries, the Warsaw Pact affords the peoples of all the countries of the socialist community dependable guarantees against imperialist encroachments on their socialist achievements and national sovereignty. By establishing the Warsaw Pact the countries of the socialist community have opposed the forces of imperialism with their combined political and military power. Based on the principles of socialist internationalism and embodying the idea of collective defence of socialist achievements, the Warsaw Pact is at the same time directly related to the task of fundamental restructuring of the entire system of international relations on the principles of peaceful co-existence, since the establishment of a security system in Europe is one of its central goals.

Regarding the Warsaw Pact as a guarantee of peace and security in Europe, the socialist countries unswervingly pursue a policy of strengthening and perfecting this organization in keeping with Lenin's counsel that defence of socialist achievements against the aggressive ambitions of imperialism is one of the laws and prerequisites of success in socialist construction. Had they not established this international alliance, the socialist countries would have found themselves disunited in the face of the imperialist forces united in NATO.

Leonid Brezhnev said in this connection: ''We are firmly against the world's division into opposing military blocs and the arms race. Our attitude on this score is well known. But we must make it clear that as long as the NATO bloc continues to exist and as long as militarist elements continue their arms drive, our country and the other signatories of the Warsaw Treaty will continue to strengthen this political-military alliance.''[19] The other Warsaw Pact member states hold identical views. Nicolae Ceausescu, General Secretary of the RCP and President of the Socialist Republic of Romania, declared at the 12th Congress of the Romanian Communist Party in 1979 that Romania needs military co-operation with the other Warsaw Pact member states for defence against imperialist aggression and for promoting the policy of peace and *détente*.[20]

The activities of the Warsaw Pact are by no means confined to dealing with purely military, defence problems. Operating within its framework is an instrument for political co-operation, the Political Consultative Committee (PCC), which is the Organization's supreme governing body. The PCC operates in compliance with Article 1 of the Treaty, which proclaims the willingness of its signatories to work for guaranteed international peace and security. At its meetings, which are usually attended by top political leaders of the European socialist countries, the PCC takes decisions setting the guidelines for an agreed policy of the socialist community on the international scene.

As was pointed out in the report of the CPSU Central Committee to the 25th Party Congress, ''The Warsaw Pact Political Consultative Committee is an important form of co-operation among leaders of our parties and countries.... . The significance of the initiatives advanced by our Political Consultative Committee in recent years is self-evident. Many of them have been the basis for decisions taken by major international forums or are reflected in a number of important bilateral interstate acts."[21] In particular, the PCC has greatly contributed to formulating a common stand of the socialist countries on the problem of European security. The Warsaw Pact member-states act in concert at the United Nations and other international organizations. This makes for implementation of the aims and principles proclaimed in the Treaty.

As was demonstrated by the anniversary session of the Warsaw Treaty Political Consultative Committee held in Warsaw on 14-15 May 1980, on the threshold of the 'eighties the Warsaw Treaty Organization continues to operate as the key factor of peace in Europe. It consistently comes out in favour of developing and deepening the process of *détente.*

The nations of the socialist community take pains to extend their all-round co-operation. The indestructible militant alliance of the Communist parties of the socialist countries, their common world outlook and common aims are the basis for this close co-operation, its spirit and guiding force. Today the ties between the fraternal parties present an impressive picture of deep-going, diverse and regular contacts between thousands upon thousands of fighters for their common cause, of builders of socialism and communism — ranging from party leaders to executives of local party organizations, down to those of factories and collective farms. These ties ensure a valuable exchange of experience, helping towards more confident progress and multiplying common forces. The leaders of the Communist parties of the socialist community of nations maintain permanent contacts among themselves. Co-operation between these parties is free of any division into dominating and subordinate countries, into parties which give orders and those that take them. However, the immense political experience of the CPSU in the domestic and international spheres has made it the most prestigious party among the Communist parties of the socialist community of nations. Erich Honecker of Germany has said that the CPSU is "the most battle-hardened and experienced contingent of the international Communist movement. Therefore, our

Party has always regarded constant strengthening of its close militant alliance with the Party of Lenin as the main criterion of proletarian internationalism.''[22] Regular meetings between leaders of the Communist parties of the socialist countries, both bilateral and multilateral, make possible joint work in mapping out the paths of further progress towards a lasting peace and communism.

Of paramount importance among them are the Crimean meetings between First and General Secretaries of the Central Committees of the Communist Parties of the European socialist countries and the Mongolian People's Republic. In the course of their discussions a programme is drawn up for concerted action of the fraternal parties and countries on the international scene. The significance of these meetings is crucial not only to the socialist community of nations but also to the cause of peace throughout the world.

For instance, in July and August 1979 Leonid Brezhnev had friendly meetings in the Crimea with Gustav Husak, Erich Honecker, Nicolae Ceausescu, Edward Gierek, Todor Zhivkov and Yumjagiyn Tsedenbal. Along with the talks General Secretary Brezhnev had with János Kadar during the visit of a Soviet party and government delegation to the Hungarian People's Republic on 30 May — 1 June 1979, the Crimean meetings and discussions of 1979 were an important stage in further strengthening co-operation between the fraternal countries in fulfilling both domestic and international tasks. As was pointed out in a resolution of the Central Committee of the Soviet Communist Party, the Crimean meetings of 1979 again demonstrated the unshakeable allegiance of the fraternal socialist states to the policy of peace and peaceful co-operation. A consistent line of curbing and winding down the arms race, a clear-cut orientation on *détente,* on supplementing political with military *détente* — such are the vital directions of socialist foreign policy which were strongly reaffirmed in the course of the Crimean meetings.[23]

The 25th Congress of the CPSU was a striking demonstration of the indissoluble unity of parties and countries of the socialist community, and of the world Communist movement as a whole. In their numerous messages of greetings to the Congress, the Communist party leaders emphasized the importance of the mission history had assigned to the CPSU and the world's first socialist state. Rodney Arismendi, First

Secretary of the Central Committee of the Uruguayan Communist Party, said in particular: '

> Many new facts in world development have shown that the USSR and the CPSU continue to be the main bulwark in the fight of the peoples for peace, independence, democracy and socialism.
>
> In saying this we do not underestimate the independence and patriotic character of each concrete revolution or deny the historical and political distinctiveness and independence of each party. We only emphasize what has been created by history itself, what is of decisive importance to the present alignment of world forces and is vital for the strategy of the three main revolutionary streams of modern times, and what is inseparable from proletarian internationalism.[24]

In his speech at the 25th Congress of the CPSU, Le Duan, First Secretary of the Vietnam Party of Labour, said: "Today the Soviet Union is the mightiest socialist power of the world. It has played, and plays now, an exceptionally great role in strengthening the might of the revolutionary forces of our time. It renders support to the national liberation movement, to the struggle for democracy and social progress, frustrates the incendiary plots of imperialism, and upholds peace in Europe and all over the world."[25]

The Soviet Union plays a special part among the countries of the socialist community not as a "superpower", which allegedly ignores the interests of its "junior partners", but as a truly great power, which blazed the trail towards socialism and bears the brunt of the struggle against the forces of reaction and war. Referring to the special role of the CPSU and the Soviet Union in strengthening the unity of the countries of the socialist community and the significance of their unity as a guarantee of foreign-policy successes of the GDR, Erich Honecker declared at the 9th Congress of the SUPG in May 1976: "Relying on the solid political, economic and military potential of the Soviet Union and the fraternal socialist countries rallied around it, our joint foreign policy has scored historic successes during the last five years.... . The socialist German Democratic Republic has won broad international recognition. The GDR works on an equal footing at the United Nations and other international organizations and maintains diplomatic relations with 121 states."[26]

The growing unity and cohesion of the fraternal socialist countries enable them to influence more and more effectively the development of international relations, to reduce the opportunities for the capitalist powers to pursue an imperialist policy. As one of the most remarkable phenomena of the present era, the socialist community of nations is a factor making an increasingly crucial and indelible imprint on all international affairs today. It is precisely the unity of the countries of the socialist community, which has augmented the power of world socialism and its prestige and influence on international affairs, that ensures, as in the past, the maintenance of peace, curbing imperialism, nipping in the bud its attempts to restore capitalism in individual socialist countries and to suppress the national liberation movement.

The co-ordination of the foreign policies of the fraternal socialist countries and their strong alliance have greatly added to their influence on world development. Today practically all steps of any importance for promoting peace and mutually beneficial co-operation between states are associated directly or indirectly with the initiatives and active joint moves of the socialist states. The role played by the entire socialist community as a decisive factor in the development and restructuring of the global system of interstate relations is growing, along with the consolidation of the national sovereignty and independence and the enhancement of the international prestige of each socialist country.[27]

Aware of the fact that the unity of the socialist countries is the main force in the struggle for peace and for the establishment of principles of peaceful co-existence in international relations, its opponents are trying to split the socialist community of nations. Bourgeois anti-communist propaganda backs nationalism, regarding it as irresistible. In a book significantly entitled *Nationalism — the Last Stage of Communism,* the American Sovietologist E. Lengyel calls for fomenting nationalist sentiment and estrangement in relations between the socialist countries, for encouraging their "independence" from the USSR.[28] In another American book published in 1972 it is alleged that "an underlying disarray of the conflicting and ever more differentiated interests of national communist élites" exists in the socialist commonwealth of the COMECON countries.[29] A number of foreign authors persistently peddle the idea of a "loosening" allegedly taking place in the alliance of the socialist member countries of COMECON and the Warsaw Pact as a result of the increased sentiments of "national egoism" in the socialist community of nations.

These fabrications are disproved by the realities. As was declared at the 25th CPSU Congress, in the socialist world "...the overall tendency is unquestionably characterized by a growing cohesion of socialist countries".[30] The biased interpretation by ideologists of anti-communism of the problems and development prospects of the socialist community of nations is scientifically untenable and speculative in character. The profound and steadily growing friendly ties between Party and state organs, between collectives and enterprises, research institutions, public organizations, among millions upon millions of citizens allow to speak of an entirely new phenomenon — a genuine fraternal alliance of peoples, united by common convictions and common aims.

Ideological subversion by anti-Communists lends special importance to developing co-operation among the countries of the socialist community in the ideological field as well. It plays a great part in the ideological education of the working people, in the struggle against bourgeois and revisionist ideology. Conferences of Central Committee secretaries in charge of international and ideological affairs have become routine. They were held in Prague (March 1975), Warsaw (January 1976), Sofia (March 1977), Budapest (February-March 1978), and Berlin (1979). These conferences discuss the key directions of co-operation in the field of ideological work, co-ordinate the positions of parties and countries on many foreign policy problems. All this helps consolidate the socialist community of nations, enhance its prestige on the world arena, where it acts as the main force in reshaping international relations.

The successes in the struggle against imperialism, for peace and socialism will indisputably grow along with the further consolidation of the power and unity of the fraternal socialist countries. Therefore, a first priority is to expose and struggle relentlessly against those who are undermining the unity of the socialist community of nations. The accomplishment of this task will have a crucial bearing on the continued enhancement of the role played by the socialist community in international relations.

*   *   *

M.A. Suslov, Politburo member and Secretary of the CPSU Central Committee, has written:

> A crucial feature of our time is that all world development is taking place under the decisive influence of existing socialism. . . . .
>
> First, there are the great historical achievements of victorious socialism and, at the same time, the increasingly favourable external and internal conditions for their further development, for the successful unfolding of the working people's class struggle in the capitalist world, for new victories of the democratic and national liberation movements, for decisive social changes both in the citadels of capitalism and in the extensive world zone that was once imperialism's colonial hinterland and reserve and has now become an important springboard of social progress.
>
> Second, objective prerequisites have formed for the restructuring of the entire system of international relations on the principles of peaceful coexistence of countries with differing social systems, for ensuring complete equality and mutually advantageous co-operation between all countries and peoples, and, above all, for ridding humanity forever of the danger of a world war.[31]

The change in the alignment of forces of the two social systems in the world arena is the decisive factor in moving the leaders of the bourgeois world from positions of the Cold War to those of peaceful co-existence. Today it has become crystal clear to them that it is impossible to settle the historical dispute between capitalism and socialism by force of arms, that the continued stepping up of international tension is senseless and extremely dangerous.

The consolidation of the positions of the Soviet Union and other countries of the socialist community has confirmed Lenin's vision of a future when socialism would be ". . .capable of exercising a decisive influence upon world politics as a whole",[32] and has lent a new dimension to the role played by the masses in present-day international relations. There is an unprecedented increase in the involvement of the general public in solving the problems of war and peace, which is striking evidence of democratization of world politics.

The ruling circles of the West find it increasingly difficult and at times simply impossible to take major foreign-policy decisions ignoring public opinion. Thus *New Dimensions of World Politics,* recently published in the West, admits that there are internal restraints in Western societies. An ethic of anti-militarism intensely held by part of the population in the West has to some extent put a higher cost on the use of force by political leaders.[33]

Public participation in world politics takes the form of mass movements for peace, for disarmament, and so on. Current changes in the world situation and the changeover to *détente* are mainly the result of activities of the public at large. The active interest of the general public in international affairs is stimulated by their awareness of the fact that wars, particularly the world wars, were appalling disasters for the peoples. Today, when enormous stockpiles of thermonuclear weapons have been built up, threatening whole countries and peoples with extinction, when the life of every human being on earth depends on the maintenance of peace, we see a sharp increase in public concern for a negotiated settlement of international problems. In addition, active popular interest in world developments is stimulated by the development of improved mass communication facilities, the advancement of the working people's educational standards and self-awareness.

All this is primarily associated with the course of social development itself, mankind's entry into a period of transition from capitalism to socialism. Marx and Engels wrote that "Together with the thoroughness of the historical action, the size of the mass whose action it is will increase".[34]

The exploiter classes have always sought and still seek today to debar the general public from discussion and settlement of the major problems of international relations, to guard the sphere of foreign policy against interference by the "mob", and to plan this policy regardless of the interests of those concerned most of all — the ordinary working people.

It is a great achievement of Soviet foreign policy that it stimulates the awakening of the masses, their involvement in the active struggle for peace and the prevention of war. From the early days of Soviet government its foreign policy has been characterized by an appeal not only to governments but also to peoples. Motivated entirely by the interests of the working class and all working people, Soviet foreign policy is addressed, as in the past, to the mass of the people. This aspect of Soviet foreign policy has been calumniated by bourgeois ideologists quick to label as "propaganda" the Soviet Union's proposals of the most radical character meeting the interests of all nations. It was precisely the profoundly democratic essence of such initiatives and the broad public response they evoked that so much irritated and confused the imperialist foreign policy-makers. Such was repeatedly the case, for instance, with the Soviet proposals for general and complete disarmament. The constructive initiatives of Soviet diplomacy, which are easily understood as meeting their interests by millions of people in all countries, are supported by all democratic, progressive, and peace forces and stimulate their activity in the sphere of international affairs.

It is a fact that the present-day system of international relations functions in a situation where the masses are more deeply involved in world politics than ever before. Today this involvement is so great that political leaders of the capitalist countries are obliged to solicit public support for their foreign-policy moves. Hence the increased attention to mass media and propaganda and the intensified efforts to manipulate public opinion and canalize it in the required direction.

The Communist and Workers' parties in the capitalist countries play a crucial part in the massive anti-war movement, which itself has assumed a new qualitative dimension. Among its activists are people from all walks of life holding diverse political views, including members of the business community. This is further vivid evidence of the widened social base to the massive peace movement. The mass movements have left an imprint on the settlement of major international issues. Their demands and their influence were taken into account in concluding the international treaties banning nuclear tests in the atmosphere, outer space and under water, nuclear weapons proliferation, etc. The massive campaigns for ending the American war of aggression in Vietnam and for calling an all-European conference on security and co-operation became an influential factor in world politics. The Moscow Congress of Peace Forces, the Brussels Assembly of Representatives of Public Opinion for European Security, the World Women's Congress in Berlin, whose noble principles united dozens of mass movements, parties, and public organizations, have left their mark on the development of modern international relations.

Addressing the 1973 World Congress of Peace Forces in Moscow, Leonid Brezhnev, who is an outstanding peace champion and a winner of the Lenin International Peace Prize and the Joliot–Curie Prize of the World Peace Council, declared: ''...the present changes in the world situation are largely the result of the activities of public forces, of the hitherto unparalleled activity of the people, who are displaying sharp intolerance of arbitrary rule and aggression and an unbending will for peace."[35] The CPSU and the Soviet Government highly appreciate the contribution of the mass public movement for peace and facilitate in every way its development, expansion, and consolidation.

The role played in the present-day international relations by the developing countries is discussed in a later chapter. We only emphasize here that their struggle against imperialism, colonialism and neo-colonialism has also become an important factor in restructuring the world system of international relations. The role of these countries in the common struggle for peace and the security of nations was duly appreciated in the report of the CPSU Central Committee to the 25th Party Congress.

Such are the objective prerequisites and factors which necessitate and make it possible to subject world politics to radical reforms, whose essence was described in the resolution "For Peace, Security, Co-operation and Social Progress in Europe" adopted by the Conference of European Communist and Workers' Parties. The resolution said: "The democratization of international relations and the development of international co-operation on the basis of equality and of mutual benefit to all peoples are aims of great importance in the struggle for the establishment of an international community free from imperialism and neo-colonialism."[36]

The record of history shows that the objective necessity of peaceful co-existence of states having different social systems does not materialize by itself. A force is required to translate this objective trend of international development into reality. This force is the foreign policy pursued jointly by the Soviet Union, the homeland of the October Revolution, with other countries of the socialist community. Having assessed the overall alignment of forces in the world, the CPSU concluded that it was possible to achieve a radical improvement in the international situation, then clearly defined the main tasks to be accomplished on the way towards this objective and set them out in the historic Peace Programme of its 24th Congress. These tasks were later developed and finalized in the Programme of further struggle for peace and international co-operation, for national freedom and independence that was adopted by the 25th CPSU Congress. These comprehensive programmes are designed to bring about an improvement of the world political climate, a restructuring of the global system of international relations to establish on earth a truly lasting and just peace for the present and future generations of men and eventually to banish war from the life of human society once and for all.

The Foreign-policy Programme of the CPSU as the Basis for Reshaping International Relations

The CPSU and the world Communist movement as a whole have defined with scientific precision the essence of the changes which have taken place in the world and the prospects they have opened up in order on this basis to draw up a concrete programme of struggle for peace, to begin practical work in reshaping international relations on the principles of peaceful co-existence of states with different social systems. The problems of war and peace, the concept of peaceful co-existence were elaborated in depth in the resolutions of the 19th and 20th CPSU Congresses and in the documents of the Meetings of Communist and Workers' Parties in 1957 and 1960. The conclusion to the effect that forces capable of preventing a global war had come on the world scene was of fundamental significance.

The Programme of the CPSU adopted by its 22nd Congress in October 1961 formulated the central goals of Soviet foreign policy: to secure a situation of peace for building a communist society in the USSR and developing the world socialist system and, acting in concert with all peace-loving nations, to deliver mankind from the menace of nuclear holocaust. It indicated that forces capable of preserving and promoting universal peace have arisen and are growing in the world. Possibilities are arising for essentially new relations between states.

Imperialism knows no relations between states other than those of domination and subordination, of oppression of the weak by the strong. It bases international relations on dictatorialness and intimidation, on violence and arbitrary rule. It regards wars of aggression as a natural means of settling international issues. For the imperialist countries, diplomacy has been and remains a tool for imposing their will upon other nations and preparing wars.

Socialism opposes imperialism with a fundamentally different policy. As is stated in the Programme of the CPSU, its underlying principles of peace, equality, self-determination of nations, and respect for the independence and sovereignty of all countries, as well as the honest and humane methods of socialist diplomacy, are exerting a growing influence on the world situation. Today, when imperialism has ceased to dominate international relations while the socialist system is playing a steadily growing role, when the influence of states which have won their national independence and of the general public in capitalist countries has increased, there is a realistic possibility for the new principles advanced by socialism to triumph over the principles of aggressive imperialist policy. A situation where not only large but also small states, where the countries which have taken the path of independent development, where all states aspiring towards peace regardless of their strength are capable of pursuing an independent policy, has arisen for the first time in history. Emphasizing that peaceful co-existence of the socialist and capitalist countries is an objective necessity for the development of human society, that war cannot and must not serve as a means of settling international disputes, the Programme of the CPSU formulates the following tasks in the field of foreign relations: to prevent another world war and create the requisite conditions for banishing war from the life of society, for establishing "healthful international relations", and for general and complete disarmament under effective international control. "The CPSU and the Soviet people as a whole will continue to oppose all wars of conquest, including wars between capitalist countries and local wars aimed at strangling popular emancipation movements, and consider it their duty to support the sacred struggle of the oppressed peoples and their just anti-imperialist wars of liberation."[37]

The meeting of European Communist and Workers' Parties at Karlovy Vary in April 1967, after analysing the developing international situation, declared: "The experience of the last few years has borne out the Communists' thesis to the effect that another world war is not inevitable and can be prevented by the joint efforts of the world socialist community, the international working class, all states opposed to war and all peace forces. These forces have grown considerably."[38] The Cold War conceptions had proved untenable. The aggressive policy of imperialism had been undermined by the active foreign policy of the socialist countries. In the interest of setting up an international security system based on the principles of peaceful co-existence of states having different social systems, the meeting resolved to work for securing a recognition of the existing realities in post-war Europe, namely, the inviolability of the present frontiers, the existence of the two sovereign and equal German states — the GDR and the FRG — and the invalidity of the Munich Agreement from the time of its conclusion. In the interest of securing the development of peaceful relations and co-operation among all European states on the principle of respect for their sovereignty and equality, it was necessary to press for a treaty to be concluded renouncing the use or threat of force in inter-state relations, and settling all disputes exclusively by peaceful means; and also for a nuclear weapons non-proliferation treaty as an important step in the direction of ending the arms race. The forum of European Communist and Workers' parties also supported the proposal for convening a conference of all European states on security and peaceful co-operation in Europe.

Describing the significance of the meeting of representatives from twenty-four Communist and Workers' parties of Europe, the Czechoslovak Foreign Minister B. Chnoupek writes that the conference at Karlovy Vary "produced a programme of action to restructure relations among European states and set up a collective security system on the principles of peaceful co-existence".[39]

The Communist Party of the Soviet Union also made a substantial contribution to working out the programme of anti-imperialist struggle adopted by the international Meeting of Communist and Workers' parties in Moscow in June 1969. The Meeting emphatically declared that imperialism was powerless to regain its lost historical initiative, to reverse the world development; that the high road of mankind's progress was indicated by the world socialist system, the international working class, and by all revolutionary forces. The struggle for world peace is a major component of the concerted actions of the anti-imperialist forces.

The defence of peace is inseparably linked up with the struggle to compel the imperialists to accept peaceful co-existence of states having different social systems, which demands observance of the principles of sovereignty, equality, territorial inviolability of every state, big and small, and non-interference in the internal affairs of other countries, respect for the right of every people freely to choose their social, economic and political system, and the settlement of outstanding international issues by political means through negotiation.[40]

The participants reaffirmed the task of complete eradication of colonialism and prevention of its revival in a new disguise.

In a speech on 14 June 1974 Leonid Brezhnev declared: "An appraisal of the general alignment of forces in the world led us several years ago to the conclusion that a real opportunity existed for bringing about a fundamental change in the international situation."[41] It was precisely the purpose of the Peace Programme drawn up by the 24th Congress of the CPSU held in March-April 1971 to achieve a change in the development of international relations, relying on the power, cohesion, and activity of world socialism, on its growing unity with all progressive and peace forces. That is a turn away from the Cold War to a relaxation of world tension, which marks the start of a fundamental restructuring of international relations. Just as the Leninist foreign policy the Peace Programme is permeated with humanism, with concern for the welfare of men and their right to live in peace. It is a programme of action for influencing the international situation to guarantee a truly lasting peace on earth for many generations of men.

The Peace Programme is a document of great historic significance and tremendous revolutionizing force. Based on the Leninist conception of peaceful co-existence of states having different social systems, it reflects the organic unity of the struggle for peace with the struggle for social progress, the objective requirements of world development and the central aims of Soviet foreign policy. To banish war from human affairs, to allow every people to shape its own destiny in freedom, to curb the imperialist aggressors, to outlaw the use or threat of force in international relations — such are the tasks facing the progressive forces as formulated in the Peace Programme. Meeting the aspirations of the people in the socialist countries, the international working class and the national liberation movement, the Peace Programme has a class character inherent in Soviet foreign policy.

The Peace Programme sets out a wide range of tasks demanding immediate attention:

1. To stamp out the seeds of war in South-east Asia and in the Middle East and facilitate a political settlement in these regions on the principles of respect for the legitimate rights of states and peoples exposed to aggression. To give an immediate and determined rebuff to any acts of aggression and violence on the international scene, taking full advantage of the UN machinery. To renounce the use or threat of force to settle issues under dispute by concluding instead appropriate bilateral or regional treaties.

2. To proceed from the final recognition of the territorial changes in Europe as a result of the Second World War, to achieve a radical swing to a relaxation of tension and peace on this continent, to secure the convocation and success of an all-European conference. To do everything possible to guarantee collective security in Europe. At the same time, the Soviet Union reaffirmed its willingness, expressed jointly with the other signatories to the defensive Warsaw Pact, to disband the Pact at such time as the North Atlantic Treaty Organization should do so, or as a first step, to abolish their military organizations.

3. To conclude treaties banning nuclear, chemical, and bacteriological weapons. To press for a universal end to nuclear weapons tests, including underground tests. To help establish nuclear-free zones in various regions of the world. To work for nuclear disarmament of all nuclear powers, and for calling a conference of the five nuclear powers — the USSR, the USA, China, France, and Britain — to resolve this problem.

4. To step up the struggle for ending the race in the production of armaments of all kinds, to call a World Conference to discuss the disarmament problems in their entirety, to dismantle military bases in foreign territories, to reduce the armed forces and armaments in the areas where military confrontaton is particularly dangerous, primarily in Central Europe. To work out measures lessening the risk of accidental breakout or preconceived arrangement of military conflicts and their growth into international crises and war. To negotiate a reduction in military spending, of the larger states in the first instance.

5. To insist on the complete implementation of the UN resolutions on the abolition of the surviving colonial regimes, to subject racism

and apartheid to universal denunciation and to boycott their remaining outposts.

6. To deepen relations between states on the basis of mutually beneficial co-operation in all fields, including the efforts to solve such problems as environmental protection, harnessing of energy and other natural resources, development of transport and communications, prevention and eradication of the most dangerous and widespread diseases, research and exploration of outer space and the World Ocean.

The Peace Programme ushered in a new phase in the foreign policy of the Soviet Union. It owes its distinctive character to its active combative spirit. The Soviet Union countered the aggressive policy of imperialists with its own policy of active defence of peace and strengthening international security. Foreign Minister Andrei Gromyko pointed out in this context that the Peace Programme was intended to contribute actively to a radical improvement in the world political climate, to a restructuring of the entire system of international relations so as to establish on earth a truly durable and just peace for many generations of men and eventually to banish war from the life of human society.[42]

That is why it was given support by the mass of the people throughout the world. All the nations of the socialist community embraced it as their own programme and did their utmost to help implement it. The developing countries expressed their full support. The leaders of the capitalist world had to give serious consideration to the Soviet Peace Programme, which indicated a way to lead international relations out of the stalemate of the Cold War to the broad expanses of peaceful co-operation of states belonging to the two opposite socio-economic systems. It became perfectly clear to them that a relaxation of international tensions was the only alternative to nuclear war.

However, the CPSU, the fraternal parties of the socialist community, and all peace forces had to exert tremendous efforts to achieve success in implementing this historic Programme, which made the early 'seventies a turning-point in world politics, a new stage in the development of international relations.

The progress in implementing the Peace Programme was primarily the result of the growing and deepening influence of the socialist states on the international situation. Speaking at the 25th CPSU Congress, Leonid Brezhnev pointed out that "...the socialist countries' influence on world affairs is becoming ever stronger and deeper. That. . . is a great boon to mankind as a whole, to all those who aspire to freedom, equality, independence, peace and progress."[43] The years between the 24th and 25th Congresses of the CPSU were a period of steady advance of the socialist countries, of consolidation of friendship, unity and cohesion among them, tending to augment their influence in the modern world.

The progress in implementing the Peace Programme, the beginning transition from the Cold War to *détente* allowed the Party to formulate new foreign-policy tasks in further efforts to reshape the system of international relations. After a profound and comprehensive analysis of the results of the foreign-policy activities carried out by the Party and the Soviet State in the period since the last congress, the 25th CPSU Congress revealed the main tendencies in present-day world development and mapped out the path of further struggle for peace and international co-operation, for the freedom and independence of nations. The Congress reaffirmed the foreign-policy line charted by the Party, declaring that the policy of *détente* would be pursued with still greater determination so as to curb the aggressive, reactionary forces, consolidate universal peace, guarantee the rights of the peoples to freedom, independence, and social progress. The Programme set forth by the 25th Congress as a logical extension of the Peace Programme is thoroughly realistic and based on an in-depth analysis of realities. At the same time, it is pervaded with a spirit of optimism and faith in the possibility of a lasting peace being established on earth. Guided by the Party's experience and assessment of the specific international situation which had taken shape towards the mid-seventies, the Programme sets the guidelines for all peace forces to accomplish the pressing difficult but perfectly feasible tasks facing them.

The Programme of further struggle for peace and international co-operation, for the freedom and independence of nations adopted by the 25th CPSU Congress as a logical extension of the Peace Programme advanced by the 24th Congress sets out the following crucially important tasks as matters of top priority:

1. While steadily strengthening the unity of the fraternal socialist states and developing their all-round co-operation in the construction of a new society, to increase their active joint contribution to the consolidation of peace.

2. To press for an end to the growing arms race fraught with the danger of war and for a switch to a reduction of arms stockpiles and to disarmament. For this purpose:

(a) to do whatever is necessary to complete preparations for a new agreement between the USSR and the USA on strategic arms limitation and reduction, to conclude international treaties for a total and universal ban on nuclear weapons tests, for banning and destruction of chemical weapons, for banning the development of new weapons types and systems of mass destruction, as well as for a ban on modifying the natural environment for military and other hostile purposes;

(b) to undertake new efforts to stimulate talks on troop and arms reduction in Central Europe. After reaching agreement on first practical steps in this direction, to continue in the years to come the cause of *détente* in the aforesaid region;

(c) to work for a transition from the current constant increase in the military spending of many states to its steady reduction;

(d) to take whatever steps are necessary to have a World Disarmament Conference convened as early as possible.

3. To pool the efforts of peace-loving nations to stamp out the remaining seeds of war, primarily to achieve a just and lasting peace settlement in the Middle East. In the context of such settlement, the states concerned are to consider the question of ending the arms race in the Middle East.

4. To do whatever is necessary to deepen *détente,* to have it embodied in concrete forms of mutually beneficial co-operation among states. To pursue actively a line towards implementing the Final Act of the All-European Conference to develop peaceful co-operation in Europe. In accordance with the principles of peaceful co-existence to continue consistent efforts to develop mutually beneficial long-term co-operation with capitalist states in various fields — political, economic, scientific, and cultural.

5. To work for security in Asia to be guaranteed by the joint efforts of states of that continent.

6. To campaign for the conclusion of a World Treaty on the Non-Use of Force in International Relations.

7. To deal as a matter of first priority with the crucial international task of eradicating all vestiges of the system of colonial oppression, all restriction of the equality and independence of nations, all remaining enclaves of colonialism and racism.

8. To press for an end to discrimination and all artificial obstacles to international trade, all manifestations of inequality, dictatorialness, and exploitation in international economic relations.

The programme of further struggle for peace and international co-operation, for the freedom and independence of nations advanced by the 25th CPSU Congress reflects not only the Soviet Union's ardent desire for peace, the consistency of its peace policy, but also the realistic character of Soviet foreign policy, which formulates practical tasks meeting the pressing demands of the times. It reflects Lenin's call for "...the greatest possible number of ... decisions and measures that would certainly lead to peace, if not to the complete elimination of the war danger".[44] The Programme is further conclusive evidence of the loyalty of the CPSU to the Leninist principles and traditions of Soviet foreign policy, the continuity of its line on the international scene. The purpose of the Programme is to take full advantage of the changes which have taken place in the world so as to reinforce and deepen the process of *détente,* to make it irreversible, to encourage practical restructuring of international relations on the principles of peaceful co-existence of states having different social systems.

The Constitution of the USSR, adopted on the eve of the 60th anniversary of the October Revolution, contains a programme of foreign policy. This historic document lends the force of law to the principles and aims of Soviet foreign policy. As laid down in the Constitution, the Soviet State consistently pursues the Leninist peace policy, coming out for strengthening the security of nations and broad international co-operation. The aims of Soviet foreign policy are to provide favourable conditions for building communism in the USSR, to consolidate the positions of world socialism, to support the struggle of the peoples for national liberation and social progress, to prevent wars of aggression, to achieve general and complete disarmament and to implement consistently the principle of peaceful co-existence of states with different social systems. The Constitution of the USSR forbids war propaganda.

The Constitution clearly brings into focus the class-motivated, revolutionary character of Soviet foreign policy stemming from the very nature of the socialist state. The class basis for Soviet foreign policy today is the well-harmonized interests of all Soviet people — a new historical community of men with the working class in the vanguard. As the Soviet State developed from a dictatorship of the proletariat into a state of the whole people, the social-class foundation of this policy widened, since it came to rely on the support not only of the working class but also of the people as a whole. The expansion and consolidation of the social foundation of Soviet foreign policy are a legitimate process reflecting the steady advance of society in the period of transition from socialism to communism.

The Constitution of the USSR declares that the Soviet Union as a component part of the world socialist system, of the socialist community, develops and strengthens friendship and co-operation, comradely mutual assistance with the socialist countries on the principles of socialist internationalism, and is actively involved in economic integration and the international socialist division of labour.

The Soviet Union's relations with other states, this historic document declares, are based on the following principles: mutual renunciation of the use or threat of force; sovereign equality; peaceful settlement of disputes; non-interference in internal affairs; respect for human rights and fundamental freedoms; the equality and right of nations to shape their own destinies; co-operation among states; scrupulous fulfilment of obligations arising from the universally recognized principles and standards of international law, and from international treaties concluded by the Soviet Union.

Thus, the increase in the power of socialism, primarily of the largest socialist state — the Soviet Union — the consistent policy of the Soviet Government and the CPSU and of the governments and parties of the fraternal socialist countries have brought about changes in international relations, set the stage for *détente* and made it the leading trend in world politics. It is precisely socialism steadily intensifying its influence on the process of social development, that is the crucial factor in reshaping the world order initiated by the October Revolution of 1917.

7

Political and Military *Détente* —
The Key Issues of World Politics

As THE world was moving into the 1970s, deep-seated processes of social development set the stage for major radical moves towards restructuring the global system of international relations. Clearly, without the energetic and purposeful effort made by progressive forces, above all by the socialist countries, and without the salutary effect they had on the overall international situation neither the objective laws governing world development nor the positive trends they had set in motion would have been able to come into play to the extent they did.

As K.Y. Chernenko, member of the Politburo of the CPSU Central Committee, pointed out: "It is a salient feature of the CPSU's work that its domestic and foreign policies form an integrated whole. They are closely bound up with each other, interdependent and directed towards the achievement of a common goal. The Party's home policy is geared to the realization of its policy slogan 'Everything in the name of man, everything for the benefit of man'.[1] To secure the most favourable external conditions for the successful tackling of this task, the CPSU has been steadily working to consolidate peace and international security, to expand friendly co-operation among nations and to maintain peaceful co-existence with capitalist countries. This policy has produced excellent results.

Positive Shifts in World Politics

Let us look at some of the tangible results of the Soviet Union's foreign policy and its work on implementing its Peace Programme which give us reason to regard the 1970s as marking a new important stage in the evolution of international relations. First of all there has been the victory of the people of Vietnam over US imperialism. Imperialism's biggest venture since the end of the Second World War aimed at bringing to its knees a socialist country and at suppressing a national-liberation revolution, failed dismally. The victory of the Vietnamese has unified the two Vietnams into the Socialist Republic of Vietnam. Vietnam's victory opened up new horizons before the whole of South-east Asia. Following Vietnam, Laos and Cambodia won their freedom. Le Duan emphasized that the total victory in the war against US aggression for the salvation of the homeland was "inseparable from the powerful support and all-round, vast, valuable and effective assistance of the Soviet Union".[2]

Thus the historic victories the peoples of Indo-China won over imperialism with reliance on all-round support and assistance from the Soviet Union and other socialist countries opened up the prospect of enlarging the family of socialist states, of more countries and peoples taking the path of socialist development.

The termination of US aggression and the withdrawal of the combined forces of the USA and its satellites from South Vietnam, which had failed to break the heroic resistance of the Vietnamese, were undoubtedly a consequence of the general weakening of imperialism and its inability to stem the tide of national and social liberation by force of arms.

The task of destroying the seeds of war in the world which the Soviet Union set itself in its Peace Programme also applies to the situation in the Middle East where an explosive situation persists. The year 1973 saw yet another flare-up of hostilities in the area caused, like the preceding three wars, by Israel's policy of aggression and annexation. In conditions of *détente* that prevailed at the time it became possible on that occasion to extinguish hostilities relatively quickly, but secure peace in the area can only be achieved if Israel pulls out of the Arab lands it has conquered, restores the legitimate rights of the Arab people of Palestine, and lets them create a national state of their own, guaranteeing in all this the security of all states in the area.

The peoples of the world highly rate the contribution made by the socialist countries, above all by the Soviet Union, to the effort of eliminating military conflicts and seeds of tension. Addressing the 25th CPSU Congress, Fidel Castro said:

> By firmly adhering to Lenin's ideas, the USSR has grown into the most reliable bastion of world peace and at the same time into the most reliable shield protecting small and weak nations from imperialism's aggressive ambitions. But for the existence of the Soviet Union the capitalist powers faced with a shortage of raw materials and an energy crisis would have immediately started a fresh scramble for a redivision of the world. Had it not been for the Soviet Union it would have been impossible to even conceive of either the measure of independence the smaller nations are enjoying today, or the successful struggle of the peoples for winning back control over natural resources or their powerful voice in the concert of nations. The extent to which peace has now been assured, the great privilege the new generations of men now enjoy, having avoided the fate of being plunged into the abyss of a world holocaust, the hope for a future in which the co-operation of all nations will be established — the peoples owe all this, above all, to the triumph of Lenin's ideas in your country and their consistent implementation in Soviet foreign policy.[3]

The changes that occurred in alignment of forces on the international scene strengthened the positions of socialism in Europe where the trend towards *détente* and consolidation of peace has been particularly in evidence. Nor is it a matter of chance. It is in Europe that socialism has the strongest positions and the concerted policy of the socialist countries has made the most impact. The recognition of the German Democratic Republic's sovereignty in international law, something that socialist countries had steadily worked for during more than 20 years, the bankruptcy of the notorious Holstein Doctrine came as a major victory for the international political line of the socialist countries. The establishment of normal diplomatic relations between the GDR and FRG and the admission of both German states to the United Nations served to consolidate the positions of socialism in the world and also contributed to the establishment in European affairs of the principles of co-operation based on full equality and mutual benefit, making the United Nations a more universal organization in line with the provisions of its Charter. Apart from that, the recognition in international law of the Western frontiers of the GDR, Poland, and Czechoslovakia and the acceptance of the shameful Munich deal as null and void from the first were of major importance. In this way the formal seal was put on the most important results of the struggle of European peoples for liberation during and after the Second World War. Speaking of the socialist countries' joint struggle on the international scene in recent years General Secretary Husak of the Czechoslovak Communist Party said: "We are greatly satisfied with the fact that the co-ordinated actions of the countries of the socialist community to implement the Peace Programme mapped out by the 24th CPSU Congress, have contributed decisively to bringing about positive shifts in the international situation and consolidating the international position of the Czechoslovak Socialist Republic."[4]

A powerful blow has been dealt at the intrigues of West German militarists and revanchists who for a quarter of a century had poisoned the European atmosphere by refusing to recognize the historical realities that took shape during the post-war period. The ground has been prepared for a stable peace and good-neighbourly co-operation in Europe and beyond it. Today, the inviolability of European countries is a principle recognized by all who signed the Final Act of the Helsinki Conference on Security and Co-operation in Europe — in effect all the European countries with the addition of the USA and Canada. In the words of the Final Act: "...The participating States regard as inviolable one another's frontiers as well as the frontiers of all states in Europe, and therefore they will refrain now and in the future from assaulting these frontiers." (Translated from the Russian.)[5]

Socialism is now firmly established in Cuba whose prestige and standing in the world have grown. The imperialists' attempts to isolate the republic and to impose an economic blockade on it have failed, largely because of the help and assistance the young socialist republic received from the socialist countries.

Among the outstanding achievements of the socialist countries' co-ordinated foreign policy is the holding of a successful conference on security and co-operation in Europe with the participation of the USA and Canada. After long and tough negotiations, the Helsinki Conference on 1 August 1975 adopted an historic document which was signed by the heads of thirty-three European states, the USA and

Canada. This document which represents a collective understanding on a wide range of pressing problems formulated the following ten principles which the Conference participants undertook to observe in European affairs:

1. sovereign equality, respect for the rights inherent in sovereignty;
2. refraining from the threat or use of force;
3. inviolability of frontiers;
4. territorial integrity of states;
5. peaceful settlement of disputes;
6. non-intervention in internal affairs;
7. respect for human rights and fundamental freedoms, including the freedom of thought, conscience, religion, or belief;
8. equal rights and self-determination of peoples;
9. co-operation among states;
10. fulfilment in good faith of obligations under international law.[6]

It should be emphasized that the Soviet Union is the only country in the world which has incorporated all ten principles in its Constitution as a basis for its relations with other countries. This is the way the Soviet Union has translated into reality the provisions of the Final Act.

The adoption of these principles governing friendly relations and co-operation between countries, principles rightly described as a code of moral laws for the international community, is a landmark event which will undoubtedly have a positive impact not only on European affairs but throughout the world. Soviet Foreign Minister Gromyko noted:

> The understandings reached at the Conference place relations between the participating countries on a sound basis of peaceful co-existence. They define specific areas and forms of co-operation in different fields of human endeavour and lay the foundation of a lasting peace on the European continent. Summing up the record of history to date, they provide a broad and clearly-defined platform for action on a unilateral, bilateral and multilateral basis for many years, and possibly decades to come".[7]

In sum, the Final Act of the Helsinki Conference is, naturally enough, a compromise reached by thirty-five countries belonging to the two polarized socio-economic systems. But it is a compromise springing from the recognition by the capitalist countries of the need to build relations in the modern world on the basis of peaceful co-existence as the only feasible basis. The validity and acceptability of this compromise lies in the fact that it has been reached in the interests of world peace while not obliterating differences in the ideologies and social systems of the signatory states.

The Final Act clearly defines the structure of effective European security and co-operation which can only be based on strict observance of recognized standards of international behaviour, on the inalienable right of each state to decide its internal affairs as it sees fit and to establish its internal laws. No nation has the right to dictate to other nations how they should live and what political and economic order they should have. The promulgation of this right, which is one of the fundamental principles of restructuring the present pattern of international relations along democratic lines, represents a major achievement for the Leninist policy of peaceful co-existence. Together with the other principles it serves as a point of departure for further efforts to develop and deepen *détente*, to turn it into an irreversible process of overall positive development in Europe and throughout the world. Leonid Brezhnev and Todor Zhivkov, after a discussion of international problems during their friendly meeting in the Crimea in August 1976, pointed out that: "The summit conference in Helsinki laid a solid foundation for restructuring relations between European states on the principles of peace, security and co-operation."[8] Admittedly, the decisions adopted in Helsinki cannot by themselves bring about a progressive restructuring of relations among the states which attended the Helsinki Conference. That would require hard work and daily efforts to translate into reality the ten principles of international community living. "Materialization of *détente* giving it tangible content is the crux of the matter and is what should make European peace really durable and unshakeable. For its part the Soviet Union, in the words of the statement issued jointly by the Politburo of the CPSU Central Committee, the Presidium of the USSR Supreme Soviet and the Council of Ministers of the USSR on the results of the Helsinki Conference, expects that all Helsinki participants will carry into effect the understandings reached and that for its part it will do likewise."[9]

In accordance with the decision of the Helsinki Conference, a review meeting was held in Belgrade in late 1977 and early 1978. The final document issued by the Belgrade meeting confirms the need for all Conference participants to translate into reality the Helsinki proposals. The Soviet Union noted with satisfaction that the Belgrade meeting protected the Final Act from attempts to revise it, to alter its content and meaning, and that it rejected attempts to legalize interference in the internal affairs of states.

The Soviet Union will continue to insist on the implementation of the proposed measures to strengthen security and expand co-operation in Europe. At the Belgrade review conference the Soviet Union tabled other important proposals: for a simultaneous halt by all countries to the manufacture of nuclear weapons of any kind and gradual reduction of the existing stockpiles of these weapons pending their complete elimination; for banning all nuclear tests with a simultaneous moratorium on nuclear explosions for peaceful purposes; for the mutual renunciation of the manufacture of neutron weapons. In the Soviet plan of action for military *détente* in Europe are important recommendations that the countries which attended the Helsinki Conference should conclude a treaty whereby they would refrain from a first nuclear strike, and would not enlarge the opposing military and political groupings and alliances in Europe by the admission of new members. The Soviet Union came forward with a proposed ceiling of 50,000-60,000 troops for military exercises. The other Soviet proposals called for confidence-building measures in the military field under the Final Act to cover the Southern Mediterranean provided the countries of the area so desired. The USSR urged the countries which attended the Helsinki Conference to hold special consultations to examine this programme.

The USSR favours the implementation of such major all-European initiatives as the proposed conference of European states on co-operation in the fields of environmental protection, power development, transport, and also seeks to encourage mutually profitable economic, commercial, scientific and technical co-operation.

In the humanitarian field, too, the Soviet Union advocates a further expansion of co-operation in keeping with the Final Act: personal contacts, information and cultural exchanges, education. This co-operation must be maintained on the basis defined by the Final Act as trust between states grows and *détente* gains momentum.

The record of international conferences with the object of arriving at a political settlement has proved their value. Only the resistance of imperialist circles, interested in perpetuating international conflict and for that reason blocking *détente* and efforts to restructure the present pattern of international relations, makes less than fully realized the possibilities offered by international conferences. Facts indicate that the Soviet Union, together with the other socialist countries displaying initiative and persistence, has taken the lead in this important area of effort to translate into reality the Helsinki understanding. In accordance with the principles worked out by the Helsinki Conference, the Soviet Union has concluded a series of major agreements with some of the participating European countries. Examples include the agreement between the USSR and France on the prevention of accidental or unauthorized employment of nuclear weapons which was signed in July 1976. On 10 October 1977 the USSR and Britain signed an agreement on the prevention of accidental nuclear war. The Soviet proposal to give advance notice of military exercises and to invite foreign observers to attend them was an important step in the direction of greater trust between European states.

Since 1972, when Soviet–American relations began to improve, the two countries have signed sixty-one inter-governmental documents regulating contacts in different areas, including a series of important documents on strategic arms limitation. In May 1972 a series of treaties and agreements of fundamental importance were signed during the Soviet–American summit in Moscow. The Basic Principles of Relations Between the USSR and the United States laid a basis in international law for the development of bilateral relations between them and stated that the two nations "will proceed from the common determination that in the nuclear age there is no alternative to conducting their mutual relations on the basis of peaceful co-existence".[10] The USSR and the USA undertook to settle their differences by peaceful means, to avoid military confrontation and to exercise restraint in their relations. For the first time an agreement was reached on measures to limit the nuclear missile race on the principle of equal security of both states. The leaders of the two powers declared that "differences in ideology and in the social systems of the USSR and the United States are not obstacles to the bilateral development of normal relations based on principles of sovereignty, equality, non-interference in internal affairs, and mutual advantage."[11]

During Leonid Brezhnev's visit to the USA in June 1973 new agreements were concluded on Soviet–American co-operation in a variety of fields. The most important of these was the Agreement on the Prevention of Nuclear War. The Associated Press commented at the time that the leaders of the world's two most powerful nations had pledged to conduct their relations in such a manner as to prevent nuclear war, and that the purpose of the agreement was to create conditions under which the danger of a nuclear war breaking out anywhere in the world would be reduced and ultimately removed.[12]

The agreements and understanding reached by both countries have been exerting a positive influence on the international situation as a whole. It was under the influence of favourable changes in Soviet–American relations, the result, above all, of fruitful negotiations at summit level, that a major advance was achieved towards international *détente*.

However, the development of Soviet–American relations has latterly been hampered by a series of unfavourable developments. There are influential forces in the USA who are opposed to better relations with the USSR and international *détente*.

Of major importance for improving the political climate in Europe and for easing international tension was the signing in 1971 of the Principles of Co-operation between the USSR and France and the Soviet–French Declaration which incorporated the basic elements of the policy of peaceful co-existence. The spirit of constructive co-operation established between the two countries pervades the political and other spheres of Soviet–French relations. The policy of concord and co-operation between the USSR and France was in many respects the starting-point for *détente* and reshaping of East–West relations on the basis of peaceful co-existence.

The results of Leonid Brezhnev's visit to France in July 1977 supplied fresh evidence of the fact that Franco–Soviet relations have become a permanent factor of world politics. The documents signed at Rambouillet, notably the Joint Soviet–French Statement on International *Détente* and the Soviet–French Declaration on the Non-proliferation of Nuclear Weapons, were a major contribution to the cause of peace and to maintaining the momentum of international *détente.*

Significant progress has been achieved in relations between the USSR and the Federal Republic of Germany since the conclusion of the Moscow Treaty of 1970, which normalized these relations. Today the FRG is the Soviet Union's biggest trading partner in the West. The question of West Berlin, a city that was a source of tension in the past, has a direct bearing on Soviet–West German relations. The conclusion in 1971 of the four-power agreement on West Berlin, confirming that the city was not part of the Federal Republic and could not be administered by it, contributed to defusing the situation and normalizing relations between the GDR and the FRG.

The joint declaration signed at the end of the visit to the FRG by Leonid Brezhnev on 4–7 May 1978 speaks of the determination of both sides to maintain and develop political co-operation between the FRG and the USSR on a solid and permanent basis. Appearing on West German television, Leonid Brezhnev said: "Whether the positive processes which began in international relations in the early 1970s will be maintained and developed depends to a considerable extent on our two countries."[13]

The USSR made good progress in developing its relations with Britain, Italy, Canada, Japan, Austria, Belgium, and other capitalist countries. The traditional good-neighbourly relations between the USSR and Finland, a fine example of peaceful co-existence between states with different social systems, advanced further. Motivated by a desire to establish good-neighbourly relations, the Soviet Government proposed to its Japanese counterpart in February 1978 to exchange opinions on the possibility of concluding a treaty of good-neighbourliness and co-operation between the USSR and Japan. Such a treaty, if signed, would accord with the best interests of the Soviet and Japanese peoples and would constitute an important step towards strengthening international peace and security.

The Soviet Union has always advocated co-operation with countries of the capitalist world to combat aggression, to prevent military conflicts or to settle them when they flare up. In the period between the two world wars, imperialism frustrated all attempts to start such co-operation. It was only the threat of world domination by fascism that compelled the Western powers to form an anti-Hitler coalition together with the USSR. After the Second World War, American imperialism ended co-operation with the USSR, launching a "cold war" against it. Today when the alignment of forces in the world has radically changed in favour of the USSR, which, the West now admits, has achieved nuclear parity with the USA, the imperialists are only too well aware of the suicidal consequences of a world nuclear war. Hence they tend to favour stable political co-operation with the USSR and the socialist world, which trend has been confirmed by the foreign policy of the major capitalist powers in recent years. There are other reasons for maintaining stable political co-operation between socialist and capitalist countries; with every passing year the objective need for stable relations between countries and peoples grows. Stability is essential both for meeting mutual interests and for tackling the global problems of economics, energy, material resources, and science and technology that face mankind.

Political co-operation between states having different social systems has been somewhat sporadic in the past and was only maintained in times of war danger or when war actually broke out. The situation is different today. Various forms of political co-operation are developing these days in a situation where no direct threat emanates from third countries. Political co-operation is called upon to ensure a negotiated settlement of conflicts and problems, and not just those of the military variety as was formerly the case.

Political co-operation between socialist and capitalist countries today is developing in new forms. One basic form is holding of regular political consultations between Soviet leaders and their counterparts from capitalist countries. The USSR has signed special protocols on political consultations with a number of Western countries. The signing of documents providing for regular political consultations furnished a legal basis for developing important political contacts between East and West.

The United Nations Organization played a major role in efforts to encourage international political co-operation in the 1970s. The world body adopted a series of resolutions on problems of security and on measures to convert the principles of peaceful co-existence into recognized standards of international behaviour. The United Nations as the most authoritative international forum has worked out measures to achieve the peaceful settlement of international conflicts and to end acts of aggression in different parts of the world. This indicates the considerable potential of the UN and its related agencies to contribute to efforts to preserve peace and encourage international co-operation.

The effectiveness of the United Nations springs above all from the role played by the Security Council in accordance with the UN Charter. But as the authors of *The United Nations: Past, Present and Future* (published in the USA in 1972) pointed out, the Security Council as the world body's most important organ relies "on the strength of its composition and powers, and devotes itself to its pledge of greater political effectiveness and of saving succeeding generations from the scourge of war". Under the UN Charter, which is based on the principles of unanimity among the permanent members of the Security Council on matters pertaining to the maintenance of peace and security, the permanent members are in duty bound to co-operate with one another in order to enable the Council to arrive at agreed decisions. However, during the Cold War into which the Western powers had dragged the United Nations, both the possibilities for such co-operation and its effectiveness diminished. It was precisely because of lack of co-operation among the permanent members of the Security Council, the authors emphasize, that the Security Council failed to function effectively.[14]

Comparing the performance of the World Body then with it today in conditions of international *détente*, we cannot but note its much greater effectiveness and its increased contribution to efforts to maintain world peace and encourage international co-operation.

Under *détente*, the United Nations is able to conduct its activities more efficiently, and in a businesslike atmosphere and far more constructive spirit than ever before. The vigorous efforts of the USSR to implement its foreign-policy programmes to strengthen peace and the security of nations have been a major contributing factor. Some of the main provisions of these programmes have been embodied in important political decisions adopted by the General Assembly and the Security Council. In recent years the General Assembly on the initiative of the Soviet Union has adopted the following resolutions which are of great importance for the future and which have contributed significantly to international *détente*: on convening a world disarmament conference, on the non-use of force in international relations and banning the use of nuclear weapons for all time, on cutting the military budgets of the permanent members of the Security Council by 10 per cent and using part of the funds thus released to give more aid to the developing countries, and on banning the development and production of new weapons of mass destruction and their systems.

At recent sessions of the UN General Assembly the USSR tabled new proposals to strengthen world peace and international security.

The all-important task here is to safeguard from attempts to wreck it what *détente* has already achieved. It is important to work energetically for the implementation of existing multilateral treaties and agreements and the UN decisions aimed at accomplishing this goal. Another direction of the work for world peace and harmonious relations among nations is to initiate bold efforts to curb the arms race as a preliminary to disarmament. Efforts to maintain the momentum of *détente* presuppose such actions by countries as would contribute to an early negotiated settlement of conflict situations and would prevent such situations. Attempts to strengthen and expand existing military blocs run counter to the spirit of *détente*. Aware of this, the USSR and other socialist countries have come forward with a proposal for all countries to refrain from actions which would lead to an enlargement of existing and the creation of new closed groupings and military and political alliances. Further progress of *détente* calls for the emancipation of the remaining colonial countries and peoples, for the elimination of racist regimes, apartheid and the vestiges of colonial oppression and discrimination in whatever form.

The Soviet Union has always proceeded from the assumption that the United Nations is an instrument of peace called upon, in the words of its Charter, to "save succeeding generations from the scourge of war''. To enhance the role of the UN in the effort to develop and consolidate *détente,* on 28 September 1977 the USSR placed before the General Assembly a draft declaration on "Deepening and Strengthening International *Détente''.*

The Soviet Union has always advocated strengthening the United Nations and has consistently opposed forces which seek to undermine its role in the present system of international relations.

Naturally, the USSR has never regarded the World Body as the only instrument for settling all international problems. The problems that arise are so diverse and spring from such a wide variety of causes so different in terms of scale, acuteness, specificity, and number of countries directly involved that the United Nations on its own cannot guarantee their effective solution.

Democratization of international relations, an historically inevitable process which has been accelerated by *détente,* makes it imperative to employ other forms of multilateral political co-operation apart from an active role for the United Nations. To this end the USSR and other socialist countries have been active in international conferences and meetings devoted to individual subjects.

In recent years these conferences have on repeated occasions contributed to strengthening international *détente* and developing international co-operation in a variety of fields. These conferences have examined important problems such as prevention of the further spread of the arms race, environmental protection, the world food problem, and the problem of raw materials.   ·

Political co-operation between countries with different social systems which has been making good progress in the direction of preventing a new world war and a negotiated settlement of outstanding international problems is a stabilizing factor of the world situation. The level of political co-operation achieved to date offers favourable opportunities for further progress in restructuring the present pattern of international relations. This is a perfectly logical development: the basic principles and guidelines formulated in bilateral and multilateral political documents act as a regulator of East-West co-operation in its various forms. Without any exaggeration, the gains of political *détente* have prepared the ground for *détente* in the military field, for broad economic, scientific, and technical co-operation and for extensive cultural exchanges.

Political *détente* has exposed the crisis of the structure of imperialist military blocs. This crisis springs from deep-seated economic and political causes, although it has been brought on by a changing world situation and the progress of mankind towards disarmament. Imperialist blocs with their military organizations and mechanisms run counter to the essence of the contemporary stage of international relations. Few people in the West today really believe in the mythical threat of "aggression from the East". *Détente*, which the USSR and the socialist community as a whole have been steadily pursuing, has exploded the myth of "inevitable Soviet attack" and has undermined the foundations of NATO and other aggressive imperialist blocs.

That this is so has been admitted by many Western experts on international relations, who say now that the policy of *détente* has "weakened Western unity",[15] and that the further progress and expension of it leads to "increasingly more independent behaviour of the major European countries" and "an almost complete removal of fears of the Communist invasion of Western Europe".[16]

But instead of drawing logical conclusions on the need to abolish imperialist military blocs, Western experts on international relations come up with prescriptions designed to strengthen them. George Ball, for one, recommends putting *détente* with the USSR "on ice" in order to shore up NATO and strengthen the bonds between the USA and Western Europe.

Of late the opponents of *détente* have stepped up their efforts to sustain dangerous international conflicts, above all, in the Middle East. This has produced a series of negative developments in the area. The separate talks between Egypt and Israel supported by the USA hamper efforts to achieve an overall settlement of the Middle East conflict.

The USSR has always worked for a comprehensive settlement in the Middle East with the participation of all the parties concerned, including the PLO.

The people of the world are watching with deep anxiety as the seeds of international tension sown by the dangerous policies of influential circles in the USA and other Western powers fall thick and fast, all of which obstructs efforts to develop international *détente*.

Disarmament — the Command of the Times

Without a relaxation of military tension, political *détente* can be neither complete nor durable. That is why the USSR and peace-loving forces throughout the world consider it essential to spread *détente* to the military field primarily by curbing the arms race and initiating disarmament.

The struggle for disarmament has always been a major foreign-policy concern for the Soviet Union. Consistent efforts for *détente* made by the Soviet Government in the period between the wars (the first stage of these efforts) were recognized and highly appreciated by peace forces everywhere. But in that period the resistance of imperialist circles of the West made it impossible to achieve any concrete results.

New conditions more favourable for disarmament efforts developed after the end of the Second World War (the second stage) in response to a radical change in the alignment of forces on the world scene in favour of socialism, peace, democracy, and national independence. The advent of thermonuclear weapons and other means of mass destruction also contributed to turning the solution of the disarmament problem into a crucial factor for the future of world peace and the survival of the human race. Aware that another war involving weapons of mass destruction would be a calamity for mankind and would inflict damage many times that of the Second World War, which claimed over 50 million human lives, people everywhere began to take active steps for disarmament, for a ban on nuclear weapons, for reduced armaments and armed forces and for cuts in military expenditure. The growing political awareness of public opinion coupled with its determination to avert the horror of a new world war and to halt the arms race, backed by the active and dedicated work for peace of the Communist and Workers' parties and other progressive forces, combined into a factor the ruling circles of the Western powers could not very well ignore. A no less important factor was America's loss in the late 1940s of its nuclear monopoly, the growing economic and military potential of the USSR, and increased Soviet political weight in world affairs for Western imperialist circles to reckon with.

The alignment of forces thus changing in favour of peace and socialism, Soviet diplomacy launched a campaign to settle problems of armament and to secure a lasting world peace. As early as 1946, Soviet delegates at the UN were repeatedly tabling proposals to ban nuclear weapons and renounce their use. The Soviet Government's declaration on general and complete disarmament put before the 24th Session of the UN General Assembly in September 1959 was a major move by the USSR. The ruling circles of the imperialist countries, however, virtually rejected these proposals. They would not go beyond paying lip-service to the need for disarmament and for lessening the burden of the arms race. Still confident of their military and strategic superiority and clinging to the illusion that the Atlantic Ocean put America safely out of range of Soviet nuclear bombers while NATO bases deployed around the USSR allowed her Air Force to hit the Soviet Union's vital centres, Western strategists and diplomats refused to co-operate in efforts to reach agreement on mutually acceptable disarmament measures.

So it was that in the second stage of disarmament efforts, too, popular hopes for curbing the arms race were dashed.

In the early 1960s the strategic balance in the world began to tilt towards the USSR as a result of the strengthening positions of world socialism and the spectacular scientific and technological success scored by the USSR in putting the first-ever artificial earth satellite into orbit. The advent of ICBMs exploded the myth of American invulnerability. The steadily changing alignment of forces in favour of socialism created qualitatively new conditions for tackling disarmament problems. The imperialists now had reason to contemplate more and more often the outcome of a military showdown with the socialist countries. Eventually Western politicians began to take a more realistic approach to disarmament.

In the changed world situation the USSR and other socialist countries intensified their efforts to reach agreement with the West on at least limiting the arms race. Leonid Brezhnev emphasized:

> It would be a good thing, of course, to have general and complete disarmament, including the solution of the problem of nuclear weapons and military blocs. Unfortunately, our Western partners are not yet ready for such a solution. But do we have to sit idly and wait for manna to drop from heaven? Not at all. The "all or nothing" principle is no good whatsoever in modern world politics. In this field we must keep pushing forward all the time, making use of every possible opportunity.[17]

Disarmament is an extremely complex and multi-dimensional problem. One of its facets is limiting the arms race in terms of quality, technically known as the "vertical" arms race. Limitation of this kind prevents the development of new weapons, and shuts out the more barbarous methods of warfare and weapons from military arsenals. Another aspect is quantitative limitation of the arms race, the so-called "horizontal" arms race. This limitation should result in a physical reduction of the available armaments. Both aspects are closely interrelated.

In the 1960s and early 1970s (the third, or contemporary, stage) considerable progress was made in the disarmament field culminating in the conclusion of a series of multilateral agreements. The treaty banning nuclear weapon tests in the atmosphere, in outer space, and under water (the Moscow Test Ban Treaty), signed by the USSR, the USA, and Britain on 5 August 1963 was a major advance. To date 106 countries have acceded to it. On 27 January 1967 the treaty on principles governing the activities of states in the exploration and use of outer space (including the Moon and other heavenly bodies) was signed, the first of a series of agreements converting outer space into a zone of peace and international co-operation.

The importance of the Nuclear Non-proliferation Treaty, which came into force on 5 March 1970 and which has since been signed by nearly 100 countries, can hardly be overestimated. Its prime significance lies in the fact that it forms an obstacle to the spread of nuclear weapons and guarantees effective international monitoring of the adherence of states to what they signed to. The Treaty aims at reducing the danger of nuclear war. Yet the problem of nuclear non-proliferation is still on the agenda. W. Epstein, a consultant to the UN Secretary General on disarmament, in a recently published monograph on the subject points to the danger of the spread of nuclear weapons.[18] The author believes that China and India are likely to be followed by other countries in developing nuclear weapons of their own. The proliferation of nuclear weapons is being encouraged by international monopolies which supply up-to-date nuclear technology and reactors to South Africa, Israel, Brazil, and certain other countries. The fact is that reactors used to generate harmless electric power also produce plutonium as a by-product, and this is the raw material for making atom bombs.

A consistent advocate of the exclusively peaceful uses of nuclear energy, the USSR has been co-operating in this field with many countries. But the Soviet Union strongly opposes the idea of peaceful uses of nuclear energy helping nuclear weapons to spread. To prevent this, a combination of efforts by many countries backed by a carefully thought-out international system of safeguards and controls is required.

It is essential of course that the Non-proliferation Treaty should become truly universal, involving all countries without exception, the nuclear powers in the first place but also the "near-nuclear" countries, or those technologically capable of producing nuclear weapons of their own. Only the close co-operation of all countries in this matter can effectively prevent the spread of nuclear weapons across the world. Needless to say, as more and more countries gain access to nuclear weapons the risk of nuclear war grows in proportion.

The treaty banning the emplacement of nuclear weapons on the sea-bed and the ocean floor was signed in early 1971. The signatories undertook not to instal or deploy nuclear weapons or any other weapons of mass destruction on the seabed and the ocean floor and in the subsoil thereof outside the 12-mile zone of the seabed. They undertake not to deploy launchers and installations specially designed for the storage, testing or employment of such weapons. A special control system was developed to monitor adherence to these undertakings.

Détente and the arms race are incompatible. It is impossible over time to combine international *détente* and the relentless build-up of national military potential, the modernization and stockpiling of weapons of war.

The present pattern of international relations cannot be radically changed without ending the arms race. The peace of the world cannot be based on the concept of mutual terror which calls for stockpiling and modernization of armaments *ad infinitum*. The record of history shows that peace relying on armaments has always been precarious and inevitably degenerates into fresh wars.

An arms race produces undue gravitation towards "power politics" and exerts a negative influence on the entire fabric of international relations, giving rise to a nexus based on military power. Such relationships, relying on armaments and formalized in military blocs, breed international tension and may lead to a catastrophe.

The security of states and peoples from war is the be-all and end-all of international security. This principle was formulated by the Soviet delegation to the Disarmament Conference in February 1933. Today, the goal of an effective system of international security is far more attainable than it was either in the inter-war period, or at the height of the Cold War. The changing alignment of forces on the world scene in favour of socialism is making all attempts to resort to violence and coercion in international relations increasingly futile, and such attempts are now completely pointless when directed against the socialist countries. In other words, the social guarantees of international security have increased vastly.

The fundamental change in the technical characteristics of modern weapons has also had an enormous influence on the definition of international security. Under the combined impact of social and political change and the scientific and technological revolution which has invaded military technology, some elements in the traditional concept of a security system and the means of maintaining it have been modified. The elevation of armed force to the status of an indispensable principle of security has neither historical antecedent nor political future. A definition of international security as a system of non-military measures ensuring the effective prevention of armed conflicts is the only realistic one in today's circumstances.

In this context we should point to the qualitative changes that have occurred in military technology under the impact of scientific and technological progress. The technical revolution in the military field has produced weapons whose destructive capacity exceeds by far anything that the world has known before. As a result a situation has arisen in which the belligerents are fully capable not only of assured mutual destruction, but of threatening the very survival of the human race. A nuclear missile war cannot be a rational instrument for achieving political ends in international relations. A world war today is no longer a rational extension of politics, to use Clausewitz's famous phrase, for the exploiter classes. For all its propensity towards adventurism, imperialism does not seem inclined to sign its own death warrant. Needless to say, recognition of this new reality does not find immediate reflection in the practical policies of the leading capitalist countries, where important forces are still at work to prevent disarmament and military *détente*.

At one time Western strategic thinking was dominated by theories about the alleged benefits of massive military expenditure for the capitalist economy. The proponents of these theories argued, for instance, that this was an effective antidote against depression.[19] By now, however, the military sector of the economies of major capitalist countries has become a huge non-productive segment of the national economy, a force eroding the entire economic mechanism. According to UN statistics the world spends an estimated 300,000 million dollars on military purposes annually. According to the Stockholm International Peace Research Institute (SIPRI) the world's annual arms spending amounted to 480,000 million US dollars in 1979. In 1980 it will attain the 800,000 million mark, which will mean a five-fold increase (in stable prices) over 1950.[20]

As a result, the scale of extended reproduction has been curtailed and economc growth has slowed down. Marx wrote that "military expenditures are in economic terms tantamount to a nation throwing part of its capital to the winds".[21]

Even Western experts have admitted the folly and irrationality of an ever-increasing burden of military spending. Thus, Seymour Melman, a Columbia University professor, in his book significantly called *The Permanent War Economy. American Capitalism in Decline* wrote that by the 1960s the US economy had gone full circle: from a means of solving the problem of surplus capital and labour it developed into a prime generator of surplus capital and labour and this eventually led to rising unemployment, increased export of capital and price rises in the country.[22]

The negative effects of the arms race which is being whipped up by aggressive militarist circles are exemplified not only by more and more material resources being annually syphoned off into non-productive spheres but also by exacerbation of the food, raw materials and energy problems, by deterioration of the ecological situation and by failure to meet the urgent social and economic wants of most of mankind, thus increasing the need for effective agreements in the disarmament field.

It should be emphasized that objective prerequisites for disarmament are by no means confined to the changed balance of military power between the two polarized social systems in today's world. In their realistic assessment of the alignment of forces in the world which is of fundamental importance for tackling the disarmament problem, the Communists proceed from a recognition of the decisive role in the alignment of class forces played by the world Communist, working-class, national-liberation, and broadly democratic and public movements. It is precisely thanks to the advances made by the leading class forces of today's world, thanks to the successes they have scored on the international scene, that far-reaching positive changes have occurred in the overall relation of forces in the world tending towards socialism and more favourable conditions have developed for tackling the disarmament problem.

The peace forces of today's world have contributed greatly to bringing about real possibilities for curbing the arms race and averting the threat of nuclear war. The pressure they have put on the ruling circles of Western powers has made these become more realistic in assessing the dangers of an uncontrolled and frenzied arms race. Political *détente* and a marked improvement of the international climate stemming from recognition and practical implementation of the principles of peaceful co-existence between states with different social systems have come as a victory for the forces of peace and progress. The measures limiting the arms race carried out in the 1960s contributed to political *détente* in relations between countries with polarized socio-economic systems; they relaxed tensions and strengthened trust between them.

So it was that by the start of the 1970s a number of new elements came into play in the international situation setting up more favourable conditions for further progress in tackling urgent disarmament problems, and for a new step forward on the road to general and complete disarmament, that guarantee of world peace.

The 25th Party Congress, in defining the immediate tasks in the field of military *détente*, pointed out that ending the arms race and initiating disarmament remained one of the principal areas of concentration for the Soviet Union's foreign-policy activities. This task has never been more urgent than it is today.

The new Soviet Constitution states that the Soviet Union strives for general and complete disarmament.

The Soviet Union's struggle for military *détente* is proceeding in difficult conditions. Quite apart from the objective problems springing from the essential complexity of international limitation of armaments, such as how to put into effect the principle of non-violation of security interests of the parties concerned, the development of adequate criteria for comparison, the finding of an effective common denominator for limitations on different weapons systems, the development of adequate verification and monitoring arrangements, Soviet diplomacy came up against open resistance to *détente* on the part of the forces of reaction and war, those enemies of peace.

One form of this resistance is represented by theories advanced by certain quarters in the West in a bid to justify the arms race and, in fact, calling for its intensification. We refer specifically to the doctrine of "super-armament" expounded by the lunatic fringe of anti-Communists represented by R. Strauss-Hupe and Senator Henry Jackson. The American "hawks" have countered the Soviet programme of military *détente* with a concept of unlimited development and modernization of armaments. Pentagon circles preach that international *détente* is not the only alternative to the Cold War either in the political or military field, and that the arms race allegedly improves the prospects of peace.[36]

Western ideologues and politicians claim that the "balance of terror" has been the first cause of international *détente*. If the world wants *détente* to continue, they suggest, it is necessary to consolidate "the balance of terror", "mutual intimidation". The West German author W. Raven, for one, writes: "Intimidation far from being the opposite of *détente* is its prerequisite. If the pursuit of *détente* tempts its adherents to abandon intimidation, *détente* itself will be the first casualty."[24] Raven is echoed by another West German political scientist, Nils Andrén, who warns against further steps towards armaments reduction. He writes: "*Détente* between the superpowers is a child of nuclear weapons and the terror balance. A very fundamental question for which, so far, history has not yet provided an answer is whether it is necessary to keep the parents alive in order to ensure the survival of the child."[25] In other words, there is no need to disarm for the sake of preserving and developing *détente*.

The advocates of an unrestricted, open-ended arms race who are prepared to plunge mankind into the abyss of a nuclear holocaust are backed by proponents of the doctrine of "arms control". These latter propose a continuation of the arms race subject to regulation by a series of international agreements and treaties. The concept of "a controlled arms race" which was developed in the late 1960s by Thomas Schelling, the American foreign-affairs analyst, called for learning to live in a world of armaments without resorting to them unduly. Views are also current in the imperialist circles whereby the proliferation of nuclear weapons allegedly strengthens peace and security through "proportionate multilateral terror". These ideas are aimed at justifying the creation of "independent nuclear forces" in Western Europe, a long-cherished goal of the West German revanchists. These concepts reflect the intention of the military-industrial complex of the USA and other Western powers to sabotage practical disarmament measures which could make it difficult to go on extorting super-profits from the arms race.

The convention adopted in March 1975 banning the development, production, and stockpiling of bacteriological (biological) and toxin weapons followed by their destruction was a major break-through in the efforts to curb the arms race. The Disarmament Committee as early as March 1971 examined the Soviet draft of the convention which was supported by other socialist countries. The draft furnished the basis for the final text of the convention approved by the UN General Assembly. The Convention is of historic significance, being the first measure of real disarmament in the history of international relations. The implementation of this Convention will remove and destroy an entire category of weapons of mass destruction — the bacteriological weapons. To date, over 100 countries have acceded to the Convention.

A distinguishing feature of this Convention is that its signatories undertake to pursue in a spirit of good will talks on reaching early agreement to take effective measures to ban the manufacture of other weapons of mass annihilation. In March 1972 the socialist countries submitted for the consideration of the Disarmament Committee a draft convention banning the development, production, and stockpiling of chemical weapons to be followed by their destruction. The Convention, if concluded, will constitute a new step forward on the road to real disarmament and result in the removal from military arsenals of yet another terribly dangerous category of mass annihilation weapons. However, considerable efforts will have to be made to overcome the stubborn resistance of those forces on the international scene who, while paying lip service to the need to ban chemical weapons, are actually dragging their feet over the resolution of this urgent problem by imposing prolonged and fruitless discussion of technicalities, before this goal will be achieved.

Encouraging progress was made in tackling the problem of nuclear disarmament, notably in imposing a complete ban on nuclear weapons testing. An important breakthrough in this area was the signing on 3 July 1974 of the Soviet–American treaty on the limitation of underground nuclear weapons tests. Under the treaty both sides undertook to halt the underground testing of nuclear weapons in the yield range above 150 kilotons, to limit the testing of nuclear weapons below that threshold to a minimum, and to confine the testing of such weapons to specified test sites. The two sides also agreed to pursue negotiations on ending the underground testing of all types of nuclear weapons.

The USSR submitted for the consideration of the 30th session of the UN General Assembly (1975) a draft "On the Signing of a Treaty on the Complete and Universal Banning of Nuclear Weapon Tests". The draft provides for banning nuclear tests in all media, in the atmosphere, in outer space, under water and under ground. The treaty, if concluded, will come into force following its ratification by a specified number of countries including all the nuclear powers. A comprehensive ban on nuclear weapons tests should not create obstacles in the way of peaceful uses of nuclear energy.

The Soviet Union's draft treaty met with broad support at the UN General Assembly session and was approved by 94 votes to 2 — China and Albania voting against. The resolution adopted by the General Assembly appeals to all the nuclear powers to initiate in the near future talks on a total ban on nuclear weapons testing.

The problem of control and verification is the main obstacle erected by the Western powers in the way of reaching agreement on ending nuclear weapon testing.

In an effort to remove this obstacle and clear the way for a total ban on nuclear weapon tests the Soviet Government in its Memorandum of 28 September 1976 on ending the arms race and initiating disarmament declared itself ready to join in the search for a compromise-based control formula acceptable to all parties, whereby decisions concerning on-the-spot inspection would be made with due regard for the principle of voluntary agreement by the parties concerned to such an inspection while ensuring that all parties to the treaty are satisfied that no one cheats. Proceeding from this principle, the USSR complemented its draft treaty submitted in 1975 with a clause whereby a state party to the treaty whose compliance with the terms of the treaty is in doubt on account of the nature of seismic phenomena detected on its territory may agree to an on-the-spot investigation of such phenomena if it accepts the motives behind this as convincing. Such an on-the-spot investigation should follow a procedure laid down by the host country. This problem was the subject of Soviet–American negotiations in Geneva in 1977 on a total ban on nuclear weapon tests.

Of major importance in the context of efforts to limit the "vertical" arms race has been the Soviet Union's proposal on banning the development and use of new extremely dangerous weapons and methods of warfare which would have catastrophic effects on the environment and health. The fact is that the current scientific and technological revolution has not only opened up breathtaking vistas for progress in every area of human endeavour, but has also created unprecedented opportunities for developing new weapons capable of inflicting irreparable damage on civilization. Scientific and techno-logical progress have reached a point where there is a real danger of devices more horrible than nuclear weapons being developed. Human reason and morality clamour for immediate action to bar the development of such weapons. The American press has reported facts testifying to the timeliness of the Soviet proposal submitted for the consideration of the 30th Session of the UN General Assembly on banning the development and manufacture of new types and systems of weapons of mass destruction. The *Christian Science Monitor* also reported the feasibility of developing explosive devices based on trans-uranium elements. Such weapons, although smaller in size than existing nuclear weapons, will have a far greater destructive capacity, the full extent of which even scientists engaged on the project cannot predict with certainty.[26] There is evidence suggesting that in the near future high-energy laser weapons may be developed with portable power units capable of blinding or annihilating. Malcolm R. Currie, Director of the Pentagon's research staff, said: "A remarkable series of technical developments has brought us to the threshold of what will become a true revolution in conventional warfare."[27] Politicians and public leaders, scientists and experts in many countries are unanimous in regarding the development of new weapons of mass destruction as the greatest potential threat to mankind today. No effort should be spared in the struggle against it.

During the discussion of the Soviet proposals at this session and in the Disarmament Committee some of the delegates called for a more precise definition of what constitutes novel weapons of mass destruction and their systems. The Soviet Government in its Memorandum of 28 September 1976 on ending the arms race and initiating disarmament stated that such weapons include those based on qualitatively new principles as regards use and effect. Examples of these are radiation, infra-sound, and genetic weapons. As for new weapons systems of mass destruction neither the new types nor those based on already-known scientific principles are to be developed.

The 31st Session in 1976 again took up this question. The Assembly adopted a resolution sponsored by the USSR and calling once more on the Disarmament Committee to speed the drafting of an agreement banning the development of new types of weapons of mass destruction and related systems.

Closely related to this question is the problem of banning environmental modification techniques for hostile purposes, otherwise known as "ecological warfare". The Western press has reported research in the USA into environmental modification for military purposes. The United States has already used such ecological warfare on a wide scale in Indo-China, exemplified by special operations to intensify rainfall by artificial means to inflict maximum damage on the economies of North and South Vietnam, Laos and

Cambodia, as well as those to induce cyclones with speeds of over 160 km per hour. Projects are contemplated which, if carried out, would make it possible to induce freak tidal waves capable of devastating whole towns in the coastal zone.

To prevent these and similar forms of environmental warfare, which if employed will irreversibly upset the ecological balance on a global scale, the USSR acted against the danger of "weather war" while research in this area was still in the experimental stage. The USSR also submitted to the 30th Session of the UN General Assembly the draft of an international convention banning active modification of the natural conditions prevailing over the earth's land mass, on the ocean floor and the seabed, within the earth's interior, in the water environment, and in the atmosphere, along with such modification of any other elements of the environment as may prejudice international security. The General Assembly approved by 126 votes a resolution recommending the Disarmament Committee to initiate work on the agreed text of the proposed convention along the lines of the Soviet draft.

The Soviet proposal, once implemented, would shut off the road to the creation of new dangerous weapons of war and methods of warfare and would thus contribute to curbing the arms race. Foreign Minister Gromyko stated: "The conclusion of such a convention would prevent the development of new methods of warfare and at the same time help solve a problem facing all mankind — how to protect the human environment."[28]

During the discussion of this question in the Disarmament Committee, the governments of the USSR and the USA in August 1975 submitted the joint draft of a convention banning environmental modification for military or any other hostile purposes. After thorough discussion, the Committee referred it to the 31st Session of the UN General Assembly which approved it on 10 December 1976.

On 18 May 1977 representatives of thirty-four countries, the USSR and the USA among them, signed a convention in Geneva undertaking not to resort to environmental modification for military or any other hostile purposes with a view to destroying the environment, or damaging it in any way, and not to encourage or incite other countries or international organizations to do so. There is no deadline on accession to the convention and it is open for signing by all countries wishing to do so.

Since the launching of the Peace Programme and of efforts to restructure the entire system of international relations, some progess has been made in limiting the "horizontal" arms race. This progress has taken the form of a series of international documents. Specially important among them is the Nuclear Non-proliferation Treaty which came into force on 5 March 1970. Several major countries including Federal Germany, Italy, and Japan have acceded to it. Israel, South Africa, Brazil, and some other countries have flatly refused to follow suit. The adoption of further effective measures to stop the spread of nuclear weapons across the globe would doubtless improve the international situation.

The socialist countries insist on scrupulous observance of the Nuclear Non-proliferation Treaty and on converting it into a truly universal treaty signed by all countries. It is in this spirit that the socialist countries participated in the Geneva conference of signatories in May 1975, which reviewed its observance over the preceding 5 years.

The goal of preventing the spread of nuclear weapons was also furthered by the Soviet–American Declaration of 17 February 1975 and by the Soviet–French Declaration of 22 June 1977 on the non-proliferation of nuclear weapons. The Soviet Memorandum of 28 September 1976 stressed the need to tighten up safeguards against the spread of nuclear weapons.

The setting up of nuclear-free zones is an effective measure against the spread of nuclear weapons on a regional basis. At the same time it is directly related to the problem of banning nuclear weapons, since the creation of such zones would impose territorial limits to the theatres of potential nuclear war. The Soviet Union has supported the idea of creating nuclear-free zones in the Balkans, in the Mediterranean, in Northern Europe, and in the Baltic. At the United Nations together with other socialist countries the USSR voted in favour of making the continent of Africa a nuclear-free zone as well as for setting up a similar zone in the Middle East.

The 29th Session of the UN General Assembly (1974) adopted a resolution sponsored by India on creating a nuclear-free zone in South

Asia "taking into account the special features and geographic extent of the region". The USSR, as the 25th CPSU Congress stressed, opposes the setting up of military bases by any power in the Indian Ocean.

One of the major tasks set by the Soviet Union's Peace Programme is to reach agreement on cutting military budgets, by the major powers in the first instance.[29] To this end at the 28th Session of the UN General Assembly in 1973 the USSR tabled a proposal for cutting by 10 per cent the military budgets of the permanent members of the Security Council and for using part of the resources thus saved to give more aid to the developing countries. Such a cutback would be a substantial disarmament measure. It would enable countries reducing their military expenditure to channel the resources this would save into meeting social and economic needs. It has been estimated that the developing countries would receive some 1.5 billion dollars' worth of additional aid. The main obstacle here is the resistance of the United States, China, and certain other countries which seem to prefer endless academic discussions of what constitutes a military budget. The proposal to cut arms expenditure has thus become, as it were, a touchstone of the good faith and sincerity of countries in matters of disarmament and strengthening peace, of their serious intention to contribute to further progress along the road to international *détente*.

While refusing to cut their military budgets, the NATO countries are steadily increasing military spending year after year.

In 1978 NATO's arms expenditure totalled 189,000 million dollars. NATO plans to boost its military spending to 254,000 million dollars by 1990.[30]

In this situation the Soviet Union had to build up its defences to deter a possible aggression by the imperialist powers. The following trend is noteworthy in this context: during the 1970s the Soviet budget increased overall in expenditure but the proportion allotted to defence was reduced.

The USSR's defence spending in 1970 was 17,900 million roubles, in 1975 — 17,400 million and in 1979 — 17,200 million roubles.[31]

As Leonid Brezhnev stressed on 20 February 1978, "In strengthening our armed forces we in no way exceed the actual requirements of our security and the security of our socialist friends. We are not threatening anyone and are not imposing our will on anyone. If *détente* continues and other countries are ready to disarm, we shall not be found laggardly."[32] The imperialists have been vainly seeking to distort the strictly defensive character of Soviet military measures by putting about a "Soviet military threat".

As early as 1971, at the time of the 26th Session of the UN General Assembly the Soviet Union proposed to convene a world disarmament conference to examine the full spectrum of disarmament measures. This proposal was incorporated into the Peace Programme which was adopted by the 24th CPSU Congress. The chief aim of the proposed disarmament conference should be to identify the positions of the world's nations on the various aspects of disarmament, and to initiate an active search for practical ways of tackling the problem. The conference could contribute substantially to resolving urgent disarmament problems by involving a maximum number of countries in discussions of every aspect of disarmament.

*   *   *

The USSR and other socialist countries have been steadily working towards military *détente* in Europe where major armed forces of NATO and the Warsaw Pact equipped with the more formidable weapons, including nuclear arms, are concentrated. At the USSR's initiative, negotiations on mutual force and armaments reduction in Europe opened on 30 October 1973 in Vienna. The Vienna talks are attended by nineteen countries: eleven countries — the USSR, East Germany, Poland, Czechoslovakia, the USA, Britain, the Federal Republic of Germany, Canada, Belgium, the Netherlands and Luxembourg — are concentrating on thrashing out concrete agreements, while eight other countries — Bulgaria, Hungary, Romania, Turkey, Greece, Italy, Denmark, and Norway — are attending the talks as observers.

In November 1973 East Germany, Poland, Czechoslovakia, and the USSR tabled proposals for reaching agreement on substantial cuts of troop strength and armaments without prejudicing the security interests of any country: during 1975 the participants in the Vienna talks (eleven countries) should cut their combined armed strength by 20,000 men. In 1975 and 1976 they should cut the remaining troop strength by a further 5 and 10 per cent. All categories of armed forces and armaments stationed in Central Europe, notably, those equipped with nuclear weapons, should be subject to reduction.

The Western countries, in a departure from the agreement reached at the early stages of preliminary consultations whereby any agreement on cuts should be based on reciprocity and equality of reductions consistent with the principle of non-violation of the security of either side and the inadmissibility of gaining unilateral military advantage, submitted a "working document", which, if adopted, would upset the balance of forces in Central Europe in favour of NATO. They proposed "asymmetrical" force and armaments reductions to achieve "overall ceilings" on the numerical strength of land forces. Drawing on arbitrary computations, Western diplomats and military experts insisted that the socialist countries withdraw from the zone of reduction two and a half times more troops than the Western countries would take out.

As the Vienna talks progressed, Western diplomats made a move calculated to score a pure propaganda point. They declared themselves ready to cut a proportion of the US tactical nuclear weapons deployed in Central Europe on condition that the socialist countries accept the Western formula of mutual force reductions in its entirety. The Western proposal was designed to make the East accept a balanced (i.e. "asymmetrical") formula of force and armaments reduction.

The West's manoeuvring for unilateral military advantage is the main obstacle in the way of a mutually acceptable agreement.

In 1975 the Vienna talks were placed on the solid foundation of equality of all the participants by the understanding reached at the Helsinki Conference on Security and Cooperation in Europe as formalized in its Final Act. Proceeding from a comprehensive and realistic account of the balance of forces in Central Europe, and to break the Vienna deadlock, the socialist countries on 19 February 1976 tabled a new proposal: in that year to reduce only Soviet and American forces. The troop strength of the armed force of the other participants in the Vienna talks was for the time being to be "frozen", and reduced in the second stage, 1977-78.[33]

Eventually all participants would cut the numerical strength of their forces by an equal percentage.

The socialist countries proposed further that both sides should cut the number of tanks and aircraft carrying nuclear weapons as well as the number of missile-launchers with standard complement of nuclear ammunition.

Force reductions were to be carried out by withdrawing whole army units and elements rather than a specified number of servicemen from different units as suggested by the West. The 25th CPSU Congress emphasized: "Our proposals rest on the only realistic basis of preserving the present balance of forces in Central Europe, a rough equilibrium. The implementation of our proposals will not prejudice the security of either side. It is to be hoped that all this will draw a suitable response from the Western powers and that it will be possible at last to move from talking about reducing armed forces and armaments to actually doing it."[34]

More recently the Vienna talks have been proceeding in a situation complicated by NATO's continued military build-up which shows that its member countries are dead set on securing unilateral advantages and military superiority over the Warsaw Treaty states. The West, as its latest proposals at the Vienna talks (20 December 1979) show, is clearly dragging its feet in a bid to prevent the achievement of effective and equivalent armaments and force reductions in Central Europe. Actually, the West has of late been shifting its ground on the substance of the issue. What is more, the Western negotiators in Vienna have even reneged on the proposals they themselves submitted earlier. Thus, whereas in December 1979 they expressed their readiness to guarantee in the proposed agreement envisaging the reduction of Soviet and US troop strength in Central Europe at the first stage, that all the Western countries directly represented at the Vienna talks would substantially contribute to the overall reductions by the West in stage 2, today they do not guarantee that stage 2 will take place at all. Virtually, the West is trying to confine the proposed reductions to just Soviet and American land forces.

What is more, while the USSR, which since the Vienna talks began has not increased its troop strength in Central Europe, is expected to withdraw 30,000 of its servicemen, the USA is to pull out only 13,000 which does not even offset the increase in the US troop strength which had occurred in the interim and which according to the January report of the US Secretary of Defence Harold Brown within the FRG alone since 1976 had reached 26,000 servicemen.

The West European NATO countries and Canada going back on their own earlier proposals now refuse to "freeze" their troop strength which constitutes three-quarters of NATO's effective potential in Central Europe after the USSR and USA have started their respective withrawals in stage 1. Instead they insist that the USSR whose troops stationed in Central Europe represent about a half of the combined potential of the Warsaw Treaty countries in the area should undertake a binding commitment to continue to limit its troop strength there.

The West's new proposals leave out the question of limiting and restricting armaments, and in the first instance the earlier proposed reduction of the US stocks of nuclear ammunition and some of their delivery vehicles deployed in Central Europe. Thus, yet another essential element on which agreement has already been reached is set aside.

In view of the need to make statistics on Soviet and American forces quoted by both sides at the Vienna talks fully comparable it is important to note that the whole statistics problem has been artificially created by the West. While casting doubts on the official troop-strength figures quoted by the socialist countries the West claims without adducing proofs that the latter allegedly have a substantial preponderance over the NATO forces and on this flimsy ground has demanded "asymmetrical" (greater by a factor of 3-3.5) troop reductions by the Warsaw Treaty countries. The exchange of official statistics in 1976 showed that as of 1 January 1976 there was a rough balance between the armed forces of the Warsaw Treaty at 987,300 including 805,000 officers and men of the land forces and NATO's forces at 981,000 (including 791,000 officers and men of the land forces). However, of late some NATO countries, notably the USA, have substantially increased their troop strength in Central Europe with the result that the earlier supplied statistics used by the Vienna negotiators no longer reflect the true position today and cannot be the basis for estimating the extent of troop reductions to be carried out. That is why the Warsaw Treaty delegates to the Vienna talks proposed on 21 February 1980 an exchange of updated statistics reflecting faithfully the actual troop strengths of both sides as of 1 January 1980.

When the 21st round of the Vienna talks got under way on 14 May 1980 the Warsaw Treaty negotiators made every effort to break the deadlock and achieve concrete and mutually acceptable results. To this end on 10 July 1980 the USSR, GDR, Poland and Czechoslovakia tabled far-reaching compromise proposals affecting the more pressing aspects of the problem of armaments and force reductions in Central Europe and preparing the ground for concluding in the near future the first agreement on reducing Soviet and American forces stationed in the area.

Under the terms of these latest initiatives in stage 1 Soviet and American forces in Central Europe are to be cut by 20,000 and 13,000 servicemen respectively with due account being taken of their actual strength. If one adds to that the Soviet contingents whose unilateral withdrawal from the GDR has recently been completed, a total of over 50,000 Soviet servicemen would leave Central Europe.[35] When troop reductions affecting the forces of all the signatories of the proposed agreement in both stages are complete, equal collective ceilings of troop strength at 900,000 servicemen for both NATO and Warsaw Treaty would be established.

Of major importance has been the exchange of updated statistics on the numerical strength of the armed forces of all countries directly represented at the Vienna talks in Central Europe as proposed by the socialist countries. Now the Vienna negotiators have at their disposal adequate statistics on the basis of which to work out an agreement.

In declaring their readiness to cut a substantially greater number of troops in stage 1 than will the West, the Warsaw Treaty countries expect West European countries and Canada to undertake, as the USSR, the GDR, and Poland are prepared to do, to freeze their troop strength in the period between the two stages and to reduce it in stage 2 to an extent necessary for reaching equal collective ceilings of their respective troop strengths.

The problems facing the participants in Vienna must be resolved, however complex and formidable they may be. Not only the socialist countries but all the countries and peoples of Europe have a vital stake in this. The success of the Vienna talks on force and armaments reductions in Central Europe will contribute subtantially to the progress of *détente*, to efforts to strengthen peace and security in Europe and beyond.

The Soviet–American talks on strategic arms limitation held a very special place in the Soviet Union's disarmament efforts. The progress of these talks had a tremendous impact on the resolution of the disarmament problem as a whole, since the USSR and the USA are by far the biggest nuclear-missile powers. The Soviet–American negotiations which began in November 1965 resulted in a series of agreements which marked a new stage in the progress towards military *détente*. The nature of these agreements was determined above all by the commitments made by the USSR and the USA to limit their more sophisticated weapons systems which formed the hard core of the military might of both.

The questions covered by the Soviet–American agreements fall into two basic groups: limitation of strategic defensive arms and limitation of strategic offensive arms. In May 1971 the Soviet and American governments agreed to concentrate on preparing a treaty limiting the deployment of anti-ballistic missile (ABM) systems, as a first step to be followed by agreements on limiting strategic offensive arms. This order of priority was dictated by the fact that the deployment of ABM systems would have inevitably augmented the offensive nuclear missile potential of both sides.

An agreement on limiting ABM systems was signed in Moscow on 26 May 1972. Under the agreement, which is of unlimited duration, sides undertook not to deploy a country-wide ABM system nor to develop a skeleton for an ABM shield. The parties undertook to confine their ABM systems to two complexes in each country: one complex deployed around its capital city and one around its ICBM silos. The number of anti-missile missile launchers in each of the complexes was not to exceed 100 units.[36] The ABM Treaty was a major step towards inhibiting the strategic arms race. In this way, active factors intensifying the strategic arms race both in the defensive and offensive areas were significantly weakened and thousands of millions of dollars and roubles originally intended to finance the deployment of ABM systems went unspent. Two years later a new advance was achieved in the area of limitation and reduction of ABM systems. On 3 July 1974 the USSR and the USA signed in Moscow a protocol to the Treaty on Limiting ABM Systems whereby the two sides agreed to have one instead of two ABM complexes with a ceiling of 100 units on the number of anti-missile missile launchers. Radical limitation measures culminating in physical reduction of the strategic offensive arsenals of the USSR and the USA opened up favourable prospects for further agreements on the limitation of strategic offensive arms.

The first breakthrough in this area was the signing on 26 May 1972 of the Interim Agreement on Limiting Strategic Offensive Arms. Unlike the radicality of the ABM Treaty, this 5-year agreement, while imposing no limits on recently developed systems, limited those offensive strategic arms of which both sides had significant stockpiles. The situation was complicated further by the fact that for a variety of reasons the development of individual types of strategic arms by both sides had not been quite symmetrical. What is more, the strategic armaments development programmes of both countries were at different stages of completion and differed significantly in terms of quality.

Under the terms of the Interim Agreement, the USA and the USSR undertook not to start the deployment of additional ICBM silos as of 1 June 1972. They also undertook to limit the number of submarine-based ICBM launchers. The agreement represented an advance in the efforts to decelerate the strategic offensive arms race. It created effective obstacles to the "quantitative" race even though it left unresolved the question of modernization: the terms of the Interim Agreement allowed both sides to replace existing ICBM land-based silos or submarine-based ICBM launchers with improved systems. Thus the question of limiting strategic offensive armaments received a temporary and partial solution. That is why right after the conclusion of the 1972 Agreement the USSR and the USA took steps to reach a long-term agreement imposing both quantitative and qualitative limitations on strategic offensive arms.

Seven years of tough and painstaking negotiation culminated on 18 June 1979 in the conclusion in Vienna of the SALT-2 Treaty between the USSR and the USA. Evaluating the significance of SALT-2, Leonid Brezhnev has emphasized that it is "realistic and concrete. Its essence lies in limiting the quantity of armaments and inhibiting their modernization. The treaty rests on the principles of parity and equal security of both sides.... The product of efforts made over many years, it constitutes a fair balance of interests. Each provision... each word in the text of the Treaty has been carefully weighed and worked through dozens of times."[37]

An analysis of the limitations on the strategic armaments imposed by SALT-2 shows the compromise character of many of them. Yet this in no way detracts from the treaty's significance as a whole. SALT-2 is important if only because it puts up a roadblock in the way of the further stockpiling of the most destructive and costly overkill weapons. In this sense SALT—2 is the most radical international act of its kind.

In this context that part of the joint Soviet-American communiqué of 18 June 1979 which states that neither side is pursuing nor will in future pursue military superiority as it might destabilize the situation dangerously and lead to a higher level of armaments and would not contribute to the security of either side, takes on special importance.

SALT-2 is also important in that it lays the foundation for further progress towards a new agreement on the limitation of strategic armaments. Speaking of the prospects of SALT-3, Leonid Brezhnev has said that this treaty "will represent a further step towards inhibiting the development of new weapons and will provide not only for limiting the growth of armaments but their mutual reduction by both sides as well.[38]

Finally, SALT-2 has provided a fresh impetus to international *détente* as it helps ameliorate the international climate as a whole and strengthen world peace. That is precisely the reason why the opponents of *détente* and of complementing it with measures to limit the arms race were immediately up in arms against it.

According to *Foreign Affairs*, "One of the factors underlying the campaign against SALT-2 in the United States was clearly that old attachment to American strategic primacy that had prevented Soviet–American negotiations on strategic arms control from getting under way before 1969."[39] In opposing SALT-2 its critics attack *détente per se*. Realistic-minded people in the West understand this wall. Hedley Bull, Montague Burton Professor of International

Relations at Oxford, writes, "...One's impression of the SALT-2 debate in America is that ... the chief issue at stake is *détente* itself — whether the United States should still strive to relax tension and broaden the scope of co-operation with its adversary or should enter a new phase of combativeness. The latter prospect is viewed by America's European and Pacific allies, and by most of the international community apart from China, with fear and alarm."[40] It now looks as if some people in the USA are seeking to resolve this debate to the detriment of peace and international co-operation.

Unfortunately, the arms race is still going on and is assuming more dangerous forms. New modifications and types of weapon of mass destruction are being developed and we know well on whose initiative. This intensifies the arms race, increases mutual distrust and makes the adoption of disarmament measures more difficult.

The Soviet Union, while looking to its defences, is not seeking and will not in future seek military superiority over the other side. As Leonid Brezhnev emphasized in his address at a celebratory meeting marking the 60th anniversary of the October Revolution:

> It is not our intention to upset the rough balance of armed forces prevailing today, say, between East and West in Central Europe, or between the USSR and United States. But in exchange we insist that no one else should try to upset it in his favour. Needless to say, the preservation of the existing equilibrium is not an end in itself. We want to see the arms race slowed in order to scale down military confrontation. It is our intention to substantially reduce and eventually remove the threat of nuclear war, that greatest menace to mankind.[41]

On that occasion Leonid Brezhnev on behalf of the Soviet Union called for reaching agreement on a simultaneous halt by all nuclear powers to the production of nuclear weapons and on a gradual reduction of available stockpiles culminating in their complete removal.

A number of other measures designed to promote military *détente* brought progress in Soviet–American relations and further advance in the area of mutual undertakings to limit strategic arms. The agreement reached by the USSR and the USA on 30 November 1971 paved the way towards the prevention of accidental and unauthorized employment of nuclear weapons under the control of both countries. The agreement also covered organization and technical arrangements, the exchange of relevant information, and procedures for inquiries and consultations. The USSR–USA Agreement on the Prevention of Incidents on the High Seas and in Air Space (1972) reduced the risk of dangerous clashes between warships and aircraft of both sides.

A major landmark in the efforts to strengthen international security was the signing on 22 June 1972 of the Agreement on the Prevention of Nuclear War. Of unlimited duration, the Agreement went far beyond the framework of bilateral relations as it facilitated the progress of *détente* and the efforts to establish an atmosphere of trust and mutual understanding in the world. The USSR and the USA agreed that they would refrain from the threat or use of force against each other in circumstances which might place in jeopardy international peace and security. The Parties agreed that they would be guided by these considerations in the conduct of foreign policy and in their actions on the international scene.[42]

Article IV of the agreement on the prevention of the risk of nuclear war is of fundamental importance. If at any time strained relations between the USSR and the USA, or between either of them and third countries, should lead to the danger of nuclear conflict, the USSR and the USA should immediately initiate urgent consultations with a view to making every effort to prevent the risk of war. The joint Soviet-American Communiqué makes a point of emphasizing this agreement. Both sides believe that "it represents a historic landmark in Soviet-American relations and is a major contribution to strengthening the basis of international security as a whole. The Soviet Union and the United States declare themselves ready to consider additional measures to consolidate peace and to eliminate for all time the threat of war and especially the threat of nuclear war."[43] The principles formulated in the Agreement of renunciation of the use of force and adoption of resolute measures to prevent nuclear war constitute an important additional factor reducing the risk of an armed clash between the two countries.

A new major contribution to the work for disarmament was made by the USSR at the 31st Session of the UN General Assembly, when it submitted a draft treaty on the renunciation of the use of force in international relations along with a memorandum covering a comprehensive programme of measures to secure peace and initiate disarmament with a view to giving tangible substance to *détente*.[44]

The USSR urged the nations of the world to redouble their efforts to end the arms race and initiate disarmament. For its part the USSR declared itself ready to reach agreement on the most radical disarmament measures culminating in general and complete disarmament. The Memorandum stressed that the important thing was to move on from talking about ending the arms race to actually doing it.

*   *   *

Viewed in historical perspective, the treaties and agreements mentioned above add up to a major breakthrough in disarmament efforts. Admittedly, these treaties and agreements are limited and fall short of resolving many major disarmament problems, nor do they rule out the threat of war. However, even limited, partial agreements make for the step-by-step resolution of pressing problems. The importance of those partial measures adopted to date transcends the framework of military *détente*. It is hard to overestimate their positive impact on international politics and the stimulating influence they have had on efforts to create a climate of trust and co-operation. They are an active factor for securing peaceful co-existence between countries with different social systems.

The agreements, treaties, and understandings reached in this area to date, the principles they embody and the measures adopted in the sphere of disarmament, form the embryo of an international system of arms limitation paving the way for steady progress towards general and complete disarmament. The important thing now is to involve all the world's nations in international agreements and treaties limiting both the quality and quantity of armaments, banning the more barbarous weapons and blocking effectively the spread of nuclear weapons. To achieve this goal, the USSR has proposed the convening of a world conference to discuss the full range of disarmament problems.

One notes that the principles of limiting the arms race are being increasingly recognized by political and scientific circles of the West which traditionally took the view that the security of a country or group of countries could only be guaranteed at the expense of the security of other countries. Professor George Coffee of Columbia University, writing in *International Affairs,* urged his readers to realize that security was "not a zero sum game in which one can gain only at the expense of one's adversary but a game in which both can gain through co-operation and compromise."[45] The disarmament measures carried out to date confirm this. Today as never before it is becoming ever more clear that the security of countries can only be realistic if it is equal for all.

The concept of international security at the present stage in the evolution of international relations cannot be considered in isolation from the process of disarmament. Seen in the historical and political context international security should be understood as a system of measures guaranteeing the effective prevention of armed conflicts. In this interpretation, disarmament and the abolition of military blocs are effective forms of guaranteeing international security.[46] It will be seen that the exclusion of coercion by force of arms and of resort to armed force is a major point of difference between this concept of international security and the traditional one. Such elements within international security as multilateral non-military co-operation between countries to prevent conflicts and guarantee peace, abandonment of the use of force in international relations, and measures to limit the arms race and reduce the danger of nuclear war are playing a growing role.

However, as long as the danger of war persists, as long as America and her NATO allies continue their military build-up and the socialist countries are obliged to look to their defences, their efforts to build up their defence potential form a deterrent against the forces of aggression and reaction and a major factor in stabilizing the international situation.

The struggle for disarmament, as, indeed, the efforts of the USSR and other peace forces to bring about a lasting peace and international *détente,* has not been a smooth-running process with no delays or setbacks. The cold warriors have not given up their attempts to take the offensive and step up the arms race yet again.

*   *   *

Summing up the foregoing, we may safely say that the importance of the disarmament measures adopted to date goes beyond the framework of limiting the arms race, as they have had a major positive effect on international politics. Measures to limit the arms race favour normal political development by freeing international and world politics from the undue influence of military and technical factors. These measures stimulate the creation of a climate of trust and co-operation, help the changeover from confrontation to *détente,* and prepare the ground for reshaping international relations on the basis of peaceful co-existence between states with different social systems.

Already progress made in limiting armaments as a result of agreements achieved thus far is having a serious economic effect since it inhibits the growth of military spending and offers encouraging opportunities for funnelling the resources thus released into civilian sectors of the economy. According to Senator Percy, the conclusion by the USSR and the USA of the 1972 ABM Treaty has enabled the USA (as we have seen) to save some 100,000 million dollars originally earmarked for the Safeguard system.[47] The implementation of the Soviet-proposed ban on the production and stockpiling of chemical weapons followed by their destruction will result in impressive savings. It has been estimated that anti-chemical warfare measures to protect 100-200 million people cost at least 15-20,000 million dollars.[48] General and complete disarmament offers truly breathtaking opportunities for tackling urgent social and economic problems facing the world.

The current Soviet disarmament efforts have convincingly demonstrated the dialectics of the inter-dependence and inter-connection of political with military *détente*. They have shown that military *détente* is unthinkable without a matching political atmosphere, and that military *détente* cannot endure and be stable unless it is backed up by effective measures to lower the level of military confrontation between the two world systems. Therefore, since they form an integral part of this process, the limitations imposed on the arms race to date should be viewed in the context of its intimate connection with the on-going efforts to restructure radically the present pattern of international relations.

The goal of ending the arms race, of initiating disarmament and military *détente* is urgent as never before. The achievement of this goal remains one of the key areas of concentration for the foreign-policy activities of the CPSU and the Soviet Government. The Soviet Union's unflagging efforts to translate into reality the ideals of the Great October Socialist Revolution, to secure world peace and bring about disarmament, have won it the gratitude and affection of people all over the world who see the Soviet Union as a dedicated champion of peace, disarmament and military *détente*.

Thus we see that the 1970s were a period of fruitful activity by the CPSU and the Soviet state to avert the danger of a new world war. That the threat of such a war has receded is the main achievement of Soviet foreign policy. The efforts of the Soviet Union and other socialist countries have resulted in measurable progress towards restructuring the present pattern of inter-state relations, away from confrontation and towards a relaxation of world tensions. This progress is evidenced by the settlement of and successful search for a solution to a number of major international conflicts, by the conclusion of treaties and agreements slowing the arms race and narrowing its sphere, and by the conclusion of agreements to reduce the risk of military conflict.

This does not mean, of course, that the threat of a world nuclear war may be considered removed. All the same, encouraging progress has been made in lessening this threat. Changes for the better in the world situation, which were particularly in evidence in the 1970s and which have come to be known as international *détente*, are tangible and concrete. Leonid Brezhnev has pointed out:

> These changes are exemplified by the recognition and formalization in international documents of a kind of code of rules governing honest and fair relations between countries, which sets a barrier in international law and in moral and political principles across the path of those who are inclined to try their luck in military ventures. These changes are exemplified in the achievement of the first, albeit modest, agreements which close off some of the channels of the arms race. They are also exemplified in a whole nexus of agreements covering many areas of peaceful co-operation between countries having different social systems.[49]

Take whatever aspect of present-day international relations we may, be it crucial global problems or those affecting individual parts of the world, everywhere the basic trend is seen indicating that Leninist principles of peaceful co-existence are becoming part of the practice of relations between countries having polarized social systems. In conditions of the current peace offensive mounted by the socialist countries on the basis of these principles, a process is at work despite the resistance of the reactionary forces of imperialism towards a fundamental reshaping of the present pattern of political, economic and cultural relations between countries of different social systems, and this creates favourable conditions for the movement of all countries towards social progress. However, the record of history indicates that to achieve lasting and durable world peace is not easy and requires an inflexible sense of purpose, great persistence and dedication, as well as fresh efforts by the peace-loving nations.

8

International Economic
Co-operation — A New Stage

The Scientific and Technological Revolution and Co-operation Between Socialist and Capitalist Countries

A fundamental restructuring of the present pattern of international relations on the basis of peaceful co-existence between countries of different social systems is above all a matter of creating a suitable political climate favourable to the development of every form of international intercourse. Without finding a successful solution to political and military problems, it is impossible to develop relations between countries in other areas of international life. Without progress in political *détente* there can be no advances in co-operation between socialist and capitalist countries in the economic, scientific, technical and cultural fields. As Leonid Brezhnev has said: "We always remember, and we believe others should also remember, that broad-based and fruitful development of economic and cultural contacts, that an effective solution to human problems, is only possible if the threat of war is removed."[1]

A durable peace is a system of relations whereby the countries involved are obliged to adhere to recognized standards of international law, to renounce the use of external force, to refrain from interfering in the internal affairs of one another no matter what the pretext, and to carry out mutual arms and troop reductions in the interests of world peace and security. The essential material foundation of a durable world peace is made up of close international co-operation in the econòmic, scientific and technical fields, and of business co-operation to mutual advantage between states.

The Helsinki Conference gave close attention to this basic tenet. Central to the underlying principles and provisions of the Final Act were matters relating to the "second basket", measures for international co-operation in the economic, scientific, and technical fields.

The Helsinki Conference emphasized that international co-operation in these fields based on mutual advantage is a major stabilizing factor within peaceful relations. The Final Act of the Helsinki Conference states that the signatories "will give due attention to measures for the promotion of trade and the diversification of its structure... will encourage the expansion of trade on as broad a multilateral basis as possible, thereby endeavouring to utilize the various economic and commercial possibilities", "to encourage the development of industrial co-operation between the competent organizations, enterprises and firms of their countries". These questions were again examined by the Review Conference in Belgrade.

Expanding economic and scientific and technical co-operation with the rest of the world has become an integral element of the Soviet Union's economic policy. It is no concidence that the *Basic Guidelines for the USSR's Economic Development for 1976-80* should state as one aim: "To adopt the necessary measures for effecting the provisions of the Final Act of the Helsinki Conference directed towards the expansion and development of international co-operation in the field of the economy, science and technology, in environmental protection and in other spheres."

Détente implies a restructuring of international relations on the sound principles of peaceful co-existence, mutual respect and mutual benefit. There is an essential dialectical bond between *détente* and broad international co-operation, since *détente* brings into play potential opportunities inherent in free, stable, and equal international exchange. Mutually beneficial international economic, scientific, and technical co-operation prompts the countries involved to act with restraint on contentious political issues. That is why the USSR and fellow socialist countries attach not only economic but also political importance to mutually beneficial economic co-operation with advanced capitalist countries on the basis of full equality. They see it as a major guarantee of durable world peace.

The policy of developing international co-operation in every area of human endeavour, of stimulating an active involvement in it of the socialist countries, is dictated by both the political and the economic interests of those countries and effectively serves the goal of promoting social progress, peace, and the security of nations. This policy is integral to Lenin's concept of peaceful co-existence.

The potential for economic co-operation between socialist and capitalist countries is good. It was the creation of the material and technical basis of mature socialism and the Soviet Union's consistent efforts to expand its economic co-operation with the rest of the world that turned this sphere of activity into a major sector of the national economy which forms a solid basis to its co-operation with other countries. The successful progress of economic, scientific, and technical co-operation has augmented the foreign-trade potential of other socialist countries.

Secondly, the West is increasingly coming to appreciate the benefits of expanding economic co-operation with the East. As Ernst Mommsen, Chairman of the West German Krupps, has pointed out: "The aspect of stability of trade with the East deserves special attention from the Western standpoint. Foreign trade with the industrialized countries of the West is subject to cyclical ups and downs due to changing market situations. . . . By contrast, trade with the East, where a centralized system of economic management avoids such cyclical fluctuations, is to my view a positive factor affording an injection of stability into our foreign trade. This is of major importance for ensuring job security for our workers and employees."[2]

In a situation marked by crisis phenomena besetting the West's economies, the development of co-operation with socialist countries serves to alleviate the position of millions of working people in capitalist countries. It has been estimated that trade with the Soviet Union has created at least 2 million jobs in West European countries. This is of no mean importance at a time when the industrialized capitalist countries, according to official statistics, had over 18 million unemployed in early 1979.

While expanding economic relations with the socialist countries will not cure capitalism of its hereditary ills, it does fully accord with the interests of the popular masses of capitalist countries by helping to alleviate the burden of their serious economic hardship which may deteriorate into dangerous political problems. It will be remembered that it was precisely the Great Depression of 1929-33 that paved the way to the rise of nazism in Germany, plunging the nations into the Second World War.

The present and future state of the economic, scientific, and technical ties between socialist and industrialized capitalist countries is having and will continue to have a major influence on the fortunes of international *détente* as it contributes to the consolidation and expansion of the essential material foundation of peaceful co-existence.

TABLE 1

Socialist and Industrialized Capitalist Countries in the World Economy
(1975 data)*

	Socialist countries	Capitalist countries[a]
Area	25.9	24.0
Population	32.1	18.6
Contribution to world		
production	40.0	50.8
to world exports	10.0	65.7
to world imports	11.3	67.2

*Sources: *Capitalist and Developing Countries.* [a]*handbook*. Moscow, 1973.
    World Economy and International Relations, 1976, Issue 8 (Statistical supplement).

In accelerating the development of their productive forces, a key factor in the steady improvement of living standards, and strengthening their positions in competition with the capitalist world, the socialist countries place emphasis on self-reliance exploiting the advantages of the socialist mode of production and continually expanding co-operation among themselves. The record to date demonstrates that the socialist community is capable of maintaining rapid economic growth, being fully independent of the capitalist world economically and technologically. But this does not mean, of course, that the USSR and other socialist countries oppose co-operation with the industrialized capitalist countries, as the Austrian economist W. Hendrix when he alleges that "autarkic planning has been engrained from the first in the socialist mode of thinking"[3] would have us believe.

The USSR and other fraternal socialist countries see stable and diversified economic, scientific, and technical co-operation with industrialized capitalist countries as making for their economic development. The main report of the Central Committee to the 25th CPSU Congress pointed out: "One of the salient features of our time is increasing utilization of the international division of labour for the development of each country irrespective of the size of its national wealth and its level of economic advancement. Like other countries, the Soviet Union is seeking to exploit the advantages offered by external economic relations in order to mobilize further opportunities for successfully tackling its economic problems and for gaining time, for boosting production efficiency and accelerating scientific and technological progress."[4]

Guided by the Leninist ideas of restructuring the entire pattern of international relations including economic, scientific, and technical relations, the CPSU and the Soviet state have been steadily working for establishing truly democratic principles in relations between states. International economic, scientific, and technical relations can be based only on the principles of sovereignty and full equality of the countries involved, on full respect for their laws, for their social and political systems. These relations should rest on mutual benefit and should help each country involved to develop its productive forces and improve living standards in rational and effective ways. The problem of identifying direction and terms for developing international co-operation in the field of economic activity, science and technology is of first importance as it largely determines not only successful co-operation but also its conversion into a major factor in stabilizing world peace.

As a counterweight to those international economic relations which were fashioned under capitalism and which rested on the selfish interests of monopoly groups and individual enterpreneurs, on the dictates of the strong, the socialist countries approach international co-operation from a fundamentally different angle. Behind-the-scene deals, agreements playing off one set of partners against the other, market speculation — all these features so familiar in the behaviour of countries seeking to manage international economic life for selfish ends, to oppress and exploit economically weak countries, are alien to socialist countries. These countries in no way regard international economic, scientific, and technical exchanges as benefiting one side only to the other's disadvantage. On the contrary they believe that in the modern world all countries stand to gain from a mutually beneficial exchange, even though in this each partner is governed by his own interests.

Socialist and capitalist countries with their polarized social and economic systems are part of a global economic system which is in the course of change. Within the framework of a global economic system, they expand and improve co-operation in economic, scientific, and technical fields.

In studying the nature and character of global economic relations, the founders of Marxism–Leninism took it that the development of these relations was stimulated by the requirements of material production and the progress of productive forces, that it was an objective and progressive global trend. Under the impact of this trend towards the internationalization of economic life, each country was interested in taking full advantage of the international division of labour with a view to developing its own productive forces in the most efficient and comprehensive way.

The current scientific and technological revolution has brought with it new factors of the international division of labour in addition to the traditional ones. The dramatic expansion of the range of industrial products coupled with their increasing technical sophistication, notably in the engineering, electronics, electric power development and chemical industries makes it impossible for even the biggest industrialized countries to maintain sustained and economically efficient manufacture of the full world range of products.

The further progress of the scientific and technical revolution which is augmenting the trend towards the internationalization of economic activity calls for wide growth in international economic, scientific, and technical co-operation. That revolution has involved the two world social and political systems on account of specific laws governing the evolution of both. It helps form and strengthen international ties in the economic, scientific, and technical fields.

The objective need for expanding economic, scientific, and technical co-operation between socialist and industrialized capitalist countries is being increasingly dictated by the logic of the scientific and technological revolution and its inherent laws. To quote Leonid Brezhnev again: "One can only keep pace with the times and measure up to the demands and opportunities of the scientific and technological revolution by relying on the broad international division of labour. Today this is, perhaps, axiomatic. Hence the need for mutually beneficial long-term and large-scale economic co-operation, both bilateral and multilateral. ... We further advocate this kind of co-operation because we see it as a good method of providing a secure material back-up for peaceful relations among nations."[5]

Today, the degree of specialization of modern science is so great and the sphere of practical application of the results of scientific research so all-embracing that even countries with the most developed scientific and technical potential are no longer able to advance with equal success in every area of scientific research. This emphasizes the imperative need for an across-the-board expansion of scientific and technical co-operation between the socialist and the industrialized capitalist countries with their great scientific and technical potential and numerous trained personnel. Without such co-operation the further progress of science would be difficult if not impossible.

Scientific and technological co-operation emerging as a distinct trend after the end of the Second World War, is now a major element in the present system of international economic relations. The rapid scientific and technological revolution is prompting different countries to pool their efforts both on a regional and global basis for greater success in tackling common economic, technical, and ecological problems. Such collaboration enables the participating countries to derive maximum benefits from the international division of labour, to avoid the irrational waste of effort and resources resulting from duplication of scientific and technological projects. Scientific and technological monopoly is a luxury that no country today can afford. Eventually it inhibits progress in science and the advancement of the productive forces of each country.

Made up of countries with different social systems, today's world is not homogeneous. But mankind is facing a series of problems whose resolution is vital to the future of the human race. These include the provision of adequate food, raw materials, and energy for the world's growing population. Then there is the problem of the economic backwardness of Asia, Africa, and Latin America, the legacy of colonialism. The successful resolution of this problem is essential for normal international relations in the future, for mankind's progress as a whole. Finally, there are problems of shielding mankind from numerous dangers posed by the onward rush of uncontrolled technological progress, in other words preservation of the human environment and conservation of nature. As Leonid Brezhnev put it: "These are real and serious problems. With every decade that passes, these problems will become more acute unless a sensible solution is found by collective efforts through planned international co-operation."[6]

Despite the formidable complexity of the problems facing the world today, the situation can be improved to a considerable extent by collective efforts of the world's nations through international co-operation based on full equality. Addressing the 6th Special Session of the UN General Assembly in April 1974, Andrei Gromyko stated that the USSR invariably and consistently advocated a pooling of efforts to tackle problems affecting the interests of all mankind. In his words: "The USSR declares its readiness to participate both on a bilateral and multilateral basis in discussions of ways and means of overcoming the energy crisis, bearing in mind that the interests of all countries should be adequately met. Perhaps in no other area is there a greater need to restructure the present pattern of international economic relations with a view to basing them on principles of genuinely equal and mutually beneficial co-operation."[7]

The exacerbation of global energy, raw materials, and food-supply problems has placed on the agenda more thorough study of the resources of the World Ocean, accounting as it does for three-quarters of the globe's surface, to ensure these resources are more rationally and efficiently made use of. Already the World Ocean supplies an estimated 13 per cent of the total protein for human consumption, some 20 per cent of the world's oil, over 70 per cent of its bromium, and 60 per cent of its magnesium output. The ocean contains practically everything required to support the human race. Its role in transport cannot be over-emphasized. A rational exploitation of these and other resources calls for joint efforts of many countries, in the first instance of those which possess the necessary economic, technical, and scientific potential. At present the socialist and the industrialized capitalist countries have this potential.

The World Ocean is a biologically integrated and carefully balanced ecological system. The present scale and methods of its exploitation may, if continued, do irreparable harm to this delicate balance. Therefore it is essential to develop international economic, scientific and technical co-operation among all interested countries in resolving the above-mentioned problems.

Many of the dilemmas of environmental protection are no respecters of national frontiers. To tackle them successfully would be impossible without economic, scientific, technical, and political co-operation of the countries affected. Environmental pollution is particularly heavy in industrialized capitalist countries, on account of the uncontrolled operations of monopolies which pay little or no attention to environmental protection and nature conservation.

The rapidly unfolding scientific and technological revolution accentuates the need and gives added opportunities for developing long-term economic, scientific, and technical co-operation to accelerate progress in many other areas of human endeavour where collective efforts are essential. Cases in point include space exploration, transport, notably air transport, the peaceful uses of nuclear energy, and control of the most dangerous and widespread diseases.

Long-term and stable economic, scientific, and technical co-operation between socialist and industrialized capitalist countries directed at these and other problems will doubtless help their eventual resolution and enable the countries involved to save time, effort, and resources in the process. All this at the end of the day will benefit the whole of mankind, and will contribute to more lasting world peace and international security. The Soviet Communist Party at its 24th and 25th Congresses declared the Soviet Union's readiness to actively participate in a concerted, international attack on these problems. The USSR has been steadily working to fulfil the CPSU's instructions and expand its co-operation in the economic, scientific and technical fields with the rest of the world.

Expansion of Economic, Scientific, Technical and Cultural Co-operation

Broad international co-operation in the economic, scientific, technical, and cultural fields is a salient feature of the stage we have reached in the evolution of international relations. Apart from the expanding scale of this co-operation, new forms of developing it have emerged and enriched its content to make this co-operation an essential aspect of the ongoing fundamental restructuring of the fabric of international relations.

These relations lie in a sphere at once complex and multi-dimensional. Foreign trade, production relations, capital movements, currency dealings, international services, the exchange of scientific discoveries and inventions, together with yet more forms of relations between countries create an intricate nexus of global economic relations which represents a dialectic unifying a great many contradictory processes and factors. The progress of international economic relations is characterized by an unstable equilibrium subject to periodic disturbances from the operation of laws governing the development of capitalism. However, the contradictory nature of capitalist economics is not the only factor upsetting the balance of today's world. There are a number of political reasons as well. One has been the drastic curtailment by the capitalist countries of business co-operation with the socialist countries during the Cold War. For a long time this inhibited international economic co-operation, slowing down the internationalization of global economic activity and damaging the interests of all countries regardless of their socio-economic system.

For many years the imperialists tried to block the economic development of the socialist countries by hampering their participation in the international division of labour. Developments since then have shown the utter futility of these attempts and compelled a realistic reappraisal of the state of the world. As John Rockefeller, the American financier, rightly observed: "For the last twenty years we have cut off most trade, most exports, and this has not brought them [the socialist countries] to their knees, has not forced them to come begging to us, and has not prevented them from rearming and becoming more powerful in the world."[8] A similar situation arose early in 1980 when the Carter Administration imposed severe restrictions on trade with the USSR. But these discriminatory restrictions are bound to fail.

The difficulties the capitalist world are encountering impel it towards economic co-operation with the socialist countries. However, the changed approach of capitalist countries to economic co-operation with the socialist world does not signify change in the basic attitude of their ruling classes to socialism. The struggle between socialism and capitalism still continues at the present, new stage in the evolution of international relations, but is being increasingly conducted within a framework that does not conflict with the task of maintaining world peace and mutually advantageous co-operation.

Lenin observed more than once that global economic relations were becoming a more powerful force than either the will or decisions of any of the bourgeois governments and classes hostile to socialism, and that this superior force was compelling them to establish economic relations with the socialist world. As early as the latter half of the 1960s, the policy of curtailing trade with the USSR and other socialist countries began to give way in the majority of capitalist countries to a policy aimed at achieving a measure of normalization and encouraging commercial and economic links with the socialist world. In the early 1970s, when political *détente* in international relations was stimulating the passage to stable political co-operation between countries with different social systems, this process gained momentum. Discussion of problems involved in expanding economic relations, conclusion of ever-wider economic agreements increasingly became the top priority for summit meetings between the leaders of socialist and capitalist countries.

In the 1970s trade between East and West expanded rapidly as socialist and capitalist countries concluded hundreds of agreements on economic co-operation. As a result the trade turnover between

Comecon and the EEC grew from 7,500 million dollars in 1970 to 70,000 million dollars in 1977.[9]

Since the early 1970s the USSR has substantially expanded its trade, and scientific and technical co-operation with the industrialized capitalist countries. This is best seen (Table 2) in the growth of trade turnover between the USSR and this group of countries.

TABLE 2
Soviet trade with advanced capitalist countries
(thousand million roubles in current prices)*

	1970	1971	1972	1973	1974	1975	1976	1977	1978	1979
Exports	2.2	2.5	2.5	3.7	6.3	6.1	7.8	7.8	8.7	12.5
Imports	2.5	2.6	3.4	4.6	6.1	9.7	10.9	10.9	11.0	13.2
Turnover	4.7	5.1	5.9	8.3	12.4	15.8	18.7	18.7	19.7	25.7

Source: *Foreign Trade of the USSR in the Postwar Period.* Moscow, 1972, p. 14. *Economic Gazette*, 1980, No. 13, p. 20.

As Table 2 indicates, between 1970 and 1976 the USSR's annual trade with advanced capitalist countries grew fourfold to reach 18,700 million roubles in 1976. Since 1976 there has been a slow-down in the growth of trade. The increase in the USSR's trade with advanced capitalist countries in 1979 by 6000 million roubles as compared with the 1978 level is largely attributable to a sharp rise in prices.[10]

The Soviet Union's biggest trading partner among the industrialized capitalist countries is West Germany. The USSR's trade with the FRG reached 2900 million roubles in 1977, a sixfold increase compared with 1970. In 1978 it rose to 3300 million roubles.

Japan is the USSR's second largest trading partner among the advanced capitalist countries. In 1977 Soviet trade with Japan amounted to some 2400 million roubles.

The USSR's trade with Finland stood at 2200 million roubles in 1978, with Italy — some 2000 million roubles, with France — 1800 million roubles and with Britain 1500 million roubles.[11]

The USA was in the sixth place in the USSR's trade with industrialized capitalist countries in 1977 (when the trade turnover stood at more than 1500 million roubles).[12] Between 1971 and 1975 the volume of Soviet–American trade exceeded that in the preceding 5 years by more than eight times and reached 5400 million roubles. The following statistics give a good idea of the importance of the change in Soviet–American trade: because of the discriminatory restrictions and the economic blockade imposed by the USA on the USSR and other socialist countries the volume of trade between the USSR and USA in 1951 was a minuscule 22 million roubles.[13]

While noting the progress of Soviet–American trade, we should qualify that by saying that as yet this trade does not match the full economic potential of the two countries either in terms of volume and other parameters or in terms of the role the two countries play in the world economy. A severe impact on the progress of Soviet–American trade has been exerted by the laws on trade and government export credits passed by the US Congress in December 1974 which made the grant of most-favoured-nation status to the USSR and the provision of government export credits conditional on Soviet consent to certain unacceptable terms which have no bearing on trade and economic relations. In the second half of the 1970s the US Administration's hardening line on Soviet–American relations as a whole impeded commercial and economic links between the USSR and USA. In early 1980 the US Administration virtually embargoed trade with the USSR under the pretext of "punishing" the USSR for the help it had given to the government of the Democratic Republic of Afghanistan.

While noting the rapid expansion of trade between the socialist and the capitalist countries, we remark the fact that this trade is still rather modest when set against the economic potential and role in the world economy of these countries. East–West trade still represents only 6 per cent of the world trade turnover, and this at a time when the socialist and capitalist countries involved account for over 90 per cent of the world's industrial production.

The present stage of commercial and economic relations between socialist and industrialized capitalist countries is characterized not only by a steady expansion of trade, but also by new forms of co-operation. These latter reflect a quantitative as well as qualitative shift in this area of international life, the result of an ongoing restructuring of the global system of inter-state relations which has touched every area of world economics and politics.

Long-term and large-scale projects are becoming a salient feature of the new stage in the economic relations between socialist and capitalist countries. Long-term programmes (usually dated for 10 years) of commercial, economic, industrial, scientific and technical co-operation form the organizational and legal basis of large-scale co-operation between socialist and industrialized capitalist countries. In May 1978 USSR and West Germany signed a 25-year agreement providing for a significant expansion of economic relations between them up to the year 2000. The agreement gives a new dimension to the Soviet Union's economic, scientific, and technical co-operation with other countries and is having a major stabilizing effect on political relations in the world.

To date, a total of 1200 contracts for industrial co-operation have been signed between countries which participated in the Helsinki conference and each year adds another hundred such. At the moment 220 long-term inter-governmental agreements on economic co-operation are in hand. By contrast, in the early 1960s there were only 23. Today hundreds of Western companies and banks have their representatives in socialist countries, 180 of them in the USSR alone. At the same time 20 banks in the West are handling operations on behalf of the socialist countries.

Industrial co-operation with developed capitalist countries was pioneered by Hungary and Poland in the mid-1960s. Now Hungary has over 300 industrial co-operation agreements with capitalist countries, Poland 200, Romania 150, Bulgaria 30, and Czechoslovakia 25. In 1970 a Soviet organization concluded an agreement with the French firm Alcatel on the manufacture and marketing of programme-controlled machine-tools. Under the agreement the Soviet side manufactures the machine-tools while the French side produces and supplies the associated control systems. Industrial co-operation between socialist and capitalist countries now covers the building of ships, the manufacture of hydraulic excavators, power equipment, electronic computers, and so on. The USSR is helping to build nuclear power stations and an iron-and-steel works in Finland, an iron and steel complex in France, and a major hydro-electric power station in Iceland.

The development of industrial co-operation presents excellent opportunities for expanding business relations. However, to exploit such opportunities calls for a greater measure of mutual trust and for strict observance of often flexible organizational arrangements. It should be remembered that co-operation is often marred by the attempts of some Western firms to gain unilateral advantages by trying to foist onto the socialist countries only those technologies and production lines which heavily pollute the environment, require low-skilled manning staffs, and do not readily lend themselves to mechanization.

Discussing new forms of external economic relations which have emerged in recent years and which are dominated by "buy-back" deals between Western firms and the USSR, the 25th CPSU Congress stated that "they substantially add to our potential and, as a rule, yield the best effect".[14] Under such compensation agreements, new enterprises wholly owned by the USSR are built in co-operation with foreign firms, the former receiving credits, equipment, and licences from its Western partners and repaying them with part of the products manufactured by these enterprises.

The USSR has concluded scores of such buy-back deals with many industrialized capitalist countries for the execution of major industrial projects in a variety of industries. Their total value exceeds several thousand million roubles. Under compensation agreements, the USSR is carrying out a series of major projects some of which are the biggest of their kind in the world. These include first and foremost a 5000-kilometre trans-European gas pipeline with an annual transmission capacity of 30,000 million cubic metres of natural gas. Major firms of West Germany, Italy, France, and Austria are helping build this pipeline. US, West German, Italian, and French firms assist the USSR in building automobile plants. Other joint industrial projects currently in hand include a major fertilizer complex being built in co-operation with American firms; a major iron and steel complex near Kursk being built with a number of West German companies; a gas pipeline to link Iran, West Germany, Austria and France via the USSR and Czechoslovakia being built with West German, French, and Austrian technical assistance; a pulp-and-paper complex at Ust-Ilyim being carried out with French participation. Japan is helping the USSR to develop coal mining and timber industries in the Soviet Far East.

For its part the USSR participates in the execution of thirteen major construction projects including a metallurgical complex at Fos-sur-Mer, an oil refinery at Anbesse, a large-capacity forge plant at Issoir, all in France; an iron and steel complex, two nuclear power plants and a trunk gas pipeline in Finland.

The mutual benefit derived by both sides from buy-back deals is beyond question. Under these deals the USSR's foreign partners acquire a stable market over time for their products. In a situation marked by dwindling marketing opportunities in the capitalist world due to stiffening competition and price instability, this offers the foreign firms added opportunities to strengthen their economic position.

Mixed companies are playing an increasing role in stepping up the deliveries of industrial products from socialist countries to West European markets. There are such companies in France, Finland, Sweden, Belgium, Norway, and some other countries. In France several mixed companies are operating: Aktif-Auto (to promote Soviet farm machinery, road-building and construction equipment), Rusbois (timber), SOSO (chemicals) and Stanko-France (marketing machine-tools, forges and presses). There are commercial centres for the sale and servicing of Soviet-made motor cars which promote Soviet car exports in Finland (Konela), Sweden (Matrico), Norway (Konela Norgebil), Belgium (Scaldia-Volga).

The co-ordination of economic programmes by government agencies of the co-operating countries and the adoption of crucial decisions on economic co-operation at government level are entirely novel in the economic relations between socialist and industrialized capitalist countries. This new quality of co-operation, characteristic of relations between socialist countries, is gradually coming to mark East–West economic relations, lending them greater stability.

Co-operation between Comecon and capitalist countries is noted for yet another major quality: the socialist countries are pursuing this co-operation not for any passing considerations. For them, such collaboration is no temporary phase, but reflects their long-term interest, based as it is on long-term national economic development plans.

For the West a long-term approach to the development of economic co-operation with socialist countries is also important because such realities of the capitalist world as competition, the search for new markets, the problem of maintaining the operation of industries at full capacity and ensuring full employment are all long-term factors. Therefore, that the number of long-term agreements on economic co-operation between socialist and capitalist countries should have exceeded the total of conventional trade deals between them is a perfectly logical development.

Monetary relations occupy a special place in East–West economic life. Their importance can hardly be over-estimated, as they form the nerve system of economic co-operation and may either promote or inhibit its progress. Monetary relations are a particularly sensitive barometer of the political atmosphere. The scale, forms, and means of monetary relations between countries with polarized systems reflect the political relations between them as well as the state of commercial, economic, scientific and technical co-operation that exists.

Experts on international monetary relations have noted that the credit policy of the West towards socialist countries has undergone significant change under the impact of international *détente*. Once a political weapon, most obviously so in the Cold War period, credit is gradually becoming a means of normal economic co-operation based on mutual benefit. Thus in recent years France has made available to the USSR 3200 million, Italy 1800, Japan 1500, and Canada 500 million dollars.

The financing of American exports to the USSR and other socialist countries is still at a fairly low level owing to discriminatory restrictions imposed on the socialist countries.

There are serious obstacles in the way of economic, scientific, and technical co-operation between socialist and industrialized countries of the West. The EEC is a closed integrated grouping of nine industrialized countries of Western Europe which have fenced themselves off from the rest of the world with high import customs tariffs. As a result the EEC countries discriminate against socialist countries in their tariffs policy. The socialist countries currently have to pay the EEC for exports of manufactured and semi-manufactured goods 9 per cent on top of value.

Socialist countries also lose money on farm exports to EEC

countries by paying a massive surcharge equivalent on average to a 35 per cent customs duty, a record rate in the industrialized capitalist world.

The progress of economic co-operation between Comecon and the EEC has raised a series of organizational and legal questions that bear on identifying the areas in which the two economic groups desire to co-operate. It is essential to build these relations on a non-discriminatory basis with due regard for the interests of both in the resolution of urgent problems.

We have already spoken of the objective need for international co-operation in science and technology as being integral to the pattern of global economic relations. The opportunities for co-operation in this area are excellent on account of the impressive success scored by the Soviet Union and other socialist countries in the field of science and technology.

However, there are not a few politicians in the USA and other Western countries who oppose scientific and technical co-operation with the USSR and other socialist countries, seeing it as "helping the enemy". These politicians approach *détente* and its manifestations in every area of international life "from positions of strength", following the dangerous stereotypes of the Cold War period. They allege that *détente* is a "one-way street" bringing benefits to the USSR alone, which according to them, desperately needs Western technology.

The opponents of *détente* and expansion of Soviet–American economic, scientific, and technical co-operation build on a weak foundation their plans to hamper the construction of communism in the USSR by breaking off contacts. It is a fact that the Soviet Union scored outstanding success in science and technology in a period when scientific and commercial contacts between the USSR and the USA were non-existent. Developments since then have demonstrated that the Soviet economy and science are fully capable of coping with problems facing them without economic contacts with the West.

It should be added, however, that the present scale of economic, scientific, and technical co-operation between socialist and industrialized capitalist countries is grossly out of proportion with their potential. The reason for this is to be sought not in economics or science but rather in the throw-backs to the days of the Cold War, in the disruptive activity of reactionary forces which oppose international *détente* and attempt to make the development of trade and scientific and technical contacts with the USSR and other socialist countries conditional on the USSR giving them a blank cheque to interfere in their domestic affairs.

Thus, despite the undeniable success that has been scored thus far in expanding economic, scientific, and technical links between socialist and capitalist countries, the tremendous opportunities for mutually advantageous co-operation and the advantages of the international division of labour are far from being exploited to the full. It should be said that practically all industrialized capitalist countries are resorting to various forms of discrimination in their economic, scientific, and technical contacts with the USSR and other socialist countries. The range of the discriminatory measures used is wide enough. A severe inhibitor of trade between socialist countries and developed capitalist countries is the imposition by most of these countries of restrictions on imports from the USSR and other socialist countries.

A number of countries, notably those on NATO's co-ordination committee for the control of strategic exports to socialist countries (COCOM), have lists of "strategic" goods not exportable to the USSR and other socialist countries. Various discriminatory tariffs imposed on exports from socialist countries, including refusal to grant them most-favoured-nation status, severely hamper trade between socialist and industrialized capitalist countries.

Many of these countries have imposed restrictions on the export of certain lines of goods to the socialist countries along with restrictions on credit and the licensing of exports. The United States is practising an especially wide variety of discriminatory measures to inhibit trade and scientific and technical co-operation with the USSR and other socialist countries. American external economic practices contain, perhaps, the greatest number of survivals and legacies of the Cold War in the sphere of economic, scientific, and technical links, above all with the USSR, of any Western country.

Thus, two distinct trends are in evidence in economic, scientific, and technical co-operation between East and West: one is towards their expansion, the other towards freezing them, to the point of curtailment. The struggle of these two trends has a direct bearing on international *détente*. The first trend is contributing to give material substance to *détente* while the second undermines it.

The present condition of economic co-operation between socialist and industrialized capitalist countries indicates that the trend towards its expansion over the past decade is steadily gaining momentum, being based, as we have shown, on the objective factors of social, historical, production, scientific, and technical development. The eventual triumph of this trend is not in doubt.

However, it should also be noted that in recent years the opponents of *détente* have put numerous obstacles in the way of expanding economic, scientific, and technical co-operation between East and West to hamper efforts to consolidate *détente*. Quite powerful forces are attempting to prevent the expansion of East–West economic co-operation. The active resistance of the military–industrial complexes of the leading imperialist countries and the aggressive NATO bloc is a severe brake on the progress of co-operation.

While paying lip service to *détente*, spokesmen for the military–industrial complex and the NATO leadership claim that *détente* can be a reality provided the West keeps on building up its military power to offset the combined military potential of the Warsaw Pact member countries. Using anti-Communist slogans and the myth of Soviet military threat, they are seeking to poison the political atmosphere in the world in order to freeze and curtail economic co-operation with socialist countries. Their arguments for doing so are highly unoriginal: they allege that expansion of economic and scientific and technical co-operation with the USSR and other socialist countries is helping a potential military opponent. Therefore, they conclude, this co-operation should be severely limited, if not ended altogether. These forces propose to cut the scale and volume of co-operation, to restrict its forms and give up the quest for new ones, as well as to impose all sorts of restrictions and bans, to make political demands on socialist countries prejudicial to their sovereignty, and much else.

The refusal to grant the USSR most-favoured-nation status is not motivated by any economic considerations. The Soviet Government rejects as totally improper and unacceptable American attempts to make commercial and economic links with the USSR conditional on the latter meeting American demands in matters that have nothing to do with trade and economic relations and lie exclusively within the sphere of Soviet jurisdiction. This sort of claim to interference in the domestic affairs of another state can yield nothing but harm and inhibit trade and economic relations between the two countries.

The Soviet Union has strongly rebuffed this policy. Thus, the attempts to exact a "political tribute" from the USSR exemplified by the Jackson–Vanik amendment to the 1974 Trade Act failed. *Business Week* wrote: "The authors of the amendment made two serious mistakes. They assumed that under pressure from Congress the Russians would be prepared to capitulate in public. They also assumed that the USSR could not do without American industrial goods and technology."[15]

Speaking of the opportunities the US missed as a result of the adoption of the Jackson–Vanik amendment, ex-President Ford sadly observed that "as a result, Western Europe and Japan have stepped into the breach...".[16] Experts of the USSR–USA Trade and Economic Council have estimated that because of the discriminatory restrictions imposed by the US Congress, the USA lost 2000 million dollars' worth of Soviet orders. *Business Week* wrote that the Americans fear that while Washington stalled on easing restrictions more and more orders would go to European and Japanese businessmen offering low-interest credits.[17]

In recent years, those opposed to an expansion of economic co-operation between East and West have joined hands with various reactionary forces including the Zionist circles of many capitalist countries, scientists, politicians, and journalists who have thrown in their lot with the cold warriors, reactionary émigré organizations, and such like. At first they did not object to expanding economic co-operation with socialist countries, trusting to convert this co-operation into an instrument for interference in their domestic affairs, into a tool for subverting the pillars of socialism.

When they saw that the socialist countries were frustrating their plans, they began to press for a curtailment of economic co-operation with the East, pointing to alleged violations of human rights in the socialist countries. The realities of life in the USSR, the new Soviet

Constitution which proclaims and guarantees the exercise of the full range of human rights in every area of political, economic, and cultural life, give the lie to these insinuations.

Finally, in some capitalist countries, notably in the USA, many people cherish strange ideas that economic difficulties, notably rising unemployment, have been brought on by economic co-operation with socialist countries. This line of attack is being used by reactionary trade-union bureaucrats in the George Meaney mould who claim that imports from the USSR and other socialist countries "eat up" jobs that unemployed Americans would otherwise have had if the USA had produced the goods involved.

However, it is common knowledge that unemployment in capitalist countries springs from inherent features of capitalism which cannot exist without a reserve army of labour. The clumsy attempt to blame unemployment in capitalist countries on their economic co-operation with socialist countries is preposterous.

Chancellor Schmidt of West Germany said in an interview that West Germany's trade with the USSR and other socialist countries, thanks to its significant expansion in recent years with a social–liberal government in office, had created jobs for some 300,000 people. The political significance of this trade lies in the fact that it meets the commercial interests of both sides, being the bedrock of *détente* and the normalization of relations, and makes these relations understandable for everyone. Commercial interests are a good defence from the policy of reverting to the days of the Cold War.[18] Despite the difficulties in its way, East–West economic co-operation has been making steady progress as recent statistics clearly indicate. The USSR and other socialist countries are optimistic about its future.

The 25th CPSU Congress defined as a major task an ever-deeper involvement of the USSR's national economy in the international division of labour and the further efforts to place its economic co-operation with the rest of the world on a long-term footing. This objective has been incorporated into the Tenth Five-Year Plan. Prime Minister Alexei Kosygin put it thus in his report to the 25th Congress:

Our primary attention will be devoted, as before, to the development and consolidation of co-operation with the socialist countries. The twenty-year comprehensive programme for socialist economic integration and the co-ordinated plan of multilateral integration measures adopted by the Comecon session in the summer of 1975 are taking on increasing significance for our co-operation....

In the conditions of international *détente*, our economic relations with the developed capitalist countries, which have a good basis for expanding on the principles of the Final Act of the Conference on Security and Co-operation in Europe, are also acquiring new qualitative aspects. We shall continue the practice of concluding large-scale co-operation agreements on building industrial projects in our country and on the participation of Soviet organizations in building industrial enterprises in Western countries. Other promising forms of co-operation include agreements on a compensation system, especially so if the recovery of investments in the new enterprises is rapid, the agreements on various types of industrial co-operation and joint scientific research and design.[19]

Further vigorous and purposeful efforts must be made to expand and improve mutually beneficial economic co-operation which forms the essential basis of peaceful co-existence between countries with different social systems, to consolidate the gains achieved by positive development in this area. Only this approach can help to further lessen the threat of war and eventually produce a new pattern of international relations, more sound and in harmony with the aspirations of the world's nations.

The 1970s saw significant progress in the field of cultural relations between socialist and capitalist countries as more and more countries became involved in cultural exchange. Cultural exchanges expanded and became more intensive and their forms more varied. Cultural exchanges are now a key area of the foreign policy of countries and the subject of treaties and agreements.

In the past 5 years the USSR expanded its cultural exchanges with the rest of the world by some 50 per cent. At the moment the USSR is maintaining cultural contacts with 120 countries. Needless to say, nothing like that could even have been dreamt of in the days of the Cold War.

A salient feature of today's international cultural exchange is that it is becoming an indispensable element of peaceful co-existence of countries having different social systems, and an effective instrument for strengthening peace, friendship, and mutual understanding among nations. International *détente* helps achieve international cultural exchange, and that has a positive feedback effect by helping to create a climate of mutual trust and goodwill.

This important function of international cultural exchange has been formalized in a series of international documents in the early 1970s. Thus in 1970 UNESCO called upon all countries to step up activities through cultural and information media in support of peace, international co-operation and mutual understanding, and to take appropriate measures against the production, publication, and circulation of works inciting hatred between nations, and violence and war.[20]

The international UNESCO Conference on cultural policy in Europe held in Helsinki in the summer of 1972 pointed out that cultural contacts among European countries promote better knowledge of one another, greater trust and mutual understanding, and in this way contribute to *détente* and the disappearance of tension in Europe. The Conference recommended that all European states should regard cultural co-operation as a contribution to European security, and should actively use cultural exchanges and the media to promote ideas of peace, friendship and mutual understanding.[21]

In developing cultural relations with the rest of the world, the USSR and other socialist countries have been strictly adhering to these principles. The USSR strongly opposes the persistence of such legacies of the Cold War as "psychological warfare", the use of the media to poison relations between countries and conduct subversion.

Cultural co-operation between socialist and capitalist countries made encouraging progress in the 1970s. Even so, there was a measure of imbalance in cultural exchanges. The reasons for this imbalance include the attempts of certain forces in the West to exploit cultural exchanges for the purpose of camouflaged subversion, and the resistance of Western circles to an expansion of cultural exchanges with the socialist world.

The USSR and the socialist countries are advocating such principles in the field of international cultural exchange whose strict observance is essential for the further expansion of international cultural co-operation: respect for sovereignty, domestic legislation, and the national peculiarities of each country, non-interference in its internal affairs, and reciprocity. Leonid Brezhnev outlined the Soviet Union's position on this issue with total clarity when he said: "One often hears that the West attaches importance to co-operation in the cultural domain, and especially to exchanges of ideas, the spread of information, and to contacts between nations. Permit us to declare here in all earnest: we too are in favour of this, provided of course that such co-operation is conducted with due respect for the sovereignty, laws, and enrichment of the peoples, for greater trust between them, and for ideas of peace and good-neighbourly relations."[22] Given this, the development of international cultural exchanges will benefit the cause of peace and co-operation among nations and will become a key factor in the democratic restructuring of the present pattern of international relations.

In line with the Final Act of the Helsinki Conference, the USSR and other socialist countries have adopted further measures to expand the exchange of books, films, and works of art. As for the capitalist countries, their high-sounding rhetoric about the importance of exchanging spiritual values was not matched by their deeds. On the whole, the population of socialist countries are better informed about life in the West than is the public in capitalist countries about socialist reality. The reason for this lies chiefly in the fact that the ruling class in capitalist countries is not interested in helping the working people at home to learn at first hand the truth about socialist countries, about their public and cultural life, and their political development.[23]

These, then, in broad outline, are some of the major results and main features of the progress of economic, scientific, technical, and cultural relations between socialist and capitalist countries under *détente* and of the progressive restructuring of international relations on the basis of peaceful co-existence of countries with different social systems.

9

The Developing Countries in the Modern World

ONE of the major changes in recent international life has been the conversion of former colonies and dependent countries from the objects of imperialist policy they once were into fully fledged subjects of international relations. The involvement of these countries in the mainstream of world politics, their independent performance on the world scene without any imperialist intermediaries, have considerably diversified this process, making it more dynamic and comprehensive.

The changing alignment of forces in favour of socialism in the world has been a crucial factor in the failure of the imperialist powers to keep their grip on giant colonial empires. The collapse of the colonial system of imperialism in the 'fifties and 'sixties ended the more obscene forms inherent in capitalism of relations between countries, the forms of direct subordination of colonies to mother-countries. The process of decolonization which developed vigorously from the 1950s-60s dealt a mortal blow to the traditional patterns of colonialism. However, the imperialists did not give up the hope of keeping the peoples of former colonies in submission. By exploiting the economic and political weakness of newly independent countries, the imperialist powers attempted to retain their military, political, and economic presence so as to be able to influence the new domestic and foreign policy. The neo-colonialist strategy of imperialism in this period found expression in a cobbling together of military–political blocs in Asia, in drawing into them the newly independent countries, in

265

propping up reactionary and puppet regimes, and in economic penetration of these countries. To retain their grip on the peoples of Asia and Africa in the post-colonial era, imperialist circles fanned national, regional, and inter-communal strife and differences passed on from the colonial period. It is no secret to any that the Western powers were behind the 1961-4 Congo crisis, the conflict in Laos after the 1962 Geneva Conference, and others.

The struggle of the imperialist powers against national liberation movements in Asia, Africa, and Latin America and the support and backing they gave to domestic reaction often took the form of direction intervention. This was a feature of the neo-colonialist policy of imperialism in the 'fifties and 'sixties towards countries fighting for their independence. However, as the international situation evolved, imperialist attempts to secure a position of dominance in developing countries through the direct use or threat of force were becoming less effective. The reason was that the steadily growing military and political power of the socialist countries and their increasing assistance to the newly independent countries were gradually creating objective conditions under which direct armed intervention by the imperialist powers was restricted or ruled out altogether.

Yet it would be premature to claim that armed intervention has been completely discarded from the arsenal of foreign-policy instruments at the disposal of imperialist powers in their relations with developing countries. From time to time threats emanate from Western capitals to use armed force against young independent countries whose policies do not suit the imperialist circles. Suffice it to recall the scandalous announcement by the former US Secretary of State that under certain conditions American armed intervention is not ruled out against the oil-rich countries of the Middle East seeking to use their mineral wealth for national advancement. But this kind of threat, which 10 or 20 years ago might have helped the imperialists achieve their aims, today is counter-productive as it only stiffens the resolve of developing countries to protect their national interests from being encroached on by imperialist monopolies. Naturally, things would have been quite different had the developing countries been obliged to defend their political and economic independence in a face-to-face confrontation with the immeasurably superior forces of imperialism.

The help and support they received from the socialist countries have made a crucial contribution to the efforts of developing countries to defend that independence and make the imperialist powers renounce their more aggressive methods of conducting relations with these countries. The growing role of recent colonies and semi-colonies in world affairs is a key feature of contemporary historical development. This positive process springs from a variety of factors, not least from the circumstance that as more and more colonies and semi-colonies gain independence and the total of such new countries grows, the combined population of the Third World grows with it. Of the almost 150 UN member states, 115 are developing countries whose combined population accounts for 60 per cent of the world's total. But other factors seem to have been more important.

In recent years, the peoples fighting for their complete national and social emancipation have scored a marked success. Imperialist attempts to subvert the freedom and independence of the peoples of Indo-China by force of arms failed dismally. Portugal's colonial empire, the world's last surviving one, has collapsed. The peoples of Guinea-Bissau, Mozambique, Angola, the São Tomé, Principe, and Cape Verde Islands have gained independence. The racialist regimes of Southern Africa are being undermined. Popular movements in Namibia and Rhodesia entered a new stage. The anti-apartheid campaign in South Africa has become more active. The concerted efforts of imperialism and Zionism to suppress independent development of the Arab countries have failed. Most of the African and Asian countries, having won political independence, are working steadily to achieve economic independence. These countries are nationalizing the property of foreign capitalists, tearing down the colonial economic structure and making a start on developing a diversified economy. Industrialization and expansion of the public sector, land reform, the overcoming of survivals of feudalism, measures to improve living standards — such things are what is novel in the development of the newly independent countries. Progressive forces in these countries are steadily working to stamp out the vestiges of colonialism, to democratize public and government institutions, to strengthen political self-sufficiency and conduct an independent foreign policy. Most of the developing countries, members of the non-aligned movement, embrace the principles of peaceful co-existence.

India, Sri Lanka, and Nigeria have made notable progress in their efforts to attain economic self-sufficiency and to strengthen their political freedom. India has almost quadrupled its industrial output since independence. The public sector of its economy accounts for all of heavy engineering output and for one-quarter of total electric-power generation. A number of developing countries are following the socialist path. Algeria, the Congo, Guinea, the PDRY (South Yemen), and other countries have made encouraging progress along the road of non-capitalist development. The positive social and political evolution of the young states, many of which are embarked on socialist development, reinforces their contribution to the struggle for world peace and security of nations, and involves them more deeply in the global revolutionary process as well as in efforts to restructure the present pattern of international relations.

A major factor in the growing influence of the developing countries is their changing position in the world economy, more specifically in industrial production and within the system of external economic relations of capitalist countries.[1] The deepening crisis of capitalism coupled with serious energy and raw-materials shortages has brought out an important truth: the economies of even major imperialist powers are directly dependent on the terms on which they will retain access to the raw-material and energy resources of developing countries. Indeed, the contribution to the total consumption by America, the EEC countries and Japan of iron ore, aluminium, chromium, cobalt, copper, tin, tungsten, oil, and natural rubber made by external sources of supply varies between 75 and 100 per cent. This new situation enables the developing countries to use their energy and raw-material resources to achieve their goals in various areas of international political and economic relations. These countries are stepping up their efforts to radically restructure the present pattern of international economic relations on more democratic and equitable lines, and they are increasingly taking joint action in this.

Events have dashed imperialist hopes for reducing the political independence of developing countries to a mere show, to the acquisition by them of emblems, national anthems, flags, and such-like trappings of sovereignty. The countries which have thrown off the

yoke of colonial dependence are pressing on with their determined
struggle for full equality and dignity among the other members of the
world community. Pointing to this trend, Leonid Brezhnev
commented that for the majority of developing countries: "It may
definitely be stated that they are defending their political and
economic rights against imperialism with mounting energy, seeking to
consolidate their independence and to raise the social, economic and
cultural standards of their peoples."[3]

Apart from giving political support to developing countries, the
USSR is assisting them in their efforts to solve their economic
problems, notably in the development of national industries, the
bedrock of economic independence. The Soviet Union is transferring
to developing countries on favourable terms significant quantities of
up-to-date technology. It has helped train some half a million
specialists for the Third World. The stability and reliability of
economic links between the USSR and these countries have stood the
test of time.

The alliance of developing countries and the socialist community is
growing stronger under the impact of international *détente*. Their co-
operation is advancing both economically and commercially with
sixty-four countries of Asia, Africa, and Latin America, where it
assists some 1050 projects in various industries, 480 of them already
operational. By 1977 Soviet economic and technical aid to the
developing countries had grown by 520 per cent from the 1960 level.

The political aspect of relations of the USSR and other socialist
countries with the emerging countries has acquired a new dimension.
With certain of these countries, the USSR has concluded treaties of
friendship and co-operation. Many of them are working side by side
with the USSR for peace and *détente*, for the freedom and
independence of nations. The active involvement of these countries in
the work of the UN where they form the majority, is further proof of
their increased role in world politics.

The record of international development since the end of the
Second World War has demonstrated the intimate connection between
the growing power and the peace-oriented policies of the socialist
countries and the successful progress of revolutionary struggles for
national independence thorughout the world. National liberation

revolutions triumphed in Asia and Africa at a time when the world socialist system was becoming a decisive factor of international life. The consistent peace-oriented policy of the USSR and other socialist countries, apart from helping newly-independent states to ward off imperialist attacks, has contributed to the elimination of the imperialist powers' monopoly in economic relations with these states.

Many developing nations have become active in the battle against imperialism, allies of the socialist countries in their efforts to restructure radically the present pattern of international relations on the basis of Leninist principles of peaceful co-existence. The Soviet Union and other socialist countries have been giving, and will continue to give, every support to all peoples fighting for freedom. This is the embodiment of the internationalist unity of world socialism and the national liberation struggle of peoples which is developing in depth and breadth.

Détente in Strengthening the World Positions of Emerging Countries

Many countries of Asia, Africa, and Latin America are insistently demanding the establishment of a new world economic order, a radical restructuring of the entire pattern of international relations on democratic lines to ensure that the roles of overlordship and submission, once imposed by imperialism on inter-state relations and incompatible with relations among sovereign countries, are eliminated once and for all.

The new alignment of forces in the world has provided favourable conditions for an effective struggle by the emerging countries to accomplish this goal. In his speech to the 25th Congress, Leonid Brezhnev pointed out: "It is clear now that, the alignment of class forces on the world stage being what it is, the newly independent countries are fully capable of resisting imperialist dictatorialness and of obtaining fair and equal economic relations."[3] They are standing up for their political and economic rights in ever more vigorous confrontation with the imperialist powers so as to buttress their independence and raise the social, economic and cultural standards of their peoples.

The course of world development enables them to see the need for such a change in the present pattern of international relations as the means to finish off neo-colonialism. In this area the interests of the socialist and the developing countries fully coincide. This forms the basis of their anti-imperialist alliance, which will go from strength to strength despite the intrigues of imperialist forces seeking to tear the developing countries away from the socialist community, to isolate them on the world stage, and to leave them defenceless against imperialist incursion.

Many in the West are speculating about the alleged conflict of policy-interest between emerging and socialist countries over international *détente*. Some allege that *détente* does not accord with the interests of emerging countries. Attempts to play socialist countries off against the Third World are doomed to failure by the course of historical development: there is no antagonistic conflict of interest between socialist countries fighting for a restructuring of international relations and developing countries implacably opposed to imperialism and neo-colonialism. That this is so is proved by an examination of what *détente* and the transformation of international relations on Leninist principles offer the emerging countries.

Socialism for the first time in human history set the task of achieving a genuine equality in international relations, one that covers not only relations between the leading powers but those between all members of the world community irrespective of economic, military, and scientific potential. The opponents of international *détente* have developed the so-called theory of the "two superpowers", whereby the USSR and the USA allegedly seek to harmonize their relations solely to be the better able to impose their will on the smaller and developing countries. This theory is untenable, for it aims at obscuring the fundamental difference between Soviet and American foreign policies. The USSR, a great and powerful country, is a socialist state to which imperialist ambitions to keep smaller countries and their peoples in submission are alien. The USSR is using its might to further the interests of peace and social progress, fighting resolutely against imperialist aggression in whatever form.

When the socialist countries first set the task of injecting into the practice of international relations the principles of peaceful co-existence between states with different social systems, the principles of full equality and co-operation, they realized that they were furthering not only their own interests and those of the broad sections of the population in the capitalist countries, but those of the developing countries as well. The socialist countries start from the tenet that in conditions of world peace the countries fighting for freedom, independence, and social progress would have more favourable opportunities for expanding contacts within the world community on the basis of full equality, for defending their interests and opposing colonialism and racism.

The 24th and 25th CPSU Congresses adopted decisions which proved once again that world socialism was resolutely advocating the emancipation of oppressed peoples, defending the sovereignty of newly independent nations, was working for normalization of relations between states to establish political and economic equality and was insisting on a final end to imperialist and racialist arbitrary rule in international relations.

It is difficult to overestimate the co-ordinated actions of the socialist countries in bringing to a halt the long war in Indo-China. The peoples of Indo-China link their successes to the massive support and assistance they got from the USSR and other socialist countries. The victory scored by the peoples of Indo-China had a tremendous impact on the course of events in the Third World. It demonstrated the strength and potential of national-liberation movements, their inexhaustible power. It lent new impetus to the struggle of the young countries of Asia and Africa for independence and restored health to the situation in South-east Asia. It is a fact that the Soviet Union's support has enabled the Arab countries to effectively oppose the Israeli aggressors for a number of years, containing Tel Aviv's expansionism and that of its imperialist backers and protectors.

The moral, military, and political support given by the socialist countries to national liberation movements in the former Portuguese colonial possessions helped those countries not only to gain independence but to retain it in the battle against the combined forces of imperialism and local reactionaries seeking to make this independence a fiction. The assertions of certain statesmen, government officials, and ideologists of the capitalist world claiming that the socialist countries' aid to the patriotic forces of Angola in their struggle against local reactionaries and imperialist intervention complicated the international situation and checked the further progress of international *détente* do not hold water. It is hard to understand how the gain of genuine independence by a country can possibly impede further efforts to strengthen world peace and security. If anything, the end of imperialist intervention in the affairs of the sovereign people of Angola, to allow them to decide their destiny for themselves and make a free choice of the path of development, itself contributes to a strengthened peace and to the elimination of seeds of tension and conflict in this part of Africa capable of spilling over national borders and threatening in general.

Therefore, as the joint communiqué issued at the end of the visit to the USSR by the Angolan Prime Minister Lopo do Nascimento in May 1976 rightly emphasized, the Angolan people's victory over the forces of imperialism and reaction was of great political significance for the further struggle of African peoples towards the final elimination of the vestiges of colonialism and racism in Africa. The close bonds of brotherly friendship and co-operation which grew up between the Soviet and Angolan people in the years of armed struggle waged by Angola's National Patriotic Forces for freedom and independence matched their vital interests and contributed to the cause of peace and security of all nations.[4]

The establishment of a just and democratic world order is unthinkable without complete eradication of the relics of colonialism, apartheid, and racism. Despite the fact that the global system of colonial oppression has been done away with, it is too soon yet to speak of a complete disappearance of colonialism in all its forms and manifestations. Colonialism is still poisoning the international situation and breeding many international conflicts.

The racialist régime in South Africa is trampling upon the legitimate rights of Namibia and the African majority of South Africa, and is trying to drown in blood their liberation struggle, committing acts of aggression against neighbouring states. These actions have created a major flashpoint in Southern Africa.

The peace-directed foreign policy pursued by the socialist countries is speeding the process of decolonization to its end, that is to say, resolving one of the key problems for what Lenin described as "a new scheme" of international relations.

Referring to the socialist world's contribution to this process the *Diariu di Luanda* has written: "Their unity of action with the socialist states and other progressive forces in the world is the earnest of success for the African countries' anti-colonial and anti-imperialist struggle."[5]

It should be emphasized, however, that in pressing for the establishment of principles of peaceful co-existence in international relations, for disarmament and prevention of military conflicts and aggressive acts, the socialist countries recognize the sacred right of peoples to fight (if necessary with arms in hand) for their emancipation from colonial oppression, for their independence. Peaceful co-existence does not mean that aggressor and victim should be lumped together for purposes of maintaining peace "at any price". The victim has every right to resort to all means of defence to maintain freedom and independence in the face of imperialist aggression, and that includes the right to armed defence. This and only this is the Soviet Union's concept of peaceful co-existence and its implications for foreign policy.

The CPSU, in following its Leninist foreign policy of peaceful co-existence of socialist and capitalist countries, sees its supreme duty in furnishing support and aid to people fighting for their freedom and independence, for social progress. The CPSU says in its Programme that it "Considers fraternal alliance with the peoples who have thrown off the colonial and semi-colonial yoke to be a cornerstone of its international policy. This alliance is based on the vital common interests of world socialism and the world national liberation movements. The CPSU regards it as its internationalist duty to assist the peoples who have set out to win and strengthen their national independence, all peoples who are fighting for the complete abolition of the colonial system."[6] This policy was reaffirmed by the 25th CPSU Congress.

The establishment of the principle of peaceful co-existence as a dominant trend in the evolution of international relations makes easier the task of completing the elimination of the colonial system. Just such favourable conditions prevail in the world today. Stressing this, Giselle Rabesahala, General Secretary of the Independence Congress Party of Madagàscar, said at the 25th CPSU Congress: "We know that the national liberation movement's successes of recent years result from the heroic struggle of the peoples of the developing countries. We want to stress, however, that they were achieved in a generally improved international climate and in conditions of *détente* that resulted from the tireless efforts of the Soviet Union and the CPSU, from their consistent implementation of the Peace Programme adopted by the 24th Congress."[7] Successful national-liberation struggles contribute in turn to the progress of *détente* and to efforts to strengthen world peace and the security of nations. Speaking at the 25th CPSU Congress, Yusuf Dadoo, Chairman of the South African Communist Party, said: "The policy of *détente* is inseparable from the struggle of the oppressed peoples for freedom and national liberation. A lasting peace and the elimination of all possibilities of world or regional armed struggles can only be fully achieved when all peoples are rid of the burden of imperialist domination. This is why the glorious recent victories by the peoples of Vietnam, Mozambique, Cambodia, Laos, Guinea-Bissau, and Angola are historic blows for world peace as well as for national liberation."[8]

Détente is having a salutary influence on the political climate throughout the world. Witness the termination of the October 1973 (Yom Kippur) war in the Middle East. Commenting on the role of the *détente* factor in that conflict, Leonid Brezhnev said: "If the current conflict in the Middle East had erupted in a setting of general international tension and strained relations, say, between the United States and the Soviet Union, it could have been much more dangerous and might have reached a scale imperilling world peace."[9]

The opportunities and prospects offered by international *détente* to the developing countries are quite impressive. *Détente* enhances the role of these countries in world affairs by helping them consolidate their political independence and facilitating the creation of conditions for positive action on the socio-economic problems they face. All of which enables the developing countries to strengthen their world positions and play an increasingly influential part in world affairs. In contributing to the positive processes affecting the development of the world situation and in joining the socialist countries in efforts to democratize international relations, the developing countries help the development of *détente* in depth. The leaders of these countries, in advocating the policy of *détente*, are fully aware of its beneficial effect.

In improving the political climate in the world, international *détente* is preparing the ground for concrete measures to limit the arms race. In this way, colossal resources available to all countries including the developing ones can be released and channelled into constructive ends. As we have mentioned above, multi-billion sums could be made available to the Third World in the event of the implementation of the Soviet proposals to cut by 10 per cent the budgets of the permanent members of the Security Council and use part of the resultant savings to give more aid to the developing countries. If this were done, vast sums could be spent on the war against hunger, illiteracy, and economic backwardness in the Third World.

In an attempt to prove that international *détente* brings no benefits for the emerging countries, the opponents of peaceful co-existence claim that improving relations between the USSR and the USA allegedly leads to both countries "neglecting" the interests of the developing world. J.H. Howe, former member of the State Department's Policy Planning Council and Director of the US Aid Programme to East Africa, said that considerations related to the Cold War, which were the main reason for aiding the poor countries in the 'fifties and 'sixties, were now regarded as considerably less important.[10] Howe added that abandonment of the Cold War policy had resulted in the USA neglecting its relations with the emerging countries and in curtailment of American aid to these countries in recent years.

The theme that *détente* and improved Soviet–American relations bring no benefit to the emerging countries was echoed by the *Christian Science Monitor,* which wrote that the developing countries were the casualties of *détente*.[11]

In actual fact, however, the real reason for the reduction of Amerian aid to the developing countries has nothing to do with any "diminished interest" allegedly taken in them as a result of America's abandonment of cold-war policies. American imperialists still have a vested interest in chaining the developing countries to capitalism's chariot. Depending on changes in the world situation, only the forms and means of achieving their ends *vis-à-vis* the developing countries undergo change among the imperialists.

To a certain extent the reduction of American aid to the newly independent countries has been due to the American imperialists' prolonged and costly gamble in Indo-China, which had severely undermined the American economy and finances. But the main reason for this reduction was that American imperialist circles were dissatisfied with the stance of these countries towards major international problems.

The White House makes no secret of the fact that, in future, American aid to developing countries will be conditional on how far they support the USA on major political issues at international forums.

The *US News and World Report* issue of 31 March 1980 wrote: "...A beefed-up (American) aid program is essential if the US is to challenge Russia's bid for influence among so-called non-aligned nations of the Third World."[12] But for the Soviet Union and the rest of the socialist camp, the American imperialists and their counterparts in other Western powers would have continued to exploit the colonial peoples of Asia, Africa, and Latin America.

Détente between socialist and capitalist countries cannot be an obstacle in the way of the social and economic development of Asia, Africa, and Latin America. On the contrary, *détente* is indispensable to their further progress. Peaceful co-existence between the countries with different social systems, along with international *détente*, are major factors in the further successful progress of the developing countries struggling to consolidate their independence and make further headway in social and economic development.

Having fully realized the irreconcilable nature of their differences with the former colonial powers and those industrialized capitalist countries which continue to exploit them by neo-colonialist methods, the developing countries are adamant in insisting on the complete elimination of relics of colonialism, racism, and apartheid. Their refusal to compromise on matters of principle, coupled with the attacking nature of their foreign policy and their resolute action against imperialism, result directly from the radically changing alignment of forces on the world stage in favour of the forces of peace and socialism.

The Contribution of the Developing Countries to the Reshaping of International Relations

Addressing the 25th CPSU congress, Leonid Brezhnev stated in this connection: "It is quite clear now that with the present correlation of world class forces the liberated countries are fully able to resist imperialist autocracy and achieve fair — that is, balanced — economic relations. Another thing is also clear: that their contribution to the common struggle for peace and the security of the peoples, already considerable, will very likely become even greater."[13]

The developing countries are active in the struggle for peace and security and for democratizing international economic relations in a variety of ways: at the UN and its specialized agencies, in the non-aligned movement, in the Organization of African Unity and in collective actions on the economic front. Their work is made more effective by close co-operation with the USSR and other socialist states.

Thanks to the concerted efforts of socialist and developing countries, the UN has adopted important resolutions on the maintenance and consolidation of peace, on disarmament, on the eradication of colonialism, and on condemning and curbing imperialist aggression. In recent years the UN, at the initiative of the socialist countries backed by the developing nations, adopted a declaration on strengthening international security, a resolution on the renunciation of the use of force in international relations, on banning for all time the use of nuclear weapons and a resolution on convening a world disarmament conference. Successive General Assembly sessions, UN committees, and specialized agencies have adopted decisions sponsored by developing countries or backed by them, designed to stamp out the vestiges of colonialism, racism, and apartheid, to eliminate the seeds of tension and to create favourable conditions for the social and economic progress of the nations of the world.

The anti-imperialist stance of the developing countries which have a solid majority at the UN has made it impossible for the major capitalist powers to exploit the notorious "voting machine" with the help of which the imperialists had for years been able to rubberstamp such UN resolutions as suited them. Significantly, American diplomats who in recent years have been finding themselves in increasing isolation took to complaining about "the tyranny of the majority at the UN", referring to the firm position of the developing countries on major international issues. Thus, despite the resistance of the US and its allies, the 30th Session of the UN General Assembly passed a resolution outlawing fascist ideology and Zionist practices and condemned Zionism as a form of racism and race discrimination.

In recent years the United Nations has been the scene of an all-out offensive by the combined forces of socialism and national liberation movements against imperialism. The developing countries take a good deal of credit for the conversion of the UN into a world forum for discussing crucial issues facing today's world, where the forces of reaction often find themselves in total isolation. The admission to the world body of a large number of young independent states which share the socialist countries' ant-imperialist stance has enabled the organization to contribute better to the reshaping of the present pattern of international relations on democratic principles.

The anti-imperialist character of the developing countries' foreign policy is best seen in the non-aligned movement. The anti-imperialist thrust of this movement springs not only and not so much from the "anti-imperialist inertia" which, some bourgeois authors allege, is the result of the preceding anti-colonial stage of the national liberation movement. The fact is that the newly independent countries are insisting on equitable economic and political conditions for their social and economic development. For this reason their interests are diametrically opposed to those of the imperialist powers which seek to perpetuate relations of inequality so as to be able to continue plundering the resources of the Third World.

The non-aligned movement, which emerged as a counterbalance to the military and political groupings of the imperialist powers, into which the latter had sought to corral young independent states, implies more than mere non-participation in blocs. The movement is the product of the struggle against imperialism, colonialism, and racism, of the policy of solidarity with peoples fighting for their independence. The first Bandung Conference of the Heads of State and Government of Non-Aligned countries (1955) proclaimed in its "Declaration on Promoting Universal Peace and Co-operation" the following as the goals of the movement: to work for peace, for general disarmament, for banning the tests and use of weapons of mass destruction, to fight against all forms of colonial oppression, and to eliminate the vestiges of colonialism and racialism.

The non-aligned countries in their Belgrade Declaration of 1961 spoke of the responsibility of all countries for the maintenance of world peace. They branded war as a crime against humanity, and stressed that the principles of peaceful co-existence were the only alternative to the Cold War and a possible nuclear catastrophe. The Belgrade Conference supported the socialist countries' call for general and complete disarmament under strict international control.

The noble principles of the non-aligned movement coupled with the determination of the developing countries to become sovereign members of the world community rather than objects of the policy of this or that colonial empire, prompted the overwhelming majority of the newly independent countries to join the movement.

The non-aligned movement took an uncompromising, highly principled stand on the struggle against imperialist policy. At their Third Conference in Lusaka in 1970, the non-aligned countries declared their support for the struggle of the peoples of Indo-China for freedom and independence, and condemned Israeli aggression. The anti-imperialist thrust of the decisions adopted by the Fourth Non-Aligned Conference in Algiers in 1973 is especially noteworthy. The Conference's political declaration emphasized "the need for co-operation between the non-aligned countries and all countries and all forces opposed to colonialism and neo-colonialism, with a view to providing active and material support for the armed struggle of African liberation movements".[14] The world press commented that the Algiers Conference resolution on the Middle East situation and the Palestinian problem was a strong and unequivocal statement of position on the issue from the developing countries. The resolution declared all Israel's measures in occupied Arab territories null and void. It condemned the Western powers, notably the USA, for their military, economic, political, and moral support for Israel and demanded on immediate halt to this support and assistance. The Conference also adopted a number of major political documents including resolutions supporting the heroic struggle of Vietnam.

Efforts to consolidate world peace, initiate disarmament, and make the present pattern of political and economic relations in the world more democratic are central to the activities of the non-aligned movement. The Third Non-Aligned Conference adopted a political declaration on peace, independence, co-operation, and democratization of international relations. The Fourth Conference of the Heads of State and Government of non-aligned countries stressed that the current deepening of East–West *détente* and the progress towards the settlement in Europe of problems inherited from the Second World War represent a major success for the peace forces throughout the world. The Conference stressed the universality of the principles underlying East–West *détente*.

Seeing the work for disarmament as a key area of their efforts for peace and security, the non-aligned countries resolutely advocate disarmament and an early convocation of the proposed World Disarmament Conference. In its Declaration, the Algiers Conference emphasized that the non-aligned movement advocated general and complete disarmament, notably banning the manufacture and use of nuclear weapons and their delivery vehicles, the destruction of all existing nuclear weapons' stockpiles and a total ban on nuclear tests in all media throughout the world.

The Fifth Non-Aligned Conference met in Colombo in August 1976 and was attended by delegates from over eighty countries including the PLO.

In a message to the Chairman of the Colombo Conference, President Brezhnev wrote: "As repeatedly stressed in the fundamental documents of the CPSU, the Soviet Union sets a high value on the anti-imperialist, anti-colonial, and anti-racist orientation of the non-aligned movement and on its contribution to the consolidation of world peace and international security, to the independence and progress of the liberated countries."[15]

The vast majority of delegates to the Colombo Conference noted that *détente* and the progressive establishment of the principles of peaceful co-existence were the dominant trends in international relations. The delegates of India, Sri Lanka, and other countries called for redoubling efforts for peace, national independence and social progress, for spreading *détente* to involve the whole world. They also called for disarmament and protested against the establishment of foreign military bases in the Indian Ocean.

The anti-imperialist, anti-colonialist character of the non-aligned movement was reaffirmed in the final documents of the Conference, notably, in its Political Declaration, in the Economic Declaration, and in the Programme of Action for the economic field. The Political Declaration reiterated that the non-aligned movement's chief goal was "the maintenance of peace and security among nations" and the establishment of "a new and just international order".

The Sixth Non-Aligned Conference held on 3-8 September 1979 was a milestone. For the first time in the 18-year history of the non-aligned movement a conference of its heads of state and government met in Latin America. It brought together a record number of delegates — ninety-four countries and liberation movements attended; counting those present in the capacity of observers and guests brought the total of delegations to over one hundred. Most of the issues discussed by the conference had a direct bearing on American policy in Asia, Africa, and Latin America and this caused the USA to react with nervous sensitivity to the conference's deliberations. *Newsweek* magazine wrote: "...The conference troubled its attentive observers in Washington... United States officials saw the Havana summit as a kind of trial in absentia..."[16]

The political declaration which was part of the conference's final document expressed satisfaction at the positive changes that had occurred in the 1970s as a result of international *détente* and stressed that the principles of peaceful co-existence must be made the cornerstone of international relations. At the same time the declaration stressed the need to spread *détente* to other regions of the world.

The document strongly condemned the support given by the USA, Britain, and other Western powers to the racist regime in South Africa, support designed to prevent the people of Namibia and the indigenous population of the Republic of South Africa to exercise their right to self-determination and independence. The declaration says that these powers aid and abet the apartheid system and have been indirectly involved in the acts of aggression committed by the racists of South Africa against Angola, Mozambique, Botswana, Zambia, and other independent African countries.

The Havana Conference condemned the Camp David agreement and the separate peace treaty between Egypt and Israel, seeing them as infringing the inherent rights of all the Arabs, including the Arab people of Palestine, and contributing to perpetuating the Israeli occupation of Arab territory. The document demands that the United States dismantle its war bases in Cuba and Puerto Rico which threaten peace and security in Latin America.

The non-aligned movement called for an undeviating implementation of the UN decisions and those passed by the Security Council on liquidating apartheid in South Africa. The conference backed the idea of self-determination for the people of Western Sahara who are fighting against the occupying invaders under the leadership of the Polisario Front.

The forces of imperialism and reaction have failed to exploit for splitting purposes differences of opinion among the members of the non-aligned movement springing from differing socio-political regimes and foreign-policy orientations of the developing countries. The Havana Conference showed that the non-aligned nations were still opposed to imperialism over the key issues of world politics.

The movement of non-aligned countries, which include the majority of developing countries, is now one of the most important factors in world politics. It renders an active contribution to the fight for peace, security, *détente*, and equal co-operation, for the establishment of a just system of international political and economic relations, and to the struggle against imperialism, colonialism, neo-colonialism, and all forms of domination and exploitation.

Co-operation with socialist countries is a guarantee of further successes of developing countries in their anti-imperialist struggle. Not surprisingly, the imperialists are sparing no effort in an attempt to drive a wedge between the Soviet Union and the developing countries. This attempt is coming up against strong resistance from most of the non-aligned countries. Speaking at the Algiers Conference, Fidel Castro emphasized: "Any attempt to score off non-aligned countries against the socialist camp is profoundly counter-revolutionary and plays into the hands of the imperialists. To destroy our friendship with the socialist camp means to weaken the non-aligned countries, to leave them at the mercy of the still powerful forces of imperialism.... . Mutual understanding with the socialist countries coupled with unity of action of the countries fighting for their independent development is indispensable to the success of our common struggle."[17] (Translated from the Russian.)

The imperialists are seeking to blunt the anti-imperialist edge of the non-aligned movement, to oppose it to the socialist countries, to foment discord and strife among the non-aligned countries. They are being helped in this by the ultra-revolutionaries who are trying to impose on the non-aligned movement the notorious doctrine of the "hegemony of the superpowers" and the concept of "equal responsibility" of all economically developed countries irrespective of whether they are imperialist or socialist, for the poverty and economic backwardness of the developing world. The Colombo Conference was the setting for strongly contested argument over this issue. After prolonged and often heated debates, the Conference adopted documents on political and economic problems which confirmed that by and large the non-aligned movement had retained its progressive character.

The non-aligned movement is the biggest and most influential political movement in the developing world. At the same time recent years have seen a noticeable increase in the role of regional organizations and associations of developing countries as their influence on world politics grew. The Organization of African Unity (OAU), which brings together all the independent countries of Africa except for the Republic of South Africa, is now a major factor of international life.

To be sure, the OAU just like the non-aligned movement as a whole, is not all of a piece either in the social and economic structure of its constituent member-countries or in terms of the ultimate goal of its governing political forces.

Anti-imperialism, for all that, remains the basis of the general principles of co-operation among African countries irrespective of their social and political orientation. Anti-imperialist trends within the OAU have intensified markedly. The African countries are stepping up their efforts to eliminate the vestiges of colonialism and racism, to oppose imperialist aggression and economic inequality. Whereas a few years ago the idea of a dialogue with the racialist regime of South Africa was supported by certain African countries, today it is rejected by all.

Despite strong imperialist pressure, the 26th Session of the OAU Ministerial Council hailed the independent People's Republic of Angola and called on all OAU countries to grant on an individual and collective basis political, diplomatic, economic, technical, and material aid to the new independent state.

The imperialists will not come to terms with the anti-imperialist thrust of the OAU. The forces of imperialism and their lackeys in Africa are now putting their money on splitting the unity of African countries. To this end, the imperialists are stooping to the dirtiest of methods including acts of banditry, setting up of break-away and splinter groups, and fanning of domestic feuds in certain African countries. To further their reactionary plans, the imperialists are also exploiting the onerous legacy of the colonial past. A salient feature of the political map of today's Africa is the fact that in some instances state frontiers do not follow ethnic lines. This is a legacy of the colonial partition of the African continent when the imperialist powers carved up Africa at will, disregarding the ethnic and historical background of its peoples. After independence, African countries retained the frontiers of the former colonial possessions. One of the basic principles of the OAU Charter is respect for territorial integrity and inviolability of existing frontiers. But for the wisdom and statesmanship displayed by African leaders over this complex, contentious issue, the dark continent would have been plunged into a seething cauldron of incessant strife and feuds.

By now, no one doubts that events in the Horn of Africa triggered off by Somali's aggression against Ethiopia in 1977/8 were an attempt by the imperialist powers acting hand in glove with reactionary Arab regimes to undermine African unity and sabotage the principles and Charter of the OAU. By encouraging the chauvinist ambitions of the

Somali leadership, the imperialist powers together with reactionary forces in the Arab world hoped to make Somali a cat's-paw with which to kill off the national democratic revolution in Ethiopia and entrench themselves in North-east Africa.

Anti-Imperialist trends characterize not only the OAU. In the 1970s Latin American countries were likewise taking an increasingly anti-American stand, at government level. Latin American countries are stepping up their opposition to the domination of American monopolies and Washington's interference in their domestic affairs. In August 1975 the Conference of 25 Latin American countries, including Cuba, adopted a decision to set up a Latin American economic system without the USA. This new regional organization is called upon to promote co-operation among Latin American countries with a view to accelerating their national development and strengthening their economic independence. The Soviet Union supports their efforts to consolidate political and economic independence and welcomes their increasingly great role in international affairs.

The idea of creating "peace zones" in South-east Asia and other parts of the developing world looms large in the foreign-policy programme of developing nations. The campaign for the creation of "peace zones" is eroding military and political groupings set up by the imperialists and is having an improving effect on the entire international situation. As the process of *détente* spread beyond Europe in September 1975, the SEATO bloc collapsed, followed by CENTO in 1979.

The Soviet Union and other socialist countries are working steadily for an improved political climate in Asia.

The principles of Asian security formulated by the Soviet Union met with support among the peace-loving countries of the continent. The declaration on the further development of friendship and co-operation between the USSR and India signed in June 1976 pointed out that efforts to strengthen peace and security in Asia should be based on renunciation of the use of force, respect for sovereignty and the inviolability of frontiers, non-interference in the internal affairs of countries and peoples, and on broad-based co-operation in the economic and other fields observing complete equality and mutual benefit, those same principles which have proved effective in Europe.

The idea of strengthening peace and security in Asia by collective efforts has both its supporters and opponents. The Maoists, for instance, claim that this idea is directed against the interests of China. The Soviet Union has repeatedly stated that the proposed Asian security system has no aim other than turning Asia into a continent of peace by involving in this security system all Asian countries, including China.

The 25th CPSU Congress declared that the Soviet Union stands ready to normalize its relations with China on the basis of peaceful co-existence. The normalization of relations between the USSR and China will without doubt have a positive effect on the situation in Asia and the world as a whole.

The present international situation confirms that to tackle the problem of Asian security is both topical and realistic. The successful progress of world socialism combined with the intensification of anti-imperialist actions by the developing countries have created favourable conditions for the implementation of the Bandung principles in the continent of Asia. The active participation of developing countries in the search for ways of ensuring security in Asia justifies an optimistic view of future developments in this part of the world.

As the emerging countries are stepping up their efforts for peace and security, for democratizing international relations and for political equality, the crisis of the neo-colonialist economic policy pursued by the imperialists *vis-à-vis* developing countries is becoming increasingly apparent. The winning by these countries of political independence has prepared the ground for the elimination of imperialist oppression in all its forms and manifestations. However, this independence has not by itself ended this oppression. As developing countries become a major factor of world politics via their growing political independence, so the futility of imperialist efforts to perpetuate the status of these countries as agrarian and raw-material appendages of Western capitalism becomes increasingly clear. The objective march of history has prompted the national-liberation movement to join the battle for genuine economic independence.[18]

The fact is that after winning national independence the former colonies continued to be an object of imperialist exploitation; only the form of exploitation changed as the methods of external economic coercion became invalid. The neo-colonialist policy has resulted in the perpetuation of the economic backwardness of the developing countries, in the catastrophic growth of their indebtedness to foreign powers, grinding poverty and unemployment for their populations. The economic gap separating developing countries and the industrialized capitalist countries, far from being narrowed, keeps widening. The Commission on International Development set up by the World Bank in the late 1960s and headed by the former Canadian Prime Minister Lester Pearson noted in a report: "The widening gap between the developed and developing countries has become a central issue of our times.... . The climate surrounding foreign-aid programmes is heavy with disillusionment and distrust.... . We have reached a point of crisis."[19]

The following statistics give an idea of the economic plight of the emerging countries. In the first half of the 1970s the developing countries contributed less than 10 per cent of world industrial output while making up 65 per cent of the world's population. Because of Third World technological backwardness, productivity of labour is a mere 8-9 per cent of that in the industrialized capitalist countries.

In the early 1970s the deprived sections of the population of the Third World numbered some 1200 million people, i.e. some 67 per cent of its total population. An estimated 700 million (39 per cent) lived in grinding poverty and suffered from chronic malnutrition. This disturbing problem far from being eradicated, is growing ever more acute.

Apart from deep-seated domestic reasons largely engendered by colonialism, the problems facing the developing countries today are a consequence of the continuing exploitation of these countries by the imperialist powers. Experts of the Club of Rome headed by a leading authority, J. Tinbergen, have estimated that the developing countries, due to the uneven pattern of the international division of labour, lose up to 100,000 million dollars annually,[20] and are losing more and more with every year. Thus, the purchases of foreign technology by the developing countries now cost them between 3000 and 5000 million dollars a year. The UN Secretariat estimates that by the year 2000 this outlay is expected to grow by 20 to 35 times.[21] The external debt of the Third World to the industrialized capitalist powers is growing rapidly. Whereas in 1955 their combined debt was 38,100 million dollars, in 1975 it was 140,000 million dollars. Today it is in excess of 250,000 million.

At the turn of the 1970s the antagonistic nature of contradictions between the imperialist and developing countries, arising from the unequal position of the latter within the world capitalist economy and from the widening economic gap between the two groups of countries, became fully apparent. About the same time more favourable conditions developed for the emerging countries to step up their struggle against the inequitable system of international economic relations which the imperialists had imposed upon them. Because of a radically changed alignment of forces on the world stage in favour of socialism and the tide in international relations running towards *détente*, the imperialists often find it impossible to use force to protect their economic interests in the developing countries or to prevent the latter from bringing their mineral wealth and other national resources under their own control.

In this situation the developing countries, leaning on the socialist world's political support and economic co-operation, mounted an offensive against the imperialists' economic positions in their midst. At successive sessions of the UN General Assembly and other international forums, the developing countries pressed for and obtained the adoption of a series of major documents including the resolution on the inalienable sovereignty of peoples over their resources, the declaration on the establishment of a new international economic order, the Charter of economic rights and duties of states, the Programme of Action, and others. Analysis of these documents will show that the emerging countries are fully resolved to put an end to unequal economic relations.

These days the struggle of developing countries is unfolding under the slogan of a new world economic order whose main components include full sovereignty over domestic natural resources, the introduction of higher prices of the raw materials exported by developing countries, increased inflow of financial resources into these, easier access of Third World products into markets in the industrialized countries, improved terms of technology transfer, and tighter controls over the operations of the multinationals.

It should be noted, however, that representatives of some developing countries in a departure from the principle of the universality of demands may consider it in order to oppose discriminatory restrictions in international commercial and economic relations without extending this principle to the relations between socialist and capitalist countries. Any departure from the universality principle, any softening of the intolerant attitude to discrimination in whatever form carries the danger of undermining the common front of the developing countries in their struggle for full equality in international economic relations. The document submitted by the socialist countries to the UNCTAD-V session in Manila in May 1979 noted that "discrimination against socialist countries in the markets of the capitalist West differs little from the discriminatory practices against the public sector of the developing countries in these markets. That is why the ongoing restructuring of international economic relations in its commercial, political, and structural aspects can be effective given its comprehensive implementation and mandatory application to all the flows of world trade including East–West trade."[22]

At the Manila session the socialist countries came out in favour of implementing as a matter of urgency the following measures:

— elimination of discrimination and any other artificial obstacles from international trade, the eradication of inequality, dictation and exploitation in whatever form from international economic relations. What these relations require is new, modern regulatory standards which make adequate provision for the rights and interests of all groups of countries, with special reference to the particular problems of the developing countries;

— restructuring the present pattern of the world economy and international trade with a view to assuring their more balanced development, including accelerated industrialization of economically backward regions and improving living standards for all peoples. The socialist countries just as the developing ones are interested in such a restructuring which would be in line

with the requirements and demands of the modern world;
— strengthening national sovereignty over natural and manpower resources, restriction of the operations of the transnational corporations and the carrying out of domestic changes within the developing countries themselves as a complementary measure to the restructuring of international economic relations;
— changing the existing unfair and unequal mechanism of international economic relations to democratize the associated agencies and institutions.

The socialist countries' approach to the new world economic order is determined by their treating the proposed restructuring of external economic relations as indissolubly linked with the changing overall international political climate, as an integral component of the historical process of restructuring inter-state relations along democratic lines. This restructuring is associated with the establishment in international relations of such basic principles as the sovereign equality of states, self-determination of peoples, inadmissibility of seizure of foreign territory, non-interference in the domestic affairs of states, freedom of choice in deciding under which economic and social systems people will live and the inadmissibility of discrimination on these grounds, unconditional sovereignty of states over their own economic resources including the right to nationalization, condemnation of colonialism and apartheid, and others.

That is precisely the reason why the USSR attaches prime importance to maintaining the momentum of international *détente* and to ending the arms race as an indispensable condition for world peace. With the solution of this task, which will have exceptionally important consequences in a variety of fields, the socialist countries associate their hopes for a realistic opportunity to find additional resources to be used as aid to developing countries since only in conditions of peace is it feasible to look for ways of resolving the problems facing mankind today, including the practical question of the establishment of a new world economic order.

The persistent efforts of Third World countries to obtain equal status in international economic relations have yielded encouraging results. The imperialist powers have been compelled to compromise and meet the Third World half-way as is seen in their reluctant acceptance of the quadrupling of oil prices by OPEC.

Incidentally the OPEC decision in 1973 to quadruple the price of oil demonstrated that the developing countries had at their command a striking means of persuasion over the industrialized capitalist countries. As J.H. Howe put it, this decision rocked the capitalist world "as no other event since the Cuban missile crisis".[23]

Significantly, the Third World countries, in pressing for restructuring the present pattern of international economic relations, are increasingly coming to realize that boosting productive forces through industrialization is the principal line of advance in their efforts to overcome their economic backwardness.

At the Lima Conference they set the goal of increasing their contribution to world industrial output to 25 per cent versus the current 7 per cent by the year 2000. This will require the maintenance of annual growth rates of industrial production in the Third World at 10 per cent as against the 6-7 per cent they were in 1960.[24]

The struggle for the establishment of a new world economic order based on equality among sovereign states and on their mutually advantageous co-operation is central to the larger fundamental restructuring of the entire system of international relations for which the socialist countries have been working. Consequently, the success of the struggle is unthinkable without further strengthening the alliance between the developing countries and the socialist camp. In this context the danger and harmfulness for the developing countries of the concept of a world divided into "rich North" and "poor South" is all too obvious.

The "North–South" theory is being exploited by the imperialists in an attempt to disclaim responsibility for the economic plight of the Third World. Using this theory, the imperialists and their lackeys attempt to saddle all the industrialized countries including the USSR and other socialist states with "equal responsibility" for the present economic predicament of the developing countries. The aim of this manoeuvre is obvious: the enemies of peace and social progress would like nothing better than to disunite the principal anti-imperialist forces, to sow discord among them. Andrei Gromyko has commented in this connection: "As previously, the USSR will oppose attempts to drive a wedge between the national-liberation movement and its natural ally the socialist community. We shall never accept, either in theory or in practice, the spurious concept of the division of the world into 'poor' and 'rich' countries, which places on one and the same footing the socialist countries and those capitalist countries which have extracted massive amounts of wealth from the countries formerly under colonial rule." [25]

The Soviet Government's statement of 4 October 1976 on reshaping international economic relations made a point of stressing that the interests of the socialist and developing countries in this area basically coincided. [26] The programme for the establishment of a new international economic order put forward by the Third World expresses its legitimate aspirations to extend the elimination of colonialism to the economic sphere so as to end its exploitation by the industrialized countries of the West and establish conditions enabling the developing countries to overcome their economic backwardness. The document underlines that unjustified attempts to involve the socialist world in a scheme whereby the world is divided into rich and poor countries in a bid to equate the socialist countries with the imperialist powers in the matter of historical responsibility for the economic backwardness of the developing countries, for the consequences of colonial oppression, and the neo-colonialist exploitation of these countries, are designed to justify and whitewash the exploitative policy of the imperialists towards the Third World. In the words of the Soviet Government statement: "There are not, nor can there be any grounds for demanding from the Soviet Union and other socialist states what the developing countries are demanding from the developed capitalist states, including mandatory transfer of a fixed proportion of GNP in economic aid." [27]

The assistance given by the socialist countries to the developing world is not compensation for previously inflicted damage on the latter, nor is it an act of atonement for past sins. It is the assistance of a friend and ally in the struggle against a common enemy — imperialism, colonialism, and neo-colonialism. Naturally, the Soviet Union's potential for extending economic aid to the Third World is not unlimited. It should be remembered that the USSR is already carrying a heavy burden of commitments to maintain peace and security of nations in the face of encroachment by aggressive imperialist circles.

The just demands of the developing countries for meaningful resources to be placed at their disposal to help them to overcome their backwardness should be met, in the first instance, at the expense of the profits of capitalist monopolies and the non-productive expenditures on the arms race which the imperialist have forced on the world.

The Soviet Government's statement of 4 October 1976 notes that further progress in political and military *détente* will facilitate the normalization of the world economic situation. In its turn progress in restructuring international economic relations will contribute to developing the process of *détente*. The USSR is fully aware of this connection and takes it into account in its foreign policy.

The developing countries together with the socialist community are waging a determined struggle for reshaping the entire system of international relations, political and economic, along democratic lines. Their active participation in this has lent a new dimension to the process. The growing unity and cohesion of the developing countries, the national-liberation movement, the socialist countries, and the international working-class movement is a guarantee of further progress towards the ultimate objective of a just and democratic world peace.

The imperialists are powerless to reverse the course of history. Back in the period when the first waves of national liberation were rising in the East, Lenin wrote that "...No force on Earth will succeed in restoring the old serfdom system in Asia, nor in sweeping off the face of the Earth the heroic democratism of the popular masses of Asian and semi-Asian countries."[28] Leonid Brezhnev, in his Report on the occasion of the 60th anniversary of the October Revolution in 1977, said: "Today we may confidently state that no force in the world will succeed in sweeping off the face of the Earth the fruits of the heroic struggle for liberation waged by the peoples of the former colonies and semi-colonies of imperialism. The cause of popular liberation is unconquerable and the future belongs to it. The torch kindled by the October Socialist Revolution in Russia will never be extinguished on this front of world history."[29]

10

Reshaping International Relations and the Battle of Ideas

THE stiffening and further extension of the struggle between the two opposite socio-economic systems over the main directions of reshaping international relations in the 1970s has had its repercussions in the ideological sphere as well. The last decade has seen a veritable eruption of bourgeois conceptions widely varying in form, terminology, and declared goals concerning a new world order, peaceful co-existence, and *détente*. In the present situation of a battle of ideas intensifying on the international scene, the political-academic complex existing in the leading imperialist powers has advanced to a leading place in the direct process of planning and supporting with propaganda the foreign policy of imperialism. The emergence of a large number of new theories and conceptions, as well as their "politicizing" — their evermore complete utilization as instruments for ideological and political struggle — is attributable to a number of factors.

The realization by the ruling quarters of the imperialist states, under the pressure of the realities of international life along with internal socio-political processes, of deep-going changes in the alignment and balance of forces in the international arena led them in the 1970s to admit the untenability of the theoretical foundations of the foreign policy pursued in the Cold War period. "The post-war order of international relations — the configuration of power that emerged from the Second World War — is gone. With it are gone the conditions which have determined the assumptions and practice of United States foreign policy since 1945",[1] President Nixon had to admit in 1971. His admission largely reflected the views of the entire ruling class of the biggest imperialist power. The crisis of the former "assumptions", the theoretical background of the foreign policy of the United States as the leader of the capitalist world has produced an intellectual vacuum of its own kind in the foreign-policy planning of the entire capitalist world. The ruling quarters of the Western powers have come to realize more acutely the need for new ideas to give them a guideline for action in the changed international situation and make possible a new approach to the implementation of foreign policy. Supplying the ruling quarters of the capitalist states with ideas and conceptions called upon to enhance the efficiency of their foreign-policy moves has become a highly important function of the "brain trusts" of the West. It was not accidental, therefore, that such foreign-policy planning centres of the capitalist states as the "trilateral commission", "the Bilderberg meetings", "the Commission of Critical Choices for Americans", and others were established or stepped up their activities in the 'seventies.

Another highly important factor which stimulated the interest of bourgeois ideologists in developing theories and conceptions of international relations was the deep-going moral and political crisis that gripped Western society in the 'seventies. This crisis became manifest both in the growing discrediting of the foundations of the social order in the capitalist countries themselves and in the disillusionment of the general public in the Western countries with their foreign-policy objectives. Quite eloquent in this context is the following admission by the leading American financier Nelson Rockefeller: "The increase in the tempo of change and the vastness and complexity of the wholly new situations which are evolving with accelerated change, create a widespread sense that our political and social system has serious inadequacies."[2] (Translated from the Russian.)

The US "dirty war" in Indochina, the scandalous exposés of the Watergate affair, and the CIA activities overseas dealt a devastating blow to the myths of the "civilizing mission of the West in the world" which had been circulated by bourgeois propaganda for decades. As

Marshall D. Shulman, chief adviser at the US Department of State and former Director of the Russian Institute at Columbia University, declared, the moral and political crisis of Western society in the 'seventies "...in extreme measure ... has reinforced the loss of confidence in democratic (i.e. bourgeois — N.L.) societies as the chosen people of human progress, and in the capacity of self-government to cope with the growing complexities of national and international life".[3]

The results of public-opinion polls in the United States and other capitalist countries in the first half of the 'seventies furnish conclusive evidence of a revaluation of the Cold War stereotypes. For instance, the Gallup Institute, acknowledging in 1973 the dissipation of the Cold War atmosphere in the United States, pointed out that the attitude of American citizens to the Soviet Union was far more favourable than it had ever been since the Second World War and that such a reversal in public opinion was unprecedented.[4] In the meantime, in many West European countries a notable consolidation of the left forces and erosion of the anti-Communist and anti-Soviet stereotypes were in evidence. The ideas of socialism and peaceful co-existence had been gaining ever wider recognition among various strata of the population. As shown by polls carried out, in particular, in West Germany in the first half of the 'seventies, the number of persons who expressed themselves in favour of socialism in that country increased 17 times over between 1970 and 1973.[5]

In the light of the aforesaid political and ideological trends in the capitalist world in the 'seventies, perfection of the propaganda camouflage of imperialist foreign policy, its provision with a more or less dependable "logistic" support, as well as more effective measures to quell the anti-imperialist sentiments among the masses abroad has become an important function of the numerous theories and conceptions of reshaping international relations evolved by bourgeois ideologists. The widely advertised bourgeois conceptions of "reformation" or "reshaping" of international relations must, as visualized by the ruling quarters of the Western countries, create at least a semblance of seizing the initiative in the struggle for reshaping the international system from the forces of social progress and prove to the population in the capitalist countries that monopoly capital is also progressive. This function of the bourgeois conceptions of "reshaping" international relations can be described in Lenin's words to the effect ". . .that historical situations arise when reforms, and particularly promises of reforms, pursue only one aim: to allay the unrest of the people, force the revolutionary class to cease, or at least slacken, its struggle".[6]

The very fact that the Western circles, primarily those of the United States, have come forward with the idea of a "new world order", of creating a "new world structure" is indirect evidence of their recognition of the radical change in the alignment of forces in the international arena in favour of socialism and the impossibility to preserve the old system of international relations where the imperialists acting without impunity unleashed wars and committed acts of aggression, interfered in the internal affairs of other countries and peoples and suppressed the working people's liberation struggle. It would be an over-simplification, however, to conclude that the authors of the conceptions of a "new world order" are motivated by a desire to reconcile the ruling quarters of the imperialist powers to the changes which have taken place in international relations. On the contrary, the chief aim of all bourgeois conceptions of reshaping international relations is to find more effective ways of achieving the traditional class objectives of imperialism, to forestall further shifts in the alignment of world forces in favour of socialism and democracy.

In virtue of the methodological pluralism characteristic of bourgeois political science, the contradictory political positions of its ideologists, the conceptions of a "new world order" do not constitute a heterogeneous, integral, and internally consistent theory. However, a few trends or schools may be identified along the general lines of the efforts of Western scholars to evolve various conceptions of a "new world order".

In the last few years, the school advocating the conception of "interdependence" has come to the fore in a number of Western countries. At the same time, the "trilateral commission" set up in 1973 by representatives of the political, business, and scientific circles of the United States, some West European countries, and Japan is the true co-ordinating centre for applying the conception of "interdependence" to different regions or spheres of international relations. Theoreticians of the "trilateral commission" interpret a "renovated international system" as a system of rules, requirements and procedures applied in international relations, which would leave the possibility of taking current decisions — within the framework of rules — to the member states of the system or even to private firms and individuals. This system of rules would limit current working decisions in such a way that the decisions of individual states would combine into a single and useful whole rather than contradict one another.[7]

However, the authors of the report "Towards a Renovated International System", which has created quite a sensation in the West, avoid mentioning directly what rules will be drawn up and enforced to create their projected "interdependent" world, who will do this work, and how it will be done.

This is, however, discussed by other bourgeois scholars. Let us examine, in particular, the "system of rules" they are proposing for relations between the imperialist powers and the young states and compare these "rules" with facts from the foreign-policy practices of developed capitalist states.

First of all, the authors and advocates of the conception of "interdependence" cannot ignore the fact that with the world alignment of forces changed in favour of socialism and with the steadily growing power of the socialist community of nations, the imperialist powers are not in a position to employ against the developing countries the same methods of undisguised blackmail and military coercion they so widely used but 10 to 15 years ago. Therefore, while regarding the maintenance of the existing neo-colonial system of relations as their central objective, many government and political leaders in the West under present conditions rely on covert methods to attain their traditional goals. Hence the conception of "interdependence" is advertised as an "invitation for a dialogue" with the young states and as a "renunciation of confrontation" with them. This aspect of the conception under review was quite clearly formulated by the former US Ambassador to the United Nations Andrew Young: "My permanent task is to find common language with the Third World nations, particularly in Africa, to make them allies of the United States and secure their support for the American stance. . ." (Translated from the Russian.)

Emphasizing the importance of setting up relations of "interdependence" with the Asian, African, and Latin American countries, bourgeois scholars point out as the chief factor the growing need of the industrialized capitalist states for raw materials and fuel resources, which are concentrated mainly in the developing countries. In addition to economic considerations, however, the authors of the schemes of an "interdependent world" have in view objectives of a social-class character of crucial importance for imperialism. Making certain concessions to the young states in the economic and political spheres, the neo-colonialists expect that encouragement of industrial development, wider access of manufactured goods from the developing countries to the markets of industrialized capitalist states, and similar measures will provide a more acceptable platform for a broadly interpreted compromise with the national bourgeoisie. Offering this "new" platform for a *rapprochement* with the ruling quarters of a number of Asian, African, and Latin American countries, the neo-colonialists hope that in the situation of an intensified class struggle in the young states the national bourgeoisie will seek more eagerly than before an alliance with imperialism in the struggle to preserve its own positions. The thesis of the theoreticians of "interdependence" on the incompatibility of revolutionary transformations in society with international stability understood as maintaining relations of "interdependence" should be interpreted precisely as an attempt to find common language with the big bourgeoisie and other reactionary forces in the developing countries. The American scholars Richard Rosecrance and Arthur Stein, for example, frankly say that revolutions undermine interdependence.[8]

What are the specific recipes offered by theoreticians of "interdependence" and how are they related to the practices of the present stage of restructuring international relations?

First, the advocates of this conception (such as Lincoln Bloomfield, Nazli Choucri, Miriam Camps, and others) appeal to the ruling quarters of the industrialized capitalist states to modify slightly their policy in relation to the developing countries so as to create the prerequisites for a "dialogue" with them. They recommend these quarters, in particular, to curtail the most offensive forms of political "interdependence", such as the military presence of imperialist powers in young states; to scale down the level or modify the forms of economic presence through both government and private channels; to consent to conclude international agreements on trade in raw materials; to diversify the ties between the imperialist states and the suppliers of the main raw materials.[9] It can be seen that some of these recommendations viewed individually are similar to the demands some developing countries have been making for quite a while. The implementation of the complex of these measures in the context of the class strategy of imperialism, however, has nothing in common with the aspirations of the peoples of Asia, Africa, and Latin America. In fact, the development of relations of "economic interdependence" encouraged by the ruling quarters of the Western countries pursues the objective of strengthening the ties of the state monopoly bourgeoisie with the social élite of some developing countries, which is taking advantage of the aggravation of the energy and raw-materials problems to secure its own enrichment. In the 'seventies this direction of neo-colonialist policy not only became clearly outlined but also acquired a largely new character. Attempts are being made through financial deals on an unprecedentedly large scale to "harmonize" the interests of the ruling quarters and the big bourgeoisie of some young states with the ambitions of the ruling class of the imperialist powers. Such deals are backed up by concerted political moves against the progressive forces in many regions of the "development zone". As justly pointed out by the Soviet scholar K. Brutents, "we are witnessing, in effect, the emergence of a new reactionary international social coalition of a specific character".[10]

Another field in which theoreticians of "interdependence" are unusually active is the construction of such schemes of reshaping international relations that would oppose the socialist states to the developing countries and place the socialist community of nations on the same footing with the imperialist powers as regards the historical responsibility for the economic backwardness of the former colonies. Professor Richard Gardener of Columbia University, in particular, is quite prolific in drawing up recommendations to this effect. Proceeding from the false premise of "equal responsibility" of the socialist countries and the former metropolitan countries, this

theoretician of "interdependence" is urging the developing countries
to make economic and financial claims on the Soviet Union.

Such provocative "recommendations" are absolutely unfounded.
The Soviet Government's statement "On Restructuring International
Economic Relations" said in this context:

> There is not, nor can there be any grounds for claiming from the Soviet Union
> and other socialist countries what the developing countries are claiming from the
> industrialized capitalist states, in particular, the handover to the developing
> countries through economic aid of a fixed share of gross national product. First,
> the socialist states cannot be held responsible for the economic backwardness of
> the developing countries they have inherited from colonial times. Second, these
> states have never been involved, nor are they involved now, in the economic
> exploitation of any country. Third, the socialist countries have nothing to do
> with the disastrous impact produced on the developing countries by economic
> depression, monetay crises and other manifestations of economic anarchy within
> the capitalist system.[11]

Finally, another important field of the theoretical and practical
activities of the strategists of "interdependence" is planning measures
to harness the developing countries more securely to the economic
mechanism of the capitalist system by means of various economic
associations. The idea being most actively circulated at present is one
of setting up a so-called "Euro-African" association composed of the
West European member countries of the EEC and the associated
African member states of this community. The "Euro-African"
conception is supported by those circles in the developing countries
who hope to consolidate their positions at home and abroad through
greater reliance on the imperialist powers. "Considering the national
resources and intellectual potential of Europe and Africa, one can
understand what enormous power will be wielded by such an
association... existing in the form of a symbiosis", President
Senghor of Senegal declared at a meeting of the Council of Europe.[12]
Such plans are based on idealization of the conception and practices
of "interdependence", which is in effect a disguised form of neo-
colonialist exploitation of the peoples of the young states.

Summing up the principles of the conception of "interdependence"
it should be said that all of them are designed one way or other to
inhibit progressive transformations of the system of international
relations, to perpetuate the existing ties between the young states and
the imperialist powers, to mitigate the contradictions between the

imperialist powers and co-ordinate their actions on a wide range of problems and, finally, to impose on the socialist countries such forms of "co-operation" that would in fact infringe their interests and oppose them to the developing countries.

Another large group of conceptions of a "new world order" are those of a "balance of power". They are discussed in the works of Hans J. Morgenthau, George Liska, Morton Kaplan, David Easton, Henry Kissinger, William R. Kintner, and other scholars. This trend is also to be seen in other studies on the theory of international relations published in the West. For instance, the collective research "The Theory and Practice of International Relations" maintains the idea that international relations were based on a "balance of power" in the past and are based upon it to a varying degree today. Although this conception, as the authors write, has come under criticism, a "balance of power" remains a factor in international affairs.[13] Proceeding from the "balance of power" theory, Alastair Buchan, Professor of International Relations at Oxford University and a former director (1958-69) of London's International Institute for Strategic Studies, writes about the end of the "bipolarized world" that emerged from the Second World War and a transition to a multipolar world. He traces the causes of this to China's revival as a great power, Japan's rise to the rank of the world's third biggest industrial power, the completion of the decolonization process and the loss by the United States of its military supremacy in Asia and its economic domination of the world.[14]

Many Western students of international relations refer to the latter's evolution in the direction of multipolarity. The emerging multipolar system of international relations, as they claim, is rooted in the rapid quantitative and qualitative changes in the strategic military field, the changing structure and alignment of forces in the world arena, the rising nationalism and the "diffusion of strength in the world". The problem of relations between "North and South" between the "rich" and the "poor" nations, they maintain, is a source of growing international tension. All this leaves its imprint on the modern world, converting it from a bipolar to a multipolar society.

Western writers analyse scrupulously the advantages and flaws of the bipolar and multipolar systems of international relations. Some theoreticians allege that the bipolar system is more stable and hence safer, since the actions of a single opponent are more predictable than those of a few in a multipolar system. Others argue that a multipolar system ensures greater stability, since a greater number of potential foes will be a stronger deterrent against the unacceptable behaviour of any state in the world arena. The American scholar Arnulf Baring sees hidden danger in the substitution of a multipolar for a bipolar system of international relations. "Some day, I am afraid", he writes, "we will long for the days of the frozen bipolarity and stable conditions of the Cold War. Only an overly optimistic observer can call the model of the world we are heading for polycentric. It is, in fact, chaotic."[15]

Naming the United States, the USSR, China, Western Europe, and Japan as the main protagonists in the multipolar "power centrist" structure of the world, bourgeois theoreticians construct various models of a "balance of power" between the aforesaid poles, which, as they see it, must constitute the foundation of a "new world order": USA–USSR–China (the triangle of rivalry), USA–Western Europe–Japan (the triangle of co-operation); USA–Western Europe–USSR (the Western triangle); USA–USSR–China–Japan (the Eastern quadrangle), USA–USSR–China–Japan–Western Europe (the stable pentagon). The last of these variants attracted the interest of many authors, who claim that the five-digit formula of the "balance of power" system may be a good foundation for a future stable "new world order" that will assure peace.

The true meaning of this five-cornered formula, just as of other geometric constructs of bourgeois political science, however, is different. Proceeding in effect from the notorious "balance of power" theory with its exclusive reliance on military factors, bourgeois theoreticians expect to create an equilibrium that in a situation of definite tension between the centres of power in the world arena would enable every interested side to pursue its own objectives. Nor do they conceal the fact that the United States is cast for the part of the main regulator, the fulcrum of the balance. In these plans special importance is attached to the great-power policies of certain anti-Soviet circles.

The conception of a "balance of power" system is meant not to secure a peaceful "world order" but to sustain and step up friction between states or groups 'of states, to exploit situations of conflict to attain the traditional goals of imperialist foreign policy — supremacy, unilateral economic and other advantages. Its ultimate objective is to perpetuate the positions of capitalism, to check the development of world revolution and the continued change of the alignment of forces in favour of socialism.

It will be recalled that in the latter half of the 'seventies the "balance of power" conception became overgrown with new details called upon to refurnish it in some way and adapt it to the changes in the international situation. Bourgeois scholars engaged in formulating new "rules", which were to be observed by the participants in the "balance of power" system — primarily the USSR — so as to "strengthen international stability".

For example, the American scholar Joseph Whelan, who at the request of Congress has carried out a monumental research on "Soviet Diplomacy and Negotiating Behaviour: Emerging New Context for US Diplomacy", holds that the USSR should exercise "restraint" toward the developing countries as the decisive condition for successful functioning of the "balance of power" system in the 1980s, because in the 'seventies Soviet policy in the Third World allegedly operated in its plans and consequences against international stability.[16]

This thesis is closely related to another which Zbigniew Brzezinski advanced in 1978 concerning the existence of a so-called "arc of instability" which, as he claims, can be drawn on the map from Chittagong in Bangladesh, through Islamabad and further to Aden. The situation in all countries of the "arc", he maintains, is characterized by "internal instability" caused by the "influence of Soviet power". Brzezinski attempts to prove in his constructs that the mythical "Soviet expansion" in the area of the "arc of instability" may choke off the Western world by barring it access to the oil fields of the Middle East.[17]

For all their scholarly garb, such constructs are completely divorced from reality. The "arc of instability" theory is in effect a rehashed variant of the "domino theory" formulated by American ruling quarters as far back as the 'fifties, which long provided the theoretical platform and a propaganda smokescreen for the aggression in Indochina. If crises do exist in the Middle East today, they are caused not by "Soviet influence" at all but by the actions of the United States itself threatening the freedom of the Iranian people, organizing subversive activities against the Democratic Republic of Afghanistan, and widening its military presence in this region.

Among bourgeois writers there are critics of the "balance of power" concept as the foundation for a "new world order". They describe it as inacceptable and are searching for other blueprints to establish it. Criticizing the foreign-policy concepts current in the West, primarily the "balance of power" theory, the British scholar J.W. Burton says that alliances as one of the cornerstones of the balance-of-power policy have been made irrelevant by the advent of nuclear weapons.[18] Therefore he rejects the idea of collective security, describing it as "balance-of-power in disguise". Burton suggests that the new model of international relations should be based on non-alignment.

Indisputably, the wide variety of international relations, the entire complexity of the alignment of forces cannot be reduced to a bipolar system, a confrontation between two powers — the USA and the USSR. The international situation today is characterized by a multiplicity of forces, each furthering its own interests. However, the increase in the polycentric tendencies — the emergence in the capitalist world of new centres of power and imperialist rivalry and the greater involvement of medium-sized and small states — by no means cancels out the main antagonism in the modern world, its division into two systems and their historical confrontation. It is this confrontation that determines the deep-rooted objective foundation of the world alignment of forces, despite all the twists and turns of international development.

It is necessary to point out another specific feature characteristic to a varying extent of both the conception of "interdependence" and the modern modifications of the "balance of power" theory. This is the efforts of their authors to play down the importance of national sovereignty or to get it renounced altogether. In its extreme variant this idea is expressed in the old formula of a "world government" which proved worthless primarily because of its unrealistic character in a world divided into two systems — socialism and capitalism. Bourgeois scholars recommend a "new world order" to be based on a renunciation by states of their national sovereignty. They refer to the alleged "erosion" of national sovereignty by the widening and deepening international ties, military, political, and economic co-operation among countries. They welcome this "erosion" as indispensable for a stable "world order". Recent changes in the structure of the international community, the American scholar R.J. Vincent writes, suggest hypotheses challenging both national sovereignty and the principle of non-intervention as a form of its protection.[19] The idea of supranational government is called upon to serve and protect the interests of the multinational imperialist monopolies.

Other Western theoreticians of international relations proclaim an inevitable "convergence" of the opposite socio-economic systems. In devising a "new world order" they concentrate on the political and organizational aspects of the world community, attaching prime importance to mutual adaptation of the two different socio-economic systems. The anti-socialist implications of such projects are self-evident.

A relatively new trend in the quest for a theoretical basis for a "new world order" is the conception of building it through reconstruction of the worldwide system of international economic relations. Such conceptions have been generated by the exacerbation of the crisis situation in the capitalist economy and the specifics of the present stage of relations of the capitalist countries with the socialist and the developing countries. In the last few years these relations have shown an obvious discrepancy between the old capitalist order of international economic relations, on the one hand, and on the other, the widening sphere of business co-operation with the socialist countries, as well as the vital needs and requirements of the developing countries.

Some Western scholars, as well as certain others, tend to reduce the processes taking place in the world arena to a conflict between "rich" and "poor" nations, obscuring thereby the difference of principle between the capitalist and the socialist states. They view industrial development and *per capita* income rather than the socio-political system prevailing in a given state as a criterion for its characterization. The establishment of a "new world order" is identified with measures to level off disparities in the economic advancement of countries. They ignore the central question of restructuring international relations — the affirmation of the principle of peaceful co-existence of states having opposite social systems, as well as the related problems. Yet it is peace and security that are a *sine qua non* for mutually beneficial and well-balanced international economic co-operation contributing to more rapid development of countries. Of course, there is a feedback: closer international economic co-operation works for a relaxation of tension and peace.

While acknowledging that change in international economic relations is inevitable, bourgeois ideologists seek to prevent it from undermining the foundations — the capability of the imperialist circles to exert economic pressure to attain their political objectives in international affairs and keep the developing countries within the capitalist economic orbit, the sphere of expansion of the biggest monopolies of the imperialist powers.

As can be seen, the bourgeois schemes of a "new world order" by no means meet the need for truly reshaping relations between states having different social systems on the principles of peaceful co-existence and broad constructive co-operation. They can only produce a negative effect and hinder the positive trends showing in international affairs. For instance, the American political scientists Gerald and Patricia Mische see the main task of maintaining this "order" in keeping up the alleged "global process of convergence".[20] In their view the principles of a "new world order" must be "supra-national" and "supracultural". The converged "new world" would, they claim, put an end to the struggle between the two socio-economic systems, which is an "anachronism" today.

This purpose is also served by the latest bourgeois conceptions of *détente,* another series of which were produced by ideologists of imperialist foreign policy in the latter half of the 'seventies.

As is known, any advance in the direction of a more durable peace, greater security and wider peaceful co-existence of states having different social systems is resisted by reactionary capitalist ideologists and politicians. This is borne out by the record of the past and the current state of international relations between states of the two opposite systems where international reaction is making frantic efforts to push the world back to Cold War times or to take advantage of *détente* to promote its selfish interests. Hence the zigzags, vacillations, reversals, and other negative phenomena in the foreign policies of some capitalist countries.

In this situation the enemies of *détente* have stepped up their activities on the ideological front. They have set up various committees, groups, councils and commissions to evolve new doctrines and conceptions in an attempt to explain theoretically the current negative trends in relations between countries with opposite social systems and to prove that these trends are causing no harm to *détente* and the international situation in general. Numerous attempts are also in evidence to modify or rather distort the very notion of *détente* and to emasculate the meaning attached to it when the process of relaxation of international tension got under way.

For example, in a book published in the West in 1976 the concept of *détente* is interpreted as a limited confict before the end of the century within the USSR– China– West triangle.[21]

The authors of this work come up with the notions of "minimal" and "maximal" *détente*, claiming, as has become habitual with the opponents of *détente*, that the Soviet Union stands to gain from *détente* more than the United States. On this premise they propose different, more effective ways and means of implementing a policy of *détente* viewed as a "limited conflict". The key point in their recommendations is haggling with the USSR over the terms of grain and high technology deals. The United States is advised to demand Soviet concessions in matters of arms control and a settlement in the Middle East, South Africa, and other regions.

The authors insist that now relations with Western Europe and Japan, as well as finding a solution to the economic, energy, and food problems must be more important to Washington than anything else. Therefore, the United States should not put *détente* with the USSR at the top of the list of foreign-policy priorities.

Détente is not the main political problem, they claim. Bilateral relations with the USSR, a change from confrontation to co-operation should not be given first priority in the near future.... . Therefore, the United States should scale down the present level of significance of relations with the Soviet Union.[22] West–West rather than East–West relations must be central to the United States.[23]

The French Sovietologist Patrick Wajsman also warns against the "excessive attraction" of relations between East and West and argues that the interpretation of *détente* should meet the interests of the Western world.[24]

The latest modification of bourgeois views on the essence of *détente* in relations with the USSR and other socialist countries is the conception of "re-ideologization" of international relations, or "ideological confrontation". Until a relatively recent time the approach of bourgeois theoreticians to the problems of world politics had been influenced by the conception of "de-ideologization", that is, a renunciation of ideological struggle. This conception boiled down to an effort made under the pretence of a general "abandonment of ideology" to undermine the influence of Marxism–Leninism and secure more favourable conditions for the infiltration of bourgeois ideology into the socialist countries.

Today the conception of "de-ideologization" is being increasingly displaced by conceptions designed not simply to intensify the ideological struggle in international relations but to turn it into an "ideological war" or at least "ideological confrontation". Their advocates are stressing the need for the foreign policy of bourgeois states to be adapted to the exigencies of the ideological struggle and for still greater emphasis on ideological propaganda in foreign policy.

It is precisely this function that the so-called "moral policy" proclaimed by the Carter Administration has been performing in the latter half of the 'seventies. "There is only one nation in the world which is capable of true leadership among the community of nations, and that is the United States of America. But this leadership need not depend on our inherent military force, or economic power, or political persuasion. It should derive from the fact that we try to be right and honest and truthful and decent."[25] This is how the President himself formulated the key principle of this policy. The leading theoretician of "morality" within the US ruling quarters has lately been Zbigniew Brzezinski.

He formulated the theoretical postulates of the "moral policy" in the book *Between Two Ages. America's Role in the Technetronic Era,* and a series of articles published in American foreign-policy journals, as well as — after his appointment as National Security Adviser to the President — in lengthy interviews with a number of American and West European newspapers.[26]

Referring to a crisis in the established American values and institutions, particularly the traditions of liberal democracy, Brzezinski has undertaken to formulate a new ideological platform of the American ruling class — the so-called "rational humanism". One of its main principles is recognition of the aspiration of all members of society towards actual rather than formal equality. This champion of "rational humanism" claims that in the United States itself every condition needed for such equality is already available, so the task facing America now is to create similar conditions in the rest of the world, since "...a nation concerned with social justice... cannot help but become similarly committed on an international level".[27] Proceeding from this principle, Brzezinski describes the essence of the objectives of the US "moral policy": the role of the United States in world affairs must not be confined to the maintenance of the *status quo* or a balance of power; it must rather consist in lending the process of change a positive direction, and an effort to secure an equitable and creative harmony between freedom and equality.

It is indisputable that concepts of "rational humanism" and such-like ideas promulgated by bourgeois ideologists are untenable in the scientific sense. The central thesis of "rational humanism", to the effect that America's ruling class (which is precisely what Brzezinski has in mind, referring to the American nation) can be in the vanguard of progress towards social justice at home does not hold water. What justice, indeed, can be sought by a handful of moneybags, who in the first half of the 'seventies constituted a mere 0.3 per cent of the American population but owned (to speak of direct ownership alone) 22 per cent of the nation's wealth. What kind of justice is it indeed with 60 per cent of the people owning only 7.5 per cent of America's wealth?

It is important, however, not only to expose the demagogy of the advocates of "moral policy" but also to define the specific objectives attached to it by the American ruling quarters.

It appears that on the international plane America's ruling class expects to dispel with its "moral policy" primarily the intense anti-American sentiments which developed with the mass of the population of Western Europe and the developing countries in earlier years. This is exactly why the advocates of "moral policy" are talking so much about the alleged abandonment by the United States of its attempts to impose its will on other peoples and its changeover to what they describe as the convincing force of American moral leadership. ". . . We must recognize that our power to influence resides — now in the 1970s — overwhelmingly in our example", declared William P. Bundy.[28] This reliance on the "power of example" combined with loud admissions of a curtailment of American might serves a perfectly obvious goal — to create a semblance of a reduction in the "share of coercion" in American foreign policy, to prove its evolution in the direction of greater commitment to peace and non-violent actions in pursuit of altruistic goals common to all mankind.

Another foreign-policy objective the advocates of "moral policy" evidently seek to achieve is more active employment of American class allies abroad in a situation where the possibility for American imperialism to wield its own power is substantially limited. In view of this objective, there has been a shift in emphasis in the interpretation of the US security conceptions formulated in his time by Harry Truman. Whereas in the late 'forties the principle of interventionism was proclaimed as the foundation of US security, now the accent is placed on the fact that the stability of the international system (and the tranquillity of America) depend on the character of relations between the governments and the masses in other countries. To guarantee its own security the United States must take advantage of the aspirations of various social groups and strata in other countries towards the "ideals of democracy" (that is, bourgeois democracy) to have the relations between the peoples and governments in these countries restructured in a way useful to the American bourgeoisie. Thus, the American ruling quarters have open to them what may be termed a policy of "inverted globalism": with the traditional objective of establishing a world order suited to the American ruling class remaining unchanged, the main instrument for its achievement is to be sought not in the power of the United States itself but in the potential of those groups and strata in other countries whose interests theoreticians of "moral policy" believe to be close to or identical with those of the American bourgeoisie.

The advocates of the conception of "moral policy" attach special significance to the employment of techniques that have the character of subversive activities and "psychological warfare". Among the most favourite means being intensively used in imperialist foreign policy today are regular demands that the USSR and other socialist countries should respect human rights.[29]

It is easy to see that these zealots of human rights under socialism are concerned in effect with problems of a different kind, namely, with ways of providing a favourable climate for the anti-socialist activities of various turncoats and their patrons, for undermining the foundations of the socio-political system of socialism, for widening the channels of infiltration of bourgeois propaganda into the socialist countries, for interference in their internal affairs. Not only do they shut their eyes to the flagrant violation of human rights in the Western world but they are also taking great pains to conceal the fact that for over 60 years now socialism has been pressing for humanization of international relations, for securing such international law and order as would provide the optimum conditions for protection not only of the political but also of the most vital social rights of the individual — the right to work, to education, to free medical care, and other benefits.

A Return to the Cold War and Gunboat Diplomacy

The latest conceptions of *détente* under review, which have been formulated by representatives of influential circles in the capitalist countries and have a fairly great impact on foreign-policy making in the Western world reflect the truly intricate and contradictory character of the process of *détente* and restructuring international relations on just and democratic principles. The Soviet Union, however, sees not only this aspect of this process.

Leonid Brezhnev declared in August 1977: "We see the negative aspects of world developments, but we by no means believe that they alone determine the world situation. Indeed, simultaneously many-sided peaceful co-operation is developing successfully between dozens of states belonging to different social systems.... . Matters in this field may be going without sensation, yet progress is in evidence, and it would be a mistake to underestimate it."[30]

Thus, the world continues its progress along the path of *détente*. This is logical, because it corresponds to the objective laws of social development. Consequently, at this juncture of international political development the primary task is to consolidate *détente,* to secure its long-term prospects, and to make it irreversible.

It is symptomatic that some representatives of the sober-minded circles in the Western world are clearly aware of this fact. For example, the well-known American Sovietologist George F. Kennan, formerly US Ambassador to the USSR, a professor at the Institute for Advanced Study, Princeton, who has recently founded the Kennan Institute for Soviet Studies in Washington, maintains that relations with the USSR are central to American foreign policy, since they have a crucial bearing on the prevention of nuclear war which looms cloud-like on the horizon. Kennan advises the US Administration to avoid measures and gestures that might be interpreted by the USSR as meddling in its domestic affairs and might interfere with the completion of the "main task of American statesmanship with relation to Russia, which is... to reduce the danger posed for both countries and for the world by the present military rivalry".[31]

Another American analyst, Arthur Macy Cox, also speaks from realistic positions. In his new book entitled *The Dynamics of Détente* he maintains that a policy of *détente* is the only sensible policy today, while an end to the arms race and the implementation of disarmament are pivotal to this policy. In view of the manoeuvering of the American foreign-policy ideologists around the problems of *détente,* Cox emphasizes the following principle of essential importance to all foreign policy. "The main reasons for moving ahead with *détente* to end the Cold War and the arms race are that we will have better security and will live in a more peaceful and productive world."[32] The appeals of realistic-minded Western experts for practical steps to be taken to stabilize *détente,* to reduce the war menace, and to end the arms race certainly deserve support. In the matter of deepening the positive shifts in international relations today such steps assume steadily increasing importance. Brezhnev has said in this context: "International relations today are at a crossing, as it were, of ways that may lead either to growing trust and co-operation or to growing mutual fears, suspicions, and arms build-up — ways that may lead in the final analysis either to a lasting peace or, at best, to balancing on the brink of war. *Détente* makes it possible to choose the way of peace. It would be a crime to miss this opportunity. So the most vital and pressing task today is to stop the arms race which has spread throughout the world."[33]

*   *   *

The Marxist-Leninist scientific conception of the development of the worldwide system of international relations today, which was formulated by the 24th Congress of the CPSU and further developed in the resolutions of the 25th Congress, enables a correct approach to solving the vital problems of today. This conception is being carried into effect by the Soviet Union jointly with all other countries of the socialist community.

> Only a democratic peace, a just peace, can be a genuinely lasting peace. Such a peace must be based on respect for the rights, sovereignty, and legitimate interests of all countries without exception, be they big or small, be they members or non-members of political groupings — and not on some poles of strength and rivalry, about which it has become fashionable to speak in some quarters. It is not a matter of learning more subtle methods of manipulating the so-called balance of forces, but a matter of excluding the use of force from international relations. This requires the pooling of the constructive efforts of all countries.[34]

From the viewpoint of socialist policy the central goal of a fundamental restructuring of international relations must be to remove the seeds of conflict from relations between states with different social systems, to intensify various forms of co-operation in their relations, as well as in relations among all peoples, countries, and states, and to lend this co-operation a stable character. The central component, the linchpin of co-operation between states having different social systems is their joint actions to prevent another world war. A new pattern of international relations cannot be established without military *détente*, ending the arms race, a settlement of conflicts, stamping out the existing and preventing the appearance of new seeds of war.

The implementation of measures to limit and end the arms race and eventually achieve general and complete disarmament must be the primary indispensable component of military *détente* in international relations. A series of treaties and agreements on arms limitation have been concluded in the last few years. All of them put together and the complex of measures they provide for can be viewed as the embryo of such a system, an important element of the emerging new structure of international relations. In its present form this system affects only a few sectors of military activity and far from all states possessing large military arsenals. Hence the great urgency attached to the problem of securing the effectiveness and universal application of the partial measures agreed upon, of supplementing them with new agreements containing wider commitments to limit armaments so as to narrow steadily the material basis for military confrontation.

Co-ordination of measures to reduce the danger of armed conflict is another essential component of the emerging new relations in the sphere of military *détente*. With the existing practice of mutual consultations and co-ordination the risk of direct confrontation and war breaking out by accident is diminished. In a situation of military *détente* differences and disputes between states must be settled by peaceful means, while the existing methods of negotiated settlement should be applied on the basis of a free and voluntary choice of procedure most acceptable to the sides in every specific case by mutual consent and in the interest of a speedy and fair settlement.

The fulfilment of this task is closely bound up with a number of other vital problems involved in consolidating international peace, in particular, with that of dissolving military–political alliances and setting up collective security systems. The military–political relations among capitalist states, in the form of exclusive alliances, are by themselves generating a dangerous state of confrontation.

The approach to a fundamental restructuring of the system of international relations primarily as a system of stable political co-operation among states ruling out eventually the necessity for military coercion logically entails the development of diverse economic, scientific, and technical ties between states. Such co-operation is called for by the following objective factors: the expansion of the possible spheres of co-operation between countries; the need for joint efforts to solve a number of increasingly pressing current problems of power development, transport, communications, developing raw material resources, environmental protection, the exploration and use of the World Ocean and outer space, intensifying agriculture, preventing and eradicating diseases, and so on.

Because of their character and scope these problems cannot be solved by any country alone and require a collective effort.

One of the major factors of restructuring the system of international relations plagued by inequality, exploitation, and neo-colonialism is economic equality. The system of international relations taking shape today will not be viable if it preserves economic inequality, and if economic pressure and discrimination continue to exist as its structural elements.

There is a close inter-relationship between reshaping international economic relations on the principles of justice, on the one hand, and political and military *détente*, on the other: a relaxation of political tension complemented with military *détente* facilitates international economic co-operation; the latter in turn can effectively contribute to the establishment of a stable system of political co-operation among states. As declared in the final communiqué of the Berlin Conference of Communist and Workers' Parties of Europe, "Broad international co-operation becomes ever more necessary for safeguarding peace, achieving a just settlement of international conflicts, strengthening security and implementing practical steps towards disarmament. This co-operation is necessary to further the establishment of new and equitable international economic relations."[35]

The United Nations is called upon to play an important part in developing various forms of co-operation among states primarily in promoting peace and international security. Andrei Gromyko has said that "today the UN should concentrate on developing the process of *détente* in the world arena. The Soviet Union is working to enhance the prestige and role of this organization as the key instrument for strengthening peace, is upholding the lofty goals and principles of the United Nations Charter, is pressing and will continue to press for their implementation and for a strict compliance by all states with their obligations assumed under the UN Charter.''[36]

Thus, the Marxist–Leninist conception of *détente* and restructuring international relations is distinguished by a comprehensive approach to world processes, a thorough consideration of the entire totality of factors responsible for the development of new trends, the actual complexities and contradictions in relations between countries, the differences in ideology in particular.

It should be emphasized that this conception of reshaping international relations is based on a sober recognition of the fact that this process is and will be taking place in a situation of incessant ideological confrontation between the two world systems. The struggle between ideologies, however, is not an insurmountable obstacle to improving relations between socialist and capitalist states. As is known, for all the profound ideological differences between them appreciable progress has been achieved in their mutual relations. This fact belies the claim of bourgeois ideologists to the effect that the ideological struggle and ideological differences make improvement of relations between states with different social systems impossible in principle.

It should be stressed, however, that in a situation of fundamental reshaping of international relations this struggle must run a course different from that of the times of the Cold War and acute international tension. Indeed, defence and propaganda of one's ideals have nothing in common with a malicious distortion of facts, shameless slander, attempts to interfere in the domestic affairs of socialist countries — something bourgeois propaganda actively engaged in during the Cold War years and the enemies of *détente* are doing in our day.

The ideological struggle must rule out subversion and blackmail, as well as the methods of the so-called black propaganda. The interests of developing all-round co-operation between states require the sphere of ideological struggle to be cleared of the instruments and techniques of subversion characteristic of psychological warfare which the imperialist circles used in the past and are using today. In the field of international politics it is important to develop mutual relations in a way precluding an extension of ideological differences to relations between states, so that the ideological struggle in the international arena could not grow into international military-political conflicts.

The Marxist-Leninist conception of restructuring the system of international relations is remarkable for the force and scope of its impact on various spheres of life. Restructuring of international relations is bound to lead not only to the establishment of lasting peace and international co-operation, to mankind's deliverance from the scourge of war. It creates the most favourable climate for progressive change in the world, facilitates social progress, offers the masses excellent opportunities for achieving their cherished ideal of building a classless society.

The clearly worded Marxist-Leninist conception of reshaping international relations is profoundly realistic. This is evidenced by the experience gained in the conditions of *détente*. The prospects outlined by it can be made a reality, because they express the main trend of the modern epoch — mankind's transition from capitalism to socialism.

11

Détente Today: Problems and Outlook

IN THE past 2 years the international climate has visibly cooled. There has clearly been an appreciable deterioration of the international situation brought about, above all, by the moves of the imperialist circles of the United States, who have been at considerable pains to shunt world development back into the eroded and now increasingly dangerous rut of the Cold War. Once again someone, and the "someone", unfortunately, is quite influential in the Western world, is trying to throw mankind back to the days of "fist law" in international affairs, intending like Louis XIV to engrave on the barrels of his cannon the motto "Ultima ratio regum" (The final argument of kings) or to echo Napoleon's sadly celebrated phrase "Les grandes bataillons ont toujours raison" (Large battalions are always in the right). "What they call peace is peace in name only, in reality what has existed eternally from the nature of things is uncompromising war among states."[1] These words were uttered over two millennia ago by Plato, but it seems they have just resounded in the Oval Office of the White House or on Capitol Hill.

Not a day passes without Washington trying to revive the spirit of the Cold War, to whip up militaristic hysteria. Any cause is being exploited, real or invented. Take, for example, Afghanistan. The ruling quarters of the United States, as well as of China, would resort to anything, even to armed aggression, that would interfere with the Afghan people's building a new life in accordance with the ideals of

320

the liberation revolution of April 1978. But when the Soviet Union helped its neighbour Afghanistan, at the request of its government, to rebuff the aggression and to repulse the raids of bandit gangs operating primarily from within Pakistan, Washington and Peking raised an unprecedented hue and cry accusing the Soviet Union of every mortal sin: an intention to gain a warm-water port, an ambition to lay its hands on foreign oil, and so on. The simple fact of the matter is that the imperialist plans to suck Afghanistan into the orbit of imperialist politics and to create a threat to the Soviet Union's south border have been frustrated.

American ruling quarters were embarked on an "anti-*détente* policy" long before the "Afghan crisis" broke, as is evidenced by a series of the Carter Administration's foreign-policy moves designed to revise the established structure of Soviet–American relations in favour of the United States by putting pressure on the Soviet Union. The Administration has abandoned the Soviet–American understandings concerning a comprehensive Middle East settlement and instead has opted for encouraging the separate Egyptian–Israeli deal in an attempt to chain to the chariot of its policy not only Israel but also Egypt. The United States is thus attempting to secure its positions in this strategically important and oil-rich region, positions which have been undermined by the Iranian revolution. The journal *Foreign Policy* in its November 1978 issue wrote: "...the Carter foreign policy team... entered the East–West arena confidently. It failed to examine the legacy of the containment and *détente* periods and rushed ahead with its own activism, believing that the Kremlin remained greatly impressed by US abilities to affect the USSR's security and future as a major power."[2]

The Washington session of the NATO Ministerial Council in May 1978 approved an additional, long-term armament programme designed to induce the NATO countries to increase by 3 per cent annually their real arms expenditure on a stable basis. The programme, which covers the period almost up to the year 2000, is also designed to build up an "intimidation" potential which the United States quite openly intends to use in East–West political relations.[3]

Having signed the SALT-2 Treaty with the USSR in Vienna in June 1979, the United States at the Brussels NATO session in December 1979 pushed through a decision to produce and deploy in Western Europe a new generation of its medium-range nuclear missiles in an attempt to upset the balance of forces in Europe ·in favour of the United States and its NATO allies. The US statement on the intended withdrawal of 1000 American nuclear warheads from Western Europe made in Brussels at the time does not change anything. What this measure means in practical terms has been explained by Radio Europe I. In its comment on that promise it said that the withdrawal of these nuclear warheads which are "fit for the scrap heap", "obsolete and hopelessly inadequate for the needs of the moment", is aimed at "clearing the decks" for deploying Pershing-2 and cruise missiles which have a greater range.[4]

Further evidence of aggressive American intentions is the constitution of the "rapid deployment force" designed for operations in the Gulf area and other "flash points", i.e., for suppressing the national liberation movements in those areas.

Another source of heightened international tension is the United States' playing "the Chinese card". At the NATO Council session in May 1978 US government officials openly declared that there was a connection between the interests of the USA and NATO and those of the Peking leadership who openly oppose *détente* and call for preparations for a war against the USSR. Since then American official assessments of China have referred to it as nothing short of a "strategic counter-balance to the USSR", a "potential second front" which could be opened against the USSR and even, be it noted, "NATO's 16th member".[5] In his State of the Union message to Congress in January 1980, President Carter said that when he took office in 1977 he placed emphasis on the need for the USA to reassert its leadership in the world. To quote President Carter, "I'm determined that the United States will remain the strongest of all nations."[6]

American ruling quarters have launched a frenzied arms race to secure military superiority over the USSR. In the fiscal year beginning October 1980, more than 164 billion dollars were allocated for military spending, 20 billion up on 1979. Already, the Senate suggests boosting the arms bill to 173.4 billion dollars. The planned outlays for the Pentagon for the next 2 years stand at 196.9 and 209.3 billion dollars respectively.[7]

By imposing a new and more dangerous round of the arms race on the world, Washington hypocritically points an accusing finger at the supposed "rapid growth" of the Soviet Union's military spending, citing data so unbelievably groundless that as George Kennan said it is amazing that they should come from men in positions of responsibility.[8] It is a fact that since 1970 the Soviet Union has been reducing its military spending. Whereas in 1970 the USSR spent 17,800 million roubles on defence, in 1978 the figure was 17,200 million. Over this period the share of military spending in the Soviet Union's national budget declined from 11.5 to 7 per cent.[9]

The advantages offered by its socialist economic system enable the Soviet Union to maintain an impressive defence potential and keep its armed forces at the required level of preparedness on relatively smaller military outlays than in capitalist countries.

The imperialists' hopes for gaining military superiority over the USSR and the rest of the socialist commonwealth have been dashed. The record of history confirms this. It is senseless at the present time to try and gain a strategic advantage over the USSR by developing new weapons. Those who intend to secure military superiority over the USSR in its way will do well to remember that the Soviet economy, science, and engineering are of a sufficiently high standard to develop within a short time any type of weapon on which the enemies of peace will put their money. The senselessness of any new round of the arms race is proved not only by the Soviet Union's ability to rapidly close this or that "technological gap" but also by the fact that the very notion of "military superiority" over a potential enemy in the nuclear age is illusory.

The socialist countries do not pursue military superiority. But if a new spiral of the arms race is thrown on them they will have no option but to respond to the challenge with suitable counter-measures.

*   *   *

Now that the international situation has deteriorated and the imperialists are clearly bent on testing the will of the peoples for peace and their determination to pursue *détente* and good-neighbourliness the question naturally arises: has this unfavourable twist in the development of world politics come as a surprise to those who have consistently worked for *détente* seeing it as an objective necessity, and for restructuring the present pattern of international relations on the generally recognized principles of peaceful co-existence? The answer is an emphatic "no". In his day Lenin repeatedly emphasized that history follows a zigzag course and the socialist state in the conduct of its foreign policy has to take into account the most intricate and, at times, bizarre twists in the situation, its ups and downs and even temporary setbacks and reverses.

The establishment of the principles of peaceful co-existence in relations between states belonging to different socio-economic systems and adhering to polarized political and ideological philosophies has never been treated as a process developing along straight lines. It has always been a complicated and, at times, contradictory process. As the influence and appeal of socialism grow, capitalism has been trying by all means in its power to protect and regain its positions, seeking every now and then to offset the loss of its ideological influence and its reverses in the socio-political area by flexing its military muscles and using military force, and by conducting aggressive expansionist foreign policies, all of which aggravates the international situation and gives rise to dangerous conflicts which threaten world peace and the security of nations.

The two opposed social systems represent two poles in world politics, two polarized aspects of the essential contradiction of the modern era which determines the course of world development. Struggle between them in every area of their mutual relations, including international politics, is inevitable. That is why elements of co-operation are in this area dialectically intertwined with elements of confrontation. Co-operation and confrontation are the two basic aspects of peaceful co-existence, they are facets of one process. Their unity is dialectical in character. It is impossible to treat them in isolation one from the other, to concentrate on one and ignore the other.

The record of international relations over the past decade convincingly confirms this dialectical interdependence. Despite the notable shifts during the past 10 years in the pattern of international life towards diversified co-operation between states having different social systems, the development of *détente* has not been conflict-free in any of its phases, it has never represented an idyllic climate in international politics. *Détente* has evolved as a cumulative product of the dialectical interaction of two foreign-policy courses, opposed both in terms of their class origin and of their eventual class objectives — socialist and bourgeois foreign policies. The latter, in particular, is shaped and implemented as a policy of protecting the capitalist system and expresses the interests of the dominant classes of modern bourgeois society. This policy is affected, on the one hand, by a growing perception of imperialism's inability to crush socialism militarily in the conditions of a changed alignment of forces in the world and the existence of nuclear weapons which, if used, would plunge mankind into the abyss of catastrophe. On the other hand, it is affected by a constant desire to impede the revolutionary development of the world, to inhibit it and, with luck, to reverse it. All this taken together causes bourgeois international politics to follow a zigzagging course. At one period elements of "co-operation" are in evidence in it, exemplified by a wish to reach agreement on particular problems, to arrive at accommodation with the socialist countries, while conversely at another period emphasis is laid on "rivalry" and a desire to resort to well-accustomed methods of brute force and hegemonistic ambitions gain the upper hand.

By *"détente"*, bourgeois politicians often mean a freezing and guaranteeing of the socio-political *status quo* in the world while they blame any liberation movement by peoples on the instigation of external forces, on the Soviet Union's "interference". They qualify them as a "violation of the rules of *détente*" and exploit them as an excuse for whipping up military tension, sabre-rattling and for conducting a policy "from positions of strength". This is precisely how the present American Administration, pursuing a policy of aggravating the international climate and undermining *détente*, has been behaving. However, these actions by the American ruling circles in a bid to dictate their terms to other nations are "tantamount to grave miscalculations of policy", Leonid Brezhnev warns. "And like a boomerang they will hit back at their initiators if not today, then, surely, tomorrow."[10]

The reasons for the present aggravation of the international situation are rooted in the policy followed by those reactionary imperialist circles who saw that under *détente* they were unable to accomplish their goals and that *détente* weakened their influence and positions in the world. These goals were, above all, to undermine the prestige of socialism and its impact on broad sections of the world population, in an attempt to limit its appeal and attraction.

It turned out, however, that *détente* has destroyed many of the ideological pillars which had supported imperialist policy and formed the foundation of its militarist thrust based on the use of brute force. Take, for instance, the myth of "Soviet threat" which has been used to justify the existence of the NATO bloc and its policy in international affairs. The former chairman of the NATO Military Committee, the British Admiral Peter Hill-Norton in his *No Soft Options. The Politico-Military Realities of NATO,* had to admit that it is difficult to prove the existence of this "threat" and that when *détente* began many in the West stopped believing the myth. To quote Hill-Norton: "People continually ask whether there is a threat to NATO or to its individual member-states. Others go further and assert that there is no threat."[11]

This evolution in the climate of Western public opinion seriously worried the Atlantic circles who decided to counteract by reversing the trend and once again to stimulate an atmosphere of fear and alarm among the public in which it would be easier to increase military spending, to tighten up the screws in the socio-economic area and to divert public attention from such perennial problems as unemployment, inflation, and other serious ills which in conditions of capitalist society remained unresolved.

Under *détente* many of the social problems confronting the Western world began to be perceived more acutely by the public and these problems moved to the foreground and insistently demanded urgent action to solve them. The West German political scientist M. Görtemaker put it well in his book on the history of *détente* when he wrote that *détente* "... opened up ample scope for the activities of opposition parties, groups, and trends and encouraged them to intensify their criticism of their own systems".[12] The American author T. Larson also pointed out that "*Détente* has facilitated the spread of

Marxism–Leninism in the more or less advanced industrial nations..." and that "in the less developed world it is the popularity of anti-imperialism that facilitates the spread of Marxism–Leninism...".[13]

The successes of the national liberation movements and the victories scored in the years of *détente* by patriotic and progressive forces in many developing countries also dismayed those in the West who sought to maintain imperialist influence and domination in the Third World so as to continue to exploit their natural and manpower resources invoking the excuse that the preservation of the existing international order was in the "vital interests" of the imperialist powers. Characteristically, the current big talk in US government circles about its "vital interests" has been echoed almost literally in the pronouncements of the lunatic fringe of the rightists in the USA who have been the most vociferous opponents of *détente*. Thus, in 1978 the so-called "Committee on the Existing Danger", one of the leading organizations speaking for the ambitious conservative-militarist circles in the USA, published a report clearly favouring a policy "from positions of strength" and an arms build-up to consolidate the positions of the USA in the world. The report's authors demanded a very broad interpretation of US international interests, to say the least. In the words of the report, "It is apparent therefore that no part of the world can be excluded in advance from our security concerns. The globe itself is the strategic theatre of the central conflict of our time."[14]

It should be remembered that even during the halcyon days of *détente* the reactionary forces of the West tried hard to inhibit its progress, to prevent is spread to the military field and to this end stoked up the arms race. Each successive step towards limiting the arms race had to be fought for with great persistence and had to contend with the fierce resistance of the military–industrial complex, its spokesmen and lobby in the political circles. It was precisely the steps taken by these forces in the military field that hit *détente* hardest. Although Western leaders paid lip-service to the necessity of maintaining balance and parity in the military field, in their practical actions they sought military superiority over the socialist countries with a view to pursuing a policy of blackmail and dictatorialness.

At the same time there are forces among the ruling circles of the West who favour the continuation of *détente*, being aware that it has no viable alternative at the present juncture. All glib talk about the existence of a third way along the lines of "a cold peace" fails to inspire with renewed hope many of the sober-minded Western politicians who are only too well aware of the dangers of the nuclear age, of the risk of "brinkmanship", something that the advocates of "a hard line" towards the socialist countries are again urging. The recently constituted American Commission on East–West Accord composed of prominent politicians, businessmen, and scientists including the former Chairman of the Senate Foreign Relations Committee, William Fulbright, J.K. Galbraith, the economist, Donald Kendall, President of Pepsico Inc., and the former American Ambassador to the USSR George Kennan, are calling for pursuing *détente*. The book *"Détente or Debacle: Common Sense in US–Soviet Relations"*[15], published by the commission, contains an exposition of a fairly rational and realistic concept of *détente* which should "meet fully existing realities" and be free from exaggerated expectations. *Détente*, the authors note, should develop with full account been taken of the differences in the socio-economic systems in the USA and USSR which will continue their rivalry in a variety of fields including ideology. But the important thing is to ensure that this rivalry and competition proceed "within the bounds of the rational", in other words, in peaceful forms only. *Détente* does not imply an abandonment by either side of its efforts to protect its vital national interests. On the other hand, *détente* does not imply the grant of a blank cheque to interfere in the international affairs of the other nor does it or can it imply, the authors continue, any "reward" for "good behaviour". They conclude that *détente* should not be the object of "political haggling".

After resigning as Secretary of State to express his disagreement with the Carter Administration's foreign policy, Cyrus Vance, in his commencement speech at Harvard University on 5 June 1980, strongly criticized Washington's line of interference in the internal affairs of other countries and attempts to impose its will on them. He warned that "it is naïve to believe that they [the USSR] . . . would willingly accept a position of second-best in military strength". There was a pervasive fallacy, Vance continued, that "America could have the power to order the world just the way we want it to be..., that we could dominate the Soviet Union — that we could prevent it from being a super-power — if we chose to do so".

"This obsolete idea has more to do with nostalgia than with present-day reality", Vance said. "Spread over the widest territory of any nation on earth, the Soviet Union has its own strategic interests and goals. From a state of underdevelopment and the ravages of war, it has built formidable military and industrial resources. We should not underestimate these resources..."[16]

Cautioning against "the dangerous new nostalgia, a longing for earlier days when the world seemed... to have been a more orderly place in which American power could, alone, preserve that order", Vance said that the United States should not resort to military solutions to international problems. Military power is a basis, not a substitute, for diplomacy. Undue reliance on military power diverts from a search for constructive solutions and represents self-indulgent nonsense, Vance concluded.

Vance's realism is shared by many in the United States who believe that it is time to shed the illusion that military power can be an effective instrument of foreign policy, that social changes occurring in other countries can be checked. The record to date indicates that it is futile to try to suppress forces around the world pressing for social change. Change is inevitable and irresistible.

The difficulties *détente* has run into, its deviation and even setbacks, have demonstrated the validity of the dialectical proposition to the effect that the evolution of international relations, involving as it does the scrapping and abandonment of the old and conservative, proceeds through struggle and the overcoming of contradictions.

Peaceful co-existence does not imply removal of the basic contradiction of our time, that between socialism and capitalism, it does not imply termination of the class struggle, removal of social and ideological differences, the erasure of their fundamental nature and it does not dispense with the need to put through social changes in the modern world. In this context the question of how peaceful co-existence and *détente* relate to social development and progress, to the class and national liberation struggles in the world, takes on a particularly urgent and relevant dimension.

The Leninist theory of international relations draws a clear line of distinction between these relations — between social systems and between states having different systems. Peaceful co-existence only covers the field of inter-state relations and does not extend to the sphere of social and inter-class relations. *Détente* does not and cannot rescind or change the laws of class struggle. International *détente* and the current class struggle represent two inter-related aspects of social progress during the momentous passage of mankind from capitalism to socialism.

Marxist recognition of the inevitability of confrontation in present-day international relations does not mean that any form of struggle regardless of means is in order between countries. It merely refers to forms of struggle which do not undermine peaceful relations between countries. From this basic position true Marxists have strongly condemned the imperialists' recent aggressive moves as these are incompatible with peaceful co-existence under which the superiority of a particular system is tested and ascertained not on the battlefield or in the course of preparations for a military clash but rather through competition in the economic, political, social, and intellectual and cultural areas. It is tested and determined by the ability of a system to meet the aspirations and hopes of the population, by its ability to better their standards of living, to establish social justice and ensure the real exercise by citizens of all their human rights and liberties. All mankind has a vital stake in the preservation of peace. Socialist countries need peace to build a new society, socialism, and communism. In his address to the 25th Party Congress Leonid Brezhnev put it well when he said, "We make no secret of the fact that we see *détente* as the way to create more favourable conditions for peaceful socialist and communist construction. This only confirms that socialism and peace are indissoluble."[17]

The intimate connection between the struggle for peace and for social progress is profoundly dialectical. The peace-loving foreign policy of socialist countries and the positive changes it has produced in international relations is exercising a salutary impact on the dynamics of social progress in the capitalist world and in the Third World. At the same time, the sharpening class struggle in capitalist countries and the rising tide of national liberation follow a logic of their own which is subject to the laws governing the development of capitalism, the social and class antagonisms inherent in the capitalist system. The fertile soil for class struggle and social changes is provided by the internal economic, social, and political environments of the capitalist world. The people of each country have a perfect right to fight for their national and social emancipation, to be their own masters, and to choose freely the socio-political and economic system under which they will live. Needless to say, this right implies that any country, any nation is free to ask another country to help it combat imperialist intervention, to protect its independence and uphold its freedom to follow the road it has chosen. This right presupposes the provision of such help by other countries, if asked. Always loyal to its internationalist law the Soviet Union has invariably assisted and is assisting peoples fighting to defend their independence from outside encroachments, peoples who are determined to rid themselves of imperialist domination to embark on the road of free development and social progress.

There is also a "feedback relationship" between social progress and the struggle to keep up the momentum of international *détente*. Peaceful co-existence is by no means the product of the spontaneous, uncontrolled development of events nor does it signal a change in the essence of imperialism. The peace of the world and the victory of social revolutions in the twentieth century represent an organic unity. The record of twentieth-century history indicates that the policy of peace and peaceful co-existence originated in the mainstream of the social revolution of our time. As a result of its development social forces which prepared the ground for implementing the policy have emerged and gained in strength. Socialism, the international working class and the national liberation movement are now a decisive factor behind the on-going radical alteration in the alignment of forces on the world stage and the consequent fundamental restructuring of the entire pattern of international relations. These forces are now at the centre of the momentous battle of our time — the battle for peace.

*   *   *

The ship of *détente* is steaming through the rough seas of

international relations. The reactionary forces of bellicose imperialism are out to torpedo it in order to set the clock back, to reverse world development and check social progress. But their efforts are to no avail largely because of the vastly increased economic and defence potential of the Soviet Union, and the strong socio-political and ideological unit of Soviet society. Another major factor has been the fact that the CPSU and the Soviet Government displaying self-possession and consistency have stayed the course and have not allowed anyone to throw them off the policy line mapped out by the 24th and 25th Party Congresses.

The CPSU and the Soviet Government are convinced that *détente* is unconquerable, as it brings benefits to all the world's countries and peoples and remains the dominant trend in today's international relations. Standing firm in the face of imperialist provocation while at the same time strongly opposing the imperialists' aggressive moves, the Soviet Union together with the rest of the socialist camp has been steadily working to maintain the momentum of *détente*, to achieve disarmament, to assure peace and the security of nations. The firm policy followed by the socialist community of nations in world affairs is having a tremendous salutary impact on the entire course of world development, ensuring as it does the security of peoples and their continued advance along the road of social progress. The firm resolve of the USSR and other socialist countries to keep up their peace efforts was reaffirmed in the documents of the Warsaw meeting of the Political Consultative Committee of the Warsaw Pact countries in May 1980. The decisions taken at that meeting, held to mark the Pact's silver jubilee, are instinct with a determination to preserve and consolidate *détente*; they confirm the peace-oriented proposals made earlier by the socialist camp. These decisions outlined new initiatives which demonstrate the continued readiness of the Warsaw Pact countries to pursue and deepen the dialogue with countries belonging to different social systems.

In treating military *détente* as an objective and pressing necessity the Warsaw Pact countries proceed from the realization that there are no insuperable obstacles to finding a practical solution to existing problems, given the willingness of all the parties concerned to contribute to the common effort in a constructive spirit. The countries concerned should concentrate their efforts above all, on confidence-building measures, on renouncing the use or threat of force, on limiting the armed forces and armaments of each country or groups of countries to a level required by the exigencies of national defence and on abandoning on the basis of reciprocity all attempts to gain military superiority.

For their part the Warsaw Pact countries stated in their declaration that they had never sought nor would they in future seek military superiority. They advocate the maintenance of the military balance at ever lower levels, with a view to eliminating military confrontation in Europe. Their strategic doctrine is strictly defensive and does not envisage the development of a first nuclear strike capability. The Warsaw Pact countries spelled out in more detail their 1979 proposal made at the Budapest meeting of the Committee of Warsaw Pact Foreign Ministers for holding a conference on military *détente* and disarmament in Europe. They renewed their proposal for all the countries which attended the Helsinki Conference to conclude a treaty binding its signatories not to be the first to use either nuclear or conventional weapons against the other side. The Warsaw Pact countries spoke in favour of reaching agreement at the ongoing disarmament talks and of resuming disarmament talks which had been suspended or discontinued. As a first-priority measure alongside the ratification of the SALT-2 Treaty they favour the early and successful completion of the talks on a total and universal ban on nuclear weapons tests, on the prohibition of radiological weapons, on outlawing chemical weapons followed by the destruction of their stockpiles, on the non-use of nuclear weapons against non-nuclear countries that do not have such weapons in their territory, and on non-deployment of nuclear weapons in countries where such weapons are not deployed at present.

At the same time, the socialist countries have called for an immediate opening of talks on such urgent measures of military *détente* as the conclusion of a world treaty on the non-use of force, cessation of the production of nuclear weapons followed by their step-by-step reduction until no such weapons are left, on banning the development of new weapons and weapons systems of mass destruction and on cutting military budgets, in the first instance of the major powers. Of exceptional importance is the socialist countries' proposal examining in the United Nations, for instance, measures to limit and scale down military presence and military activity in the Atlantic, Indian, or Pacific Oceans, in the Mediterranean Sea or in the Persian Gulf in order to assure untrammelled traffic along the major international communication routes.

The Warsaw Pact countries have reiterated their readiness to limit or cut back the stockpiles of any type of weapons on the basis of reciprocity. In their view there are no problems either global or regional which could not be resolved by political means.

The silver jubilee meeting of the Political Consultative Committee of the Warsaw Pact countries favoured spreading *détente* to involve all parts of the world. A summit meeting of the world's heads of state would be a substantial contribution to the achievement of this goal. Such a meeting should concentrate its attention on measures to eliminate the existing foci of international tension, to avert war. The socialist camp has been consistently advocating a fair and durable negotiated settlement of conflicts wherever in the world they may develop. The socialist countries take the view that no problem either global or regional can defy a political solution. This applies to both the Middle East problem and the US–Iran conflict. The Soviet Union and other socialist countries demand complete cessation and non-resumption of outside interference in whatever form against the government and people of Afghanistan.

The documents adopted by the Warsaw Pact countries at their summit in Warsaw indicate that the socialist countries are fully determined to pursue in the 1980s a policy aimed at consolidating peace, maintaining the momentum of international *détente* and securing disarmament. As Leonid Brezhnev emphasized:

> We have been loyal to the Peace Programme adopted by the 24th and 25th Congresses of our Party. And so as we enter the 1980s we remain committed, as we were in the 1970s, to strengthening *détente* rather than destroying it. We are for cutting armaments and not for building them up. We are for closer relations and better understanding among nations and not for alienation and hostility. We are confidently holding aloft the banner of our Leninist foreign policy — the banner of peace, freedom, and independence for the peoples, the banner of social progress.

The Central Committee Plenum of the CPSU held in June 1980

discussed a report by Andrei Gromyko "On the International Situation and the Foreign Policy of the Soviet Union". In its resolution on the report the plenum noted that an amelioration of the international situation had been achieved in the 1970s. As *détente* progressed, peaceful co-existence between countries having different social systems began to be filled with concrete economic and political content, the Cold War had visibly declined and more favourable objective prerequisites had been established for resolving disputes and international conflicts through a just negotiated settlement. The resolution continued,

> Of late, however, the aggressive forces of imperialism have countered these positive trends with a policy motivated by an unwillingness to reckon with the realities of the modern world — the progressive consolidation of the positions of socialism, the successes of the national liberation movement, and the growth of the freedom-loving democratic forces in general. Imperialism is seeking to put a brake on the objective process of the renovation of the world. The leaders of the NATO military bloc, primarily those of the United States, have set course for tipping the present military balance in the world in their favour to the detriment of the Soviet Union, the rest of the socialist community, to the detriment of international *détente* and the security of nations.[18]

The dangerous policy pursued by the militarists is most clearly manifested in the US President's Directive No. 59 on the "new nuclear strategy". Rooted in the notorious "Schlesinger doctrine", which provided for shifting the order of priority of nuclear strikes from the cities to military targets, this strategy has a number of new and highly dangerous aspects.

First, it calls for delivering "limited nuclear strikes" at a wider range of targets (with military–political command centres included).

Second, these strikes may now be delivered not only by strategic but also by "Eurostrategic" nuclear weapons.

Third, not only short but also long nuclear wars are contemplated.

Fourth, a first "knock-out" nuclear strike is recommended as the best option.

Presidential Directive No. 59, ostensibly intended to reduce the risk of nuclear war, in fact paves the way towards it, and its active prosecution. Officially proclaimed as a means of reducing casualties in the event of a nuclear holocaust, it can in fact only increase them. Advertised as a method to "stabilize" the strategic situation, this strategy tends to destabilize it. And this despite the fact that maintenance of this stability is one of the main commitments assumed by the United States and the Soviet Union in Vienna on 18 June 1979. Addressing the 35th session of the UN General Assembly on 23 September 1980, Andrei Gromyko, Member of the Politburo of the CPSU Central Committee and Minister of Foreign Affairs of the USSR, said:

> The policy the United States has chosen to follow, which can only be described as militaristic, is expressed in the so-called "new nuclear strategy". Under the smokescreen of arguments about the possibility of some "limited", "localized" employment of nuclear weapons, which are completely at variance with the facts, the architects of this strategy are seeking to implant in the minds of men the idea that a nuclear conflict is permissible and acceptable. This reckless conception tends to heighten the risk of nuclear catastrophe, which cannot but cause and is causing concern throughout the world.[19]

Directive No. 59 is an attempt by the United States to find a way out of the "nuclear stalemate" it reached as far back as the 1960s as a result of the socialist commonwealth building up a powerful defence potential. The consolidation of the Soviet Union's nuclear missile capability has been an effective deterrent against American aggressive ambitions all this time. Now that there is strategic parity between the USSR and the USA this capability acts as a still stronger deterrent. At present Washington expects to achieve strategic superiority primarily by qualitative improvement of its nuclear forces, though it does not ignore the quantitative aspect of the matter either.

All hopes to upset the military strategic balance between the world of socialism and the world of capitalism, which·represents a gain of fundamental historic importance, are doomed to failure.

Détente is a legitimate product of the alignment of forces on the world stage that has emerged over the past decade. *Détente* has struck deep roots in present-day international life and real possibilities are now available for maintaining its momentum as the dominant trend of world politics. The capitalist countries, including the United States, need *détente* every bit as much as the Soviet Union and other socialist countries do.

The June 1980 Plenum expressed confidence that objective opportunities and socio-political forces exist which are capable of preventing the slide-back to a new "cold war" and of ensuring normal peaceful co-existence among countries having different social systems and of removing the danger of a world thermonuclear conflict. The road to the solution of this task lies through negotiations based on a strict observance of the principle of parity and equal security. This view is gaining the support of statesmen in Western countries and in uncommitted nations.

Many of America's allies believed that President Carter had overreacted to the Afghanistan events and by his call for trade sanctions against the USSR and a boycott of the Moscow Olympics has damaged the cause of *détente*. They also openly called in question Carter's strategy on a Middle East settlement and his policy towards Iran. According to *US News and World Report,* the Venice meeting of the "big seven" in June 1980 revealed an unprecedented rebellion against American leadership.[20] The London *Sunday Times* qualified the differences between the USA and Western Europe in their assessments of *détente* as basic.[21]

The majority of West Europeans favour a continuation of *détente* and oppose a revival of the cold war. Indicative in this context was the Warsaw meeting (May 1980) between President Giscard D'Estaing of France and Leonid Brezhnev, a meeting that contributed towards resumption of the interrupted East and West dialogue.

Another pointer in this direction was the Moscow visit by Chancellor Helmut Schmidt of West Germany and Deputy Chancellor, Foreign Minister Genscher. In talks with Soviet leaders Schmidt said that the pursuit of *détente* remained a major objective of the FRG government. He advocated the maintenance of contacts and continuation of the dialogue with a view to expanding co-operation between East and West. In the joint communiqué at the end of the talks the two sides emphasized that, as before, they considered *détente* necessary, feasible, and useful and expressed their will to contribute in every way to the efforts to ensure the preservation of *détente* as the dominant trend in international relations. There is no rational alternative to peaceful co-operation based on full equality among states.[22]

"We face the future with optimism," Leonid Brezhnev stressed. "This optimism is well founded. We are aware that the deliberate aggravation of the international situation by American imperialists reflects their resentment at the consolidation of the positions of socialism, at the rising tide of the national liberation movement and the strengthening of forces advocating *détente* and peace. We know that the will of the peoples has overcome all obstacles to clear the road for the positive trend in world affairs, that is so aptly expressed by the word '*détente*'. This policy has struck deep roots. It is supported by mighty forces and has every chance of remaining the basic trend in inter-state relations."[23]

Conclusion

THE international system that has taken shape in the course of human history has been subject to the influence of a variety of factors: the level of productive forces and international division of labour, the class character of participating states, demographic, military, technological, political, geographical, and other factors. In each historical era the international system looked different and had characteristics and features peculiar to it. The dynamics of its evolution has proceeded in step with the evolution of the basic contradiction of each successive historical era.

The system of international relations that had emerged in the period of the formation and development of capitalism collapsed early in the twentieth century. The crisis of the international system produced by bourgeois society reflected the crisis of capitalism as an economic system.

The rupture of the chain of capitalist exploitation in Russia which occurred in 1917 marked the start of a new stage in the evolution of the international system: once a system homogeneous in class terms, it became rent by class antagonisms and included states with opposite social systems. The various historical analogies drawn by bourgeois scholars between the international system of the modern world and the systems of past eras are invalid precisely by virtue of the fact that the basic contradictions of the modern world — contradictions between the socialist and capitalist systems of society — are unprecedented both in terms of their acuteness and in terms of their impact on the fabric of international relations.

In his day Lenin wrote: "There are two forces on earth that can decide the destiny of mankind. One force is international capitalism, and should it be victorious it will display this force in countless atrocities as may be seen from the history of every small nation's development. The other force is the international proletariat."[1] Returning to this thought later, Lenin stressed: "Two camps are now quite consciously facing each other all over the world; this may be said without the slightest exaggeration."[2] The alignment of the political forces in the modern world is incomparably more complex than it was in Lenin's day. But through the intricate and variegated maze of intersecting and conflicting forces a basic great divide is clearly distinguishable — the division of the world into two polarized socio-economic systems.

Lenin saw the interaction of the two camps as forming the hard core and axis around which the whole of international life revolved, as the basis of the polarization of social and political forces in the world. Lenin pointed out: ". . . World political developments are of necessity concentrated on a single focus — the struggle of the world bourgeoisie against the Soviet Russian Republic, around which are inevitably grouped, on the one hand, the Soviet movements of the advanced workers in all countries, and, on the other, all the national liberation movements in the colonies and among the oppressed nationalities."[3]

The developments since then have inevitably introduced corrections and adjustments into the particulars of Lenin's analysis which applied to the situation which prevailed in the world at the time. But his analysis has retained its validity and relevance in all of its essentials, both theoretical and methodological. The confrontation of the two systems — capitalism and socialism — remains in the mainstream of world politics constituting its nerve trunk. For this reason Lenin's concept of peaceful co-existence covering as it does both co-operation and confrontation of the two systems and the achievement of compromises in the interests of preserving world peace, the security and well-being of the nations, has permanent value and significance. This concept underlies the struggle of the Soviet Union and other socialist countries for restructuring the present pattern of international relations on democratic principles to create a global system that would be congruent with the realities of a divided world.

The present international system has undergone substantial change in its evolution. The first cause and motive force of this change has been and still is the confrontation and interaction on the international stage of states having opposite social systems. In this process the steadily growing transforming role of world socialism is a legitimate trend of the evolving international relations.

Whereas after the First World War imperialism largely succeeded in keeping the new Soviet state out of the process of restructuring international relations and in setting up the Versailles–Washington system which suited the ruling circles of the victor powers, after the Second World War the situation underwent radical change. The defeat of fascism to which the Soviet Union had made the decisive contribution, the emergence of a world socialist system, the collapse of colonial empires and the consequent entry into the world arena of new actors — newly independent countries — these factors combined to change the environment of the evolving international relations. As the authors of a book edited by Kurt London and published in the USA in 1978 noted; the Bolshevik revolution made a yawning breach in the system of European great powers. Hitler's aggression against Russia and the aggressors' defeat by the Red Army completed the destruction of the system.[4] The Soviet Union's increased power and the changes affecting world politics ended the rules of the international game which had prevailed in the period of domination of the West.[5]

Particularly significant changes in favour of the forces of peace and socialism occurred in the 1970s. These had a telling impact on the entire fabric of international life and substantially altered its underlying principles. The alignment of forces within the capitalist system also changed as is exemplified by the sharpening and deepening inter-imperialist contradictions in every area, and the emergence of new centres of economic and political rivalry inside the imperialist camp. As the general crisis of imperialism deepened the foreign policy of the imperialist powers was increasingly misfiring. Imperialism has failed in its attempts to impede the development and consolidation of world socialism. It has failed to check mankind's progress.

The current scientific and technological revolution has also exerted substantial influence on the international system. The spectacular progress of communications and transportation, the rapid development of the military field which resulted in overkill weapons of horrifying destructive capacity that threaten the very continuance of the human race have combined to increase the need for closer interaction and inter-dependence of countries and nations and they have practically ended the age of isolation in international relations. For centuries in the past particular conflicts between states had but local significance and did not directly affect the interests of "third countries". Not any more. Today any explosive situation threatens the general peace. That is why the task of preventing an annihilating thermonuclear war is a matter of ensuring the future of the human race. Today Immanuel Kant's warning, formulated in his treatise "Towards Eternal Peace", has a disconcertingly modern ring. Kant wrote that as mankind advanced it increasingly met the choice of "...either ending all wars by an international covenant or, without that, of facing the prospect of a 'gigantic cemetery' following an annihilating war. (Translated from the Russian.)"

The trends of social development have led to the unprecedented impact on world politics made by the general public who have a vital stake in the preservation of peace. The highly principled, open, fair, and honest foreign policy and diplomacy of the socialist countries has played a conspicuous role in involving important segments of the public in the fight for peace and social progress. The increased influence of the masses on the foreign policy of advanced capitalist countries has been graphically illustrated by the international public movement against American aggression in Indochina, the broad-based movement of various political forces in Europe in support of *détente*, security, and co-operation on that continent. These grassroots movements, despite the rather unsmooth course of their evolution, on the whole added up to a force which the ruling circles of the leading Western powers could not very well ignore in the conduct of their foreign policy.

The 1970s were marked by major successes scored by anti-imperialist liberation movements. The people of socialist Vietnam won a victory which culminated in reunification of their country, popular rule in Laos was consolidated and the bloody regime in Kampuchea toppled. Ethiopia, Angola, Mozambique, and South

Yemen shook off the fetters of imperialist domination. The dictatorship in Nicaragua collapsed. The Afghan revolution, the overthrow of the Shah of Iran, and the victory of the patriotic forces of Zimbabwe have all been major milestones in the struggle of the peoples of those countries for their social and national emancipation.

These successes represent important milestones in the general struggle for peace and social progress, for restructuring the present pattern of international relations on democratic principles, a process initiated by the Great October Socialist Revolution in Russia.

References

Introduction

1. V.I. Lenin, *Collected Works*, vol. 41, p. 242.
2. *Pravda,* 1 February 1977.
3. L.I. Brezhnev, *The Foreign Policy of the CPSU and the Soviet State. Speeches and Articles.* Moscow, 1975, pp. 240-41.
4. L.I. Brezhnev. *Following Lenin's Course,* vol. 4, Moscow, 1975, p. 194.
5. V.I. Lenin, *op. cit,* vol. 37, p. 153.
6. *Ibid.,* vol. 41, p. 165.
7. *America as an Ordinary Country. U.S. Foreign Policy and Future,* R. Rosencrance (Ed.). Cornell University Press, 1976, pp. 251, 252.
8. *Pravda,* 3 November 1977.
9. V.I. Lenin, *op. cit.,* vol. 40, p. 92.
10. *Ibid.,* vol. 26, p. 303.
11. K.I. Zarodov. *Socialism, Peace, Revolution. Some Theoretical and Practical Problems of International Relations and Class Struggle.* Moscow, 1977, p. 67.
12. A.A. Gromyko, "The Leninist Strategy of Peace: Unity of Theory and Practice". *Kommunist,* 1976, No. 14, p. 16.
13. *Modern Bourgeois Theories of International Relations: A Critical Analysis.* Moscow, 1976, p. 95.
14. See: *New Dynamics in National Strategy. Paradox of Power.* New York, 1975; S. Brown, *New Forces in World Politics.* Washington, 1974.
15. See: *The Theory and Practice of International Relations,* Ed. D. McLellan, W. Olson, and F. Sonderman, New York, 1974.

Chapter 1

1. K. Marx and F. Engels, *Works,* vol. 16, p. 11.
2. *Ibid.,* vol. 4, p. 445.
3. *Ibid.,* vol. 17, p. 5.
4. *Ibid.,* p. 291.
5. *Ibid.,* vol. 12, p. 735.

6. *Socialism and International Relations,* Moscow, 1975, p. 9.
7. K. Marx and F. Engels, *op. cit.,* vol. 5, p. 212.
8. *Ibid.,* vol. 16, p. 373.
9. *Ibid.,* p. 11.
10. *Ibid.,* p. 11.
11. *Ibid.,* vol. 31, p. 71.
12. *Ibid.,* vol. 16, pp. 17-19.
13. *Ibid.,* vol. 17, p. 281.
14. *Ibid.,* vol. 22, p. 13.
15. *Ibid.,* pp. 51-2.
16. *Ibid.,* vol. 30, p. 47.
17. V.I. Lenin, *op. cit.,* vol. 19, p. 52.
18. K. Marx and F. Engels, *op. cit.,* vol. 22, p. 385.
19. *Ibid.,* p. 387.
20. *The World Economy and International Relations.* 1977, No. 5, p. 74.
21. See: F.S. Northedge and M.J. Grieve, *A Hundred Years of International Relations.* Praeger Publishers, 1971, pp. 8-9, 360.
22. V.I. Lenin, *op. cit.,* vol. 32, p. 337.
23. *Ibid.,* vol. 17, p. 230.
24. *Ibid.,* vol. 4, p. 383.
25. *Ibid.,* vol. 16, p. 68.
26. T. Bartenyev and Y. Komissarov, *Thirty Years of Good Neighbourly Relations. On the History of Soviet-Finnish Relations.* Moscow, 1976, p. 7.
27. *The CPSU: Resolutions and Decisions of Congresses, Conferences and Plenary Meetings of the CC,* 8th ed., vol. 1, pp. 344-5.
28. V.I. Lenin, *op. cit.,* vol. 19, p. 222.
29. *The CPSU:...,* *op. cit.,* vol. 1, p. 344.
30. *Ibid.*
31. V.I. Lenin, *op. cit.,* vol. 17, pp. 195-6.
32. V.I. Lenin, *op. cit.,* vol. 22, p. 156.
33. *Ibid.,* pp. 142-3.
34. *Ibid.,* vol. 27, p. 261.
35. *Ibid.,* vol. 30, p. 120.
36. *Ibid.,* p. 152.
37. *Ibid.,* vol. 23, p. 62.
38. *The Bolshevik Faction in the IV State Duma. Collected Records and Documents.* Leningrad, 1938, p. 347.
39. V.I. Lenin, *op. cit.,* vol. 23, p. 144; vol. 17, p. 231.
40. *Ibid.,* vol. 23, p. 183.
41. A.E. Badayev, *Bolshevik Deputies in the State Duma. Reminiscences.* Moscow, 1954, p. 344.
42. *Theoretical Problems of Proletarian Internationalism.* Moscow, 1972, p. 20.
43. V.I. Lenin, *op. cit.,* vol. 26, p. 1.
44. *Ibid.,* p. 316.
45. *Ibid.,* p. 327.
46. *Ibid.,* p. 107.
47. *Ibid.,* p. 108.
48. *Ibid.,* pp. 165-6.
49. *Ibid.,* p. 166.

50. *Ibid.,* vol. 31, pp. 49-54.
51. *Ibid.,* p. 114.
52. *Ibid.,* vol. 32, p. 46.
53. *Ibid.,* vol. 26, p. 304.

Chapter 2

1. K. Marx and F. Engels, *Works,* vol. 4, p. 334.
2. *USSR Foreign Policy Documents,* vol. 1, Moscow, 1959, p. 12.
3. V.I. Lenin, *Collected Works,* vol. 35, pp. 16-17.
4. *Ibid.,* p. 222.
5. *USSR Foreign Policy Documents,* vol. 1, p. 34.
6. *Ibid.,* p. 12.
7. *USSR Foreign Policy Documents,* vol. 2, Moscow, 1958, p. 639.
8. G.A. Arbatov, *The Battle of Ideas in Contemporary International Relations.* Moscow, 1970, p. 289.
9. V.I. Lenin, *op. cit.,* vol. 30, p. 133.
10. *Ibid.,* vol. 42, p. 71.
11. *Ibid.,* vol. 41, p. 166.
12. *Ibid.,* vol. 31, p. 170.
13. *Ibid.,* vol. 42, pp. 71-2.
14. See: H. Marcuse, *Soviet Marxism.* New York, 1958, p. 38.
15. *USSR Foreign Policy Documents,* vol. 1, p. 14.
16. See: F. Barghorn, *Soviet Foreign Propaganda.* Princeton, 1964, p. 86.
17. See: J. Mackintosh, *Strategy and Tactics of Soviet Foreign Policy.* London, 1962, p. 2.
18. *Pravda,* 3 November 1977.
19. F.J. Triska and D.D. Finley, *Soviet Foreign Policy.* New York, 1968, pp. 169-70.
20. See: R. Rosser, *An Introduction to Soviet Foreign Policy.* New York, 1969, pp. 126-7.
21. See: H.J. Morgenthau, *Politics Among Nations.* New York, 1948.
22. E. Sallier. *De l'oural à l'Atlantique. Le bond russe en Afrique.* Paris, 1969, p. 71.
23. G.A. Arbatov, *op. cit.,* pp. 290-291.
24. V.I. Lenin, *op. cit.,* vol. 35, p. 403.
25. *USSR Foreign Policy Documents,* vol. 2, p. 638.
26. *Ibid.,* vol. 1, p. 565.
27. V.I. Lenin, *op. cit.,* vol. 50, p. 186.
28. *Ibid.,* vol. 50, p. 186.
29. L.I. Brezhnev, *Following Lenin's Course,* vol. 4, Moscow, 1974, p. 336.
30. V.I. Lenin, *op. cit.,* vol. 40, p. 243.
31. *Ibid.,* vol. 35, pp. 116-17.
32. *Ibid.,* p. 16.
33. *Ibid.,* vol. 45, p. 447.
34. See: *ibid.,* vol. 34, p. 197.
35. *Ibid.,* vol. 35, p. 20.
36. *Ibid.,* vol. 27, p. 441.
37. See: *Papers Relating to the Foreign Relations of the US The Lancing papers 1914-1920,* vol. III. Washington, 1940, p. 346.

References 347

38. See: W. Williams, "The Isolationism Legend in the 1920s". *Science and Society,* vol. XVII, 1954, No. 1, p. 8.
39. *History of Diplomacy,* vol. 2, Moscow, 1945, p. 366.
40. See: A Bekker, *Woodrow Wilson. The World War. The Treaty of Versailles.* Transl. from English. Moscow, 1923, pp. 191-2.
41. See: L. Broad, *Winston Churchill: a Biography.* New York, 1958, p. 186.
42. *USSR Foreign Policy Documents,* vol. 1, p. 59.
43. *History of Soviet Foreign Policy,* vol. 1, 1917-45, Moscow, 1976, pp. 43-4.
44. V.I. Lenin, *op. cit.,* vol. 37, p. 190.
45. *Ibid.,* vol. 39, p. 403.
46. V.I. Lenin, *op. cit.,* vol. 35, p. 402.
47. *Ibid.,* vol. 34, p. 133.
48. *The Leninist Traditions of Soviet Foreign Policy,* Ed. A.L. Narochnitsky. Moscow, 1977, pp. 71-2.
49. V.I. Lenin, *op. cit.,* vol. 45, p. 240.
50. *Ibid.,* vol. 49, pp. 269-70.
51. *Ibid.,* vol. 32, p. 154.
52. *Ibid.,* vol. 43, p. 99.
53. *Ibid.,* vol. 42, p. 107.
54. *Ibid.,* vol. 30, p. 120.
55. *Ibid.,* vol. 41, p. 245.
56. L.I. Brezhnev, *op. cit.,* vol. 5, Moscow, 1976, p. 146.
57. V.I. Lenin, *op. cit.,* vol. 40, p. 99.
58. *Ibid.,* vol. 42, pp. 353-4.
59. *USSR Foreign Policy Documents,* vol. V, Moscow, 1961, pp. 80-81.
60. *Ibid.,* vol. III, Moscow, 1959, p. 597.
61. For greater detail see: *History of Soviet Foreign Policy. 1917-45,* pp. 143-52.
62. Quoted from: *Lenin on Friendship with the Eastern Peoples.* Moscow, 1961, p. 346.
63. *USSR Foreign Policy Documents,* vol. IV, Moscow, 1960, p. 167.
64. *Ibid.,* vol. II, p. 223.
65. V.I. Lenin, *op. cit.,* vol. 42, p. 22.
66. *Ibid.,* vol. 45, p. 71.
67. *Ibid.,* vol. 44, pp. 304-5.
68. *Ibid.,* vol. 42, p. 24.
69. *The Lenin Miscellany,* vol. XXXVI, p. 254.
70. V.I. Lenin, *op. cit.,* vol. 42, p. 70.
71. *Ibid.,* vol. 40, p. 152.
72. *Fiftieth Anniversary of the Great October Socialist Revolution.* Moscow, 1967, p. 58.
73. V.I. Lenin, *op. cit.,* vol. 44, p. 383.
74. *USSR Foreign Policy Documents,* vol. V, pp. 191-2.
75. V.I. Lenin, *op. cit.,* vol. 45, pp. 36-7.
76. *Materials from the Genoa Conference.* Moscow, 1922, p. 80.
77. V.I. Lenin, *op. cit.,* vol. 44, p. 408.
78. *Ibid.,* vol. 45, p. 241.
79. *Materials from the Genoa Conference,* p. 81.
80. V.I. Lenin, *op. cit.,* vol. 45, p. 193.
81. *Ibid.,* vol. 42, p. 23.
82. *Ibid.,* p. 60.

Chapter 3

1. Quoted from: I. Gorokhov, L. Zamyatin, I. Zemskov, and G.V. Chicherin, *A Diplomat of the Lenin Cohort.* Moscow, 1973, p. 186.
2. See: H. Hedson, *Soviet Policy Abroad — Behind the Headlines,* 1947, vol. VII, No. 3, 3.
3. See: *The USSR After 50 Years. Promise and Reality,* Ed. Hendel and R. Braham. New York, 1972, p. 270.
4. See: S. Lipset, *Revolution and Counterrevolution. Change and Persistence in Social Structure.* London, 1969.
5. See: A. Ulam, *Expansion and Coexistence. Soviet Foreign Policy. 1917-1973.* New York, 1976, pp. 133-4.
6. Quoted from: *Lenin and the Communist International.* Moscow, 170, p. 49.
7. V.I. Lenin, *op. cit.,* vol. 42, p. 22.
8. *Ibid.,* vol. 44, p. 296.
9. *Ibid.,* vol. 38, p. 139.
10. G.V. Chicherin, *Articles and Speeches.* Moscow, 1961, p. 285.
11. V.I. Lenin, *op. cit.,* vol. 44, p. 3.
12. *Ibid.,* vol. 39, p. 323.
13. I. Gorokhov *et al., op. cit.,* p. 188.
14. *History of Soviet Foreign Policy,* vol. VII, p. 199.
15. *Izvestia,* 13 December 1923.
16. *USSR Foreign Policy Documents,* vol. VII, p. 607.
17. *Ibid.,* p. 516.
18. *Izvestia,* 27 January 1925.
19. Quoted from: A. Sizonenko, *The Soviet Union and Latin America.* Kiev, 1976, p. 7.
20. *USSR Foreign Policy Documents,* vol. VIII, Moscow, 1963, p. 119.
21. A. Sizonenko, *op. cit.,* p. 73.
22. *Lenin and the Communist International,* p. 404.
23. *History of the Communist Party of the Soviet Union,* vol. 4, book 1, Moscow, 1970, p. 436.
24. *USSR Foreign Policy Documents,* vol. VI, Moscow, 1962, p. 36.
25. *The CPSU:...,* *op. cit.,* vol. 4, 8th ed., p. 15.
26. *USSR Foreign Policy Documents,* vol. VII, p. 197.
27. *Comintern Documents...,* p. 825.
28. *Ibid.,* p. 826.
29. See: *Baltimore Sun,* 2 December 1927.
30. Quoted from: V.M. Heitzman, *The USSR and the Disarmament Problem (Between the First and Second World Wars).* Moscow, 1959, p. 184.
31. *USSR Foreign Policy Documents,* vol. XIV, Moscow, 1968, p. 29.
32. *The USSR in the Struggle for Peace. Speeches and Documents.* Moscow, 1935, p. 75.
33. *USSR Foreign Policy Documents,* vol. XV, Moscow, 1969, p. 102.
34. Quoted from: *History of Diplomacy,* vol. 3, Moscow-Leningrad, 1945, p. 416.
35. L.A. Bezymensky, *German Generals With and Without Hitler.* Moscow, 1961, p. 44.
36. *History of Diplomacy,* vol. 3, pp. 464-5.
37. See: *The Memoirs of Cordell Hull.* New York, 1948, vol. 1, p. 297.

38. *The 17th Congress of the All-Union Communist Party (Bolsheviks),* 26 January–10 February 1934, p. 14.
39. V.Y. Sipols, *The Soviet Union in the Struggle for Peace and Security. 1933-9.* Moscow, 1974, pp. 39-40.
40. *History of Soviet Foreign Policy,* 1917-45, p. 308.
41. *USSR Foreign Policy Documents,* vol. XVII, Moscow, 1971, p. 589.
42. V.I. Lenin, *op. cit.,* vol. 45, p. 241.
43. *The VII Congress of the Communist International and the Struggle Against Fascism and War.* Moscow, 1975, p. 265.
44. A. Sizonenko, *op. cit.,* p. 74.
45. *USSR Foreign Policy Documents,* vol. XVIII, Moscow, 1973, p. 561.
46. *The VII Congress of the Communist International and the Struggle Against Fascism and War,* p. 385.
47. *Ibid.,* p. 259.
48. See: *The Soviet Historical Encyclopedia,* vol. 6, Moscow, 1965, p. 156.
49. See: *New York Times,* 30 November 1937.
50. *History of World War II, 1939-45,* vol. 2, pp. 73-4.
51. *V.I. Lenin and Soviet Foreign Policy.* Moscow, 1969, p. 164.
52. *Izvestia,* 14 March 1938.
53. See: *Foreign Affairs 1946,* October, p. 38.
54. *The XVIII Congress of the All-Union Communist Party (Bolsheviks),* 10-21 March 1939. Verbatim report. Moscow, 1939, p. 17.
55. *Izvestia,* 20 March 1939.
56. See: *Documents on British Foreign Policy,* 1919-39. Third Series, vol. v, p. 632.
57. See: *Foreign Relations of the United States,* 1939, vol. 1, p. 307.
58. A.J.P. Taylor, *English History 1914-45.* Oxford, 1965.
59. V.I. Lenin, *op. cit.,* vol. 44, p. 151.

Chapter 4

1. See: V.I. Lenin, *Collected Works,* vol. 36, p. 323.
2. See: *Hitler. Deutschland und die Machte.* Hrsg. M. Funke. Dusseldorf, 1976, p. 175.
3. Quoted from: *The World War of 1939-1945,* Moscow, 1957, p. 149.
4. See: A.J.P. Taylor, *English History 1914-1945.* Oxford, 1965, p. 469.
5. N.I. Lebedev, *The Downfall of Fascism in Romania.* Moscow, 1976, p. 265.
6. N.I. Lebedev, *op. cit.,* p. 265.
7. Quoted from: *History of Diplomacy,* vol. 4, Moscow, 1975, p. 150.
8. Quoted from: *History of Soviet Foreign Policy. 1917-1945.* Moscow, 1976, p. 418.
9. See: *Amerasia,* March 1941, p. 7.
10. *Soviet Foreign Policy During the Patriotic War,* vol. 1, Moscow, 1946, pp. 29-30.
11. *Documents and Materials on the History of Soviet Polish Relations,* vol. 1, Moscow, 1973, p. 198.
12. *Soviet Foreign Policy During the Patriotic War,* vol. 1, p. 141.
13. See: W.L. Langer and S.E. Gleason, *Undeclared War, 1940-1941.* Washington, 1948.
14. Quoted from: *The Leninist Traditions of Soviet Foreign Policy,* p. 147.
15. V.I. Lenin, *op. cit.,* vol. 34, p. 232.

16. *Soviet Foreign Policy During the Patriotic War*, vol. 1, p. 166.
17. *Franco-Soviet Relations During the Great Patriotic War of 1941-1945. Documents and Materials.* Moscow, 1959, p. 47.
18. See: W.D. Leahy, *I Was There.* New York, 1950, pp. 317-18.
19. See: H.L. Stimson and M. Bundy, *On Active Service in Peace and War.* New York, 1948, p. 527.
20. *Soviet Foreign Policy During the Patriotic War*, vol. 1, pp. 118-19.
21. *Teheran-Yalta-Potsdam.* Moscow, 1970, p. 96.
22. *Correspondence of the Chairman of the USSR Council of Ministers with the Presidents of the USA and the Prime Minister of Great Britain During the Great Patriotic War of 1941-1945*, vol. 1, Moscow, 1957, p. 31.
23. See: *Soviet Foreign Policy During the Patriotic War*, vol. 1, p. 425.
24. *Teheran-Yalta-Potsdam*, p. 189.
25. *Teheran-Yalta-Potsdam*, pp. 192-3.
26. L.I. Brezhnev, *Following Lenin's Course. Articles and Speeches*, vol. 3, Moscow, 1972, p. 148.
27. Quoted from: *History of Soviet Foreign Policy, 1917-1945*, p. 492.
28. See: W.D. Leahy, *op. cit.*, p. 390.
29. *Teheran-Yalta-Potsdam*, p. 386.
30. *Teheran-Yalta-Potsdam*, pp. 387-9.
31. *Izvestia*, 3 August 1970.
32. See: *The Memoirs of Harry S. Truman*, vol. 1, p. 87.
33. See: J.F. Dulles, *War or Peace.* New York, 1950, p. 30.
34. *The Soviet Delegation at the Paris Peace Conference*, Moscow, 1947, p. 214.
35. *Ibid.*, p. 343.
36. *History of Soviet Foreign Policy, 1945-1975*, p. 41.

Chapter 5

1. See: *Public Papers of the Presidents of the United States.* New York, 1961, p. 549.
2. See: *Look*, 1959, 12 November.
3. Y.M. Melnikov, *U.S. Foreign Policy Doctrines.* Moscow, 1970, p. 14.
4. See: *The Private Papers of Senator Vandenberg.* Boston, 1952, p. 494.
5. *The Policy Documents of the Struggle for Peace, Democracy, and Social Progress.* Moscow, 1964, p. 39.
6. See: *Foreign Affairs*, 1964, April, p. 475.
7. *The 20th Congress of the CPSU.* Verbatim report, vol. 2, Moscow, 1956, p. 414.
8. *The Policy Documents of the Struggle for Peace, Democracy, and Social Progress*, p. 27.
9. *The Warsaw Treaty Organization. 1955-1975. Documents and Materials.* Moscow, 1975, p. 9.
10. *Izvestia*, 24 October 1962.
11. *Pravda*, 8 July 1966.
12. L.I. Brezhnev, *Following Lenin's Course*, vol. 2, Moscow, 1970, p. 373.
13. V.K. Sobakin, *Collective Security.* Moscow, 1962, pp. 363-74.
14. Andrei Gromyko, *1,036 Days of President Kennedy.* Moscow, 1969, p. 184.
15. *The XXIII Congress of the CPSU.* Verbatim report, vol. 2, Moscow, 1966, p. 304.

Chapter 6

1. The USSR Central Statistical Board, *The USSR in Figures,* 1979. Moscow, 1980, p. 61.
2. *Ibid.,* p. 76.
3. *Ibid.,* p. 102.
4. *Pravda,* 23 February 1980.
5. The USSR Central Statistical Board, *op. cit.,* p. 87.
6. *Ibid.*
7. *Pravda,* 15 October 1977.
8. *The Soviet Impact on World Politics,* Ed. Kurt London. Hawthorn Book Inc., New York, 1974, p. 296.
9. *Materials from the 25th Congress of the CPSU,* p. 5.
10. *Kommunist,* No. 3, 1979, pp. 19-20.
11. *Vneshnyaya Torgovlya* (Foreign Trade), No. 9, 1960, p. 40.
12. See: E. Lengyel, *Nationalism — the Last Stage of Communism.* New York, 1969. *Problems, Prospects.* Moscow, 1975, pp. 19-21.
13. *Pravda,* 25 March 1980.
14. *Pravda,* 19 February 1980.
15. *Council for Mutual Economic Assistance. Thirty Years,* p. 46.
16. *Ibid.,* p. 48.
17. *The Warsaw Treaty Organization. 1955-1975.* Moscow, 1976, p. 184.
18. *Kommunist,* 1977, No. 3, p. 20.
19. *Materials from the 25th Congress of the CPSU,* p. 8.
20. *Scinteia,* 20 February 1979.
21. *Materials from the 25th Congress of the CPSU,* p. 8.
22. *Greetings to the 25th Congress of the CPSU,* p. 29.
23. *Kommunist,* 1979, No. 13, pp. 7-8.
24. *Greetings to the 25th Congress of the CPSU,* p. 337.
25. *Ibid.,* p. 18.
26. *The 9th Congress of the Socialist Unity Party of Germany.* Moscow, 1977, p. 7.
27. K.I. Zarodov, *Socialism, Peace, Revolution.* Moscow, 1977, p. 142.
28. See: E. Lengyel, *Nationalism - the Last Stage of Communism.* New York, 1969.
29. See: *The Communist States in Disarray. 1965-1971.* Minneapolis, 1972, p. 346.
30. *Materials from the 25th Congress of the CPSU,* p. 8.
31. M. A. Suslov, "Marxism–Leninism and Revolutionary Renovation of the World", *Kommunist,* 1977, No. 14, p. 23.
32. V.I. Lenin, *Collected Works,* vol. 41, p. 165.
33. See: *New Dimensions of World Politics,* Ed. G. Goodwin and A. Linklater. London, 1975, p. 38.
34. K. Marx and F. Engels, *Works,* vol. 2, p. 90.
35. L.I. Brezhnev, *The Foreign Policy of the CPSU and the Soviet State. Speeches and Articles.* Moscow, 1975, p. 608.
36. *For Peace, Security, Co-operation, and Social Progress in Europe. On the Results of the Conference of Communist and Workers' Parties of Europe.* Berlin, 29-30 June 1976, p. 43.
37. *The Programme of the Communist Party of the Soviet Union.* Moscow, 1976, p. 61.

38. *Documents of the Conference of European Communist and Workers' Parties at Karlovy Vary, 24-26 April, 1967.* Moscow, 1967, p. 6.
39. See: *International Affairs,* 1978, No. 2, p. 4.
40. *The International Meeting of Communist and Workers' Parties. Documents and Materials.* Moscow, 1969, pp. 316, 317.
41. L.I. Brezhnev, *op. cit.,* p. 718.
42. See: A.A. Gromyko, "The Peace Programme in Action", *Kommunist,* 1975, No. 14, pp. 4-5.
43. *Materials from the 25th Congress of the CPSU,* p. 5.
44. V.I. Lenin, *op. cit.,* vol. 45, p. 241.

Chapter 7

1. K.Y. Chernenko, "The Leninist Peace Strategy in Action", *International Affairs,* 1976, No. 4, p. 5.
2. *Greetings to the 25th Congress of the CPSU,* Moscow, 1976, p. 27.
3. *Ibid.,* p. 39.
4. *Ibid.,* p. 60.
5. *In the Name of Peace, Security and Co-operation. On the Results of the Helskini Conference on Security and Co-operation in Europe, 30 July — 1 August, 1975.* Moscow, 1975, p. 18.
6. *Ibid.,* pp. 17-23.
7. A.A. Gromyko, *Kommunist,* 1975, No. 14, p. 14.
8. *Pravda,* 12 August 1976.
9. *Pravda,* 30 July 1976.
10. *The Foreign Policy of the Soviet Union. Collection of documents. 1972.* Moscow, 1973, p. 84.
11. *Ibid.,* pp. 84-5.
12. Quoted from: *Izvestia,* 23 July 1973.
13. *Pravda,* 7 May 1978.
14. *The United Nations: Past, Present and Future,* James Barros (Ed). New York, 1972, pp. 16, 22.
15. S.W. Ball, *Diplomacy for a Crowded World. An American Foreign Policy.* Little Brown & Co., 1976, p. 318.
16. *New Dimensions of World Politics,* G.L. Goodwin and A. Linklater (Eds). London, 1975, p. 86.
17. L.I. Brezhnev, *On the Foreign Policy of the CPSU and the Soviet State. Speeches and Articles.* Moscow, 1975, pp. 583-4.
18. W. Epstein, *The Last Chance. Nuclear Proliferation and Arms Control.* New York, 1976.
19. See: *Contemporary Problems of Disarmament,* Moscow, 1970, pp. 335-73.
20. *Za Rubezhom,* 1980, No. 31, p. 8.
21. *The Archive of K. Marx and F. Engels,* vol. IV, p. 29.
22. S. Melman, *The Permanent War Economy. American Capitalism in Decline.* New York, 1974, p. 114.
23. See: V. Ya. Aboltin, "Imperialist Concepts of the Arms Race and Arms Control". In: *Contemporary Problems of Disarmament.* Moscow, 1970.
24. W. Raven, *Sicherheit in Spanningsfeld.* Bonn, 1972, p. 55.

25. W. Andren and K. Birnbaum, *Beyond Détente: Prospects for East-West Co-operation and Security in Europe.* London, 1976, p. 188.
26. *The Christian Science Monitor,* 1975, 19 June.
27. *The New York Times Magazine,* 1975, 23 November.
28. *Pravda,* 25 September 1974.
29. *Materials from the 25th Congress of the CPSU,* Moscow, 1976, p. 22.
30. *Mirovaya Ekonomika i Mezhdunarodniye Otnosheniya* (World Economy and International Relations), 1980, No. 6, p. 25.
31. The USSR Central Statistical Board, *The USSR in Figures, 1979.* Moscow, 1980, p. 52.
32. *Pravda,* 21 February 1978.
33. D. Proektor, "Military *Détente—* the Number One Task". *International Affairs,* 1976, No. 5, pp. 54-5.
34. *Materials from the 25th Congress of the CPSU,* p. 24.
35. *Red Star,* 25 July 1980.
36. See: *The Collected Effective Treaties, Agreements and Conventions Concluded by the USSR with Other Countries,* Issue XXVIII, Moscow, 1974, Document No. 1965.
37. *For Peace on Earth. The Soviet–American Summit in Vienna, 15-18 June 1979. Documents, Speeches, Records,* Moscow, 1979, pp. 24-5.
38. *Pravda,* 3 March 1979.
39. *Foreign Affairs,* vol. 57, No. 3, 1978, p. 445.
40. *Foreign Affairs,* vol. 57, No. 3, 1978.
41. *Pravda,* 3 November 1977.
42. *Pravda,* 23 June 1972.
43. *Ibid.*
44. V. Levonov, "The Soviet Union's Disarmament Efforts". *International Affairs,* 1977, No. 4, pp. 31-43.
45. *International Affairs,* 1976, No. 1, p. 53.
46. See: A.A. Svetlov, *Disarmament Problems and International Détente,* Moscow, 1975, p. 57.
47. *Congressional Record,* 22 March 1976, p. 3926.
48. A.A. Svetlov, *op. cit.,* pp. 89-90.
49. *Pravda,* 3 November 1977.

Chapter 8

1. L.I. Brezhnev, *Following Lenin's Course,* vol. 4, Moscow, 1974, p. 281.
2. *Vorwarts,* 11 December 1975.
3. Quoted from: *International Affairs,* 1975, No. 1, p. 59.
4. *Materials from the 25th Congress of the CPSU.* Moscow, 1976, p. 56.
5. L.I. Brezhnev, *op. cit.,* p. 327.
6. *Pravda,* 3 November 1977.
7. Quoted from: *Pravda,* 12 April 1974.
8. *US News and World Report,* 5 January 1976, p. 24.
9. *The World Economy and International Relations 1979.*
10. *Ekonomicheskaya Gazeta* (Economic Gazette), No. 13, March 1980.
11. *Vneshnyaya Torgovlya* (Foreign Trade), 1979, No. 4.

12. *The Economy and Foreign Economic Relations of the USSR,* Moscow, 1979, p. 132.
13. *The Historic Significance of the Experience in Enforcing State Monopoly of Foreign Trade in the USSR,* Moscow, 1979, p. 32.
14. *Materials from the 25th Congress of the CPSU,* p. 57.
15. *Business Week,* 23 February 1976.
16. Quoted from: *The World Economy and International Relations,* 1976, No. 4, pp. 34, 35.
17. Quoted from: *Izvestia,* 16 September 1977.
18. Quoted from: *The World Economy and International Relations,* 1977, No. 12, p. 132.
19. *Materials from the 25th Congress of the CPSU,* pp. 135, 136.
20. UNESCO, *The Final Report. The Intergovernmental Conference on the Organizational, Administrative and Financial Aspects of Cultural Policy, Venice. 24 August–2 September 1970.* Paris, 1970, p. 16.
21. See: UNESCO, *The Final Report. The Intergovernmental Conference on Cultural Policy. Helsinki 19-28 June 1972.* Paris, 1972, pp. 49-50.
22. L.I. Brezhnev, *op. cit.,* vol. 4, p. 77.
23. *For Peace, Security, Co-operation and Social Progress in Europe. On the Results of the Berlin Conference of Communist and Workers' Parties of Europe. 29-30 June 1976.* Moscow, 1976, p. 12.

Chapter 9

1. E. Tarabarin, "The National Liberation Movement: Problem and Prospects". *International Affairs,* 1978, No. 1, p. 76.
2. *Materials from the 25th Congress of the CPSU,* p. 13.
3. *Ibid.,* p. 12.
4. See: *Pravda,* 1 June 1976.
5. *Diariu di Luanda,* 4 June 1976.
6. *The Programme of the CPSU,* Moscow, 1969, pp. 50-51.
7. *Greetings to the 25th Congress of the CPSU.* Moscow, 1976, p. 444.
8. *Ibid.,* p. 390.
9. L.I. Brezhnev, *On the Foreign Policy of the CPSU and the Soviet State. Speeches and Articles.* Moscow, 1975, p. 664.
10. J.H. Howe, *The US and the Developing World.* New York, 1974, pp. 87-98.
11. *Christian Science Monitor,* 27 July 1973.
12. *U.S. News and World Report,* 31 March 1980, p. 59.
13. *Materials from the 25th Congress of the CPSU,* p. 13.
14. *Ibid.,* p. 13.
15. *Pravda,* 16 August 1976.
16. *Newsweek,* 17 September 1979, p. 12.
17. *Pravda,* 9 September 1973.
18. See: *Pravda,* 18 June 1976.
19. *Partners in Development. Report of the Commission on International Development.* New York, 1969, pp. 3-4.
20. *Employment, Growth and Basic Needs: A World Problem.* Geneva, 1976, p. 21.
21. UNCTAD Doc. TD/183/REV 1, p. 38.

22. UNCTAD Doc. TD/249/, p. 8.
23. J.H. Howe, *op. cit.*, p. 87.
24. UNIDO Publication P 1/38, pp. 12 and 28.
25. *Pravda*, 12 April 1974.
26. *Pravda*, 5 October 1976.
27. *Ibid.*
28. V.I. Lenin, *Works*, vol. 23, p. 3.
29. *Pravda*, 3 November 1977.

Chapter 10

1. *United States Foreign Policy for the 1970s. Building for Peace. A Report by President R. Nixon to Congress. 25 February 1971,* New York, 1971, p. 4.
2. *Western Europe: The Trials of Partnership,* D.S. Landes (ed.), Lexington–Toronto, 1977, p. v.
3. *Foreign Affairs,* vol. 55, No. 2, January 1977, p. 325.
4. *American Public Opinion and Politics,* Ed. Y.A. Zamoshkin, Moscow, 1978, p. 234.
5. Institut fur Demoskopie, Allensbach, *Jahrbuch der Offenflichen Meinung 1968-1973.* Allensbach, 1974, p. 331.
6. V.I. Lenin, *Collected Works,* vol. 30, p. 320.
7. R.N. Cooper, K. Kaiser, and M. Kosaka, *Towards a Renovated International System. A Report of the Trilateral Integrator's Task Force to the Trilateral Commission.* New York–Paris–Tokyo, 1977, p. 35.
8. *Comparative Modernisation.* New York, 1976, pp. 384-5.
9. *Toward a Strategy of Interdependence.* The Department of State Special Report, No. 12. Washington, 1975, pp. 21-3; N. Camps, *The Management of Interdependence.* New York, 174; F.P. Bergston, *New Era, New Issues.* "*Economic Import*", No. 1, 1975.
10. K. Brutenta, "Neo-Colonialism on the Threshold of the Eighties: 'Modernisation' of Strategy". *Mirovaya Ekonomika i Mezhdunarodniye Otnosheniya* (World Economy and International Relations), No. 8, 1979.
11. *Pravda*, 5 October 1976.
12. Quoted from C. Delmac, *L'Europe et le Tiers monde.* Henle, 1975, p. 234.
13. D.S. McLellan, W.S. Dison, and F.A. Sonderman, *The Theory and Practice of International Relations.* New York, 1974, p. 401.
14. A. Buchan, *Change Without War. The Shifting Structures of World Power,* 1974.
15. Quoted from: W. Hanrieder, *The United States and Western Europe. Political, Economic and Strategic Perspectives.* Cambridge (Mass.), 1974, p. 55.
16. *Soviet Diplomacy and Negotiating Behaviour: Emerging New Context for U.S. Diplomacy.* Committee on Foreign Affairs, House of Representatives, 96 Congress, 1 Session, Washington, 1979, p. 544.
17. *The New York Times Magazine,* 31 December 1978.
18. J.W. Burton, *International Relations. A General Theory.* Cambridge, 1965, p. 60.
19. R. Vincent, *Nonintervention and International Order.* Princeton, 1974, p. 282.
20. G. Mische and P. Mische, *Towards a Human World Order. Beyond the National Security Straitjacket.* New York, 1977.

21. *The Soviet Empire: Expansion and Détente,* Ed. W.E. Griffith. Lexington–Toronto, 1976, p. 8.
22. *Ibid.,* pp. 399-400.
23. *Ibid.,* p. 249.
24. P.L. Wajsman, *Illusion de la détente.* Paris, 1977.
25. J.E. Carter, *Why Not the Best?* New York, 1976, p. 141.
26. Z. Brzezinski, *Between Two Ages. America's Role in the Technetronic Era.* New York, 1970; "U.S. Foreign Policy: The Search for Focus". *Foreign Affairs,* vol. 51, No. 4, July 1973.
27. Z. Brzezinski, *Between Two Ages, op. cit.,* p. 255.
28. *Foreign Affairs,* vol. 54, No. 1, October 1975, p. 59.
29. *Ibid,* vol. 55, No. 2, January 1977, p. 325.
30. *Pravda* 17 August 1977.
31. G. Kennan, *The Cloud of Danger – Current Realities of American Foreign Policy.* Boston, 1977, p. 218.
32. Arthur M. Cox, *The Dynamics of Détente. How to End the Arms Race.* New York, 1976.
33. *Pravda,* 23 December 1977.
34. L.I. Brezhnev, *Following Lenin's Course. Speeches and articles,* vol. 4, Moscow, 1974, p. 389.
35. *For Peace, Security, Co-operation and Social Progress in Europe. On the Results of the Conference of Communist and Workers' Parties of Europe. Berlin, 29-30 June 1976.* Moscow, p. 43.
36. A.A. Gromyko, "The Peace Programme in Action". *Kommunist,* 1975, No. 14, p. 18.

Chapter 11

1. Plato, *The Dialogues of Plato,* Vol. 2, New York, 1937, p. 407.
2. *Foreign Policy,* Fall 1978, p. 23.
3. "NATO's Fifteen Nations". 18 March 1979.
4. See: *Mezhdunarodnaya Zhizn* (International Affairs), No. 7, 1980, p. 8.
5. *Department of Defense Annual Report,* F.Y. 1979, Washington, p. 23; *U.S. Military Posture for 1979,* p. 4.
6. *Weekly Compilation of Presidential Documents,* 21 January 1980, p. 195.
7. *Mirovaya Ekonomika i Mezhdunarodniye Otnosheniya* (World Economy and International Relations), No. 7, 1980, p. 101.
8. G. Kennan, *The Cloud of Danger.* Boston–Toronto, 1977, p. 30.
9. *Mirovaya Ekonomika i Mezhdunarodniye Otnosheniya,* 1978, No. 12, p. 19.
10. *Pravda,* 13 January 1980.
11. P. Hill-Norton, *No Soft Options. The Political–Military Realities of NATO.* London, 1978, p. 16.
12. M. Gormaker, *Die unheilige Allianz. Die Geschichte der Entspannungspolitik, 1943-1979.* Munchen, 1979, p. 191.
13. T. Larson, *Soviet–American Rivalry.* New York, 1978, p. 284.
14. *Is America Becoming Number 2? Current Trends in the U.S.–Soviet Military Balance.* Washington, 1978, p. 25.
15. *Détente or Debacle. Common Sense in U.S.–Soviet Relations.* New York, 1979.

16. Quoted from *Pravda,* 22 June 1980.
17. *Materials from the 25th Congress of the CPSU.* Moscow, 1976, p. 33.
18. *Pravda,* 24 June 1980.
19. *Pravda,* 24 September 1980.
20. Quoted from *Pravda,* 22 June 1980.
21. *Pravda,* 1 June 1980.
22. *Pravda,* 2 July 1980.
23. *Pravda,* 12 January 1980.

Conclusion

1. V.I. Lenin, *On Soviet Foreign Policy.* Moscow, 1979, p. 108.
2. *Ibid.,* p. 144.
3. *Ibid.,* p. 165.
4. *The Soviet Impact on World Politics.* New York, 1978, p. 56.
5. *Ibid.,* p. 44.

Bibliography

Classics of Marxism - Leninism

Marx, K. and Engels, F. *The Communist Manifesto* — Marx and Engels, *Works*, vol. 4.

Marx, K. *The Constitutional Manifesto of the International Workingmen's Association.* — *Ibid.*, vol. 16.

Marx, K. *An Appeal to the National Workingmen's Union of the United States.* — *Ibid.*

Marx, K. *To Abraham Lincoln, President of the United States of America.* — *Ibid.*

Marx, K. *The First Appeal of the General Council of the International Workingmen's Association Concerning the Franco-Prussian War.* — *Ibid.*, vol. 17.

Marx, K. *The Second Appeal of the General Council of the International Workingmen's Association Concerning the Franco-Prussian War.* — *Ibid.*

Engels, F. *To the Spanish Federal Council of the International Workingmen's Association.* — *Ibid.*

Engels, F. *Anti-Duhring.* — *Ibid.*, vol. 19.

Engels, F. *The Role of Violence in History.* — *Ibid.*, vol. 21.

Engels, F. *Can Europe Disarm?* — *Ibid.*, vol. 22.

Lenin, V.I. *The Democratic Tasks of the Revolutionary Proletariat.* — *Collected Works*, vol. 10.

Lenin, V.I. *Two Tactics of the Social-Democrats in a Democratic Revolution.* — *Ibid.*, vol. 11.

Lenin, V.I. *The Balkan Peoples and European Diplomacy.* — *Ibid.*, vol. 22.

Lenin, V.I. *The Question of Peace.* — *Ibid.*, vol. 26.

Lenin, V.I. *Socialism and War.* — *Ibid.*

Lenin, V.I. *On the Slogan of the United States of Europe.* — *Ibid.*

Lenin, V.I. *Imperialism As the Highest Stage of Capitalism.* — *Ibid.*, vol. 27.

Lenin, V.I. *A Turning Point in World Politics.* — *Ibid.*, vol. 30.

Lenin, V.I. *Letters from Abroad.* — *Ibid.*, vol. 31.

Lenin, V.I. *The State and Revolution.* — *Ibid.*, vol. 33.

Lenin, V.I. *Marxism and Insurrection.* — *Ibid.*, vol. 34.

Lenin, V.I. *The Tasks of the Revolution.* — *Ibid.*

Lenin, V.I. *The Infantile Disorder of "Left-Wing" Communism.* — *Ibid.*, vol. 41.

Lenin, V.I. *Better Fewer, But Better.* — *Ibid.*, vol. 45.

Political Documents (Russian Language Edition)

The Communist International in Documents. 1919-1932. Moscow, 1933.
Resolutions of the VIIth World Congress of the Comintern. Moscow, 1935.
Policy Documents of the Struggle for Peace, Democracy, and Socialism. (Documents of the Meetings of Representatives of Communist and Workers' Parties held in Moscow in November 1957, in Bucharest in June 1960, in Moscow in November 1960), Moscow, 1961.
Documents of the Conference of European Communist and Workers' Parties held in Karlovy Vary, 24-26 April, 1967. Moscow, 1967.
The Berlin Conference of the Communist and Workers' Parties of Europe. 29-30 June, 1976. Moscow, 1977.
Documents of the International Meeting of Communist and Workers' Parties. Moscow, 5-17 June, 1969. Moscow, 1969.
The CPSU in Resolutions and Decisions of Party Congresses, Conferences and Central Committee Plenary Sessions, vol. 1-10. Moscow, 1970-1972.
Materials from the 24th Congress of the CPSU. Moscow, 1971.
Materials from the 25th Congress of the CPSU. Moscow, 1976.
Documents of Soviet Foreign Policy, vol. 1-21. Moscow, 1959-1977.
The 50th Anniversary of the Great October Socialist Revolution. A Resolution of the Plenary Session of the CC CPSU. Theses of the CC CPSU. Moscow, 1967.
Towards the Centenary of the Birth of Lenin. Theses of the CC CPSU. Moscow, 1970.
On Preparations to Mark the 50th Anniversary of the Founding of the USSR. The Resolution of the CC CPSU of 21.II. 1972. Moscow, 1972.
The Thirty Years of the Soviet People's Victory in the Great Patriotic War. Documents and Materials, Moscow, 1975.
On the 60th Anniversary of the Great October Socialist Revolution. The Resolution of the CC CPSU of 31 January 1977. Moscow, 1977.
The Constitution (Fundamental Law) of the Union of Soviet Socialist Republics. Adopted at the Seventh (Special) Session of the Ninth Supreme Soviet of the USSR, on October 7, 1977.

Soviet Literature

Andropov, Yu. V. *Communist Convictions — the Great Strength of the Builders of the New World.* A speech delivered at a meeting in Moscow marking the centenary of the birth of Dzerzhinsky. Moscow, 1977.
Andropov, Yu. V. *Leninism — the Science and Art of Revolutionary Creativity.* A speech delivered at a celebratory meeting in Moscow devoted to the 106th Anniversary of the birth of Lenin. Politizdat, 1976.
Arbatov, G.A. *The Ideological Struggle in Today's International Relations.* Moscow, Politizdat, 1970.
Bakhov, A.S. *The Dawn of Soviet Diplomacy. The Organs of Soviet Diplomacy from 1917 to 1922.* Moscow, 1966.
Basov, A., Petrov, V. *USSR–USA: A Changing Relationship.* Moscow, 1976.

Bogomolov, O. "The Material Foundation of a Durable Peace". *Kommunist*, 1978, No. 2.
Bogush, E. "Marx on the Foreign Policy of the Working Class". *International Affairs*, 1958, No. 5.
Brezhnev, L.I. *Following Lenin's Course*, Vols. 1-6. Moscow, 1970-1977.
Brezhnev, L.I. *On the Foreign Policy of the CPSU and the Soviet Government*. Speeches and Articles. 2nd enlarged edition. Moscow, 1975.
Brezhnev, L.I. "Speech at the XVIII Congress of the Komsomol". *Pravda*, 26 April 1978
Brezhnev, L.I. "An Interview Granted to Vorwarts, the Weekly of the Social Democratic Party of Germany". *Pravda*, 4 May 1978.
L.I. Brezhnev's Tour of Siberia and the Far East. Moscow, 1978.
Bromlei, N. Ya, Zhukov, E.M. and Lycitsyna, L.N. *The World Socialist System. Some Problems of the Theory and History of the Formation of Socialism*. Moscow, 1973.
Burlatsky, F.A. and Galkin, A.V. *Sociology, Policy, International Relations*. Moscow, 1975.
Chernenko, K.U. "A Durable and Reliable Security for Europe". *International Affairs*, 1978, No. 4.
Chernenko, K.U. *A Year After the Helsinki Conference*. Moscow, 1976.
Chernenko, K.U. "The Leninist Strategy of Peace in Action". *International Affairs*, 1976, No. 4.
Chichérin, G.V. *Lenin and Foreign Policy*. Moscow, Politizdat, 1977.
Chubaryan, A.O. *Peaceful Coexistence: Theory and Practice*. Moscow, 1976.
Current Bourgeois Theories of International Relations. A critical analysis, Moscow, 1976.
From the Decree on Peace to the Peace Programme. 1917-1975. A Record of Soviet Foreign Policy. Moscow, Politizdat, 1975.
The Diplomacy of Developing Countries. Moscow, 1976.
The Diplomacy of Socialism. Introduction by A.A. Gromyko, Moscow, International Relations Publishers, 1973.
Efremov, A.E. *Nuclear Disarmament*. Moscow, 1976.
Fedoseev, P.N. *Marxism in the 20th Century. Marx, Engels, Lenin in Today's World*. 2nd enlarged edition, Moscow, 1977.
Frantzev, Yu. P. *The International Significance of the Great October Socialist Revolution*. Moscow, 1967.
Galkin, A. "The Masses and Foreign Policy". *World Economy and International Relations*. 1965, No. 7.
Gorbachev, B.V. "The Socialist Community as a New Type of International Relations". *Questions of the History of the CPSU*, 1977, No. 9.
Grishin, V.V. *Under the Banner of Lenin's Party Towards the Victory of Communism*. A speech made at a public ceremony marking the 54th Anniversary of the Great October Socialist Revolution, Moscow, 6 November 1971.
Gromyko, A.A. *Along the Road of October — Towards New Victories for the Cause of Communism and Peace*. A speech delivered at a celebratory meeting to mark the 57th anniversary of the Great October Socialist Revolution, Moscow, 6 November 1974.
Gromyko, A.A. *The 1036 Days of President Kennedy*. Moscow, 1971.
Gromyko, A.A. "The Leninist Peace Strategy: A Union of Theory and Practice". *Kommunist*, 1976, No. 14.

Gromyko, A.A. "The Peace Programme in Action". *Kommunist*, 1975, No. 14.
The History of the CPSU in 6 volumes, vols. 1-5. Moscow, 1964-1970.
A History of the CPSU, 5th edition. Moscow, 1977.
The History of Diplomacy, in 6 vols., vols. 3-5. Moscow, 1965-1975.
The History of Soviet Foreign Policy, 1917-1975, in 2 vols. Under the editorship of A.A. Gromyko and B.N. Ponomarev, 2nd ed., revised and enlarged. Vol. I 1917-1945; Vol. II 1945-1975. Moscow, Nauka Publishers, 1976.
The History of the USSR in 12 volumes, vols. 7-11. Moscow, 1967-1977.
A History of the World, vols. 8-11, Chief Editor: Academician E.M. Zhukov. Moscow, 1961-1977.
Inozemtsev, N. "On a New Stage in the Development of International Relations". *Kommunist*, 1973, No. 13.
Inozemtsev, N. "The Theoretical Bases of the Leninist Peace Policy". *The Proceedings of the USSR Academy of Sciences*, 1976, No. 2.
The International Policy of the CPSU and the External Functions of the Soviet State. Moscow, Mysl Publishers, 1977.
International Relations and Soviet Foreign Policy. Past and Present. Moscow, Nauka Publishers, 1977.
Kapchenko, N. "F. Engels on the International Policy of the Working Class". *International Affairs*, 1970, No. 11.
Kapchenko, N. "The Foreign Policy of Socialism and the Reshaping of International Relations". *International Affairs*, 1975. No. 3.
Karenin, A. "The 'Balance of Power' Theory". *Questions of Philosophy*, 1974, No. 2.
Khryashcheva, N.M. *The New Strategy of Neocolonialism. (Current Bourgeois theories of external economic relations of the developing countries)*. Moscow, 1976.
Khvostov, V.M. *The Problems of the History of Soviet Foreign Policy and International Relations*. Selected works. Moscow, Nauka Publishers, 1976.
Khvostov, V. "Soviet Foreign Policy and Its Impact on the Course of History". *Kommunist*, 1969, No. 10.
Kim, G.F. *The Anti-Imperialist Struggle of the Peoples of Asia and Africa Today*. Moscow, 1971.
Kirilenko, A.P. "Along the Road of October, Fulfilling the Decisions of the 25th Congress of the CPSU". *Kommunist*, 1977, No. 11.
Kirilenko, A.P. *Selected Speeches and Articles*, Moscow, 1976.
Kortunov, V. "New Factors in International Relations and Bourgeois Ideology". *International Affairs*, 1977, No. 8.
Kosolapov, V. "International Relations and Social Progress". *Questions of Philosophy*, 1974, No. 5.
Kosygin, A.N. *Selected Speeches and Articles*. Moscow, 1974.
Kozyrev, A., Nilov, N. "The UN and Détente". *International Affairs*, 1977, No. 6.
Kukin, D. "From the Historical Experience of the Governing party of the Working Class'. *Kommunist*, 1978, No. 4.
Kukin, D.M. *Lenin's Plan for Building Socialism in the USSR and its Realization*. Moscow, 1972.
Kunina, A. "A Critique of the Bourgeois Theories of the Development of International Relations". *International Affairs*, 1973, No. 1.
Lebedev, N. "The Cooperation Between the USSR and the Developing Countries in the Struggle for Democratization of International Relations". *History of the USSR*, 1977, No. 1.

Lebedev, N. "The International System: Problems of Development". *International Affairs*, 1976, No. 11.

Lebedev, N. "Lenin's Ideas on the Fundamental Restructuring of International Relations". *Modern and Recent History*, 1976, No. 5.

Lebedev, N. *A New Stage in International Relations*. Moscow, 1976.

Lebedev, N. "On the Class Nature of Peaceful Coexistence". *Kommunist*, 1975, No. 4.

Lebedev, N. "Socialism and the Reshaping of International Relations". *International Affairs*, 1978, No. 1.

V. I. *Lenin and Soviet Foreign Policy*. Moscow, 1960.

The Leninist Traditions of Soviet Foreign Policy. Moscow, 1977.

Matveev, V. "Ideology and Diplomacy Under Détente". *International Affairs*, 1977, No. 6.

Mazurov, V.T. *Along the Road of October — Towards the Victory of Socialism* — A speech delivered at a celebratory meeting to mark the 55th anniversary of the Great October Socialist Revolution. Moscow, 1972.

Military Force and International Relations, Moscow, Nauka Publishers, 1972.

Mintz, I.I. *The History of the Great October Socialist Revolution*, vols. 1-3. Moscow, 1967-1970.

Narochnitzky, A. "On the Theory and Method of the History of International Relations". *Questions of History*, 1976, No. 2.

Narochnitzky, A. "Sixty years of the USSR's Struggle for Peace and Security". *Modern and Recent History*, 1978, No. 4.

Narochnitzky, A. "Soviet Foreign policy and the Problem of European Security in the Interwar Period". *Modern and Recent History*, 1974, No. 5.

Nikonov, A. "Military Détente and the Restructuring of International Relations". *World Economy and International Relations*, 1977, No. 6.

Orel, V. "International Non-governmental Organizations Under Détente". *Soviet State and Law*, 1976, No. 10.

Petrovsky, V.F. *American Foreign Policy Thinking. A critical survey of the organization, method and content of US bourgeois research into international relations and foreign policy*. Moscow, 1976.

Petrovsky, V. " 'The Structure of the World': Formulas and Reality". *World Economy and International Relations*, 1977, No. 4.

Polyakov, Yu. A. *The Great October Socialist Revolution*. Moscow, 1977.

Polyakov, Yu. A. "Some Problems of the History of the Transition from Capitalism to Socialism". *Kommunist*, 1978, No. 4.

Ponomarev, B.N. *The Historic Significance of the Great October Socialist Revolution*. A speech delivered at the international scientific conference "The Great October Socialist Revolution and the Modern Era". *Kommunist*, 1977, No. 17.

Ponomarev, B.N. *Selected Speeches and Articles*. Moscow, 1977.

Problems of the History of International Relations and Ideological Warfare. Moscow, Nauka Publishers, 1976.

Some Problems of Contemporary International Relations. Moscow, 1974.

Public Opinion and the Problems of War and Peace. Moscow, 1976.

Questions of the History of Soviet Foreign Policy and International Relations. A collection of articles in memory of V.M. Khvostov, Moscow, Nauka Publishers, 1976.

Radulesky, G. "On the New International Economic Order". *Problems of Peace and Socialism*, 1977, No. 4.

Rybkin, S.I. *War and Politics Today*. Moscow, 1973.

Samsonov, A.M. *The Collapse of the Nazi Aggression*. Moscow, 1973.

Sanakoev, S. "Foreign Policy and the Popular Masses". *International Affairs*, 1975, No. 4.

Sanakoev, S. "The Foreign Policy of Imperialism and Bourgeois Political Science". *International Affairs*, 1978, No. 1.

Sanakoev, S.P. and Kapchenko, N.I. *On the Theory of Socialist Foreign Policy*. Moscow, 1977.

Sergiev, A. "Lenin on the Alignment of Forces as a Factor of International Relations". *International Affairs*, 1975, No. 4.

Shakhnazarov, G. "Effective Factors of International Relations". *International Affairs*, 1977, No. 1.

Sobakin, V. "The Constitutional Foundations of Soviet Foreign Policy". *Kommunist*, 1977, No. 17.

Socialism and European Security. Edited by O.T. Bogomolov. Moscow, 1977.

Socialism and International Relations. Moscow, Nauka Publishers, 1975.

Solomentsev, M.S. *Leninism — the Science of Revolutionary Struggle and Communist Construction*. A speech delivered at a Moscow meeting, devoted to the 108th anniversary of the birth of Lenin. Moscow, 1978.

Suslov, M. "Introductory Remarks at the International Scientific—Theoretical Conference 'The Great October Socialist Revolution and the Modern Era'". *Kommunist*, 1977, No. 17.

Suslov, M.A. "Marxism—Leninism and the Revolutionary Rejuvenation of the World". *Kommunist*, 1977, No. 14.

Suslov, M.A. *The Roads of Communist Construction*, vols. 1-2. Moscow, 1977.

The Systems Approach and International Relations. Moscow, Nauka Publishers, 1976.

Temkin, Ya. "The Development of Lenin's Peace Programme During the Build-up to the Great October Socialist Revolution". *Questions of CPSU History*, 1977, No. 6.

Tikhvinsky, S.L. *Chinese History and the Modern Era*. Moscow, 1976.

Tomashevsky, V.G. *Lenin's Ideas and International Relations Today*. Moscow, Politizdat, 1971.

Trapeznikov, S.P. *Social Sciences — a Powerful Ideological Potential of Communism*. Moscow, 1974.

Trapeznikov, S. "Social Sciences — on the Ideological Asset of the Party and the People". *Kommunist*, 1976, No. 12.

Trukhanovsky, V.G. *Sixty years of the USSR's Struggle for Peace and International Cooperation*. Moscow, 1977.

Usachev, I.P. *The Soviet Union and the Problems of Disarmament*. Moscow, 1976.

Ustinov, D.F. *Sixty years of Standing Sentry over the Gains of Great October*. A speech delivered at a celebratory meeting to mark the 60th anniversary of the Soviet Army and Navy, held at the Kremlin Palace of Congresses, Moscow, 22 February 1978.

Vinogradova, L. "The New World Economic Order and Theoretical Thought Abroad". *World Economy and International Relations*. 1977, No. 4.

Vygodsky, S. Yu. *The Dawn of Soviet Diplomacy*. Moscow, 1965.

The Ways of an Indestructible Friendship. Moscow, Nauka Publishers, 1977.

Zadorov, S.I. *Socialism, Peace, Revolution. Some questions of the theory and practice of international relations and class struggle*. Moscow, Politizdat, 1977.

364   *Great October and Today's World*

Zagladin, V. and Frolov, I. "The Global Problems of Today". *Kommunist*, 1976, No. 16.
Zhilin, P.A. *How Nazi Germany was Preparing its Sneak Attack on the USSR*, 2nd edition. Moscow, 1968.
Zhukov, E.M. *The Impact of the Great October Socialist Revolution on the Development of International Relations. The Historic Significance of the Revolution.* Moscow, 1957
Zhukov, E.M. "A Turning Point in World History". *Modern and Recent History*, 1977, No. 5.
Zimyanin, M.V. *Leninism — the Revolutionary Banner of Our Times.* A speech delivered at a celebratory meeting in Moscow marking the 107th anniversary of the birth of Lenin. Moscow, 1977.

Western Literature

Alker, H., Bloomfield, L.P., and Choucri, W. *Analyzing Global Interdependence*, vol. I. Mass., 1974.
Allison, G. and Szanton, P. *Remaking Foreign policy. The Organisation Connection.* New York, 1976.
America as an Ordinary Country. US Foreign Policy and Future. Ed. by Rosecrance. London, 1976.
Ball, G. *Diplomacy for a Crowded World. An American Foreign Policy.* Boston, 1976.
Basiuk, V. *Technology, World Politics and American Policy.* New York, 1977.
Beyond Détente: Prospects for East–West Co-operation and Security. Ed. by N. Andren and K. Birnbaum. Leiden, 1976.
Bosc, R. *Guerres froides et affrontements de 1950 à 1980. Analyse et perspective internationale.* Paris, 1973.
Brodie, B. *War and Politics.* New York, 1973.
Brown, S. *New Forces in World Politics.* The Brookings Institute, 1974.
Brown, S. *The Changing Essence of Power Foreign Affairs.* Cambridge (Mass.), 1973.
Brown, S. *New Forces in World Politics.* Washington, 1974.
Brzezinski, Z.K. *Ideology and Power in Soviet Politics.* New York, 1967.
Brzezinski, Z.K. *Between Two Ages. America's Role in the Technotronic Era.* New York, 1970.
Buchan, A. *Change Without War. The Shifting Structures of World Power.* London, 1974.
Choucri, N. and North, R. *Nations in Conflict. National Growth and International Violence.* San Francisco, 1975.
Clark, E. *Diplomat: The World of International Diplomacy.* New York, 1974.
Clough, R. *East Asia and US Security.* Washington, 1975.
Cox, A. *The Dynamics of Détente. How to End the Arms Race.* New York — Norton, 1976.
Détente in Historical Perspective. New York, 1975.
Détente. Ed. by G. Urban. New York, 1976.
Edmonds, R. *Soviet Foreign Policy. 1962-1973. The Paradox of a Super Power.* London, 1975.

Eubank, K. *The Summit Conferences. 1919-1960.* Norman, 1966.
Frankel, J. *Contemporary International Theory and the Behaviour of States.* Oxford, 1973.
Hayter, W. *Russia and World. A Study of Soviet Foreign Policy.* London, 1970.
Hilsmen, R. *The Crouching Future. International Politics and U.S. Foreign Policy. A Forecast.* New York, 1975.
Howe, J.H. *The US and Developing World.* New York, 1974.
International Security Systems: Concepts and Models of World Order. Ed. by R. Gray. Itasca (Ill.), 1966.
International Arms Control. Issues and Agreements. Ed. by J. Barton and D. Weilel. Stanford, 1976.
Internations Politics and Foreign Policy. Ed. by J. Roseman. New York, 1969.
Kennan, G. *American Diplomacy. 1900-1950.* New York, 1951.
Kennan, G. *The Cloud of Danger. Current Realities of American Foreign Policy.* Boston, 1977.
Kissinger, H. *American Foreign Policy.* New York, 1974.
Kissinger, H. *A World Restored: Metternich, Castlereagh and the Problems of Peace. 1812-1822.* New York, 1957.
Kissinger, H. *A World Restored: The Politics of Conservatism in a Revolutionary Age.* New York, 1964.
Kissinger, H. *American Foreign Policy.* New York, 1974.
Lafeber, W. *America, Russia and the Cold War. 1945-1975.* New York, 1975.
Lerner, M. *The Age of Overkill. A Preface to World Politics.* New York, 1962.
McLellan, D., Olson, W. and Sonderman, F. *The Theory and Practice of International Relations.* New York, 1975.
Macomber, W. *The Angels' Game. A Handbook of Modern Dipomacy.* New York, 1975.
The Middle East: Oil, Conflict and Hope. Critical Choices for Americans. Ed. by A. Odovitch, 1976.
Midlarsky, M. *On War. Political Violence in the International System.* New York, 1975.
Mishe, G. and Mishe, P. *Towards a Human World Order. Beyond the National Security Straitjacket.* New York, 1977.
Morgenthau, H. *Politics among Nations: The Struggle for Power and Peace.* New York, 1973.
Morse, E. *Modernization and the Transformation of International Relations.* New York, 1976.
National Security and Détente. New York — Crowell, 1976.
National Security and Détente. Foreword by General A.J. Goodpasten. New York, 1976.
New Dynamics in National Strategy. Paradox of Power. New York, 1975.
New Dimensions of World Politics. Ed. by G. Goodwin and A. Linklater. London, 1975.
Northedge, F. and Grieve, M. *A Hundred Years of International Relations.* London, 1971.
On the Creation of a Just World Order: Preferred Worlds for the 1990's. Ed. by Mendlovits. New York, 1975.
Petrov, V. *US-Soviet Détente: Past and Future.* Washington, 1975.

Reilly, T. and Sigall, M. *Political Bargaining. An Introduction to Modern Politics.* San Francisco — Freeman, 1976.
Reshaping the International Order. A Report to the Club of Rome. New York, 1976.
Rosser, R. *An Introduction to Soviet Foreign Policy.* Englewood Cliffs, 1969.
The Search for World Order. Ed. by A. Lepawsky. New York, 1971.
Schelling, T. *Arms and Influence.* Harvard University, 1966.
Small, M. and Singer, D. *The Images of War. 1816-1965. A Statistical Handbook.* New York, 1972.
Small States in International Relations. Ed. by A. Schon and A. Olan. New York, 1971.
The Soviet Impact on World Politics. Ed. by K. London. New York, 1974.
The Soviet Empire: Expansion and Détente. Critical Choices for Americans. Ed. by W. Griffith, Vol. IX. Lexington (Mass.), 1977.
Steibel, G. *Détente: Promises and Pitfalls.* New York, 1975.
Sterling, R. *Macropolitics. International Relations in a Global Society.* New York, 1974.
Stupak, R. *American Foreign Policy. Assumptions, Processes and Projections.* New York, 1976.
The Superpowers in a Multinuclear World. Ed. by G. Kemp. Lexington, 1974.
Teller, E., Mark, H. and Foster, J. *Power and Security. Critical Choices for Americans.* Lexington, Lexington Books, 1976.
The United Nations: Past, Present and Future. Ed. by J. Barros. New York, 1972.
U.S. Participation in International Organizations. Washington, 1977.
Ulam, A. *Expansion and coexistence. The History of Soviet Foreign Policy. 1917-1967.* New York, 1968.
Vincent, R. *Nonintervention and International Order.* Princeton, 1975.
Weeks, A. *The Troubled Defence.* New York, 1976.
Whelan, J. and Inglee, W. *The Soviet Union and the Third World: A Watershed in Great Power Policy?* Washington, 1977.
Whetten, L. *Contemporary American Foreign Policy. Minimal Diplomacy, Defensive Strategy and Détente Management.* Lexington, 1974.
The World and the Great Power Triangles. Ed. by W. Griffith. Cambridge (Mass.), 1975.
Yergin, D. *Shattered Peace. The Origins of the Cold War and the National Security State.* Boston, 1977.

Index

Index